P **ecting**

th **Video**

Producing and Directing the Short Film and Video

Peter W. Rea and David K. Irving

Focal Press
Boston Oxford Melbourne Singapore Toronto Munich New Delhi Tokyo

Focal Press is an imprint of Butterworth–Heinemann

Copyright © 1995 by Butterworth–Heinemann

&R A member of the Reed Elsevier group

Recognizing the importance of preserving what has been written, ∞ Butterworth–Heinemann prints its books on acid-free paper whenever possible.

Library of Congress Cataloging-in-Publication Data
Rea, Peter W.
    Producing and directing the short film and video / Peter W. Rea and
David K. Irving.
        p.   cm.
    Filmography:
    Includes bibliographical references and index.
    ISBN 0-240-80188-1 (acid-free paper)
    1. Motion pictures—Production and direction. 2. Video
  recordings—Production and direction. 3. Short films. I. Irving,
  David K. II. Title
PN1995.9.P7R375   1995
791.43'023--dc20   95-11927
                                                                         CIP

British Library Cataloguing-in-Publication Data
A catalogue record of this book is available from the British Library.

Part Opener and Chapter illustrations by Timothy Berry

The publisher offers discounts on bulk orders of this book.
For information, please write:

Manager of Special Sales
Butterworth–Heinemann
313 Washington Street
Newton, MA 02158-1626

10   9   8   7   6   5

Printed in the United States of America

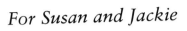

For Susan and Jackie

Contents

Preface

EFFICIO COGNOSIO (LEARN BY DOING)

There is no substitute for experience. In this book, we would like to emphasize the importance of the School of Hard Knocks. Whether you are in a film or video program or making a project on your own, this is an excellent time to be studying film- and videomaking. Profound changes are taking place in the communications field. The Academy of Motion Picture Arts and Sciences recently announced that in 1992, 72 percent of first-time directors had graduated from film school. In 1980, the figure was 34 percent. The Academy calculates that in the year 2000, the number will jump to 90 percent.

There is no better way to learn how to make a film or video than by actually doing it. Books and manuals can serve as a guide. Other films and videos can act as inspiration, and talking about and critiquing films and videos can trigger ideas. However, the two best teachers are failure and success. Experiencing the process of putting a project together, building work muscles, and understanding the craft and discipline of the process are ultimately the best ways to develop your skills.

THE POWER OF THE MEDIA

Finally, your short film or video has the potential to influence a great many people. Both media have gained great exposure in the past 20 years, and their potential is growing rapidly. All indications are that by the year 2000, products from the communications industry will be the United States's chief export commodity.

Coupled with the wide distribution of these media is the issue of the power of their content to influence. We are now grappling with crucial problems, from overpopulation to racial discrimination; from management of the earth's resources to the management of human resources. Film and video already have a powerful voice in the dialogue about these challenges. Our hope is that in expressing yourself through film and video, you will consider the world in which it will be viewed and will use your talents wisely.

Acknowledgments

We would like to thank the following people who assisted us in the writing of this book—in particular, the faculty, staff, and students at New York University, Tisch School of the Arts, Undergraduate Film and Television: Arnold Baskin, Jim Brown, John Canemaker, Christine Choy, Pat Cooper, Ken Dancyger, Carlos DeJesus, Tom Drysdale, Carol Dysinger, Everett Frost, Boris Frumin, Dan Gaydos, Fritz Gerald, Chat Gunter, George Heinemann, Ron Kalish, Julia Keydel, Marketa Kimbrell, Lou LaVolpe, Rosanne Limoncelli, Ian Maitland, Barbara Malmet, Rick McKinney, Lynn McVeigh, Brenda Miller, Lamar Sanders, Julie Sloane, George Stoney, Nick Tanis, Darryl Wilson, Brane Zivkovic, and especially Steven Sills. Also, New York University Professor Richard Schechner, who saw an early version of *Producing and Directing the Short Film and Video*.

We would like to thank Mitchell Block, John Butman, Steve Hanks, the law firm of Rudolph & Beer, Doug Underdahl, Nancy Walzog, and a special thanks to Carol Chambers for her continued support throughout the writing process and Steve West for his editing skills.

We would also like to thank Ken Bowser, Hamilton Fish, Jr., David Gurfinkel, Tova Neéman, Priscilla Pointer, and Robert Wise, for inspiration and encouragement.

For the editorial and production skills they provided to Focal Press, we would especially like to thank MaryEllen Oliver, Marilyn Rash, and Judith Riotto, who made the process of assembling these final pages a rewarding one.

Introduction

The idea of being in a darkened screening room and watching your film or video touch an audience is exciting. There is deep satisfaction in communicating on this basic level. The fantasy of creating something that has an emotional impact on others is what motivates many people to go into picture-making in the first place. There is, also, the artistic satisfaction.

Why make a short film or video? The market for "shorts" is limited. It occupies a very small niche in media sales, and rarely do shorts recoup their investments, let alone make money. For these reasons, the creation of a short work is usually motivated by considerations other than profit.

Most short works are created to give film- and videomakers an opportunity to express themselves and to display their talents. The key advantage to making a short is learning the process, honing the craft. It is a way of getting experience on a project of manageable scale. If the work turns out well, shorts can be entered into festivals. The producer and director can parlay awards and the fame of winning competitions into meetings, agents, and (ideally) employment.

How do you go about making a successful short film or video? Picture-making is a complex and demanding activity, even for the experienced. A myriad of problems inevitably arises involving script, crew, budget, casting, lighting, and so on. Each project has its own unique set of challenges. For example, one film might need a difficult location like Grand Central Station; another might call for a school gymnasium. One script might require a talented young boy who must also be meek and scrawny; another might need a homeless person. One project might run out of money before postproduction; another budget might not allow for crucial special effects. Even before starting production, you must understand sophisticated technical crafts; resource management; political and social interaction; and personal, financial, and professional responsibility.

The process of producing a film or video, be it a half-hour or a five-minute piece, has been refined over the years and developed into an art. As you will discover, there is a straightforward logic behind these steps—a logic governed by the management of time, talent, and resources. Each step is informed by pragmatism and common sense:

- *Script development*: Your script must be well crafted before preproduction can begin.
- *Preproduction*: The production must be efficiently organized before the camera can roll.
- *Production*: The project must be shot before it can be edited.
- *Postproduction*: The project must be edited before it can be distributed.
- *Distribution*: A film or videotape that is not distributed is merely an exercise.

This is only a broad outline of what must happen during the production of a short work. It describes the general flow of activity, but it does not address what these steps mean nor when and how they must be performed. Translating an idea into a film or video involves the execution of thousands of details over a long period of time. In fact, the success of any film or video project relies as much on management as it does on storytelling. Knowing where to put the camera to capture the right dramatic moment of a scene requires as much skill as marshaling the necessary people, equipment, and supplies to the location in the first place. One can't happen without the other.

This book is organized according to the general logic of how a short work is assembled. Each of the above stages is fleshed out in detail with concrete examples. Our goal is to impart to the beginner a fundamental understanding of what is required to organize and execute the production of a successful short picture. Bear in mind, though, that no two shows are alike and that there are no rules. This book is a guide, not a formula.

Each chapter presents a clear picture of what the producer and director do at any given time during the production. Unfortunately, in many beginning productions, the director and producer are the same person. Having to tackle two very different and complex responsibilities at the same time puts undue and unnecessary pressure on the novice. We discourage it.

CRAFT VERSUS ART

Moving pictures are arguably the greatest art form of the twentieth century. After all, the medium combines elements of literature, art, theater, photography, dance, and music but is in itself a unique form. For the sake of all beginning film- and videomakers who read this book, we take the pressure off by refusing to emphasize the creation of art. Instead, we stress the craft of storytelling, and telling a story well is not an easy task. Telling a short story well is even more difficult.

For us, it is difficult to think of film- and videomaking as an "art"-making endeavor. Orson Welles probably did not intend to make art when he conceived and produced *Citizen Kane*. Instead, he probably set out to make the best film he could from a particular script. The result was a well-crafted film, which was later deemed to be one of the finest feature films ever made and ultimately came to be considered "art." This label has more to do with the consensus of a critical audience long after the fact than it does with the intention of the filmmaker. Our advice to you is to set out to shoot the best short story you can, and let the audience decide whether it is art.

Let's not give Welles all the credit for the success of *Citizen Kane*. Filmmaking is a collaborative enterprise in which many creative people lend their expertise to the director's vision. Too many ingredients affect the outcome of a film to allow any one person to take credit for its success. Welles himself said that "making a film is like painting a picture with an army."

Above all, to make a successful short film or video, the entire creative team must share a passion for the material and the process. If there is no passion, the process will be no more than going through the motions of manufacturing a product. Lack of passion shows on the screen.

THREE SHORT FILMS

In this book's chapters, we try to illustrate that the potential of realizing magic on the screen is directly proportional to the quality of management in the production stages. In fact, any artistic success can be achieved only through the well-planned and well-executed management of time, talent, and resources. To help you understand this critical relationship between organization and creative success, we use examples throughout the book from what we consider to be three successful shorts: two narratives and one documentary.

The case studies are *Truman*, a 12-minute color narrative film written and directed by Howard McCain; *Mirror Mirror*, a 17-minute documentary film produced and directed by Jan Krawitz; and *The Lunch Date*, a 12-minute black-and-white narrative film written and directed by Adam Davidson. Each of these films has won competitions, and one, *The Lunch Date*, won an Academy Award. The two narratives were made as student films: *Truman* at New York University and *The Lunch Date* at

Columbia University. *Mirror Mirror* was made by a documentary filmmaker who teaches at Stanford University. Each picture can be easily rented from the distributors listed in Appendixes B and J. The scripts for the two narrative films and the transcript of *Mirror Mirror* are reprinted in Appendix C.

Why did we choose these films? They are excellent examples of well-produced and well-directed short films. As stories, they are appropriate for the short form. We chose two narratives that are similar in length but differ in storytelling styles, subject matter, and production organization. *Mirror Mirror* was included because the documentary is an important short form. Many young film- and videomakers explore the documentary as a means of self-expression. Although *Mirror Mirror* is different in nature and structure from most traditional documentaries, the form offered Jan Krawitz a unique arena in which to explore her views. The rules of production planning for the short form can be applied to any live-action (not animated) subject matter, whether it is narrative, documentary, experimental, industrial, or corporate in nature.

As teachers, we find it difficult to talk generically about production without using examples from specific films and videos. Many basic concepts and terms are alien to the beginner, and relating them to an actual production creates a common reference and a strong context. Throughout each chapter, we quote from the filmmakers' personal narratives about that part of the production process. Citing their films, which you can see and whose scripts you can read, offers concrete evidence of the range of procedures and challenges encountered in producing and directing a short film or video.

FILM AND VIDEO

Advances in audio and video technologies, especially the digital tape and editing revolution, have blurred the line between film and video. The changing technology has filmmakers shooting on film and then editing on video. Compression allows the storage of hours of material on a computer's hard drive. Smaller and more effi-

cient cameras and formats are creating a product that can be broadcast on commercial television. Much of what you see on CNN from exotic parts of the world was recorded with Hi-8 equipment smaller than most camcorders. No one knows where the convergence of telephone, cable, television, and computer technologies will lead the industry.

Video is playing an ever-expanding role in media production not only in the professional world, but also in film and television training programs across the country. Independent filmmakers now have access to sophisticated equipment that was unavailable until only recently. Many film departments use video to train students because of the financial burden of shooting film.

The process of producing and directing a short project is very similar whether it is shot on film or video. The basic production sequence can be applied. The grammar and aesthetic principles for both media are interchangeable. The industry and technologies are merging; similar opportunities can be found in both media.

TIMELINE

Producing and Directing the Short Film and Video explores both the producer's and the director's points of view. It is imperative that each know what the other is doing at all times. We have divided most chapters into two parts, reflecting the management, or "producing," skills and the storytelling, or "directing," skills required to create a successful short film or video. This organization is designed to give the novice a detailed understanding of and respect for the processes of both producing and directing, one step at a time, from idea to final print. It can also serve as a practical guide to help navigate through creative and managerial straits.

The Producer

The most misunderstood and mysterious role in the filmmaking process is that of the producer. We've been asked hundreds of times, "What does a producer actually *do?*" That his role is a mystery to most laypeople is not altogether surprising. The producer's position in the film industry is amorphous and has varying definitions. In addition, the producer never has the same job description from one project to another, and on many kinds of films and videos, it is common to see more than one producing credit.

In this book, we use the term *producer* to describe the driving force in the making of a short. We also use *producer* to describe the person who engineers all the elements necessary for the creative and business aspects of production. One of the main elements—if not the most important—is the money. The producer is responsible for raising it, budgeting it, and ultimately accounting for it to the investors. His role might be limited to the practical planning of a show, or it might include artistic collaboration. The producer might also be the director of the piece. However, if one person tackles both jobs, he must keep an eye on the "big picture." The producer's challenge is to maintain the delicate balance between script and budget.

A movie begins with either an adaptation from an existing short story, a script, an original idea, a true story, or simply an image that has dramatic and visual potential. The imagination and belief that such an idea or story can be transformed into a motion picture or tape are what begins the process. What is not widely understood is that the producer can be, and often is, the creative instigator of most short film and video projects. The producer frequently is the one who has the original inspiration that launches the whole project and then sails it home, with himself as the captain. In a general sense, we could say that without the producer, the picture would not be made. The Academy of Motion Picture Arts and Sciences gives the Best Picture Award to the producer of a film. This is the industry's acknowledgment that the producer is the person who is responsible for putting the pieces together, the person who creates the whole.

The Director

Because of the images of several contemporary superstar directors, including Spike Lee, Martin Scorsese, and Martha Coolidge, the role of the film director has taken on a romanticized image: The director shouts "Action," and the whole set swings into motion; the director chats with actors between takes and enjoys posh dinners after the day's wrap.

In reality, the director's work is never done. Because her job is to supply the creative vision for a one-of-a-kind and essentially handmade product, the choice and effect of thousands of decisions fall to her. Solving all creative problems on and off the set is the director's final responsibility, from how much light to what color blouse, from which location to how long a scream. The director alone has the "vision" of the whole film in her head, and she alone is obligated to make the sum of all her decisions throughout the process add up to its fulfillment. The director's goal is to deliver a finished film or video ready for an audience.

Although the producer strives to support the director's work and the director is the authority figure on the shoot, the director answers to the producer. However, the producer complements the director's work. When her decisions affect the budget or the schedule, the director consults the producer. The responsibilities of the producer and director often overlap. Ideally, the director and producer should be able to work well together and understand the script in the same way. Picture-making is, after all, a creative collaboration.

The director must be demanding but not dictatorial. She must do her best to draw out each cast and crew member by making him or her feel involved. The director is an active observer. She directs the actors by being part coach, part audience, and part performer. She will stand on her head if necessary to elicit a good performance. The director should have unlimited patience and be methodical, organized, articulate, and succinct. She should be broadly educated in the arts and have a working knowledge of the duties and responsibilities of each member of the team.

The director needs six things to execute a successful short: a good script, a talented cast, a devoted crew, adequate funds, good health, and luck (a major variable in any artist's work).

CHAPTER BREAKDOWNS

Chapters One and Two cover the development preliminaries that need to be dealt with prior to the preproduction phase of any project. Each chapter in Parts One and Three covering the preproduction and distribution processes, begins with the producer's responsibilities. The production and postproduction chapters in Parts Two and Three begin with the director's duties. The typical timeline graphic that follows this introduction summarizes the activities of the producer and director during the process of making a short work. Although it is difficult to determine the specific amount of time needed for each phase, the following breakdown may provide some insight.

- Financing might be immediately available or might take years to obtain.
- Scripts can come from many sources and may be ready to shoot or could take years to get into shape.
- Preproduction usually requires two to eight weeks.
- Production usually takes somewhere between a day and two weeks.
- Postproduction details take anywhere from two to ten weeks.
- Distribution can take as long as several months.

Timeline

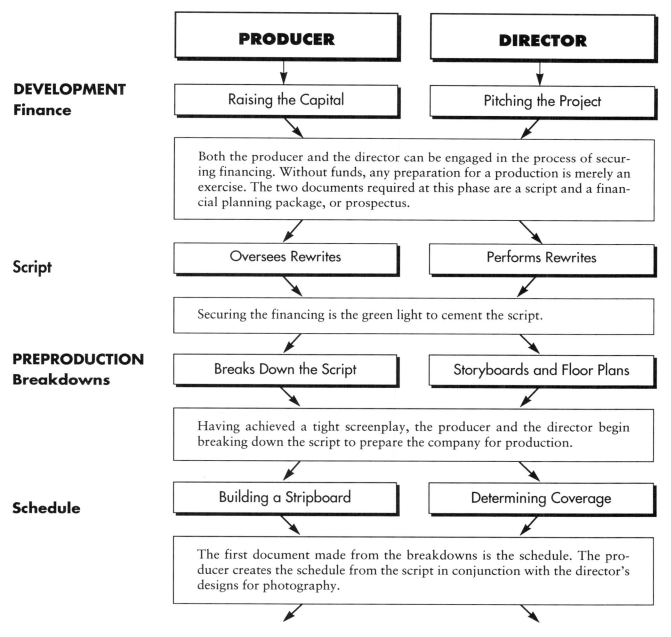

	PRODUCER	**DIRECTOR**
DEVELOPMENT Finance	Raising the Capital	Pitching the Project

Both the producer and the director can be engaged in the process of securing financing. Without funds, any preparation for a production is merely an exercise. The two documents required at this phase are a script and a financial planning package, or prospectus.

Script	Oversees Rewrites	Performs Rewrites

Securing the financing is the green light to cement the script.

PREPRODUCTION Breakdowns	Breaks Down the Script	Storyboards and Floor Plans

Having achieved a tight screenplay, the producer and the director begin breaking down the script to prepare the company for production.

Schedule	Building a Stripboard	Determining Coverage

The first document made from the breakdowns is the schedule. The producer creates the schedule from the script in conjunction with the director's designs for photography.

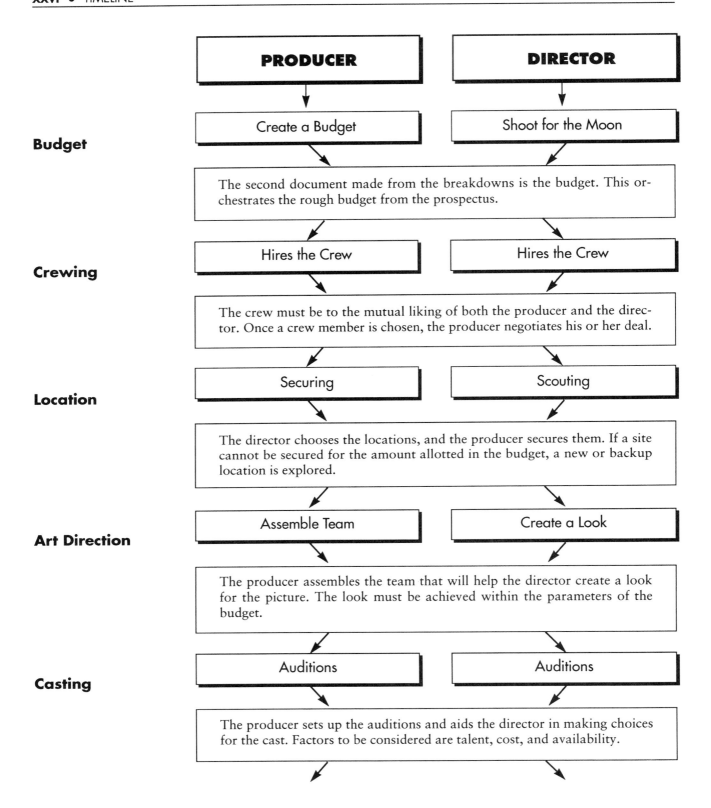

Budget

PRODUCER	DIRECTOR
Create a Budget	Shoot for the Moon

The second document made from the breakdowns is the budget. This orchestrates the rough budget from the prospectus.

Crewing

Hires the Crew	Hires the Crew

The crew must be to the mutual liking of both the producer and the director. Once a crew member is chosen, the producer negotiates his or her deal.

Location

Securing	Scouting

The director chooses the locations, and the producer secures them. If a site cannot be secured for the amount allotted in the budget, a new or backup location is explored.

Art Direction

Assemble Team	Create a Look

The producer assembles the team that will help the director create a look for the picture. The look must be achieved within the parameters of the budget.

Casting

Auditions	Auditions

The producer sets up the auditions and aids the director in making choices for the cast. Factors to be considered are talent, cost, and availability.

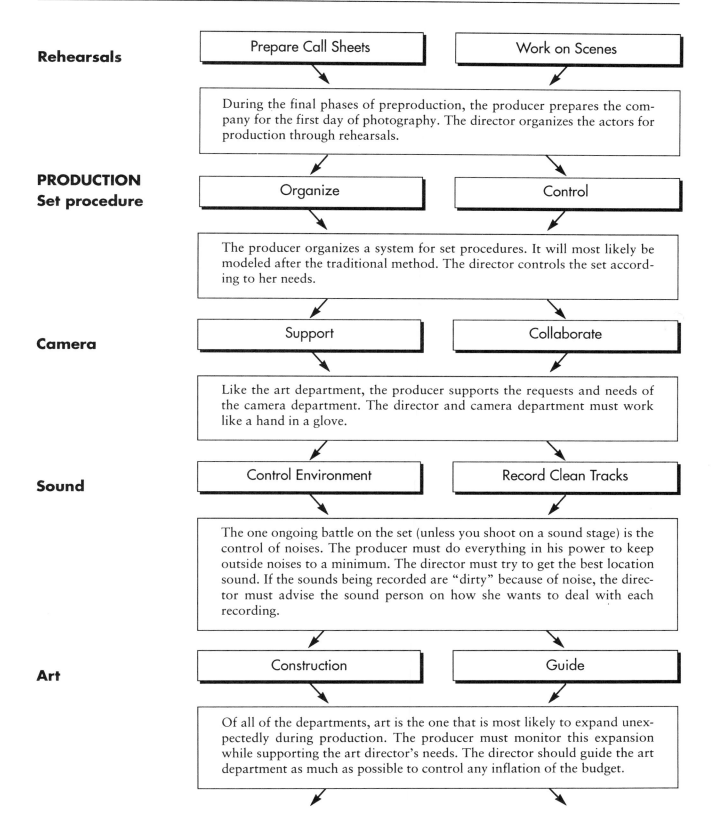

Rehearsals

| Prepare Call Sheets | Work on Scenes |

During the final phases of preproduction, the producer prepares the company for the first day of photography. The director organizes the actors for production through rehearsals.

PRODUCTION
Set procedure

| Organize | Control |

The producer organizes a system for set procedures. It will most likely be modeled after the traditional method. The director controls the set according to her needs.

Camera

| Support | Collaborate |

Like the art department, the producer supports the requests and needs of the camera department. The director and camera department must work like a hand in a glove.

Sound

| Control Environment | Record Clean Tracks |

The one ongoing battle on the set (unless you shoot on a sound stage) is the control of noises. The producer must do everything in his power to keep outside noises to a minimum. The director must try to get the best location sound. If the sounds being recorded are "dirty" because of noise, the director must advise the sound person on how she wants to deal with each recording.

Art

| Construction | Guide |

Of all of the departments, art is the one that is most likely to expand unexpectedly during production. The producer must monitor this expansion while supporting the art director's needs. The director should guide the art department as much as possible to control any inflation of the budget.

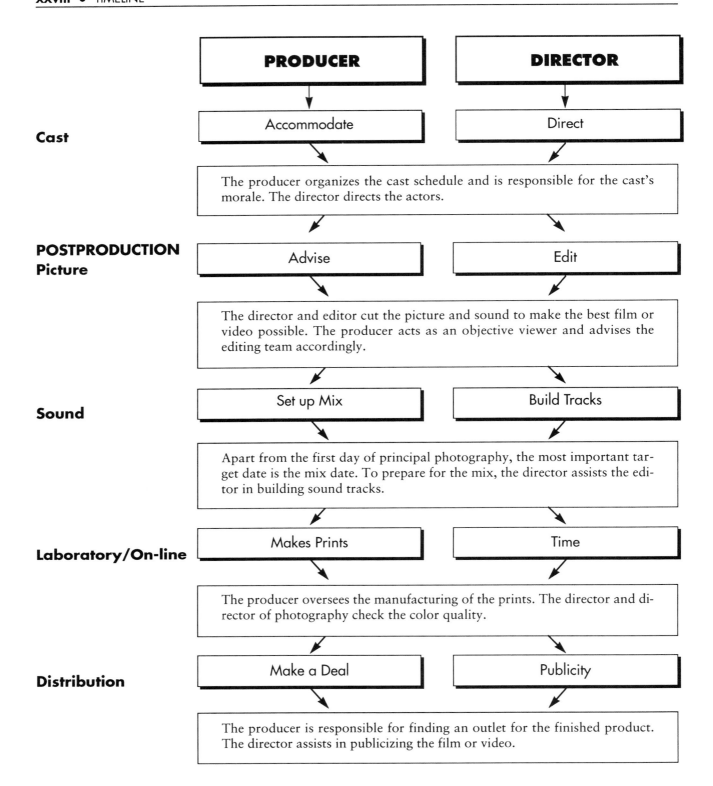

PRODUCER

DIRECTOR

Cast

Accommodate

Direct

The producer organizes the cast schedule and is responsible for the cast's morale. The director directs the actors.

**POSTPRODUCTION
Picture**

Advise

Edit

The director and editor cut the picture and sound to make the best film or video possible. The producer acts as an objective viewer and advises the editing team accordingly.

Sound

Set up Mix

Build Tracks

Apart from the first day of principal photography, the most important target date is the mix date. To prepare for the mix, the director assists the editor in building sound tracks.

Laboratory/On-line

Makes Prints

Time

The producer oversees the manufacturing of the prints. The director and director of photography check the color quality.

Distribution

Make a Deal

Publicity

The producer is responsible for finding an outlet for the finished product. The director assists in publicizing the film or video.

Producing and Directing the Short Film and Video

chapter one

Finance

We basically put a lot of things on credit cards—my credit cards.

Adam

PRODUCER

Raising the Capital

If there is one role with which the producer is traditionally associated, it is the role of fund-raiser. The producer finds the money to fund the film or video. This role is paramount because money is the lifeblood of any project. In fact, without adequate financing, there is no project. However simple the production demands might seem, it is impossible to produce something for nothing. Even if you are a one-person crew shooting videotape, you still need to purchase tape stock and rent a camera and editing equipment to complete the project.

Most beginners get turned on by romantic notions and the tantalizing creative possibilities of the visual media, but they soon find out that much of their time and energy is focused on raising funds. Independent film- and videomakers spend much of their time filling out grant applications, writing to investors, and organizing fund-raisers. Howard McCain, Adam Davidson, and Jan Krawitz struggled to secure financing for their projects. For Jan, it was a process that lasted years.

> I wrote a lot of grants over the years, and I finally got the first grant in the spring of '87. Initial money came from the Paul Robeson Fund for Film and Video. I only had two grants when I began shooting, and the subsequent three came during postproduction. I think that's significant, because I find it's always a little easier to get funding once you have something to show from the project.
>
> *Jan*

BASIC FUND-RAISING PROBLEMS

You can expect to encounter two basic problems in funding your projects. The first is the potential of either a sizable return on an investment or no return at all. Overwhelming odds support the latter. Suffice it to say that the market for short films is financially anemic. (This problem is discussed at length in Chapter 19, "Distribution.")

The second problem you will face is lack of experience. How do you persuade an investor to finance a first-time producer or director, someone who has yet to complete a project or, at best, has only a minimal track record? To look at it another way, would you hire a contractor who had never built a house?

All novices confront these two major obstacles as they start out to create their first films. The problem of inexperience is no less real or daunting than the problem of a limited market, but the producer and director definitely have more control over it. Although it might seem like a catch-22—the "Can't get a job without experience, can't get experience without a job" syndrome—there are specific ways to overcome this seemingly insurmountable obstacle. Each year, many young film- and videomakers with little experience but with lots of ingenuity, energy, and verve are able to persuade investors to believe in their talent and trust them to manage their dollars responsibly.

There is no secret formula for raising money successfully. In the pursuit of funding, it is almost guaranteed that you will come up against tremendous odds and constant rejection. Many potential investors will say "No" before one says "Yes." Some may

1

even say "Yes" at first and then change their minds. To be able to sustain excitement for your beloved project after weeks, months, and sometimes years of effort demands a strong belief in yourself, the utmost patience and perseverance, and an unbridled passion for the medium and your message.

How Much Money Will You Need?

Although short narrative films vary in cost, the average student film is approximately $750 per minute. Therefore, a 10-minute film will cost around $7,500, and a 30-minute film will cost about $22,500.

> We were doing *Lunch Date* cheaper than you would generally do a student film. Generally, I would estimate $1,000 a minute. This project was definitely budgeted for less. Adam didn't have a lot of money, and he didn't want to spend a lot of money. I think originally he wanted to spend $5,000 because it was going to be a fun project to do. He had a little extra money, and he wanted to make this film. It ended up costing more because in postproduction he wanted to spend that money. He wanted to get a good sound editor and get good music and do a good mix. But he always had the option to not do that, to just finish it cheaply, do his own sound editing and mix.
> *Garth Stein (producer of* The Lunch Date*)*

The figures are less for video productions. For documentaries, the decision whether to shoot on film or video greatly affects the price. Professional shoots, especially ones using several unions, can be very expensive. (For more on these topics, see Chapter 5, "Budget.")

FUNDING OPTIONS

Both students and independent film- and videomakers can employ similar methods for raising funds. However, some opportunities available to students are not open to independents, and vice versa. For example, some students can take advantage of their university's tax-exempt status without having to create a not-for-profit business entity. In addition, students work in a supportive environment with resources such as equipment and a sizable pool of free and willing labor. Independents must put their production teams together from scratch. On the other hand, student film- and videomakers are almost completely shut out of the grant world.

There are no rules when it comes to finding money. If you win the lottery, use it to finance your project. Putting the lottery windfall aside, here are seven possible sources of money for short films and videos.

Private Investors

This group includes any individuals who are interested in investing in your project. Private investors might be friends, family members, or associates—even complete strangers. Some people might invest because they want to see you succeed even though they understand they might not see a return on their investment. Others might be looking for a tax shelter, and still others might be shrewd businesspeople who believe in the investment opportunities and market potential of your project.

Corporate Sponsorship

Private and public corporations sometimes fund films and videos; for example, Mobil and Sony have traditionally backed public television shows. The public relations people at these corporations will guide you through the application process for various proposals. Contact as many companies as you can. To avoid wasting your time, research the types of projects each company has funded in the past (see Appendix H).

Public Foundation Grants

Some public foundations financed by federal, state, and local governments offer grants and other forms of financial aid to film- and videomakers. The National Endowment for the Arts (NEA), the National Endowment for the Humanities (NEH), and the American Film Institute (AFI) are three examples.

> I started with $5,000, and then when I was in the editing stage, I received three more grants of $3,000, $2,000, and $2,000—three grants totaling $7,000. That was my total outside funding.
> *Jan*

Private Foundation Grants

There are hundreds of private foundations in the United States, but only a few support film and video projects. Finding the ones that might be interested in your particular project requires exploration. Most major public libraries have information to assist you. Examples of sources of media fellowships are the Jerome Foundation and the Rockefeller Foundation.

Bank Loans

Banks will loan almost anyone money if the borrower provides sufficient collateral. Taking out a loan against a car, a boat, or a house can provide adequate funding for a short film or video project. The money is not a gift or an investment, and it will have to be paid back with interest.

Personal Savings

If the cost of a short work is not exorbitant, your personal savings might be sufficient. Saving money gradually in an account earmarked for your project might take less time than you think. Although a financial adviser might try to convince you that your savings are for the future or for hard times, investing in yourself is also protecting your future.

In-Kind Services and Donations

Anything that is given or donated is called *in-kind*. In-kind donations are the equivalent of hard cash. If 70 percent of your total costs are raised as currency and the remainder comes in the form of goods or services, it still equals 100 percent of your budget. Examples of in-kind donations are food from a local restaurant, deferred laboratory fees, reduced car or van rental, and a free location.

These donations are usually given in exchange for a screen credit and for the goodwill. One possible way to acquire in-kind donations is to shoot your project in your hometown. This might prompt newspaper articles with a "hometown boy/girl makes good" slant, inspiring favorable public relations with businesses that could translate into money or in-kind donations.

There is also a practice in the business called *product placement*. This is when a producer convinces a manufacturer to donate goods to the production in exchange for featuring its product in a film or video. For example, Ford might loan cars to a production for use both on and off camera with the agreement that Ford cars and trucks be used prominently in the film. Should the producer interest a clothing manufacturer, a similar arrangement might work for costuming.

Other in-kind opportunities exist for independent media artists. Here are some examples:

- Low-cost or free access to production or post-production equipment and facilities
- Financial support for artists facing work-related personal emergencies
- Information on or assistance with taxes, record keeping, accounting, or financial management
- Free legal advice or referrals

THE PROSPECTUS

To attract private or corporate support, the producer should create a proposal called a *prospectus*. The prospectus should excite potential investors by communicating on paper a strong sense of the project in a professional manner. The information gathered for the prospectus can easily be rewritten to fulfill a grant application, or tailored to the needs of a specific investor.

The prospectus should contain at least the following elements:

- Cover letter
- Title page
- One-liner
- Synopsis of story
- History of project
- Research
- Top sheet of budget
- Production schedule
- Cast list
- Brief résumés of creative team
- Description of market for project
- Financial statement
- Means of transferring funds

COVER LETTER. Use the cover letter to introduce the project to the investor. It can be targeted to all potential investors or slanted to a specific individual. The impression you make with this letter sets the tone for everything that follows. Be clear about what you want. Are you asking for many small investments or donations? What is the total amount of capital you are trying to raise?

TITLE PAGE. A good title conveys the essence of the project. Keep it short; a short title has more punch. Include artwork on the title page that catches the eye and makes an immediate impression. The right image can capture the feel and tone of your piece. Any artwork here or anywhere else in the prospectus must look professional.

ONE-LINER. A one-liner is a brief statement of your project. Following are some examples. (See also Figures 1.1 to 1.3.)

> *Truman* is a heartfelt and humorous story about an 11-year-old boy's struggle to climb a rope ladder during gym class. It involves colorful and funny vignettes that bring to life the boy's internal struggle through the dramatization of an active fantasy life.
>
> *(Truman)*

> An older suburban woman shares her lunch with a homeless man.
>
> *(The Lunch Date)*

> Faceless women reveal how they feel about their bodies in relation to the expectations of society.
>
> *(Mirror Mirror)*

SYNOPSIS OF STORY. The synopsis should be a brief narrative of the story's action. Move the story or plot forward with minimal details. The synopsis is difficult to write because you must capture the flavor of the piece and tell the story at the same time.

HISTORY OF PROJECT. Briefly describe how the project evolved. Elaborate on the subject matter and what inspires you to want to make this film or video. This section of the prospectus is especially applicable if the idea comes from another medium (stage play, short story, etc.).

RESEARCH. Research is imperative for a documentary project. Potential investors will need to understand the materials on which your story is based. Is this a true story of a living person? Is it based on a real event? Has the story been done before? What slant will the director take? Have the rights to tell this story been secured?

TOP SHEET OF BUDGET. The top sheet summarizes the budget. This summary should represent the broad categories; it is not a detailed or itemized breakdown. Too much information might prompt an investor to question why you need $400 for a special wig. You don't want to end up justifying this and every cost of the project. Investors need to trust that you are the expert. It is your business, not theirs.

Only after you have prepared an accurate budget for the script can you begin to finance the project realistically. However, you might have begun to raise money long before this by approaching investors with an early draft of the script or a "treatment" and a projected estimate of production costs. Experienced producers and production managers have the skill to examine a

Figure 1.1 Scene from *Truman.*

Figure 1.2 Scene from *The Lunch Date.*

Figure 1.3 Scene from *Mirror Mirror.*

script and estimate the cost of the project. If you have been involved in other productions of similar size and scope, you might get a sense of how much money you need before you actually work out the budget.

At the prospectus stage, the budget is likely to be an overall guesstimate. Later, it will be modified to include input from all department heads, including the director. At the prospectus stage, the director can help the producer by confirming that the bottom-line figure in the budget adequately covers her needs.

You might be able to complete the project for less than your projection, but ask for more than you anticipate needing. Who knows, you might get it and you might need it. (See Chapter 5, "Budget," for more information.)

PRODUCTION SCHEDULE. Give the approximate dates when the production will begin and end should financing become available.

CAST LIST. Draw up a list of the prominent cast members, and give a succinct résumé of their credits. The quality and ability (and in some cases recognizability) of the cast are part of the insurance that investors require to feel confident that their money is being spent wisely. Casting is essentially the domain of the director. Her input into this list is imperative.

BRIEF RÉSUMÉS OF CREATIVE TEAM. Present the pool of talent associated with the production at the time the prospectus is written. The personnel can be introduced in simple paragraphs or in complete résumés.

Writing a résumé is an art in itself. A résumé can be anywhere from a single paragraph to a full page in length. Try to find a balance between giving too much information and too little. Clearly identify each person's strengths, relevant experiences, and job description. A résumé for a producer that indicates that he can write, direct, produce, shoot, and act might overwhelm investors.

Having said that, we remind you that there are no rules. Although not all potential investors will know how to judge the subtleties of a varied background, an eclectic résumé might indeed catch an investor's eye. Work experiences as a camp counselor, location scout, or editor of a student film all point to leadership skills.

DESCRIPTION OF MARKET FOR PROJECT. Devise a distribution plan to include in the prospectus. (See Chapter 19, "Distribution," for further details.)

FINANCIAL STATEMENT. In the financial statement, you should estimate the income you expect to receive, based on your distribution plan. In addition, explain your business identity. If you can offer investors any sort of tax break, you will have a greater chance of attracting financing. Tax breaks are allowed sometimes if your company is set up as a not-for-profit entity. Consult an entertainment attorney.

MEANS OF TRANSFERRING FUNDS. At the end of the prospectus, include a letter addressed to the company from the investor, committing the investor to a specific figure. The letter should show how money can be transferred to the production account.

Presentation Is Everything

The prospectus can be peppered with graphics that support the project's concept and lend excitement to the presentation. People respond to visuals. If you can create images that connect potential investors to the idea of your piece, it will enhance their appreciation of the supporting data.

A well-written prospectus makes a professional impression. When writing the prospectus, use easy-to-understand and grammatically precise language. Stick with simple declarative sentences and clear, unpretentious words. Arrange your thoughts logically, avoid jargon, and make the ideas flow.

Don't give potential investors an obvious reason to turn down your proposal. "No" is the easiest decision to make because nothing is risked by making it. In fact, most people look for reasons to say "No." Imagine yourself on the other side of the table. Would you support someone whose business plan wasn't thought out carefully or who didn't take the time to proofread his or her work? Would you trust this person with your money?

The prospectus forces the filmmaker to think objectively about the project as a whole. The challenge becomes how to communicate an idea's potential to a complete stranger who might not be interested in the project. Beginners think that enthusiasm is enough to sell an idea. This energy can be contagious, but it must also be followed by hard information about the exact nature of the project, the talent, and the investment structure.

The prospectus is an important tool for galvanizing interest without having to pitch verbally to hundreds of people. It also identifies the sincerely interested parties whose concerns can then be addressed specifically and personally. Some producers are naturally facile and relaxed communicators. You might be one. Even if you have an innate ability to sell in person, the written presentation must be well designed. Good interpersonal skills will come in time.

The by-product of a thoroughly prepared prospectus is twofold. First, it trains you to think logically and sequentially about your idea so that when you do have the opportunity to speak face-to-face with potential investors, you will be well prepared. Second, it is an important step in the preproduction process. Now you have your first budget!

SPENDING THE MONEY RESPONSIBLY

As a producer, you have the responsibility of handling and managing the money after it has been raised. You will need to create some type of corporate identity to receive funds. This might involve something as simple as setting up a bank account into which checks can be deposited, or it can be as complex as choosing a corporate structure. Consult an entertainment attorney for details.

The business and legal skills required to handle money responsibly are based on the needs of the production. Throughout the production process, the producer supervises the allocation of cash, or the *cash flow*, through the production pipeline. This ensures that he will be able to deliver a thorough financial statement to the investors at the end of production.

DIRECTOR
Pitching the Project

Next to the film's concept, the director and her abilities are the key element that the producer touts when raising funds. If the director has a track record or other career support, such as an award for a previous work or glowing reviews, investors will treat the venture more favorably. The director must infect investors with her enthusiasm for the project. Investors often know very little about how to read a script or how to respond to production problems. What they do understand is good storytelling ability. The director who can "pitch" her film or video idea well is more apt to impress investors with her vision than someone who becomes tongue-tied or is shy. Verbal agility is crucial at the moment of "closing."

Whether you like it or not, you are now into sales. Smart investors look at the bottom line, but they are greatly influenced by the presenter. Everyone appreciates a performer and an entrepreneur. Keep in mind, however, that there is a fine line between razzle-dazzle and being obnoxious. The former is a turn-on, the latter a turnoff. Learn to observe by the reaction of those to whom you are pitching which approaches seem to work and which don't. There is nothing like asking for money; it trains the producer and director to deal with a naturally uncomfortable situation gracefully. Through the process of defining your project and shaping your pitch, you will learn how best to sell your idea.

I get really unhappy when I hear of people, not just students but independent filmmakers, who pitch an idea, start developing a particular idea, because they feel like that's what's "fundable" these days. I think the thing people fail to understand is that originality is what gets attention, not derivative filmmaking.

Jan

In the verbal and the written pitch, present a tone that grabs the target investor's attention. Use active and colorful words. Some people have a talent for this type of promotional presentation. A director's raw enthusiasm, coupled with a clear interpretation of the material, makes an effective presentation. In a verbal presentation, be enthusiastic, but speak clearly and slowly. When pitching material with a partner, know when to be silent and when to assist. If you seem like a cohesive team, your target will be impressed.

I started writing proposals. The first one was to the American Film Institute, which resulted in a rejection. I actually applied to them three years in a row and got rejected three years in a row for a historical legacy idea. But when I started refining the idea, I abandoned the whole thing, and the reason was because I felt this was too hard to do on film. It was really more like a slide show because it was all inanimate, and it worried me that I would have to rely on still material and a disembodied voice.

Jan

GENERAL FUND-RAISING SUGGESTIONS

Be Positive and Be Patient

Project supreme confidence in the picture and in your ability to execute it successfully. People are investing not only in the picture, but in you. In addition, you must be able to sustain a positive attitude over the long haul. If you are the kind of person who requires short-term rewards, this business is not for you. Perseverance and patience are the watchwords. Looking for money requires a dogged determination. You'll need the energy of the hare but the patience of the tortoise.

I thought I'd really like to make a film and figured I could probably raise enough money somehow to shoot it. I didn't think it would be very expensive. It basically came down to the fact that I was just dying to get near a camera and shoot something. What was the worst that could happen? I'd lose some money.

Adam

Act Professionally

Professionalism is a theme that we stress in all aspects of the production process, and it is also vital when you approach potential investors. You will be respected if you appear to be organized, efficient, well prepared, and articulate. You might see yourself in the role of the artist, but fund-raising is a business proposition. You are asking people to trust you with their money. If you can give the impression of knowing what you are doing, you will most likely get your foot in the door. Once in, assuming that there is quality and substance in your project idea, a coherent presentation will be critical to your success.

Be sure to allocate enough time to raise the money you need. It won't happen overnight. If you are planning to shoot in several months and have not yet begun fund-raising, you'd better hope that you win the lottery.

Be Informed

When looking for funding sources, knowing what information to seek is as important as knowing where to find it and what to do with it. The goal is to know how things work and how to work them to your advantage. Read as much as you can. Become adept at asking the right questions. Examine the budgets of pictures of a similar length.

> Total funding for *Mirror Mirror* was $12,000, and the final budget through release prints and a one-inch, but not including festival entry fees, was $14,300. The film stock, processing, location travel expenses, and the cinematographer's salary were the major production expenses. A lot of money went to research and acquisition of the archival footage. And all the postproduction costs, sound mix and all of that, probably ate up $4,000 or $5,000. Easy.
>
> *Jan*

Be dogged in the pursuit of the facts. Examine all sides of a problem; there could be more than one solution. Go to conferences. Talk to professionals and amateurs who have been successful at fund-raising, particularly with genres similar to yours. Don't be shy. Believe it or not, people like to share their knowledge with beginners as long as it doesn't cost them anything. With this information in hand, evaluate the potential investor pool.

The key is to consider everything. Focus your energies on multiple strategies. Don't pin your hopes on getting that one investor or grant. If it doesn't work out, you will be left stranded. Learn to keep many balls in the air, and learn to live with rejection. It may take 100 "No"s before you finally hear one "Yes."

> *Fund-raising tip:* Financing can be secured in two tiers. First, there's the money you need to get the project shot and "in the can." This money is raised on a script and a pitch. When the principal photography has been completed, you will require "finishing" or postproduction money. This second phase of fund-raising can be done while the project is being edited. Use the footage to show potential investors just how fabulous the picture will eventually be. As opposed to the first funds, which were raised on the ephemeral qualities of a pitch and a prayer, having footage to show makes a more solid presentation.

> I took money from my savings, I sold my motorcycle, and I borrowed money from my parents. I raised enough to get me through the first stage, which was shooting and developing the rushes.
>
> *Adam*

SOURCES FOR STUDENTS

What help is available to students? The following brief list summarizes resources you should explore.

OTHER STUDENTS. Other students are invaluable resources of solid advice and information. Who better to ask about fund-raising strategies than fellow students who are in the same position? Surprisingly, many students overlook their peers as a resource. It is up to you to brainstorm with others who are seeking production support.

INTERNSHIPS. If your film or television program is located in a media center like New York, Los Angeles, Chicago, or San Francisco, it behooves you to take advantage of internship opportunities to learn about not only the raising, but also the management, of money.

FACILITIES. Students at media programs have access to free equipment. They also have the use of production and postproduction facilities, such as stages, locations, editing rooms, mixing facilities, and screening rooms.

LEARNING OPPORTUNITIES. Keep your eyes open for ways to develop yourself. Listen to guest speakers from the industry. Take courses in a business school. Tackle writing, acting, and public speaking classes. In a pitch meeting, the topic of conversation could easily switch from your project to current events to acting techniques to writing styles. Students with varied interests and a broad background will be best equipped to converse on a number of topics and will make a favorable impression. Your ultimate goal is to know both how to communicate and what to communicate.

FUND-RAISING STRATEGIES

Find creative ways to earn money. Entrepreneurial students capitalize on their skills by creating a product to sell. Hard cash is made each week by those who know how to bake, garden, arrange flowers, do accounting, type, troubleshoot computers, and video-tape weddings.

Generate interest and create energy around your project. Set up fund-raisers, have parties, and hold screenings of your unfinished work. Use the newspapers. Create publicity by sending a press packet to newspapers and magazines.

You need not look only for big-dollar investments. Make a list of everyone you know and everyone your parents, relatives, and friends know, and ask them for a modest amount (from $15 up). They will be surprised when you ask for a small amount and will gladly donate a few dollars to the cause. If 25 friends each give $25, you'll collect $625! This is enough to buy and process five rolls of 16mm film or 60 rolls of tape stock.

> I'm in debt, but I got lucky in several ways. I was no longer paying for film school because I had become a graduate assistant. My parents didn't pay for my undergraduate education, so they were ready to pay for graduate school. Since I didn't have to pay for tuition, the money went into production. My high school friends who had done well financially helped me. So between my friends, my parents, and student loans, I paid for the film.
>
> *Howard*

KEY POINTS

1. Allow ample time to generate the funds you will need to shoot the entire picture.

2. Present your project and yourself in a professional manner. Use a prospectus—a professional business plan with which investors are familiar.

3. Research your targets for funds. If you know as much about them as they do, they will be impressed.

4. Generate enough enthusiasm to pitch the project and sustain yourself for the year or two it might take to make your film or video.

chapter two

Script

The whole preproduction process is about writing the script.

Howard

This chapter introduces you to some necessary guidelines for writing a short film or video script. It does not, however, explore in depth the nuts and bolts of writing technique. We recommend that you consult books written specifically about screenwriting for the short form. You'll find suggestions in the Bibliography.

The guidelines in this chapter are not absolutes. Violating some of these principles should not keep you from moving ahead if you feel strongly about the idea. You will be living with this project for quite a while, so it is important that you feel strongly, even passionately, about the material and its message. Remember, though, that film and video are art forms that communicate via visual images. If the script cannot visually convey a message, it might not engage an audience.

PRODUCER
Oversees Rewrites

The first step in producing a short film or video is securing a script. There are many ways you can do this. You can write one yourself, develop an original idea with a writer or director, adapt a script from another genre, or find a script that is already written. However you go about this—and we cannot emphasize this point too strongly—without a well-crafted script, you cannot have a good film or video.

Producing a documentary script involves a different process than generating a narrative text does. The specific nature of a documentary script is addressed later in this chapter.

The script is your guide through production. From it you know the story, the characters, the approximate budget, the locations, the final length, and your target audience. With a script, you can finance the production and attract the creative team that will transform the script into a final product. The first and most important member of that team is the director. Because her job is to bring a personal vision to the material, she either rewrites the script herself or supervises the rewrite until the script best suits a production based on her design.

Writing a good short script is difficult. The most common mistake novices make is trying to explore complicated or grandiose themes. They want to say it all in 10 minutes. Simple is best. The three examples provided in this book are good scripts because they are simple stories told well. (See Appendix C for the complete scripts.)

SCRIPT DEVELOPMENT

The producer supervises the development of a narrative idea until a director is brought on board to complete the rewrites and prepare the script for production. What starts out as a simple notion might go through many evolutions before it is ready to go before the cameras. The goal is to end up with the best script possible from your original idea. Be prepared to work and rework the material.

The elements that the short form can contain are limited. Before embarking on production, see and study as many shorts as possible to get a feel for the form and what can be accomplished in its time frame. (Shorts that are available for rental are listed in Appendix B, and their distributors appear in Appendix J.)

The length for shorts varies from two minutes (*Bambi Meets Godzilla*, U.S.A., 1969) to 34 minutes (*The Red Balloon*, France, 1956). The subject matter is limited only by imagination.

> Probably the biggest influence—besides all the films I'd ever seen in my life—was looking at student films, what was working and what wasn't. One thing that I thought wasn't working was that the stories went all over the place, and that there was an emphasis on the technical rather than substance.
>
> *Adam*

It is important to know what has come before. You don't want to latch onto an idea that has already been made.

> I think that I had seen a couple of films on eating disorders, and I had a feeling that I knew what was out there. I did seek out one film on beauty pageants, which was pretty irrelevant to this subject matter. But I do think that's important. I didn't want to make a film like this if there was a film that had just come out a year earlier. I did enough of a search to convince myself that there was really not one that took this particular perspective.
>
> *Jan*

Many of the great film- and videomakers were influenced by existing material. Orson Welles saw and studied John Ford's famous western, *Stagecoach*, more than 50 times while preparing to shoot *Citizen Kane*.

> I made a list of the films that really affected me as a child. One of them was *An Occurrence at Owl Creek Bridge* (which most people have seen). Then, of course, so did *The Red Balloon*. In film school, I saw many other films, such as Truffaut's *Les Miston (The Brats)*. This film didn't influence me in a conscious way but filled me up emotionally. It was so melancholy and beautiful that it made me want to run out and make films, even though I ended up making a film like *Truman*.
>
> *Howard*

WHAT IS A SCRIPT?

Think of your script as a blueprint for the final film or tape. It depicts the moment-to-moment progression of events by indicating what the audience will see and hear. Unlike a novel or a poem, the script is an unfinished work; it is only a part of the media-making process. It has no inherent literary value other than as a guide from which a film or video is wrought.

A script is to filmmaking as a blueprint is to shipbuilding or as a score is to a symphony performance. Imagine the ensuing difficulties of a shipbuilder who begins construction on a boat with only a few sketches to work from or the cacophony of a full orchestra trying to play a concert from a sketchy musical score. Just as the drawings tell the shipbuilder exactly where to place the mast and the notes on the score tell the musicians what and when and how loudly to play, so a script dictates how each member of the production team is to go about fulfilling his or her job.

WHAT DOES A SCRIPT LOOK LIKE?

The scripts in Appendix C are presented in Writers Guild of America (WGA) standard screenplay format. This format is an industry convention that has a direct relationship to how the script is photographed. (See Chapter 3, "Breakdowns," for more about screenplay format.)

A story doesn't have to be presented originally in screenplay format to make dramatic sense. You can work from an outline or from a simple scene description. This is called a *treatment*. It is the bare bones of a story told in narrative prose rather than in descriptions of individual scenes. A treatment reads like a short story and can be as straightforward as the way the case studies are described later in this chapter. However, it is imperative that the idea eventually conform to the standard script format.

A common format for documentary scriptwriting is a two-column page. On one side are listed the visuals, and on the other is listed the audio. The reader will get an idea of the show by imagining these two elements together. Documentarians learn to be especially responsive to their material. By the time the documentary gels, the story might have changed, taking a direction very different from the original outline.

> During the interview with my first subject, I asked way too many questions. After shooting 800 feet on that single interview, I reduced the number of questions from eight to four and really simplified the content. Because, despite a "test" interview, I had

overestimated how much information I could cover in a 400-foot (11-minute) roll of film.

Jan

WHERE DO SCRIPTS COME FROM?

Scripts are developed from whatever might inspire you to express and communicate something in visual and dramatic terms. All of the following sources can serve as the basis for a screenplay:

Ideas	Images
Concepts	Historical events
Adaptations from short stories	Dreams
	Fantasies
Real-life experiences	Social issues
News stories	Magazine articles
Memories	Real events

You might be inspired by a single event that occurred on a bus or train, an interaction between two people that strikes you as funny or poignant, an uncle who told you wonderful stories as a child, or a favorite teacher who was a memorable character. You might have a compelling need to express something about the social conditions in your neighborhood. The best scripts are written from the heart.

They are based on subjects about which the writer knows on a first-hand basis.

Truman focuses on conquering feelings of inadequacy in public. Most of us can empathize with Truman's transcendental moment when his perception of himself in the world undergoes a major shift, a spurt of personal growth.

> During the summer, I kept notebooks full of different ideas, random stuff. I kept drawing the picture of a little boy hanging from a rope. That image propelled me forward. I can't remember why. I also wanted to make a film that if I were an eight-year-old boy, would amuse me. The sort of film teachers would roll out on rainy days in fifth grade. I wanted it to be fun to make. I wanted to enjoy it.
>
> *Howard*

The woman in *The Lunch Date* also has a personal revelation. She and a homeless man share an unusual moment together, and then she escapes back to the suburbs. (See Figure 2.1.) This moment probably does not have the same impact on her life as the events in *Truman* do on the boy because she is older. We see her, however, experience the unexpected, which then affords her the ability to know the homeless in a new way. Both characters are changed in some way by the events of their stories.

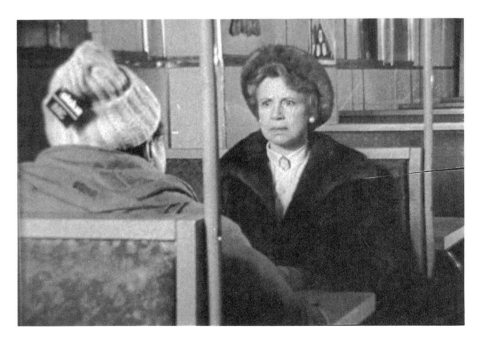

Figure 2.1 Two hungry diners, from *The Lunch Date*.

I remember that several years before, I had heard a story similar to the one I used in the film, which was a story about a person misidentifying something of someone else's as belonging to themselves. And I thought this was a pretty human mistake that anybody could make and that I had probably made somewhere along the line—assuming something about somebody else. So I played with the idea of setting this story in New York and having the two most opposite people I could think of meet.

Adam

The film *Mirror Mirror* focuses on the topic of how women perceive their bodies. The filmmaker had a specific theme to explore and set about devising a situation that would allow women to express their innermost thoughts. (See Figure 2.2.)

I believe that this self-deprecation and striving for an unattainable body type is a generalized experience among a lot of women. All you have to do is eavesdrop in department store dressing rooms or women's locker rooms to hear the laments that women have about their bodies.

Jan

HOW ARE SCRIPTS DEVELOPED?

Write down the events that you observe in your quest for a good idea or story in a notebook or diary. Mo-

ments in life happen at breakneck speed. You might think at the time that you will remember them when you go home at night, but chances are you will have forgotten some significant detail that struck you as funny or compelling. You should always be on the lookout for interesting material. Good ideas beget good ideas. The events you write down will stimulate your imagination further.

Workshops

A constructive way to deal with this accumulation of ideas and material is to "workshop them" with interested people. Invent a scenario, and present it to someone you trust or someone who might be a part of your creative team. The logical choice is someone who is already interested in writing or directing this short piece. Develop scenarios that most efficiently communicate what is happening and to whom.

Ideas that are spoken out loud have a different impact than those that are read. They can either sound better than you thought or fall flat. Not only can you test an idea or concept on an ad hoc audience, but more important, these verbalized ideas will be stimulating. A thought or image conjures up different impressions in each person's mind. If one of these ideas becomes the core of your final script, these brainstorming sessions will serve as a bond and the start of a long and fruitful collaboration that will

Figure 2.2 A masked woman surrounded by mannequins, from *Mirror Mirror.*

hopefully continue throughout the entire process.

> I had a couple of people to whom I would read my drafts, fellow students who knew what I was going for and what I had to deal with. These story sessions became the most important thing I did the whole year. That's where I got excited about the work. It was a great think tank.
>
> *Howard*

Working with a Writer

Some producers can write, and some can't. If writing is not your strength, develop your script with a writer who can put your ideas on paper more effectively than you. You might become a co-writer or act in a supervisory role. Most producers follow the latter path unless they are confident writers themselves. The give-and-take between two creative individuals can energize the process, resulting in a union in which the sum is greater than the parts.

During the process of developing and producing a project, producers work with many different kinds of creative people. No two egos are alike. Learning how to maximize people's varied talents is essential to becoming a good producer. The writer is the first of these individuals.

Any agreement with a writer to develop an idea, whether it is the writer's idea or yours, should be formalized on paper in a deal memo (see Glossary).

LEGALITIES

Rights and Adaptations (Preexisting Material)

For the privilege to profit from the commercial sale or rental of your short film or video, rights to original material must be purchased. This gives you complete control of the story in that medium. For a well-known story, commercial rights can be expensive, if not prohibitive, for a producer on a limited budget.

It is essential for you to obtain permission to use existing material or even to dramatize someone's biography unless they are within the public domain as public figures (e.g., Madonna, Elizabeth Taylor). If you read about some extraordinary man in the newspaper, get permission to write about him. You'll also need permission from the author of the article if she has exclusive information about the subject.

If you find a short story you like, make a legally binding arrangement with its author for the right to use it as the basis for your film. Contact the author's representative, perhaps an agent or an attorney, through the publisher. If the author is deceased, an agent or lawyer will represent the estate. If you have a personal relationship with the author, you might want to bypass the publisher, agent, or attorney and appeal directly to the author. This approach might also be worth trying in the case of well-known authors whose representatives categorically reject any request from unknown producers.

The work might be in the public domain and free to use if it has been 50 years since the author's death. A book is in the public domain when its copyright protection has expired. Examples are stories by Aesop, Dickens, or from the Bible. If you have any doubt as to what is or isn't in the public domain, write to the copyright office: Reference and Bibliography Section, LM-451 Copyright Office, Library of Congress, Washington, DC 20559.

Film students and beginners exhibit their work primarily at festivals, museums, or conferences. A basic use of a short work is as a springboard to future employment. It might be possible to strike a deal with the author's representative for noncommercial, or festival, rights. These are easier to attain than commercial rights. They're also cheaper—sometimes even free. Prizes at festivals are not considered profit.

Original Material

On the opposite end of the spectrum is an original story written directly for the screen. If you decide to go this route, you should purchase the rights to the material from its author, even if only for a dollar. A simple letter of agreement between you and the author will make the process legal. This letter is your protection against future disputes concerning ownership or division of any profits.

Copyright

Be sure to obtain a copyright from the Library of Congress for any original material in treatment, outline, or screenplay form. A copyright certifies that the material existed on a certain date. If someone presents the same project later, you have grounds for a claim of copyright infringement. Register only the first draft unless the story changes dramatically from one draft to another.

For the documentary producer, the rights to tell the story of a particular subject must be secured.

Rights are not necessary when dealing with historical or public figures, however. Private subjects must sign a release providing the producer with all rights necessary. If you have any question about the process of securing rights to a nonpublic figure or subject, consult an entertainment lawyer.

EXPANDING THE CREATIVE TEAM: THE DIRECTOR

When the screenplay is well into development, the producer brings in the next important member of the creative team: the director. The producer seeks an individual who is aware of the material's dramatic potential and shares or complements the producer's vision. A director frees the producer to focus on fund-raising and preproduction. The director will shepherd the script through the final stages of development, supervising the rewrites or completing them herself.

HOW DO SCRIPTS AFFECT BUDGETS?

To begin fund-raising, the producer needs to have an accurate budget that reflects the complete cost of producing the script. Changes in the script that affect the budget must be examined at this stage. Suppose, for example, that the writer requests an elephant for a particular scene. The elephant becomes one of many items that must be delivered to the set on the day when that particular sequence is to be shot. The producer looks at this script need and says to himself, "Where do I get an elephant? Won't it require a big truck and a trainer or even trainers? Where am I going to get the animal? Where am I going to put it? How much hay do elephants consume? How much will it cost?" Aware of budget constraints and responsible for the schedule, the producer might ask that a more manageable and less expensive animal be substituted. If the story is not compromised, an elephant could be replaced by a donkey, which is a smaller, more cooperative, and probably a less expensive production item. The producer should request this substitution during preproduction, rather than on the day before the scene is to be shot. (Of course, the producer might decide to keep the elephant, even at great expense, and capitalize on the publicity. Having the star arrive on the set on the back of an elephant is a great photo op-

portunity. If the picture winds up on the news, the audience will become aware of the project, and this can translate to box-office profit.)

Sometimes, compromises cannot be made without adversely affecting the project. In *The Lunch Date*, for example, the location could not be compromised. Grand Central Station is a very expensive location, but it had to be secured for two days of shooting. The film would not have had the same impact if it had been shot in the train station at Stamford, Connecticut.

DIRECTOR
Performs Rewrites

The director puts her personal stamp on all projects through the creative decisions she makes along the way, such as the choice of cast, crew, locations, and visual style. She provides the creative glue that holds the project together. However, the foundation on which all else is built is the script. A director who writes or rewrites the script contributes her focused and personalized vision to the project. In so doing, she should ensure that the final draft is the best it can be. After all, any story worth telling is worth telling well.

DIRECTOR AS STORYTELLER

A script represents the events and dramatic moments of the story, which must be translated into visual images. The director must evaluate whether the story is being told properly. Is the present draft the best realization of the central theme or concept behind the story? If the script needs work, the director must apply her own storytelling skills to reshape the screenplay.

The work to be done might vary from a slight "polish" (minor dialogue changes) to a complete rewrite (restructuring the story). If the script is in relatively good shape, the director need only prepare it to be photographed by creating a *shooting script*. This process requires numbering the scenes to reflect the locations. Each scene is given a number to make the breakdown of the screenplay precise. When this stage has been completed, the real work of preproduction can begin, that is, the stripboard, budget, and schedule.

Elements other than story content and structure can influence the development of the screenplay. The director might be inspired by a location or a particular actor. While scouting locations, she might come upon a unique setting that inspires a rewrite of a particular scene or even the whole story. After hearing a strong performer read a part, the director might decide to shape the character to better fit the talents of that actor.

> It's always, I think, about discovering the story. You write it on paper. You rewrite it. Then you start shooting it. You shoot a lot. You start editing the film together and then—where's the story? So you've got to find it all over again. You start editing things out, changing things around slightly.
>
> *Adam*

BASIC GUIDELINES FOR THE SHORT FORM

How do you evaluate a script? Only a few of the elements of dramatic writing apply to the short form. Because most beginners are not familiar with its format, let's examine these common attributes and furnish a critical point of view. The following are general guidelines; there will always be exceptions.

The screenwriting process is about research, discovery, and crystallization. Watching your story develop is an exciting experience. The final result should feel as if all the scenes are in the right place. Achieving this feeling, however, comes from patience and hard work. You will soon understand the age-old rule: Writing is rewriting. Subscribe to it. Only be satisfied with the best you can do.

Short films or videos can be developed from many different kinds of ideas. Some stories stretch the boundaries of the 30-minute format. Let's examine what *Truman, Mirror Mirror, The Lunch Date,* and a few classic shorts have in common. This will give you a greater understanding of the dramatic parameters of the short form.

Length

Is there an ideal length for a short? The best length is the one that satisfies your particular story. Work from this point. If you are concerned about the ideal length for distribution markets, submit your proposal or script to several distributors for feedback. If you have already found a market for your picture, the ideal length might be predetermined.

> *Students:* Anxious to impress people with their talent, beginning film- and videomakers often want to say too much with their short film or video project.

They tend to compress feature-length ideas into 10-minute pictures. Resist this temptation.

The Central Theme

The central theme is what the story is all about. It is the raison d'être, the cement that holds the story together. In *Truman,* the theme is conquering a fear. *The Lunch Date* is about letting go of one's prejudice. *Mirror Mirror* centers on how women see themselves juxtaposed with society's mirror. All the scenes in your film or video should be subordinate to the main theme. If a scene doesn't support your theme, eliminate it.

Conflict

A basic element common to all visual drama is the need for a specific and identifiable conflict. Conflict creates tension. Tension engages the viewer's emotions until the conflict is resolved and the tension relieved at the end of the piece.

What is conflict, and how is it created? Most narrative stories begin by establishing a problem, dilemma, or goal. Someone wants something or is unhappy or unfulfilled in some way. The process of working out this issue defines the drama. Obstacles to solving the problem intensify the conflict. The necessity of overcoming obstacles to resolve the conflict places a greater value on the lesson learned.

> What I knew from the script was the basic structure of the events that would happen. The important things to me were that the woman would get bumped, lose her wallet, miss her train, and that she'd enter this restaurant. She'd sit down, get up to get a fork, and come back, and the guy would be there. And they would share a salad, and he would get up and get coffee, and come back, and ta da. I had to figure out how I was going to reveal her mistake. That was the framework that I had. Then the lines, the bits of action, and the small details would come out of that.
>
> *Adam*

The Basic Conflicts

Different kinds of conflict are possible in a story, regardless of whether it's fictional or nonfictional:

Individual versus self (internal)

Individual versus individual (personal)

Individual versus society (social environment)

Individual versus nature (physical environment)

Each one of these conflicts, alone or in combination, draws our attention to the plight of the main character, or protagonist, when confronted by personal or other individual's demons or the forces of society or nature. The director creates a deep emotional connection between the audience and the protagonist by clearly identifying the protagonist's dilemma.

Truman employs three levels of conflict: individual versus society, individual versus individual, and individual versus self. The class represents society and is punished because of Truman's weakness. By overcoming his fear and climbing the rope, Truman is accepted to the bosom of the group. The film also deals with the conflict of individual versus individual, with the coach as the antagonist. He tries to humiliate Truman into climbing the rope, thereby forcing the boy to make his final decision.

These two levels are, however, extensions of the primary conflict that is at the heart of the story: Truman's internal conflict with himself. His need to climb up the rope (and his fear of doing so) is the reason the story exists. As an audience, we strongly identify with that need and are emotionally involved in finding out if Truman can overcome his fear and climb the rope. Once he does, the conflict is resolved, the tension is diffused, and the story ends.

The protagonist in *The Lunch Date* faces two levels of conflict: internal and personal. Her goal is to eat her salad. The obstacles are the homeless man (personal) and her prejudices (internal). This is the basis for conflict. How she deals with this unexpected situation creates a tension that will be resolved only when the woman either gets her salad or does not. The tension created by this expectation impels us to watch. We are eager to learn how she will handle this unique situation. Will she overcome her aversion to the homeless man? The transition from outrage to mutual respect is a satisfying leap for the character and the audience.

The conflict in *Mirror Mirror* is one of individual versus nature, society, and self. The goal is for the women to accept their physical appearances. Tension arises in the fact that their looks are at odds with society's standards of beauty. It is intensified by the emphasis and importance our culture places on how a woman's body looks.

In each of these stories, the filmmaker sets up an expectation by establishing a conflict. We are engaged by the main character's need to overcome the conflict and deal with the problem, and we will only be satisfied when the conflict is resolved. If the char-acters could get what they wanted easily, there would be no story.

The Dramatic Arc

Every story should have a beginning, a middle, and an end—but, as Jean-Luc Godard once said, not necessarily in that order. In *Truman* and *The Lunch Date*, each main character has a goal (the rope, the salad), and each has an obstacle (fear, the homeless man). Most narrative stories can be reduced to this basic formula of goal/obstacle/resolution, creating this progression:

beginning (setup)
middle (development)
end (resolution)

This formula creates the natural arc of all narrative and nonnarrative drama. All stories follow this progression. The problem is introduced, developed, and then resolved. When the resolution has been achieved, the story is over.

> My whole script hinges upon the fantasy sequences. They are small and contained in the final film, but they are very important in showing who the main character is. What role they play in the film constantly changed. Originally, they were the entire film. But as the story developed, they became shorter and their importance changed. They became more an element of surprise and gave clues showing what Truman was feeling. But this weeding out and connecting occurred over 13 drafts; eventually, however, the fantasies found their proper place in the story.
>
> *Howard*

The story should have some twists and turns along the way (obstacles) to add tension to its development. The events of a story are caused by either the characters or situations. The director can map these out on a graph so that no matter what scene is being shot, she can understand the dynamics of each moment and its relationship to the whole.

This map allows the director to communicate with the creative team out of sequence. For example, knowing what transpires in scene 4 will inform her work with an actor in scene 3. If the actor plays scene 3 too forcefully, he may have nowhere to go emotionally for the climax in scene 4.

Most of these principles hold true for the documentary form. A documentary also needs a dramatic arc by which it can tell a true story.

One Primary Event

Truman and *The Lunch Date* are stories told in a contained time period. By experiencing the illusion of real time, the audience is brought into the immediacy of the drama. The director's challenge then becomes to show what is outstanding about this bit of time.

A short film ideally focuses on a single event around which the action of the story revolves: in *Truman,* climbing the rope; in *The Lunch Date,* sharing a salad. The event in *Mirror Mirror* is the coming together of many women to express their feelings about their bodies. The single event is an important element in the success of each film. In a short of less than 30 minutes, it is difficult to balance any more.

By focusing on the playing out of just one event, the director can fully explore the event's dramatic potential. This simplicity of purpose frees her to give depth to the piece. The audience comes away satisfied because their expectations have been fulfilled.

> The short films I think really work all deal with single incidents. That's what I've concluded. Even the ones that are longer than ten minutes, or apparently more complicated, are really all about a specific moment in time.
>
> *Howard*

It's not always necessary to work within a confined time period to create a successful story. *Le Poulet* (*The Chicken*), a 15-minute Academy Award–winning short film written and directed by Claude Berri (B&W, 1963), takes place over a period of days. *Le Poulet* is the story of a young French boy who becomes so fond of a rooster that his parents bought for Sunday dinner that he secretly decides to convince them that it's a hen. He steals an egg from the refrigerator and places it under the rooster. This ploy works until one morning when the rooster wakes the father up with its crow. Frightened that his parents are now going to kill the bird, the boy pleads for its life. The parents, surprised and touched by the boy's attachment, decide to let him keep the bird as a pet.

> Things don't necessarily always influence you in a conscious way but sometimes excite you to do more. I had seen a lot of films, and even more in film school. I had seen *Le Poulet*, about a boy who falls in love with a chicken. (It's in the New York Public Library.) It has thirty-eight scenes in nine minutes yet is not choppy at all. The boy tries to keep the chicken alive when everyone wants to eat it. Great stuff.
>
> *Howard*

The story focuses on a single conflict that arises out of the main character's goal to keep the rooster as a pet. That conflict takes place over a week, not hours. The film is told in small vignettes that underscore the young boy's dilemma and how he attempts to resolve it.

One Major Character

Both *Truman* and *The Lunch Date* are approximately 11 minutes long. This is time to focus on only one main character. A dilemma is introduced, expanded, and resolved for Truman and the woman of *The Lunch Date*. It's true that the gym coach and the homeless man go through some sort of change, but only in direct relationship to the main character. We don't care for them in the same way as for the main characters. These secondary characters force the conflict by serving as obstacles to the protagonist's goal. Although there can be other characters, our emotions focus on one person's story in each film.

When expanded to 30 minutes, it is possible for a short film or video to deal fully with two characters, although their destinies should be interlocked in some way. An excellent example of a two-character piece is an award-winning short film entitled *Minors*, written and directed by Alan Kingsberg (1984, New York University). It is the story of a teenage girl who needs a subject for her science project and a minor league pitcher struggling to make it to the majors. The story brings these two people together. The girl, who is a baseball fanatic, convinces the pitcher that if she can teach him to throw a curve ball, he will be called up to play in the majors. She puts the pitcher through a training program, and he eventually develops a terrific curve ball. He is called up to the majors, but she is left without a project. He helps her present their pitching experiment as the science project, and it is a success. She passes her science class, and he pitches for the Yankees.

Even though there are two main characters in *Minors*, their goals intersect. Each wants something different, but the success of one is directly tied to the success of the other. The pitcher makes it to the majors because of the student, and she completes her science project because of him.

Minimum Back Story

What is back story? It is the historical information, or exposition, about the characters that is necessary to understand their motivation during the course of the story. In a short, back story must be communicated quickly and efficiently. A feature film has 30 to 40 minutes of setup time, but a short has only a few minutes. Your story and character might need to be simplified if you are unable to set up your character succinctly.

Truman is immediately presented as a young boy with a fear of climbing up a rope. We do not need to know any more about his history to relate to his present situation. The character of the woman in *The Lunch Date* is well defined by her wardrobe and demeanor. Her reaction to the street people in Grand Central Station sets up an expectation about how she will react to the man who has "stolen" her lunch. There is no need to know any more about this character to understand the rest of the film.

Internal Motives, External Action

Communicating internal problems is one of the challenges of writing for the screen. This is a visual medium. Dramatic events must be manifested visually and audibly. Both Truman and the woman from *The Lunch Date* expose their internal conflicts through their actions. Truman's outrageous fantasies are external representations of his fear. In *The Lunch Date*, the woman's prejudice is revealed when she tries to avoid dining with a homeless man. Both stories throw their characters into unexpected situations. We *see* who they are by the way they *act*.

No Talking Heads

If your story contains a lot of dialogue and very little action or dramatic movement, it might be better as a radio drama or a play. Films and videos are usually about action. Dialogue serves to support the action, define the characters, and enhance our appreciation of the images. Viewers should be able to watch a film with the sound off and still understand the story. If you are interested in adapting a play, you will need to "open up" the drama by devising actions and movement to replace many of the words and to create a visual component that doesn't exist on the stage.

Rewriting

The axiom "Writing is rewriting" is true. Stories go through evolutionary stages. They are like puzzles, worked at until all the pieces fit together. The goal is to find the right balance among the elements. Each

draft reveals something that was hidden in the previous version.

Professionals know that creating a well-crafted script takes time, patience, and devotion. The key is to get it right before walking on the set. Don't hope to work out script problems during the heat of production. During preproduction, you have the time. Take it.

> I counted thirteen drafts altogether, but I don't think that is a lot of drafts for a ten-minute film. Part of it is due to the fact that the short film form is not necessarily a very natural writing form; it's sort of a sonnet. It's very tough. Thirteen drafts is pretty much the average. Looking back through my files it's clear that in each draft the story became shorter and clearer and also moved closer to becoming a shooting script.
>
> *Howard*

Readings

Once the script is close to being finalized, the director should conduct readings to audition the material. It is one thing to write a line on paper but quite another to hear it read aloud or to see it performed by an actor under a director's guidance. What the director and actor want to discover is whether the lines ring true. How do the words flow off the tongue? Are there too many words or too few? Is the space between the words (pauses) more poignant than the words themselves?

Images before Words

The unspoken rule about visual storytelling is that if you can show it, don't say it. A director is aware that on the screen, the actor's face itself becomes part of the dialogue. A well-placed close-up could serve better than a word or phrase; an image usually speaks louder than any word. Use the words to enhance, not replace, an image.

> That's what's so great about *The Lunch Date*. I think that's why it is so successful. There's so much that the audience has to assume because nothing is spoken, and you make false assumptions. I think it's really brilliant in that way.
>
> *Jan*

In *The Lunch Date*, the original screenplay called for the woman to be accosted by a homeless person on her way to the train after the salad incident. She was to tell the man, "Get a job!" The scene was shot because it was in the script, but it is not in the final film. In the film, the woman is approached by a homeless man on her way to the train, but she completely ignores him. Why? This physical slight seemed to the director far more potent a gesture than the words, "Get a job!" Addressing the man acknowledges that he exists; ignoring him treats him as if he doesn't exist.

> I was determined to try to make this sequence work somehow. When I did that one shot of her coming into the train station, of returning after discovering her bags, I only covered it in one shot. So every take there she was saying, "Get a job!" or "Get lost!" or whatever. So I took part of the dolly shot from her earlier entrance, before she bumps into the guy, and I cut the two together. There is a slight jump, but now what she was doing was just giving him the silent treatment. And I think it worked.
>
> *Adam*

Scripts are usually overwritten because writers feel the need to put it all in. It is the director's job to trim the "fat" (unnecessary words or actions).

THE SHOOTING SCRIPT

Having supervised the rewrite or having rewritten the screenplay herself, the director must now develop the shooting script, which is a visual plan for the project. This draft is written in WGA standard format and has markings and numbers that communicate the director's vision to the producer and the camera and art departments. Up to this point, it has not been important for the script to reflect shots or visual references. The emphasis has been on structure, character, and dialogue.

The first step is to number each scene, enabling the production team to identify each scene by its numbered code. The director then previsualizes the script; that is, she creates a shooting plan for each scene. The plan should reflect how the director will "cover" each scene in the project. The term *coverage* refers to the amount and type of shots the director will need to tell the story adequately in each scene. Developing a shot plan requires that the director break down the script and create floor plans, storyboards, or both. (See Chapter 3, "Breakdowns," for more information.)

The director then marks the script with her shot plan. It will include abbreviations like *CU* (close-up, a very tight shot on an object or a character's face), *LS* (long shot, in which the camera takes in a lot of visual information), *2S* (two-shot, in which two characters are in the frame at the same time), and *OTS* (over-the-shoulder shot, which is like a two-shot except that the camera favors the face of one of the two characters).

The shooting script gives the producer information from which to construct an accurate schedule. The rest of the production team obtains from the shooting script a point of view from which to design the project.

DOCUMENTARIES

Because the development and execution of a documentary (nonfictional narrative) might take months or even years, be sure to choose subject matter about which you feel strongly and have a great desire to learn more. You might need to do extensive research to determine whether the subject matter warrants making a short film or video. You might have to view films or videos on the same or similar subjects, research newspaper and magazine articles, or conduct preinterviews.

> A crucial question I always ask myself before setting out to make any film is, Is this subject eminently "filmable" and uniquely appropriate to be treated in film? While I'm making a film, I try to foreground that issue to ensure that I am exploiting (in a good way) the unique properties of film—the interface of sound and image, and an opportunity to frame things differently from how one normally processes the world.
>
> *Jan*

The subject matter should contain inherent dramatic value that engages the viewer in the same way a narrative story does, but with real, not imagined, events. This could be an examination of an individual's or a group's struggle to overcome adversities.

> I thought I was interested in this whole notion of the "ideal" and how women in our culture are tyrannized by the belief that there exists an ideal body type and that it is ultimately unattainable. I wanted to present the ideal as something not fixed in stone, but as a representation of something separate and different from all of us. I was interested in the vagaries of the ideal. So I began to read a lot of books about concepts of beauty during different decades, trying to identify the

prescriptions for this ideal type. I read about how the White Rock girl, who adorned bottles of White Rock, was redesigned every decade so that her dimensions would reflect the changing concepts of the perfect physical type.

Jan

From research notes, an outline for the documentary can be created. This outline serves as the genesis of a script during preproduction. From the outline, a series of questions are prepared for each interview. The combination of on-camera interviews, stock footage, and cinema verité (in some cases, staged events) will comprise the visual components of the piece.

It is acceptable to write out the script in its entirety. This includes creating the answers you anticipate recording. By writing out the script, you can prepare questions that will help your subject respond according to your design. This gives the director a target during the interviews. The questions might be answered very differently than you expected, but together with the subject, you can explore fully the issues at hand.

A lot of documentarists, and particularly women, have moved into fiction films after five or ten years. They say, I got tired of sitting around waiting for people to say what I wanted them to say. I always find that so interesting because for me, that's why I will stay in documentary—because you never know what people are going to say, and I really like the unpredictability of it.

Jan

Depending on the subject, the questions you compose can be easy, or provocative. If the subject is forthcoming with the information required, the questions can be probing but cordial. If the subject needs to be drawn out, a more provocative approach might be required.

I asked my thirteen subjects the same set of four questions, changing the composition for each question. I knew that I would intercut their responses, relying on a jump-cut technique. One question was, "Describe your body from head to foot, discussing different parts as you go." Some women would start with their hair, and were very diligent about hitting every body part, and some people would start with their neck and jump to their knees, and that was OK. If they did that, I didn't ask them to talk about their breasts, waist, or hips.

It was quite revealing to observe what they chose to talk about or ignore. Some parts were complimented, and some parts were totally derided. A second question was, "If you could redesign your body to conform to the concept of your ideal, what would it look like?" I didn't realize it at the time, but the two questions are essentially the same. Because while they were redesigning, they might say, "I really hate my shoulders," for example, and that was an answer to the earlier question.

Jan

The final script for a documentary can be fully developed only in postproduction. With all of the visual and audio materials in hand, the director begins to grasp the shape that the film or video will eventually take. The audio portion of the show will be the voices from the on- and off-camera interviews, the track of the verité footage, any audiotape recorded, and possibly a narration. The assemblage of these audio elements, especially the narration (if applicable), becomes the final script.

KEY POINTS

1. Without a good script, you cannot have a good final product.
2. Proper format has a direct bearing on the production breakdowns.
3. Good scripts are not written, they are rewritten.
4. Understand the short form. As the feature-length film is to the epic poem, the short film or video is to the haiku.

part one

Preproduction

I spent a lot of hours in Grand Central, almost an entire day, getting a sense of the building. That was when I first noticed how the light streams through the windows.

Adam

You have an idea, an outline, a treatment, or a rough draft of a script that you like and are determined to shoot. You are eager to begin production and get out into the field. Assuming that you have secured the appropriate funds, you are now ready to start preproduction. During this phase, you will ready virtually every aspect for the filming process. Decisions made during this time are the most important of the whole production for they are the foundation on which everything else is built. The producer and director share many of these responsibilities. The next eight chapters indicate the specific responsibilities of each. These responsibilities are outlined in Figures I.1 and I.2.

PREPARE THOROUGHLY FOR THE SHOOT DATE

One of the major goals of preproduction is to try to anticipate anything and everything that can go wrong during a shoot. This gives you time to react sensibly to things that could not have been anticipated and are entirely beyond your control (and invariably occur, such as acts of God). These things happen because all film shoots are ruled by Murphy's Law: Anything that *can* go wrong inevitably *will*. When you plan a production, work with that assumption, and always plan for the worst-case scenario.

Preproduction is also the time to research and develop your idea, to build in all the elements instrumental to the foundation of your project, to design what it should look like, and to explore all of the variables needed to create a successful production.

Most vitally, preproduction is the time to make sure the script is the very best it can be.

Never lose sight of the fact that this is cost-effective time. All the effort you expend on preparation now will pay off during production. During preproduction, you have an abundance of something you won't have when you start shooting: time. When actually shooting, spending time is spending money. Settling on an efficient game plan and solving potential production problems during preproduction will save precious dollars later.

You can't do too much preproduction work. The more thoroughly a project is planned, the smoother the production will be. For some reason, this is a difficult concept for many novices to understand. They often return from their first major shoot dejected, having experienced just how ill-prepared they really were. They realize too late that many mistakes or disasters during production could have been averted if they had been more organized before they started to shoot. All the talent in the world won't help if your schedule isn't realistic, the meals aren't served on time, you lose the use of your location, or you don't have enough stock on hand. These are only a few of the contingencies that require forethought.

WITHOUT A GOOD SCRIPT, YOU CANNOT MAKE A GOOD FILM

Even after getting a good script as discussed in Chapter 2, there is no guarantee of producing a good film. However, a poorly thought out script has little

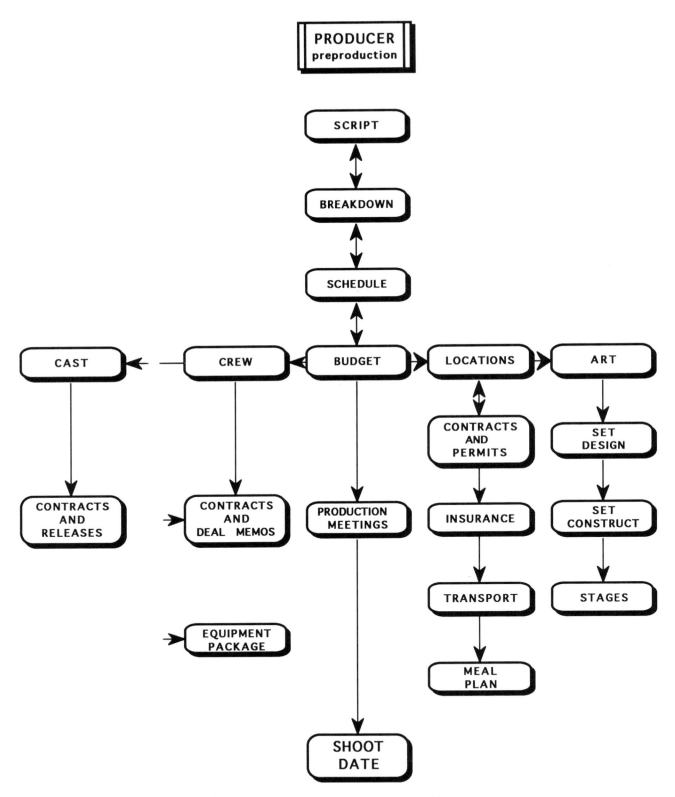

Figure I.1 Producer's preproduction responsibilities.

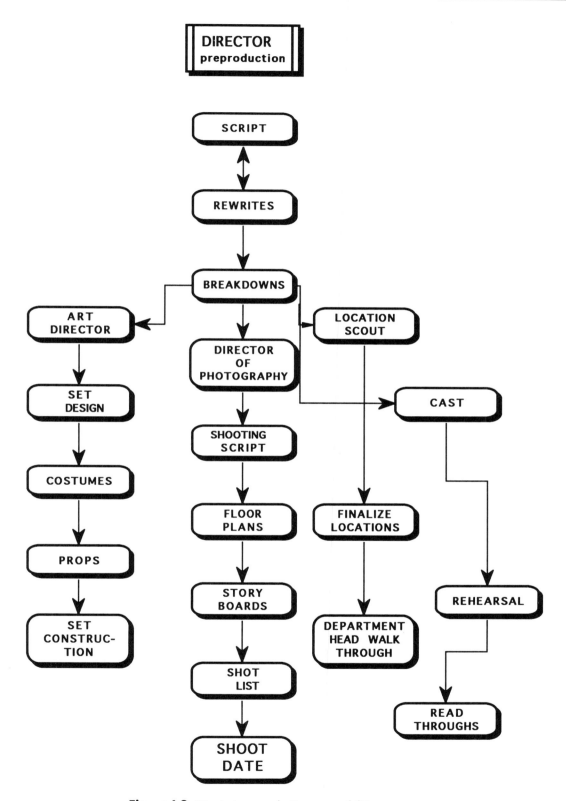

Figure I.2 Director's preproduction responsibilities.

chance of yielding a successful finished product. It is true that many serendipitous events can occur during shooting and editing that will add evocative imagery, inspired characters, and atmospheric locations to your project. The script will come to full-color life, but the progression of events—your story—will not change.

To ensure that you have the best script possible, be prepared to rewrite many times before production begins. You would be ill-advised to go out into the field with a story that doesn't live up to its full potential. The investment of time, money, talent, and effort will be wasted unless the original blueprint is solid.

Don't expect to solve lingering script problems magically during production. Unexpected surprises in action or dialogue will add measurably to the texture of a scene, but don't count on them. Rewriting the script on the set is usually too demanding for beginning film- and videomakers. The pressures of filming the original script will keep you more than occupied.

PREPRODUCTION GUIDELINES

Intangible managerial skills are as important as technical know-how in preparing successfully for production. The following are some general guidelines to help with the intangibles of preproduction. It all starts with confidence and a positive attitude.

KEEP A POSITIVE ATTITUDE. Lack of experience makes it difficult for beginning film- and video-makers to access their day-to-day preproduction progress. You might sometimes doubt that so many tasks could possibly be accomplished by the shoot date; perhaps you have one part still uncast, there is no sound recordist, and the key location has not yet been secured. Don't panic. A positive attitude is as important as efficiency and organization. Professionals understand that things can come together at the last moment. The producer situates himself at the middle of all of the activity and keeps the production team focused. He must inspire confidence that all of the elements will come together in time, no matter what the obstacles.

ALLOW ENOUGH TIME FOR PREPRODUCTION. How long should it take to prepare a short script for production? This is a difficult question because much depends on the experience of the creative team and the complexity of the script. A

story set in one room with two characters is easier to preproduce than one demanding 10 different and unique locations. However, any short project can seem overwhelming to the first-time film- or videomaker.

Aside from the time spent securing the financing, a workable formula is to allow one week of preproduction for each day of principal photography. It might take less time or more, based on script complexity and the director's experience. In the end, you will do it in the time that is available.

SET A PREPRODUCTION SCHEDULE. Use your shoot date as the final target. Create deadlines for securing cast, crew, and locations, and strive to follow them.

DELEGATE RESPONSIBILITY. Preproduction responsibilities fall on many shoulders. The producer must assign tasks to the whole creative team (art director, director, director of photography) and then keep track of their progress.

HOLD REGULAR PRODUCTION MEETINGS. Don't rely on ad hoc gatherings to keep everyone informed. Events happen too fast and plans change too often for everyone to be kept abreast via casual chats. Schedule regular production meetings, and stick to them. Keep in constant touch with the key creative staff. Don't work in a linear fashion. The production team needs to work on many things at the same time.

NEVER ASSUME ANYTHING. Double- and triple-check everything. If the producer assumes that the location manager has checked the electric supply of an apartment location, chances are only fifty-fifty that he did. Do you want to take that chance?

BREAK SOME RULES. This book is meant as a guide to a complex process. Picture-making is built on ingenuity, creativity, improvisation, and instinct. The entrepreneurial spirit is alive in the film and video business. Often, it is the breaking of a rule that leads to an exciting opportunity.

REMEMBER THAT ALL THINGS CHANGE. The process of preproduction is an evolution. The script, schedule, and budget will go through many changes before they are finalized, sometimes right up to the shooting date. The essential caveat is that once shooting begins, changes cease and you must concentrate on fulfilling the script, schedule, and budget.

At NYU, though it is probably true of any place, the first thing that occurred after settling on an idea was choosing a shooting date. The shooting date is so important because it gives you something definite, a tangible thing from which to work. From there I could create a time line, a calendar which told me by November I should have a draft, by December I should be casting, by January I should have the locations lined up. Without that, you can lose your way and postpone endlessly.

I often saw students who were not set with their dates who'd write and write, and at the end of the semester they'd say, "I need to shoot now." They left themselves three weeks for preproduction and, consequently, were doing preproduction while shooting.

I think choosing a date and sticking to it is very important because it forces you to create a funnel where everything is marching toward that moment in time. It keeps you structured, keeps you organized, and really makes you focus in on something. It keeps you from letting anything slip.

Howard

STAY HEALTHY. Putting together all of the ingredients needed to create a film or video can be exciting but stressful, especially if you're doing this for the first time. The daily stress makes demands on the body. You want to be healthy when you are in production. This means taking care of yourself during preproduction and staying at your peak. You cannot slow down production because of a cold or postpone it because of the flu.

Everything—locations, storyboards, even walking down the street and hearing a piece of music—is a springboard for your writing. You become a conduit for all of these ideas. The whole process is about focusing those ideas into ten pages, keeping the good ones, and removing the bad ones. I remember going over the shot that introduces the main character, Truman; the shot that follows the rope down the noose and then rack-focuses to Truman. Originally, it was not like that. Initially, we saw the rope, the noose, and then cut to Truman. The DP suggested the change, and it made the introduction work. Everything is for the script.

Howard

chapter three

Breakdowns

We would have a nightly meeting for an hour. We would go over the schedule, which matched the lined script, which matched the storyboard, which matched the breakdowns.

Howard

PRODUCER

Breaking Down the Script

Before a shooting schedule can be devised, the producer examines the script from all practical angles. Up to now, the development of the script has dominated the creative viewpoint; the emphasis has been on making the structure and the dialogue of the story work. Yet, although it might be dramatically effective for the main characters to have an intimate conversation in a park during a rainstorm on a bridge at night, from a practical point of view it might be quite difficult to accomplish. The producer must think about the difficulty of obtaining permission to shoot in the park and the problems of making rain, lighting a bridge at night, and recording dialogue with the sounds of rain and traffic in the background.

The producer is trained to see the repercussions of every aspect of the script. A scene in Grand Central Station (such as the one in *The Lunch Date*) might be stylistically or thematically correct, but what impact will this location have on the schedule and the budget? To evaluate the feasibility of this scene in the context of the whole picture, the producer must first extract, or *break down*, all relevant production information from the script. The combined breakdowns of all of the scenes give the producer an overview of the practical challenges of the project.

A producer can't begin to raise money for the project until he has an idea of how much it is going to cost. He can't know how much the project will cost unless he knows what equipment the film or video requires and how long it will take to shoot it.

Finally, the producer can't begin to create a schedule until the script is broken down to reveal all production information.

In essence, the producer cannot begin preproduction until the script has been completed. Although the script might change, the producer works at the breakdowns and incorporates the changes as they arise. To assist the producer, the director prepares her shot list, which will provide information for the schedule.

PRODUCTION BOOK

The producer needs easy access to the production information that he will gather during preproduction. One way of doing this is to buy a large loose-leaf notebook and a set of tabbed dividers. The first document in this book should be the script. In addition, you will eventually include a crew list, schedule, breakdown pages, props and furnishings list, cast list, budget, transportation and meal plans, insurance package, and all permits, clearances, and releases.

PROPER SCRIPT FORMAT

Before you can begin breaking down the script, it must be in proper screenplay format, which refers to how to set up the script information on a page. Professional scripts are written in a standard format to enable the production manager to evaluate the production value of each page correctly and translate it into the schedule and budget.

The format size relates to the size of the type (12-point Courier), the spacing between dialogue and action (two lines), the width of the margins, and the length of the page. (See the sample scripts in Appendix C.) The standard settings are as follows:

- Left margin: $1^1/_2$ "
- Right margin: $1^1/_2$ "
- Tab for left dialogue margin: $2^1/_2$ "
- Tab for right dialogue margin: $2^1/_2$ "
- Tab for speaker's name: $4^1/_2$ "

These elements should be capitalized in the script:

- All camera instructions (use sparingly until writing the shooting script draft)
- All sounds, including music ("The log SNAPS")
- All characters the first time they appear in every scene
- Every word in the header
  ("INT. DAY - GRAND CENTRAL STATION")
- The speaker's name, above each line of dialogue

A properly formatted screen page should equal approximately one minute of screen time. For this formula to work, the script must be typed to include a specific amount of information on each page. If you have crammed too many words of description or dialogue on one page, a 10-page script might, in fact, turn out to be a 15-minute project. Conversely, a loosely typed script will also give you an inaccurate assessment of the length of the project. Time equals money, and an accurate estimation of time is imperative for you to know how to schedule and budget a project.

Keep in mind that this "one page equals one minute" rule is only a guess. A five-page dialogue scene might run up to six or seven minutes in length, whereas five pages of action, say a chase sequence, will most likely play quicker on the screen. This rule is merely an *average* of the action and dialogue elements in the script.

BREAKING DOWN THE SCRIPT

Following are the first steps in organizing a production:

1. BREAKDOWNS
   a. Prepare breakdown sheets.
   b. Prepare strips for the stripboard.
2. SCHEDULE
   a. Place strips on the stripboard.
3. BUDGET
   a. Price each line item.

These steps are discussed in more detail in this chapter.

Step 1a: Prepare Breakdown Sheets

Breaking down the script requires that all the production elements that affect the schedule and the budget (cast, locations, props, wardrobe, etc.) be lifted from the script and placed in their respective categories on *breakdown sheets* (Figure 3.1). Each scene from the script is given its own breakdown sheet. The breakdown sheets inform the budgeting process because they single out the production requirements of each scene that will likely cost money (see step 3).

Once the relevant production information has been separated from the script, the producer need not refer back to it unless changes are made in casting, locations, or props. Dialogue changes do not affect the breakdowns unless they alter the length of a scene.

The breakdown sheets are color-coded to indicate day/exterior, night/exterior, day/interior, and night/interior scenes. If the project takes place outside during the day, you need only use day/exterior-colored breakdown sheets. The color code is a helpful scheduling tool.

The first step in the process of breaking down a script is to number the first scene (if it isn't numbered already) and draw a line in black pencil across the page at the scene's end. This visually isolates the scene you are about to break down.

Breakdown Sheet Header
Before color-coding the important information, fill in the following items at the top of the breakdown sheet:

- *Date.* The date that you are preparing the breakdown page is important when revisions are made.
- *Name of production company.* Give your production unit an identity. This can come in handy when identifying yourself on the phone, on letterheads, on cards, and most important, on the production bank account.
- *Title of script.*

```
CODE-BREAKDOWN SHEET          SCRIPT
Day Ext- Yellow          BREAKDOWN SHEET    _____
Night Ext-Green                              (DATE)
Day Int- White
Night Int-Blue
```

production company	production title/no.	breakdown page no.
scene no.	scene name	int/ext
description		day/night
		page count

CAST RED	STUNTS ORANGE	EXTRAS GREEN
	EXTRAS/SILENT BITS YELLOW	
SPECIAL EFFECTS BLUE	PROPS VIOLET	VEHICLES/ANIMALS PINK
WARDROBE CIRCLE	MAKE-UP/HAIR ASTERISK	SOUND EFFECTS/MUSIC BROWN
SPECIAL EQUIPMENT BOX	PRODUCTION NOTES	

Figure 3.1 Breakdown sheet.

- *Breakdown page number.* This will most likely correspond to the script page, but not always.
- *Scene number.*
- *Scene location.*
- *Interior or exterior* (indoors or outdoors).
- *Description.* This should be a brief and concise description, or "one-liner," of what happens in

the scene. The description plays an important part in quickly and efficiently identifying the scene.

- *Day or night.* You can also indicate dawn or dusk if appropriate.
- *Page count.* Proper page count is an important factor in scheduling. Pages are broken down

into eight sections, with one-eighth approximately equal to one inch. If a scene is smaller than one inch, it is still considered to be one-eighth of a page. Use a ruler and mark the page horizontally into inches. This will serve as a guide. Put the total page count, in eighths (for example, a scene might be 3 3/8 pages), at the end of the scene on the right side, and circle it. This will indicate the page count for that particular scene (Figure 3.2).

Lining the Script

Now that you have filled in the breakdown sheet header, the next step is to mark up the rest of the scene and transpose the relevant information to the breakdown page. You will need the following:

- Several pencils and a pen
- Transparent ruler
- Colored pencils or crayons
- Three-hole punch
- Blank breakdown sheets (use the sample breakdown sheet in Figure 3.1 as a model, or design your own)

The colored pencils are used to "line" the script, which is printed on white pages. This color coding of the script enables the reader to identify specific breakdowns at a glance.

Begin with the first scene in the script. As you line, or mark, each sequence in the script, transpose the information onto a corresponding breakdown page. Don't mark the whole script and then go back to fill in the breakdown pages. You might change the configuration of scene numbers. For example, what the writer has indicated as scene 4 you might actually mark to be a continuation of scene 3.

Make sure to <u>underline</u>, not highlight, the script. The important elements will not show through if you photocopy the script. Use colored pencils to make the following distinctions:

CAST (red). This refers to anyone with at least one word of dialogue. Each speaking character should be underlined the first time he or she appears in the scene and once on each succeeding page of the same scene. The first time a character appears in the script, his or her name should be typed in capital letters.

EXTRAS AND SILENT BITS (yellow). This refers to a "silent bit" of action (no dialogue), performed by an extra, that has an effect on the plot. For example, the homeless man who wanders around Grand

Central Station in *The Lunch Date* interacts with the main character and is a physical presence in the film, yet he has no specific dialogue.

EXTRAS AND ATMOSPHERE (green). Extras serve to fill out the frame and create "atmosphere" around which the central action takes place. Extras are used in crowd scenes and background activity. The choice of extras is important in setting the right tone for each scene. Note that working with extras might require additional crew. Holding extras for many days can become expensive. If possible, schedule crowd scenes together.

STUNTS (orange). Any physically hazardous activity that a character performs, such as a fist-fight or a fall, is a stunt. These should ideally be performed by a trained stuntperson. If you have many stunts in your project, it is wise to hire a stunt coordinator.

WARDROBE (circled). Any reference to specific wardrobe to be worn by anyone should be circled in the script. If the script indicates that costumes must be stained by food or blood, have doubles for these wardrobe items.

MAKEUP AND HAIR (indicated by an asterisk, *). This highlights any situation requiring special make-up or hair in the course of a scene or for the run of the show. Examples are wigs, facial hair, bruises, or special aging requirements. Projects set in different time periods will have special hair requirements that will have to be researched for accuracy. This should be noted on the breakdown page.

PROPS (violet). Any object indicated in the script that is handled by a character in the course of a scene, such as a knife or gun, a key, or a glass, is considered a prop. It is imperative to have backups for disposable props, such as breakaway glass and food. Props (lamps, pictures, knickknacks) should not be confused with set dressing, which is a fixed item on the set that is not handled by the characters in the course of a scene.

SPECIAL EFFECTS (blue). This can refer to explosions and fireworks, but it also relates to any physical or mechanical activity that must happen on screen. Examples include a special lighting effect, blood packs, and firearms. When a scene calls for special effects, ample time should be allocated for setup and rehearsal, and the special effects should be discharged by a special effects person.

SPECIAL EQUIPMENT (boxed in ink). Using a pen, draw a box around any activity in the script that

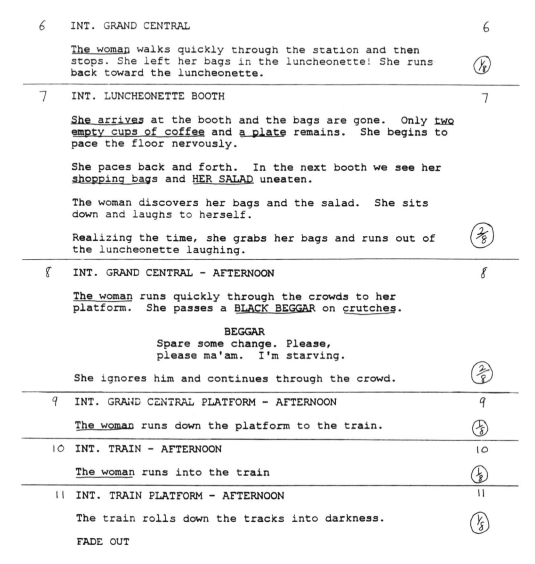

6   INT. GRAND CENTRAL   6

The woman walks quickly through the station and then
stops. She left her bags in the luncheonette! She runs
back toward the luncheonette.   (⅛)

7   INT. LUNCHEONETTE BOOTH   7

She arrives at the booth and the bags are gone. Only two
empty cups of coffee and a plate remains. She begins to
pace the floor nervously.

She paces back and forth. In the next booth we see her
shopping bags and HER SALAD uneaten.

The woman discovers her bags and the salad. She sits
down and laughs to herself.

Realizing the time, she grabs her bags and runs out of
the luncheonette laughing.   (2/8)

8   INT. GRAND CENTRAL - AFTERNOON   8

The woman runs quickly through the crowds to her
platform. She passes a BLACK BEGGAR on crutches.

              BEGGAR
        Spare some change. Please,
        please ma'am. I'm starving.

She ignores him and continues through the crowd.   (2/8)

9   INT. GRAND CENTRAL PLATFORM - AFTERNOON   9

The woman runs down the platform to the train.   (⅛)

10   INT. TRAIN - AFTERNOON   10

The woman runs into the train   (⅛)

11   INT. TRAIN PLATFORM - AFTERNOON   11

The train rolls down the tracks into darkness.   (⅛)

FADE OUT

Figure 3.2 A script page from *The Lunch Date* that has been broken down.

requires special equipment to execute a sequence, such as a dolly, crane, zoom, or Steadicam®. Special equipment needs might be specifically indicated or implicit in the way the action is described ("We move through the train station" or "Truman's moving P.O.V. up the rope ladder").

VEHICLES (light pink). This refers to "picture cars" (vehicles used by the actors in the course of the scene) as well as vehicles used as background for atmosphere.

ANIMALS (dark pink). This flags the need for an animal to perform an action in a scene. A special

trainer, or *wrangler*, is usually necessary because waiting for animals to perform specific "stunts" can be time-consuming and frustrating. The wrangler will train the animal to perform the specific task before the shooting so the scene will go smoothly.

SOUND EFFECTS AND MUSIC (brown). This refers to sound or music that must be prerecorded and played back on the set during production. This could refer to music that the actors will mouth, or *lip-sync*, or to particular sounds that you want an actor to respond to on the set, such as a door slamming or a gunshot.

PRODUCTION NOTES. This space on the breakdown sheet is provided for additional thoughts or questions about production issues reflected in the script but not covered in the categories above. It could contain questions for the director as to how she plans to cover the scene. Your job as producer is to evaluate the exact production needs of a scene in order to create a realistic schedule and budget. Leave no stone unturned. If you are unclear about something or have a question, write it down.

At the end of this process, you will have a lined and color-coded script and a set of completed breakdown pages.

Step 1b: Prepare Strips for the Stripboard

After you have marked each scene and transferred the information to corresponding breakdown sheets, you are ready to begin preparing a *stripboard*. A portion of the information you have culled from each scene can now be transposed to a *production strip* —a thin, 15-inch-long strip of cardboard. One strip represents each sequence in the script (Figure 3.3). Each strip should contain the following information about the particular scene:

- Breakdown page number
- Day or night
- Interior or exterior
- Location or studio
- Number of pages
- Scene number
- Where the scene takes place
- Who is in the scene
- What happens in the scene
- Special effects/stunts
- Extras/atmosphere
- Animals and vehicles
- Any special requirement unique to the script

Create the header first—the header serves as a key to the strips. All of the characters, extras, animals, and so on, are given a corresponding code number, which serves as shorthand so all of the information will fit on each individual strip.

Step 2: Place Strips on the Stripboard

A production stripboard is the producer's shorthand, or "show-at-a-glance." When lined up on a strip-board, each strip becomes a building block of the production schedule. A stripboard is a series of cardboard panels into which strips can be inserted and removed with ease. From these strips, shooting days can be created by grouping scenes together.

The schedule is determined by arranging the strips in the order that makes the most "production sense"— that is, that requires the least amount of time to shoot. The next chapter discusses in detail all of the variables that you must consider when creating the schedule for your project.

Color-Coding

Color-coding the strips allows you to see your project in groups of shots with a common designation. It gives the department heads an immediate visual reference of how the shoot will unfold. Indicate day or night, interior or exterior, location or studio, and anything out of the ordinary by a colored strip. At once you can see the passage of days into nights, moving from interiors to exteriors, stunts, "magic hour" shots, and major special effects, all of which have an impact on the schedule.

The production board is laid out with any color combination the producer chooses. A typical use of color is as follows:

- All day exterior scenes on powder-blue strips
- All day interior scenes on white strips
- All night exterior scenes on blue strips
- All night interior scenes on yellow strips
- All "magic hour" scenes on purple strips
- All special effects and stunt shots on red strips

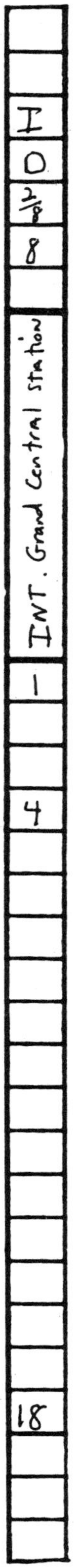

Figure 3.3 A strip.

Step 3: Price Each Line Item

From the breakdown pages, the producer can accumulate vital information from which to make an accurate budget. Every item that will cost money should be pulled from the breakdown pages and assigned an estimated price. This includes props, costumes, locations, special effects, special makeup, picture vehicles, and animals.

These lists will become important when you prepare the preliminary budget. You won't have to refer to the script again unless it goes through changes during the rewriting process. If there are changes, everything, including the breakdown pages, the strips on the stripboard, and the budget, will need to be adjusted to reflect these changes.

DIRECTOR
Storyboards and Floor Plans

Guided by the breakdown sheets, the department heads prepare for the day when a scene will be shot. The director adds to the breakdowns any information that is not reflected in the script, such as complicated camera movements, special lighting requests, and the number of extras needed.

Breaking down, understanding, memorizing, absorbing, and living the script are all part of the director's homework. Try out your ideas on video if you can. You should have a specific vision for the script and firm ideas about how you want to realize that vision. At the same time, however, you should remain flexible.

> Everything—locations, storyboards, rehearsals, even walking down the street and hearing a piece of music—is a springboard for your writing. You become a conduit for all these ideas. The whole process is about focusing those ideas into ten pages, keeping the good ones, and removing the bad ones. I remember going over the shot that introduces the main character, Truman; the shot follows the rope down the noose and then rack-focuses on Truman. Originally, it was not like that. Initially, we saw the rope, the noose, and then cut to Truman. The DP suggested the change, and it made the introduction work. Everything is for the script.
>
> *Howard*

Why does the director have to be so prepared? On set, in the heat of production, changes, additions, alterations, and compromises are made. Perhaps a lo-

cation falls through, requiring the company to move to the backup location. A cast member leaves the production, or the sun won't cooperate. Only a director who knows her material cold will be able to guide the production through troubled waters and come out the other side with a well-told story.

> I had done my homework and done my timeline. I was always very conscious of where my energies should be going at what time. I was allocating my time in terms of getting things done as they were supposed to be. It all goes back to being a production assistant on the feature, where I really saw that if you didn't have your act together you were going to sink and you were going to be pretty miserable while it happened.
>
> *Howard*

Try not to let any preconceptions or rigid planning stand in the way of chance. All of the previsualization and planning affords the director the opportunity to understand the script. If an actor or crew member has a good idea, it might be worth altering the plan to accommodate the creativity of the moment.

DEVELOPING A SHOOTING PLAN

The director is responsible for every element in front of the camera. Every creative decision flows from her vision of the script. The director defines this vision by developing a profound understanding of the script and a clear sense of its theme or central idea. It is from that point that she begins to break down each scene to discover how it will serve that central idea. There are many decisions to be made as to what the camera and actors will reveal at any given moment.

A story takes place in time and space, and the director defines that time and space. In addition, she determines the pace at which the story is told. The director is the storyteller. She must know what is important and what is not.

The director's preparation for principal photography centers on breaking the script down into shots. This shooting plan, or *shot list*, is an important factor in finalizing the shooting schedule.

How does the director convert the script to a visual plan? The process, called *previsualization*, can be done with an extremely detailed shot-by-shot storyboard or with a more general summary coupled with floor plans.

The director, having a good idea of the resources available to her, translates the script into shots by previsualizing it on paper. She confers with the director of photography, the art director, and the production manager to confirm the feasibility of her choices. Each of the director's choices will affect each department in a different way. If a dolly shot is called for, the director of photography prepares the appropriate equipment and crew. A low angle shot might require the art director to prepare a ceiling piece. The addition of a key actor in a scene can cause the production manager to reexamine the schedule. (For specifics on hiring these personnel, see Chapter 6, "Crewing.")

The director follows these seven basic steps to arrive at a shooting plan:

1. Know the script.
2. Develop a history of the main characters.
3. Break down each scene for dramatic beats.
4. Determine a visual style for the story.
5. Settle on pacing and tone.
6. Create floor plans and storyboards.
7. Make a shot list.

Step 1: Know the Script

The director must know the script inside and out. It is not enough merely to know the story line; the director must also learn the central theme, the dramatic arc, and all the beats that make up the whole. At any given time during production, she must be able to focus her actors and crew on a specific dramatic moment and be aware of how it fits into the whole. If she gives a direction that makes the moment of too great or too little importance, it will affect the entire piece.

A director dreams of a good script. The beats, the build, and the pacing in a good script are easy to determine. A poorly written script usually causes a director problems and can get her into trouble.

Step 2: Develop a History of the Main Characters

To understand the story is to understand its characters: not only what they say and do in the script, but what they might have said and done before and after. This helps the actors build a back story by creating a world for the characters to inhabit.

By creating this history, the director can "know" the characters well enough to help the actors shape their parts during rehearsals and in production. For example, is the character an eccentric? What elements in the script bring out this quality, and how is the eccentricity revealed? How can a director use the camera to illustrate this trait?

In the theater, the director and actors of a play are given a tremendous amount of rehearsal time to explore the script and the characters who inhabit the story. In a film or video, the director might have very little or even no rehearsal time. To get an actor up to speed and "in character" requires that the director know the character intimately. She needs to develop a verbal skill for communicating her ideas about the character quickly to the actor.

Step 3: Break Down Each Scene for Dramatic Beats

The director controls what the audience should be seeing and hearing at all times within the shot. Storytelling is understanding how each shot connects to the next to make a whole. Each scene has many small beats that together make up the major objective. A beat is a group of moments linked by a common objective. The director must determine the following:

- What are the beats?
- How will they be built?
- How will they be staged?
- What is the pace of each beat?
- How will the characters move from one beat to the next?
- How do all the beats together make up the scene?

When the action or objective changes, so too do the beats. Every scene has one major objective, and all of the major objectives together make up the plot of the story. Following is an example from *The Lunch Date*.

You can see from this breakdown that beat 6 is the moment in the scene when tension between the characters shifts to camaraderie. This is the climax. There is a deflation of energy in the scene upon her exit, which leads the audience to beat 7.

Beats are often shifts in the tone of the scene. A pause, an action, or an acceleration in pace can be the demarcation point from one beat to the next. The work that the actor and director do during the rehearsal process is the discovery and shaping of each

INT. LUNCHEONETTE BOOTH - DAY

The woman sits down across from the homeless man in the booth.

> WOMAN
> That's my salad.

> HOMELESS BLACK MAN
> Get out of here.

> WOMAN
> That's my salad.

(This is the end of beat 1. We wait for her next move.)
She reaches for the plate. He pulls it back.

> HOMELESS BLACK MAN
> Hey!

(Beat 2. There is a pause.)
The woman watches him chomping away at the bits of lettuce. He ignores her.

Moments pass.

(Beat 3. We wonder, "What will she do?")
She reaches over with her fork and swipes a piece of food off the plate. The woman quickly chews while keeping her composure. He continues eating.

She takes another bite. Then another. And another.

The man does not respond. Suddenly he stands and walks down the aisle.

(Beat 4. Left alone, she continues to eat.)
She continues munching away at what remains.

(Beat #5. She finishes.)
He returns with two cups of coffee with saucers. He places the cup on the table and sits.

He offers her sugar.

> WOMAN
> No, thank you.

He offers her a packet of Sweet & Low from his coat. She accepts.

> WOMAN
> Thank you.

(Beat 6. The scene has reached its climax.)
Checking her watch, she stands with her purse and leaves. He watches her exit, somewhat disappointed.

(Beat 7. The scene winds down on a sad note.)

of these beats. Shaping the beats together is "phrasing" a scene.

An excellent example of a beat in a scene is the introduction of the main character. Introducing or revealing a character can be an exciting visual moment. Take full advantage of this golden opportunity. The character can suddenly appear on a cut, you can cut to an empty frame and have the character step out of the darkness into the light, or the character can be revealed at the end of a long pan.

What is the character doing when we first see him or her? The character's behavior will give the audience a world of information.

Step 4: Determine a Visual Style for the Story

You can begin to think visually when you have an understanding of the story, the characters, and the theme. The overall visual plan for a sequence, or mise-en-scène, requires that the director decide whether the camera will be static or moving and whether the shots will be long or short. The beauty of the art of film- and videomaking is that the director's style, combined with the nature of the script, will always make for a unique approach to the text.

> There's no such thing as a compelling subject; there's only a compelling filmmaker. You can give the greatest subject in the world to a mediocre filmmaker and they'll make it boring and unfilmic.
>
> *Jan*

What is the nature or genre of your script? Are there conventions that should be followed or broken? The style in which a horror film is shot is very different from the style for a comedy. Horror films are usually dark and moody, and the camera work is often shaky or canted. Comedies are generally brightly lit, and the camera is often static or fluid, allowing the actors to perform their comedic action without camera distractions.

The director places and lights the objects and people in the frame in such a way as to create a dramatic tension. An excellent way to begin the process is to pore over paintings that express a style similar to the one you want to capture. Sharing your visual ideas with the director of photography will begin the collaborative relationship that will ultimately and ideally lead to a mutual approach. In preparing for *The Lunch Date*, the director shared his love of

Alfred Stieglitz's photographs as an inspiration for style.

The film language, or *grammar*, that the director employs includes the following elements:

FRAME. The frame can be empty, full, askew, off-balance, or in motion. The placement of characters and objects inside the frame can be balanced or unbalanced. A dramatic tension can be established, depending on how the director uses the frame, including foreground and background.

LENS. The size of the lens determines how much or how little of a sequence the director allows the audience to see. The following abbreviations are added when the script is completed. Their use distinguishes a screenplay from a shooting script. Most shots will be from this group:

- ECU—extreme close-up (eyes and nose)
- CU—close-up (complete face)
- MS—medium shot (torso)
- WS—wide shot (full body)
- LS—long shot (full body in landscape)
- XLS—extreme long shot (small body in vista)

LIGHTING. The direction and character of the light can be determined based on an initial design. High- or low-contrast lighting can shift the tone of a scene radically. (You'll find more on lighting aesthetics in Chapter 12, "Camera.")

STOCK. Black-and-white, color, or even a combination of the two is a creative choice that has a subliminal impact on the audience's appreciation of the story.

> I had thought a lot about shooting in black-and-white, but I wasn't sure. I started talking to the director of photography about the possibility of shooting in black-and-white. It turned out that it was going to be to our advantage to do it in black-and-white because without lights, black-and-white is a little more forgiving.
>
> *Adam*

FOCUS. With focus, the director both literally and figuratively informs the audience what it should be witnessing at any given moment. If a face in the foreground is out of focus and the background is in focus, the director wants us to look at the background. Imagine a wide shot of a playground on a gray day. A boy in the background bounces a ball.

He is dressed in red and is the only element in the frame that is moving. The director is making sure that the viewer's eye is on the boy.

ORCHESTRATION. The movement of the actors within the frame, coupled with the movement of the frame, shows how the director orchestrates, or choreographs, a scene. This is referred to as *blocking*. The director can block the camera, the actors, or both.

CAMERA PLACEMENT. Where the camera is placed on the set or location has an impact on the nature of any scene. A camera is usually placed at eye level to simulate the audience's perspective.

PERSPECTIVE. The use of foreground and background has impact on the dynamics of a scene. How far away or close is the subject to the frame? From whose point of view is the scene shot? That is, who is doing the seeing?

TIME. The director has the ability to stretch or compress time for dramatic purpose. She can do this through editing, camera speed, or optical printing.

SPACE. The aspect ratio of your frame is a given. Within this frame, the space can be defined by design. A good example of this is the luncheonette scene from *The Lunch Date*. The actual location was a defunct restaurant. Dilapidated and exposed to the elements, the art director managed to "define" enough tables to give the illusion that the characters were in a working luncheonette. The addition of "real" sounds enhances this illusion.

REFERENCE POINTS. Audiences feel comfortable if they have a reference point for a scene. Starting a scene with a master shot establishes the geography of the setting. (Often an establishing shot and a master shot are one and the same.) A key prop, a sign, and a map are examples of visual information that the director can share with the audience to keep the story on track.

REVEAL. As the camera moves, it is constantly revealing new information to the audience. What and how the director chooses to reveal defines her style.

TRANSITIONS. In preproduction as well as production, a director should ask, "What action does the shot I am doing now cut from, and what will it cut to?" This will lead to a discovery of the transitions either between beats or between scenes. Storyboards aid the director in determining how she would like to make transitions from scene to scene. Will the scenes dissolve into one another, fade out and then fade in, or wipe? How would the story be affected if every scene ended or started with a close-up of the main characters?

EDITING. In the editing room, a long unwanted pause can be clipped short. A response to a line on set that came too quickly can be extended by cutting to a reaction shot or a cutaway. Although the director has some control over pace in the editing room, if she wants to use a lengthy one-shot sequence without an edit, the pace is frozen on the stock or tape because the speed at which the action was choreographed is unalterable.

Here are some other factors to consider when determining a visual style:

SYMBOLISM. Some scripts call for a more formalized or symbolic approach to photography and acting. This could mean employing off-center or canted angles, low angles, slow motion, and so on. A surreal or dream sequence, such as the fantasies in *Truman*, is treated differently than the principal story.

PARALLEL ACTION. Coinciding action (action that occurs simultaneously) requires preplanning so that in the editing room, the action matches in a logical fashion. For example, if two characters leave their houses to meet at another location, one character might walk from screen left to screen right, with the other character walking from screen right to screen left. The audience will assume that the characters will eventually meet.

SUBJECTIVE/OBJECTIVE CAMERA. From whose point of view is the scene or story being told? Using the camera to tell the story from a particular point of view has a very definite impact compared to an objective camera, which takes the point of view of the director (audience).

CINEMA VERITÉ. Shooting a scene with a hand-held camera, as if a news team were on the scene, lends a feeling of immediacy to the sequence. A neorealistic style of shooting might call for a cinema verité style.

> I saw Frederick Weisman's *High School*, which was shot at a public high school in Philadelphia, and I was in a public high school in Philadelphia. I saw the film in Washington, D.C., because it wasn't allowed to be shown in Philadelphia. I saw it in 1969, and it really

did blow me away because it was consonant with the reality of my life. It was a whole different style of documentary, cinema verité, which I hadn't been exposed to.
>
> *Jan*

There's more on film grammar in Chapter 12, "Camera," and at the end of this chapter.

Step 5: Settle on Pacing and Tone

Rhythm and pace drive the audience to the emotional response that a scene demands. This is one of the director's primary responsibilities. A well-written script has a built-in style and pace. The time and space of the story are presented clearly by the author. The director merely translates the written word into pictures. This is why it is said that obtaining a good script is half the director's battle. Does the script indicate that the pace of a scene should be slow or fast, frantic or constrained?

Step 6: Create Floor Plans and Storyboards

With a thorough understanding of the script, the characters, and the visual style for the show, the director can be specific about the shots she plans to use to tell the story.

At this point, the director can work out the kind of coverage she will want for each scene. *Coverage* refers to how many and what kind of shots are needed to tell the story through each scene. To record a scene, you might use a series of rapidly edited images or a single long choreographed shot. The plan for covering a scene is a factor in scheduling the project.

> I prioritized, after I made the shot list, which were our most important shots. There were always a few little shots, or a few other angles at the end of each day, that I would have liked to have covered, but I never got the opportunity.
>
> *Adam*

Floor Plans

A floor plan is a ceiling viewpoint of the space in which you will be shooting your scene. It is laid out on an overview of the set area, and camera angles are indicated by small "V"s. The camera angles and the direction they are pointing (with indicated camera moves) allow the director and all department heads to know where the camera will be positioned (Figure 3.4).

Floor plans are useful in providing the director with an overview of how she plans to cover a sequence. Furniture pieces, walls, and set dressing can be indicated and shifted to allow the director to visualize her best angles. From this floor plan, she can prioritize her shooting, leaving extra shots, sometimes called *beauty* or *gravy shots*, until the end. If she goes overschedule, she can sacrifice a gravy shot, but she will still have the meat of the scene in the can.

The camera department can benefit from the director's floor plans by creating a complementary lighting plan. The art department will know from the floor plans which part of the set or location will be in the frame and which part will be out of the frame. The location department will see from the floor plans where the cars and trucks can be parked so that they will not appear in any of the shots.

> At this point, we brought out our little overhead maps of the gym, which was basically just a basketball court with lines drawn on it. We started laying out camera positions, determining who would be seen and what would be needed in each shot, and then we tried to group the shots in terms of efficiency: you know, those facing the same direction, so you're using the same lighting setup or the same number of kids in the shot.
>
> *Howard*

Storyboards

Storyboarding is one of the ways in which directors prepare for a production. This technique consists of making a series of sketches in which every basic scene and every camera setup within the scene are illustrated like a black-and-white comic book. Storyboards give the director and all department heads a visual record of the film before it is shot (Figure 3.5).

Having a storyboard is not essential for a dialogue sequence of two people in a room, but it is critical for an action sequence. If the director cannot draw, a storyboard artist can flesh out her visual ideas.

> I had a pretty complete shot list. As the script was getting closer and closer to a final draft, I started to storyboard. The storyboard really just mirrored the shot list, but again, it also informed the shots and changed the shots slightly. You begin to realize you don't quite need as many shots as you thought.
>
> *Howard*

Step 7: Make a Shot List

The list of the shots required for a particular sequence is termed a *shot list*. The shots indicated on the storyboards and floor plans are prioritized so that a shooting schedule can be ascertained from this list. The assistant director and production manager need to know the number of shots planned to schedule each day correctly.

> I did a combination of storyboarding and floor plans, but mainly I relied on a floor plan. In terms of storyboarding, I knew I wanted to have a close-up of her hands getting the ticket, and the stuff with the wallet falling out, and her entrance. I designed it to have the camera here for this shot, here for that shot, here for that one there. We numbered the shots and then made a shot list.
>
> *Adam*

A shot list is not a list of setups. The term *setup* refers to every time you move the camera. A shot list details every shot. From one camera position, you might change lenses and therefore have two or more

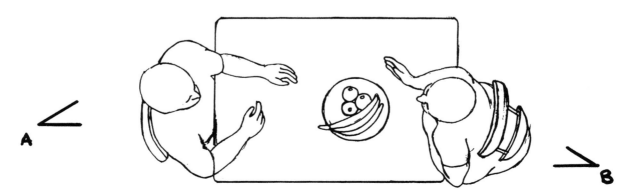

Figure 3.4 Floor plan. The camera angle on the left is a mirror of the angle on the right.

PG.____

Finish slow belly as Truman Falls out of frame on Sparrows "one" count

10-1 TAYLOR RISES INTO FRAME AND FIRES: MS. 16mm

10-4 C.U. SPARROW Reacts and turns. 16mm CAMERA AT FACE level.

10-4 He stumbles forward and we see the ARROW in his back

10-5 Kids rise up into formation and fire 16mm

11-1 SPARROW FALLS out of FRAME

Figure 3.5 Storyboards from *Truman.*

shots from one setup. Your choices when making a shot list range the entire width and breadth of camera language. Here is a partial list of elements you can explore before you decide what shots you will employ in your piece:

Staging for the Camera

MASTER. Generally, the master is a wide establishing shot of the scene. Often, an entire scene is shot in one complete master. In this case, the actors can be staged to the camera as well as staging the camera to the actors.

MINI-MASTER. In a long scene, coverage can be broken up into several short, or mini-master, shots.

FOUR-SHOT. Any scene with four actors in the frame at the same time is a four-shot.

THREE-SHOT. Any scene with three actors in the frame at the same time is a three-shot.

TWO-SHOT. Any scene with two actors in the frame at the same time is a two-shot.

OVER-THE-SHOULDER SHOT. A shot of one actor speaking to another when a portion of the second actor's shoulder appears in the foreground of the frame.

SINGLE. A single is a shot of one actor. This can be done as a close, medium, or wide shot.

CLOSE-UP. A tight shot of a portion of a frame, an object, or one actor's face and shoulders.

PAN. The camera moves horizontally to the left or right.

TILT. The camera points vertically up or down.

ZOOM. The camera has a lens that allows the subject to be brought close up or far away in the same focal plane.

DOLLY. The camera is placed on a tripod that can move up or down and pan. The dolly moves on tracks or independently.

CRANE. The camera is placed on a moving tripod that can be lifted up off the ground.

MULTIPLE CAMERAS. Some sequences (such as stunts or concerts) require that more than one camera be used at the same time.

OPTICAL AND SPECIAL EFFECTS. See Chapter 18, "Laboratory."

Your shot list might consist of one or more of these choices or a combination of shots, such as a mini-master of four characters, at the end of which the camera dollies into a close-up of the lead player. You might move in to set up a two-shot, or you might dolly from a four-shot to an over-the-shoulder and then continue to move into a close-up. Your choice of shots should be based on all of the factors mentioned above as well as an understanding of the impact the shot will have on the story and on the audience.

Once the storyboards, floor plans, or both have been approved, the director can turn to principal photography confident that she has an effective shooting plan.

THE FINAL WORD

It is not easy to transfer the script onto storyboards or floor plan sketches. Both aesthetic and practical factors must be considered. The director must ask, "How can I best cover this scene?" and, at the same time, "Do I have the resources to realize my vision for the camera choices I have made?" Aesthetic and practical considerations are often so inextricably bound together that the director makes decisions about shots in a discretionary manner. The final word rests with the director. It is part of her job.

KEY POINTS

1. Breakdowns are the link between the script and the budget.

2. The shot list, storyboards, and floor plans inform the schedule.

3. The director breaks down the script beat by beat.

4. Be familiar with visual language to cement a style.

chapter four

Schedule

I remember thinking there were four major components to building the shooting schedule. One was location restraints. Two was actor availability. Three was scene order. Four was the individual shots within the scenes, particularly with regard to how difficult they were as camera movements or how tough they were going to be for the actors.

Howard

PRODUCER

Building a Stripboard

Once the producer has dissected the script and stripped it of the essential production elements, he can create a shooting schedule. The schedule is the primary road map of the production and an essential factor in discovering how much the picture will actually cost. This chapter focuses on the variables that you will need to consider when making your schedule.

The shooting, or production, schedule shows the order in which scenes are to be shot during production. Films and videos are rarely shot in continuity, that is, in the exact order in which they appear in the script. Shooting out of continuity is a common practice in the industry because production considerations usually make it impossible to follow the script's chronology when shooting. The shooting schedule is designed so that scenes are grouped together in an order that allows for the most efficient use of time, personnel, and resources.

Production efficiency is paramount to getting the most from each dollar; there is a direct link between the number of days required to shoot the project and the budget. We will focus on budget in the next chapter, but it is important here to understand the logic of how these steps relate to one another. Don't tackle a detailed budget before you have made a schedule.

If you have correctly broken down the script into breakdown sheets and have transferred the key information onto production strips, you are ready to create a schedule. The scene strips are the tools and the stripboard is the mechanism on which the order of the scenes can be easily manipulated. The stripboard serves as a visual representation or overview of the production schedule. The beauty of this time-tested system is the ease in which strips can be maneuvered in and out of the board (whether manually or by computer) and the ability to access the entire schedule at a glance (Figure 4.1).

Don't think that this first pass at a schedule will be the final one. You are creating what might be considered a first draft. It is a launching point, not something written in stone. This initial schedule will go through many transformations during the preproduction period. Many factors influence the ideal shooting order of scenes for any particular project, and these invariably change as the shoot date approaches.

GENERAL GUIDELINES

Consider the following general guidelines as you arrange the strips on the stripboard, that is, as you put the scenes in the order in which they are to be shot. Remember, with color-coded strips, the schedule can be laid out and grouped by color, which will afford the department heads an overview of the schedule at a glance. For example, group all shots

Header   Stripboard

	No.																
Breakdown Page #																	
Day or Night																	
Exterior or Interior																	
Location or Studio																	
Scene																	
Number of Pages																	
Title: **Director:** **Producer:** **Assistant Director:** **Production Manager:**																	
Character **Artist** **No.**																	
1																	
2																	
3																	
4																	
5																	
6																	
7																	
8																	
9																	
10																	
11																	
12																	
13																	
14																	
15																	
16																	
17																	
18																	
Stunts 19																	
Sound Effects 20																	
Music 21																	
Extras 22																	
Special Effects 23																	

Figure 4.1 Header and stripboard.

from one location, all shots featuring an expensive player, all night exteriors, or all crowd scenes.

Fixed Dates

You might encounter situations beyond your control involving actors or locations that will set fixed parameters before you've even begun to formulate a schedule. Perhaps an actor has a prior commitment to start another project on a specific date before or after your picture begins, or perhaps a particular location is only available on specific dates or during certain hours. The crew of *The Lunch Date* was not permitted to shoot in Grand Central Station during rush hours. This restriction limited their shooting time to four hours in the middle of the day.

It can be very difficult to work with fixed parameters such as these. Normally, you would prefer the schedule to be totally flexible. However, if there are givens, you must adhere to them. A note pinned to the stripboard will remind everyone of fixed dates as the strips are shuffled.

> Scotty was just starting a play so she was in rehearsals and had to be out every day by five. That wasn't a problem at Grand Central because we had to be out of there by two. The last day at the restaurant we got her out in time as well. Scotty was basically in every shot. I had Clebert come down just one of the shooting days because he was just in the one scene there. I tried to stick as close as possible to continuity, where things like locations became important.
>
> For example, as I mentioned before, we were only allowed to shoot on the train platforms when the supervisor came down. So suddenly in the middle of the day, we would have to stop and go to the platform. That was day one. On the second day the supervisor didn't show up. So we went down on the platform and started shooting and then got kicked out. . . . They just didn't want us near the platform because of the danger of the electrical rails.
>
> *Adam*

Locations

Group all of your locations. The goal is to complete photography of all the scenes in any given location before going on to the next one. In the industry, this is referred to as *shooting out* a location. It doesn't make sense to travel back and forth to a location because every move the production company makes takes time and must be factored into the schedule. This was not an issue in the case of *Truman* and *Mir-*

ror Mirror because each film took place in one location. However, in *The Lunch Date*, it made sense to shoot out the cafeteria before moving to Grand Central Station or vice versa.

Organizing and executing a quick and efficient move of the entire production company, a *company move*, is an art unto itself. A skilled location manager can save a production time and money. Making a move once or twice in a day is not uncommon, but adequate time must be allocated in your schedule for such moves. A move is considered to be a company move if it is across the street, across the city, or across the county. For example, if you were to schedule two company moves across town in a day, it might take two hours to break down all the equipment, or *wrap out* of the location, and move it across town. Two moves would take up four hours, or a third of a 12-hour day.

> One of the stipulations they gave me for shooting in Grand Central Station was that they'd only let me shoot in between rush hours. I could only shoot from about 10:00 to 2:00 each day. So we had a schedule of where we would be at what times.
>
> *Adam*

If your story requires multiple locations, it is advisable to locate them as close as possible to one another. This will reduce travel time. Proximity should be factored into your creative choice of locations. This permits the establishment of a home base close to all of the locations that will serve as a production center.

If the script requires shooting at a distant location, travel days must be factored into the schedule. (See Chapter 7, "Location," for variables to consider when making this decision.)

Cast

Along with locations, the availability of actors is a major factor that influences the formation of the schedule. There are many variables you should consider when scheduling cast members. If you are working with members of the Screen Actors Guild (SAG), you must honor SAG contract rules and regulations regarding the length of a workday, travel time, meal guarantees, and turnaround time. Actors usually work a 10-hour day. The crew needs setup time at the beginning of the day and wrap-out time at the end of the day. Therefore, if an actor's schedule is pushed, so too are the hours of the crew.

When planning the schedule, make the most economical use of your talent. Actors work for a daily, a weekly, or a picture rate. If there are fewer than 10 days between shooting for an actor, he or she becomes eligible for a weekly rate; that is, if an actor works as a day player and then is called back to work four days later, the actor's contract is adjusted to a weekly player salary. You can hire an actor on a daily rate and then upgrade him or her to a weekly player, but it doesn't work the other way around. The actor on a weekly rate gets paid by the week, so that if the picture schedule carries the actor over even one day, he or she must receive the full week's rate.

Picture actors are paid a flat rate for the whole project and are available for the entire schedule, so their availability is not a factor. However, it doesn't make sense to pay an actor for two weeks if you only need her for the first and last day. It would be best to adjust the schedule and move the actor's scenes to the beginning or end of the schedule to "shoot out" the actor. It can be to the benefit of the production to do this, even if it means going into overtime with the crew to keep the actor from having to return to the set for another day. If, however, the actor's salary is less than the cost of the overtime, it would be wiser to wrap and return to the location the next day.

> We knew that we could only get the kids at certain hours each day. We promised the parents that we would be working from 8:00 to 6:00 every day, with an hour off for lunch. We really had to maintain that schedule with all the kids, so then that went for the rest of the crew, too.
>
> *Howard*

Students: Actors who work for free or whose salaries are deferred under an agreement with SAG might have full- or part-time jobs that limit their availability to your production. You might need to adapt your schedule to these constraints.

Exteriors

It is recommended that you begin the shoot with any exterior scenes. This general industry rule should be adhered to if possible. If you complete all the exterior scenes first, then when the company moves indoors, bad weather can no longer force you to change the planned schedule. If, on the other hand, you shoot all the interiors first, when the production moves outdoors, you will be at the mercy of the weather.

In this case, it would be advisable to keep at least one interior location or cover set available to move to in case of bad weather. Without a cover set, the production company has to shut down until the weather improves. A delay like this can be expensive as well as disruptive to your carefully organized schedule.

Night Shooting

It's best to consolidate all the night exteriors of each location. (Most night interiors can be shot during the day.) There are two schools of thought on how to schedule night exteriors. You can either shift the entire schedule over to nights and, instead of shooting from 6 A.M. to 6 P.M., shoot from 6 P.M. to 6 A.M., or you can organize the schedule to work on *splits*, meaning noon to midnight. This requires the company to shoot sunlight or exterior/day scenes the first half of the day, and devote the second half of the shooting day to exterior/night shots. The nature of the material might dictate only one of these alternatives.

When scheduling night shooting, you must remember that the actors require 12 hours (per the SAG contract) between the end of one day and the beginning of the next. This period is referred to as *turnaround time*. This regulation means that you can't end a day shoot and immediately begin a night one and vice versa. Weekends are often used to make the transition from a day schedule to a night schedule or vice versa. Otherwise, the required turnaround time must be absorbed into the daily schedule.

> *Scheduling:* Be aware that night shoots are hard on the body, even if the crew requests a night routine. Don't expect the crew to work as efficiently at night as they would during the day. Reduce your expectations of how many scenes you'd like to accomplish in an hour, and factor this into the schedule.

Night exterior shoots are expensive and logistically challenging. Arranging for the amount of equipment needed to illuminate a night exterior is complicated. The smaller the shot, the better your chances to accomplish the scene.

Continuity of Sequences

Although you might not be able to shoot the entire project in its order in the script, it is recommended that you shoot sequences in continuity as much as possible. This allows the actors and the director to work through the dramatic arc of a scene naturally.

It would be awkward and emotionally difficult to start the day's work with the end of an argument and then end with the beginning.

However, in filming interior scenes, try to complete as many shots as you can from each lighting setup. This is done by "shooting out" one side of the room before turning around and shooting with a new lighting setup. This might interfere with the continuity of the sequence, but it is standard procedure. It is also common sense. Having to keep changing lighting setups between each shot wastes time and energy.

Child Actors

There are strict rules governing the use of child actors. Generally, they can't work as many hours as adults can, and their parents or a teacher or social worker must be present during shooting if the child is missing school to be in the picture. Consult the SAG guidelines and child labor laws for more details.

A child's short attention span and limited energy can also be a major factor in shooting a scene. It might take longer to shoot a scene with a child, especially if the child is not a professional actor. Factor this into the schedule.

> I remember one of our first ideas was to shoot in script order to make it easier for the kids. It's such a short script, I figured we could have the luxury to do that. I was afraid that if the kids got disoriented, they would get bored, confused, and tired. We did decide to do all the fantasy scenes on the first day. We thought that was a good way to get the kids really involved in the process. They got to do three costume changes, dress up as Robin Hood, wear the Civil War costumes, do the little fire engine thing. . . . We believed that if the first day seemed exciting and appealing, we could hold their interest and make the whole shoot seem like an adventure.
>
> It also worked out well for the costume person who had to come up from New York to fit the kids and iron all the costumes; she had to leave after two days to go back to New York for another job, so that was a good piece of planning.
>
> *Howard*

Time of Year

The time of year when you are planning your production is an important consideration when scheduling exteriors. The amount of available daylight varies from summer to winter, the winter months having less available daylight, particularly in the north. To catch as much available light as possible for exteriors in winter, begin each day early.

Weather

The biggest variable in a production that features outdoor locations is the weather. Weather conditions like extreme heat, cold, snow, rain, and strong winds always have an impact on exterior photography, slowing down the company's usual pace. Cold weather will naturally slow down the movement of people and equipment, and even more so at night. Extreme cold can affect the camera's mechanism, shorten the life of a battery, and damage sensitive video equipment. You can shoot in a moderate rain, but not at a normal pace.

Research natural weather conditions (rain, snow, hurricanes, tornadoes, etc.) for the time of year that you plan to shoot. The weather bureau puts out breakdowns for annual precipitation, and farmer's almanacs are amazingly accurate when it comes to weather prediction. In addition, check the date when daylight saving time begins and ends.

There are three types of weather situations for which you should be prepared:

LIGHT. Light rain, light snow, light fog, and so on, are weather conditions that should not affect your shoot. Light rain stops and starts, and it is invisible to the camera lens as long as it is not back-lit. Light snow melts quickly. Keep the equipment and actors dry and continue shooting.

MEDIUM. It rarely rains all day. Show up at your location and wait. It might stop.

HEAVY. It is impossible to shoot in heavy weather, such as a storm. This is a good opportunity to move to a cover set.

Special Effects, Stunts, and Animals

Whenever the script requires a special effect, even something as simple as an active fireplace, special preparation and execution time must be added to the schedule. This guideline also applies to stunts and the use of animals. As a general rule, it always takes three to four times longer to prepare and shoot anything that is considered out of the ordinary.

Special effects, stunts, and animals' parts should all be rehearsed long before the shoot. This preparation will give you a chance to meet the production schedule.

Crowd Sequences

It is advisable to consolidate crowd sequences. The organization, feeding, and wardrobing of large crowds of extras (also referred to as *background*) is a logistical challenge and a large expense. Additional personnel must often be hired to support the assistant directors, the costumers, and the hair and makeup artists. Police might even be required for traffic control. Proper communication often involves the use of bullhorns and walkie-talkies. Always schedule more time than you think you'll need when working with crowds.

Special Equipment

You might need to rent additional equipment for a specific sequence, such as a Steadicam® or dolly. Steadicams require the hiring of an operator in addition to the rig. Scenes requiring any special equipment should be consolidated to save money.

Turnaround, Setup Time, and Swing Crews

Transportation to and from the set, prelighting, set dressing, and construction are all factors that you should take into consideration when setting up the stripboard. For example, it can be frustrating if the production department settles on a schedule only to discover later that it will not coincide with the construction time table. In this case, the art director should inform the production manager of the amount of time required to get the sets ready so that art department turnaround time becomes part of the equation.

Money can easily solve this sort of problem by allowing you to hire additional construction personnel. If money is tight, however, it will be back to the drawing board for the production staff to rearrange the schedule to accommodate this new information.

Much time can be saved if the production can afford to have a swing crew of electricians prerig the lights at an interior location. While the primary crew sleeps, the B team can set up the lights and "rough in" the lighting plan dictated by the director of photography. Then, when the A team arrives on the set, they merely tweak the lights, and the cameras can roll.

Novice producers usually have problems estimating how long it will take to move and set up grip and electrical equipment. Consult with as many experienced people as possible when scheduling your project. An experienced director of photography, gaffer, or key grip can be of enormous help in this area.

Other Considerations

Examine your script for any special circumstances unique to your project that will have an impact on the schedule. Each script poses its own particular set of problems. Keep an eye out for any unusual scheduling challenges.

BEGINNING THE SCHEDULE

Must you keep all of these factors in mind at all times when creating a schedule? The answer is no. The right schedule for your project evolves over time. Begin with a rough draft that takes into account the major considerations, and then gradually factor in the issues that are relevant to your particular project. Each script has a unique set of organizational challenges. Don't expect to solve all of them in the first pass. The shooting schedule might not be finalized until the week or even the day before actual shooting begins.

In fact, it is not uncommon for the schedule to continue to change during principal photography. A lost location, a sick actor, or an unexpected weather condition could force the production unit to shift around scenes and even shooting days. Beginners might have to keep adjusting their schedule because they have overestimated how much they can shoot in a day.

CREATING THE SCHEDULE

Don't start scheduling actual shooting days until you have grouped all of the scenes in a logic that is governed by the 14 important guidelines described above. This will enable you to conceptualize the "big picture" before deciding how to structure each shooting day. Follow these general priorities for scheduling:

- Start with any fixed dates of which you are aware. These will become the anchors around which you must work.
- Group your locations together, but try to place the exteriors first.
- Factor in the actors' schedules.

- Factor in the day and night schedule if appropriate. Remember that 12 hours of turnaround time is required between days and nights. Use the weekend to make this transition.
- Identify any other special adjustments your project demands, such as special effects or crowd sequences.

Begin to form the strips into days to get a rough idea of how long it is going to take to shoot the picture. Start off with an easy day if you can. Don't schedule the climactic love scene before the actors have had a chance to work together.

MAKING THE DAY

How is a *day* defined? How do you know how many pages a day your unit will be able to complete? The phrase *make the day* is an industry term that refers to successfully completing photography on the scenes scheduled for a particular day. The production unit should get off to a good start by making the first couple of days and keeping on schedule. Remember that many members of the cast and crew might not have worked together before. Going over schedule, considering all the variables, is easy to do. Successfully completing the first few days provides a psychological lift that bonds the unit and gives everyone confidence to complete the rest of the shoot.

Most feature films complete an average of between two and three script pages a day. Many low-budget features and television movies, on the other hand, average from five to 10 pages a day. Student projects usually come in at around two pages a day. Remember that these are averages. The industry is governed by what it can afford. Television budgets are small, so the tight schedules reflect that fact.

If your budget will allow, set your sights on averaging two pages a day. This does not mean that you always end up with exactly two pages completed each day. There might be days when you can accomplish only two-eighths of a page of difficult action (Figure 4.2). There might also be days when you will be able to make five to 10 pages. This is usually the case with dialogue scenes. Dialogue tends to take less time to shoot because it involves fewer lighting setups. Once the lights are in place, you can achieve a variety of shots quickly and efficiently.

> Everything went smoothly for me, I thought, in terms of getting what I wanted in the shots, feeling they were working OK—until we got to the restaurant and I did the shot of her entrance. I just couldn't get it to work. I wanted to cover it all in one shot, but it felt like it was taking forever.
>
> This was the first shot of the day. I began to panic. I felt that the time I was spending on the shot was eating into my already tight schedule. I was getting bogged down, and it threatened to put me behind, but I didn't want to settle for anything that wasn't right. It started off as a two-minute shot, so little by little, I eliminated business. Scotty started by asking for the salad, picking out the salad, speaking with the cook, etc. My problem was that I was looking at the scene in real time, not film time, which is death. Also, in a long take, one time the actors may work well, but the dolly is off. Another time the dolly hits the marks perfectly, but the focus puller misses his mark. We did eight takes, and during that time, the shot dropped from two minutes to 30 seconds.
>
> *Adam*

The two-page daily average should be accomplished in under 12 hours. It is not wise to schedule longer days than this. A tired company works less effectively than one that's well rested. Too many long days will force the law of diminishing returns. The crew's performance as they execute difficult lighting setups and complicated camera moves diminishes as the day drags on.

Student productions start out with the best intentions of working within the 12-hour limit, but something usually happens during the shoot that slows down the day. An inexperienced crew will take longer than expected to execute lighting and camera setups. As a result, the director will need to simplify her shot list to make the day.

SHOOTING DURING PREPRODUCTION

It is sometimes necessary to be in production during preproduction. If an actor needs to appear on television during a scene, the video portion of the show must be recorded in advance of the shooting day. If you are shooting a scene that requires playback of an original song, the song must be recorded before the shoot. Playback, which is music piped onto the set for the actors and musicians to lip-sync to and mime, eliminates the need for a live recording. With a live recording, mistakes might slow down the production. With playback, the director knows that the song will be perfect each time.

13 - INT GYM - DAY   13
LONG: TRUMAN stands alone in the gym.

CLOSE: His face burns. There is nothing he can say and no one to say it to.

LONG: TRUMAN stands alone again.

CLOSE: He bites his lip and starts to take a small step forward and then, in mid step, stops.
Another pause, shorter than the last, as if is about to step in front of a speeding train. Then he
wheels quickly around and is off like a shot, running for the rope.

The CAMERA DOLLYS with him, as he speeds across the gym.

HIS P.O.V.: as rushes headlong at the rope.

THE CAMERA DOLLYS back with him as he leaps up and grabs hold of the rope. He swings
back and forth once and then begins to climb upwards.

CLOSE: TRUMAN struggles upwards.

HIGH ANGLE: TRUMAN is nothing but an ant at the bottom.

                                                                                CUT TO:

14 - INT GYM - DAY   14
INT. SAME - MOMENTS LATER.

The gymnasium door opens and in steps TAYLOR. He picks up a sweat shirt, left lying near the
door and then looks up. A smile breaks over his face.

                                                                                CUT TO:

15 - INT. SAME - SECONDS LATER   15
HIGH ANGLE: TRUMAN struggles upwards.

                                                                                CUT TO:

16 - INT. SAME - MOMENTS LATER.   16
The CAMERA TRACKS down the faces of entire gym class. They stand huddled near the door,
staring silently upwards.

LONG: TRUMAN nearing the top.

CLOSE: He pulls himself up into FRAME and suddenly the tremendous NOISE of CHEERING
fills the air.

Figure 4.2 Shooting script   The CLASS is going wild. From down the hall comes sound MR. SPARROW approaching,
from *Truman.*   barking angrily.

LOCKING THE SCHEDULE

The director dictates the pace of the film. The production schedule might be greatly influenced by the
budget, that is, how many days you can afford. If
money is not a major consideration, the number of
scenes you can comfortably schedule in a day is influenced by the speed of the director and the director of

photography. You might be lucky enough to work
with a director who can knock off 30 setups in a day.
It is important, in any case, that the director be
closely involved in finalizing the schedule. She is responsible, after all, for shooting it.

All department heads should be consulted before
you lock down the board, especially the director, the
director of photography, the location manager, the

assistant director, and the art director. It is customary for all the department heads to meet before the shoot to go over each day of the schedule. This is the final opportunity they have to recommend any changes.

> It was a three-day shoot. There were things to organize, such as actors' schedules, when we could get in, how we would shoot the sequence. We knew that Grand Central would only give us the four hours a day, so we would need two days. And then a third day in the restaurant.
>
> *Adam*

The director is the key person at this meeting because she is the one who is responsible for shooting the schedule. The assistant director is the second most important person because he is responsible for keeping everyone on schedule. The director must be confident that she can make each day. Any reservations she has should be addressed at this meeting. Once the schedule is finalized, it is published and distributed to the cast and crew as the working shooting schedule.

CALL SHEET

The call sheet is the distillation of the schedule. This single sheet of paper is handed to all cast and crew members the night before each day of shooting (Figure 4.3). If the shoot is only a few days, a call sheet might reflect the entire shooting period. The call sheet is a distillation of all pertinent information regarding the next shooting day, including call time, location, actors' call times, special equipment, crew call time, and scene shot list.

The shot list segment of the call sheet is supplied by the director. All the other information on the sheet is culled from the stripboard or production schedule and breakdown sheets. The shot list is the list of scenes to be recorded during the next day's production period. It is customary for the director to review the call sheet just before it is printed for distribution. Should the director want to change the order of the scenes to be shot, she has this last opportunity to do so.

If the order is to be changed, the director should do it before the day of the shoot. If it is changed on the day of the shoot, there is no time to change the calls for actors, the crew, and the equipment.

Each day, a schedule for the following day was printed up and distributed before we wrapped. It started out with a wake-up time, then loading vehicles, call time on the set, lunch time, wrap, and finally home. We handed out one of those to every crew member. Additionally, any revisions we realized we had to make were included in that schedule.

> Every night after we went home, the director of photography, the assistant director, and the production manager (those being the key people) would go over the next day's schedule. We would talk about what we had initially intended to do and whether that was what we were still going to do. Could we foresee any new problems we hadn't anticipated? That's how we set up the schedule on a daily basis.
>
> *Howard*

The director might want to change a shot list for several reasons:

- An actor will play a scene better at a certain time of the day.
- A scene needs to be completed from the previous day.
- A light or sound problem might influence the schedule.

SCHEDULING DOCUMENTARIES

Unlike the narrative form, documentaries are scheduled on a piecemeal basis. The scheduling of shoots is based on the availability of the subject or an event. For the most part, a documentary can be scheduled on weekends or on a day-to-day basis.

Some aspects of scheduling a documentary can be easy: Book the subject and the equipment for a particular day, and then shoot. Plan a full shooting day so as not to waste the equipment rental. If you own your own equipment (which many documentarians do), the scheduling is even easier. In contrast, if your subject is tied to specific dates and times of day, then it behooves you to be there by his or her side. This might require a more rigorous schedule than a narrative shoot.

> I had to work around the schedules of my subjects. They were busy during weekdays, so I filmed them exclusively on weeknights and weekends. I tried not to schedule more than three interviews a day for our sake. Obviously, it didn't matter to them as they came in one at a time. I usually took about two hours with

CALL SHEET

Producer:

Date:

Director:

Title:

Set	Scenes	Cast	D/N	Pages	Location

Cast & Day Players	Part of	Makeup	Set-Call	Pick-up Time

Atmosphere & Extras	Set Call	Crew	Set Call

Advance Schedule or Changes	Cover Set or Weather Alternative

Figure 4.3 Call sheet.

each person. They arrived, I explained the process to them, and I tried to make them comfortable while we adjusted the lights, and so on. I didn't want to feel rushed or to adopt an assembly-line approach.

Jan

Students: The following six scheduling pointers should come in handy.

BREAK UP THE SHOOTING SCHEDULE. It may be advisable to schedule your first production, if possible, not consecutively but over several weekends or smaller periods of time. This will enable you to gauge how well you are able to "make" the planned schedule and if not, make the necessary adjustments for the next sequence. It also will enable you to see your rushes before the next shoot date. If you are not happy with what you are getting either from the performances or the camera and sound, it will allow you the time to make adjustments. For beginning filmmakers, this can sometimes prevent the crew from making the same mistakes throughout the entire shoot.

The downside of planning this way is that it makes it difficult to create momentum with your crew. It may take a couple of days for the production unit to gain a rhythm and feel comfortable with one another. Student productions may, in fact, have little choice in this matter. If actors are not being paid and have day jobs during the week, then weekends may be the only time available to them to work.

SCHEDULE RESHOOTS AHEAD OF TIME. Assume that you will need to reshoot some of your project either because it didn't come out the way you expected or because you weren't able to get it the first time around due to unexpected problems or an unrealistic schedule. Warn everyone that reshooting might be required to ensure that your crew and actors will be available. Make sure to determine the schedules of cast and crew members after the shoot. Finally, schedule reshoots far enough in advance that you are able to view all the rushes before you return to production.

> In all my films, I've never had the possibility to go back to any of the subjects because they've been location shoots all over the country. I am used to working that way. The whole notion of pickups in documentary has been completely moot for me in my work. We have never done it. The only kind of subsequent material would be stills or archival footage, but no more live shooting after the shooting period. Period.
>
> *Jan*

MAKE USE OF AVAILABLE RESOURCES. Review the schedule with your production instructor or other experienced personnel as many times as possible during this process. Most students and beginners start off with unrealistic expectations of what they can achieve in a day. They are usually too ambitious. This enthusiasm must be constantly tempered with doses of realism, common sense, and experience.

CONSOLIDATE LOCATIONS. Your schedule, limited by money and available resources, might not accommodate all the locations the script dictates, forcing you to consolidate existing locations. By combining several locations into one, you can simplify your production needs without necessarily compromising the requirements of the story.

SCHEDULE MOS DAYS. If a sequence does not absolutely require location sound, you might be able to save valuable time by shooting without recording sound on the set. In the industry, this is called *MOS*. Not having to wait for planes to pass or annoying neighbors to quiet down will shave minutes from each take and allow the production company to schedule more scenes in a day.

DON'T BE AFRAID TO POSTPONE THE SHOOT DATE. You might sense that the preproduction period is being unnecessarily rushed. Perhaps you are having problems finding the right cast, crew, or locations as the shoot date approaches. Perhaps it is your first production, and you want everything to be right. By pushing the shoot date back, you might lose a specific location or actor, but what you will gain is a smoother shoot (and a little peace of mind).

Before you think about postponing the shoot date, however, make sure that you don't have any fixed dates that are necessary for your production, such as a parade (which obviously can't be rescheduled) or a special event that plays prominently in your story.

COMPUTERS AND PRODUCTION

Computer programs have been developed that facilitate the scheduling and budgeting process. Scriptwriting, script breakdown, scheduling, and budgeting have been combined into one piece of software. This allows you to see clearly how script changes affect the schedule and the budget. Most of the professional productions today use these programs. They have become an indispensable part of organizing a production.

DIRECTOR
Determining Coverage

The director might be very involved in the process of setting up a schedule, as described in the first half of this chapter. Just as the producer factors into the schedule actor availability, prerigging, and a desire to shoot out locations, so too he must consider the director's needs. The director discusses with the producer her intended pace and approach for the first day of shooting.

The director is integral to the scheduling process in that she must be the one to finally say, "I can shoot this script on this schedule." A director's main responsibility is to make the best film or video possible based on the script. Her secondary charge is to shoot the pages scheduled for each day. Making the pages means ending a day of production having reached the goal, set during preproduction, of that portion of the script.

The director sets the pace. If you are slow, then the shoot will be slow. Your energy impels the cast and crew. It is as if the energy of the director is translated through the cast and crew and onto the screen. Therefore, an understanding of the schedule involves an acknowledgment of one's capacities. Take care of your body with ample sleep and nutritious foods so that you will have the stamina necessary for the grueling pace of a shoot.

COVERAGE = TIME = SCHEDULE

The director determines how a sequence is to be staged and shot. She might base her plan on conversations with the screenwriter, art director, director of photography, storyboard artist, editor, or indeed anyone who has a good idea about an approach to a sequence. The final decisions, however, rest with the director.

Each shot is best communicated to the department heads through storyboards, though they often change once the cast and crew arrive on the set. Therefore, it behooves the director to indicate to the producer where she plans anything out of the ordinary, including crane shots, dolly moves, and extreme high angle shots.

A producer might assume that a dialogue sequence of five pages can be executed in a single day. However, if the director plans several complicated dolly moves to cover the scene, one day might not be adequate. Conversely, a seven-page dialogue scene can be shot in one day if the photography is kept simple or is planned as one or two long takes. Remember, complicated dolly moves for every shot invite overtime.

The scene can be photographed or covered with a combination of master shot, mini-masters, over-the-shoulder shots, and one or two close-ups, or the director can light and rehearse one or two complicated dolly moves and shoot the entire scene toward the end of the day after exhaustive technical rehearsals.

If the scene is excessively storyboarded (too many shots per sequence), and especially if any one thing goes wrong (an actor arrives late, fuses are blown, etc.), then the potential to go over schedule is increased. This is not to suggest that you compromise your shot list; instead, make certain that it reflects a practical schedule.

A scene that reads on paper like an easy sequence might take on an entirely different character when envisioned by the director. For example, one director might shoot a scene in which a woman is stabbed to death in a shower in one take. After the scene is lit, she might need only 10 minutes for that one shot. On the other hand, a director like Alfred Hitchcock might design a more stylized scene that involves 88 setups and requires three days to shoot. (You'll find more on coverage in Chapter 12, "Camera.")

THE FIRST DAY

The first day of principal photography is very important because it sets the tone for the entire shooting period. On the first day, the cast and crew are galvanized behind the director's leadership. A director who can instill confidence and make the first day's pages quickly earns the respect and cooperation of the crew. The director can approve a schedule with one of three approaches:

1. *Day 1 is very light.* An easy first day gives the cast and crew time to build up a momentum and allows for the kind of first-day mistakes that are inevitable.
2. *Day 1 is an average day.* Every day is important, so a day that has an average amount of pages to shoot is a fair day. This choice does not treat the first day as anything special.
3. *Day 1 is heavy.* A deliberately heavy day in which the cast and crew have to hit the ground running is an opportunity to galvanize the company. Dead weight becomes obvious very quickly.

CONTINGENCY PLANS FOR OVERAGES

If the director falls behind on day 1, she will be playing catch-up throughout the shoot. Going over sometimes means returning to a location, another company move, additional days of principal photography, and more money.

Although the director is shooting a movie and not a schedule, there is psychological strength in meeting the day's pages. Playing catch-up is a drain on the director. Often, to get back on schedule, she will condense a scene or make judicious cuts in the script.

THINGS CHANGE

The schedule might constantly change during preproduction and production. The director should memorize the schedule as well as the script so that she can make quick adjustments to her plan.

> Each scene was numbered, as well as the shots within the scene. We then started putting the shots in the order of how we would shoot them. As it went along, there were constant little changes, based on things like the availability of the fire net or putting in a variable-speed motor and what day could we get these items for the cheapest rate. We made several revisions on the schedule as we moved closer toward the shoot.
>
> When most of our unknowns were resolved, we gave each shot a time value—how long we estimated the setup and execution of the shot would take—and we broke that down into 15-minute intervals. You could say something took two hours and 15 minutes, or 45 minutes, or a half an hour. So hopefully, we knew within 15 or 20 minutes where we should be each day. I was very, very concerned about keeping my promise to the parents that the filming be only between 8 A.M. and 6 P.M.
>
> We were fairly tight on the time, so we tried to be honest with ourselves about how long each scene would take. Based on this kind of macro to micro approach of when events had to happen and when we wanted them to happen, we could finally print up a schedule about which we felt very, very confident.
>
> *Howard*

KEY POINTS

1. The efficient use of time is directly related to production value.
2. Memorize the schedule so that you can adjust easily to alterations.
3. Settle on the priorities and coverage that will determine the basic approach to the schedule.
4. If possible, shoot exteriors first because of weather variables.
5. Shoot out interior locations if possible. It is not cost-efficient to have to come back to an interior location and relight it.

chapter five

Budget

I planned to spend about $6,500, and I came in at $6,000. This covered production.

Howard

PRODUCER

Create a Budget

Now that you have some idea of how long it will take to shoot your project and what elements will cost you money, creating a budget will be that much easier. If you have only so much money available or have set a limit on the amount of money you feel comfortable spending, put these figures aside for the moment and concentrate on creating a realistic budget for the script you want to produce. After the ink dries, see how the figures compare to your financial limitations.

Even if you have all the money in the world, it doesn't make sense to spend it all on one picture. Throwing money at a project will teach you nothing about proper fiscal management, and it will leave you less money for your next endeavor. The goal is to get the most "bang" for your buck. Spend only what you need to spend.

The script and the budget are the two cornerstones of the production. The script is the creative bible, and the budget is the financial bible. The budget defines the parameters of what can and cannot be accomplished. It contains a complete and detailed breakdown of what it will cost to finish the entire project. This breakdown includes all projected expenses for preproduction, production, and postproduction. Each and every line item, whether it is photocopying scripts or securing a location, has a price and must be itemized, categorized, and ultimately accounted for.

Script and budget are inextricably tied to one another. Script decisions become budget decisions. For example, the director wants to add a car chase. Before deciding to include the sequence, a budget must be prepared that itemizes all the expenses associated with the chase, such as the cost of the vehicles, stunt drivers, extra camera crews and cameras, water and fire trucks, police, stand-by physician and ambulance, traffic monitors, and, of course, feeding and possibly housing all these people for the days it will take to execute the sequence. The artistic value of the chase can then be weighed against its cost:

- Is the creative impact of the sequence worth the price?
- Can the present budget absorb the extra cost?
- If not, can the producer raise the additional money?

Money management performs an important role in picture-making and can play havoc with one's idea of "artistic freedom." Sooner or later, it dawns on every film- and videomaker that artistic freedom comes with a price: You must pay for every decision, every choice. This is an ironclad and immutable fact of life in the media arts. Even the lone videomaker shooting on the run with a camcorder has to eat and purchase tape stock.

The producer or production manager is responsible for drafting the budget. If you cannot afford to hire a production manager or an experienced producer, you will have to put together a budget yourself, even though the word *budget* may make you nervous. However, accomplishing this seemingly onerous task will enable you truly to understand the nuts and bolts of how a production actually runs because, like it or not, it runs on money. Putting together the financial foundation of your project can be an exciting challenge. Through the mastery of learning what things cost and why comes the satisfaction of knowing that you have gotten the best deals without skimping on the needs of the script.

Students: Because this book is written for independents (who lack the resources of a film program) as well as film and video students, we approach the budget from a perspective that is valid for all short projects. Although as a student, you might not pay for labor or equipment (other than through your tuition), knowing their commercial worth fosters a healthy respect for these resources and prepares you for the realities of the professional world after school. If your school provides some of the line items for your project, such as stock and equipment, it is a good exercise to budget these items as deferred figures. That way, you will be aware of the full cost of a production.

THE BUDGET FORM

The standardized budget form serves to simplify working up a budget. This form demystifies the process somewhat by outlining all potential expenses. The short budget form is separated into two parts. The first part is the top sheet (Figure 5.1). The top sheet offers a financial overview or summary of all the major budget categories, which are also called *accounts.* The money for each category is placed in its own account, and each budget category is given its own account number for easy reference.

The second part of the short budget form, called a *detailed budget,* is a complete breakdown of each category (see Appendix D). The detailed budget is completed first, and the total for each category is then entered under the appropriate budget column on the top sheet. For example, the total for the category "Equipment" on the top sheet reflects the cost of all the camera, sound, lighting, grip, and special equipment required for the production of the picture.

If you are creating a budget for the first time, you will need a thorough understanding of each department and how to evaluate its needs. Computing an accurate figure for each category requires an investigation into the process, as well as prices and resources available at the time and place of your shoot.

The top sheet, which serves as your complete "budget-at-a-glance," summarizes all costs related to

manufacturing the picture. The following information can be gleaned from the top sheet:

- Subtotals of all categories
- Above-the-line and below-the-line costs
- Contingency
- Grand total

Film and video budgets are typically divided into two sections: above-the-line and below-the-line. This "line" separates two fundamentally different kinds of costs associated with a production. Above-the-line costs include fees negotiated for the producer, director, script, and actors. Below-the-line costs are all expenses related to the rest of the personnel and resources required to manufacture the picture.

Above-the-Line Costs

Consider above-the-line costs to be flat fees, or amounts that are negotiated for the run of the picture. For example, the director might receive $2,000 for her services, the writer will sell the script for $1,000, and an actor can be hired for the duration of the show for $3,000. These fees are normally paid out in installments rather than at a weekly or daily rate—for example, 25 percent of the negotiated salary on signing the contract, 25 percent on the first day of principal photography, 25 percent on the last day of principal photography, and the final installment of 25 percent on completion of the work.

001 Script and Rights

As mentioned in Chapter 2, securing rights means negotiating with an author, the author's agent, the author's estate, or the author's publisher for permission to use his or her material as the basis for your short work. It is imperative that you secure the story rights if your short film or video is based on a copyrighted work. There are only three exceptions to this rule:

YOU ARE THE AUTHOR OF THE WORK. If you have written an original piece, you own the rights to it. To register your copyright, write to the Library of Congress (see Appendix F) for a registration form. There is a fee.

YOU DO NOT INTEND TO MARKET THE FINAL PRODUCT. Legal action can be taken against you only if you use copyrighted material without securing the rights and the project is sold

SHORT BUDGET TOP SHEET

Production: Date:
Length: Shooting Days:

ACCOUNT#	CATEGORY	BUDGET	ACTUAL COST
001	Script and Rights		
002	Producer		
003	Director		
004	Cast		

ABOVE THE LINE TOTAL _____

005	Production		
006	Crew		
007	Equipment		
008	Art		
009	Location		
010	Film and Lab		
	PRODUCTION TOTAL		

011	Editing		
012	Sound		
013	Lab		
	POSTPROD TOTAL		

014	Office Expenses		
015	Insurance		
016	Contingency		
	OVERHEAD TOTAL		

BELOW THE LINE TOTAL _____

GRAND TOTAL _____

Figure 5.1 The top sheet of a short budget.

or money changes hands. A film or video made for a class or screened in a noncommercial venue does not violate existing copyright laws. Consider the marketing plans for your piece, and keep in mind that securing rights after you have completed the project might be difficult, expensive, or even impossible.

Copyright laws apply to music as well. If you are making a television commercial and want to give the client an idea of how it might sound, you can use any music you like for the promotional reel. However, when the commercial is approved, before entering it into the marketplace, you must purchase the music or replace it with original music.

THE MATERIAL IS IN THE PUBLIC DOMAIN. An author's work sometimes becomes public property 50 years after his or her death. The Bible and the works of Shakespeare, Dickens, and Twain are all available at no cost. Be aware, however, that an author's heirs can extend the copyright of his or her work. An entertainment lawyer can perform a title search to check on the material's copyright status.

002 Producer/003 Director

If the producer or director is paid a salary, whether it is cash up front or a deferred sum, the amount should be entered in the budget. If no salary is involved, write in either "N/A" (not applicable) or "0.00."

004 Cast

This category refers to everyone who performs in your project, including principals, bits, and extras. Payment for these actors ranges from nothing to union wages and more. During casting, you might find that the actor best suited for an important part is a union member. In this case, you might decide to pay for the security of knowing that the role is well cast. Whether you pay for your cast or not, it is advisable to be familiar with the cost of union labor. You might not have to work with SAG actors on this picture, but this union will no doubt play a large role in most of your future projects.

The Screen Actors Guild. When you use union talent, you must sign a contract with the union or guild. Becoming a signatory with the Screen Actors Guild (SAG)—which also covers the American Guild of Variety Artists (AGVA), the American Federation of Television and Radio Actors (AFTRA), and Actor's Equity stage performers—is easy. Call SAG and speak to a representative. The guild will send the appropriate forms, and as long as you abide by the SAG Codified Agreement, you will be allowed to hire union talent.

Read the agreement carefully. The Screen Actors Guild rules governing rates, penalties, per diems, overtime, and so on, are spelled out in detail. Play by the rules, or you might have to pay penalties later. On occasion, actors tell the producer that they are willing to "fudge" their time cards without informing the union but then turn around and report the inequities.

Nonunion Talent. The only way around union rules is to hire nonunion talent. With nonunion talent, you can negotiate any deal you like with the actors. If you are working under a SAG agreement, you can only hire union talent. If you can obtain a waiver to hire nonunion actors, they will not be eligible to join the guild after working on your production if this is their first film job. The Taft-Hartley rule stipulates that after their second professional acting stint, they will be eligible to join the union.

There is a good reason why SAG is such a strong union. Its members are familiar with a difficult craft. They understand their duties and act like professionals. They are skilled in developing a character, listening to other actors, hitting marks, memorizing lines, and pacing themselves for long hours. Nonunion talent might not possess these skills.

> *Students:* Some film schools have made special arrangements with the union for salary deferment. If your picture sells, you must compensate the actor before you repay yourself for the cost of making the film or video. For example, if you employ an actor for five days, you "owe" him or her five days of scale or minimum salary, which is approximately $500 a day. If the film never sells, then you need not pay the actor anything. If you do sell the film, though, your SAG bill will be $2,500 for that one actor. Keep this in mind as you schedule talent, because there is no need to run up a big bill and have actors wait around the set if they are not needed. The Taft-Hartley rule, which allows an actor to join the guild after a second professional gig, does not apply to the student-SAG agreement.

Below-the-Line Costs

Whereas above-the-line personnel are usually paid a flat fee, below-the-line personnel are paid a weekly or daily rate. In a short film, there might very well be no fees, except possibly deferred fees, payable from profit. All other direct and deferred costs are reflected in the below-the-line section of the budget. Here is a formula for calculating the salary or rental cost for the picture:

Days at *x* rate + prep and wrap = fee

Basic Decisions

Before you can begin to put down numbers, you must make some basic decisions about the nature of your production. Every decision has a financial repercussion and will affect the hard costs of your project. It is possible that your decisions will change for a variety of reasons. For example, you might have to scale down your project to accommodate what you can raise, or you might find you have more money to spend than you had anticipated. Ultimately, your final budget will reflect what you can afford.

Will you shoot your picture on film or video? This fundamental decision will have an impact on cost, equipment, choice of crew, and the "look" of the final product (see Appendix I). Video might be less expensive during production, but film is the cheaper medium in postproduction. Video might allow greater shooting ease and flexibility, but the final product will have limited screening possibilities.

Video can be screened on a monitor or projected by a video projection system. The image on video projection becomes progressively washed out the longer the throw, or distance, to the screen. It does not compare with the quality of film projection and has yet to reach a similar size. However, technological advances in this area will continue to improve the video projection image. With high-definition television (HDTV), the image will become sharper and denser, making large projection of the video image more viable.

Discover the format needs of the market you are interested in targeting: theatrical, nontheatrical, network, cable, festivals, etc. (See Chapter 19, "Distribution," for more information.) Explore how the use of video might exclude you from some avenues of distribution. Consider shooting in video and transferring the final cut to film stock. This process is expensive, but it is an excellent avenue for the documentary, where shooting stock and processing can be limited by your budget.

If you choose to shoot on film, what format should you select? The two basic film formats are 16mm and 35mm. Some people still work in super-8mm even though fewer labs process it and the equipment is harder to rent.

The cost of shooting in 35mm is prohibitive for most beginners. It has a wonderful look, but to get 10 minutes of film, you have to shoot more than double the footage of 16mm (1,000 feet of 35mm equals approximately 400 feet of 16mm), and 35mm production equipment is expensive to rent.

For most beginners, 16mm is the preferred film format. Over the past several years, Kodak and Fuji have come out with superb new 16mm fine-grained film stocks with wide exposure latitudes, enabling them to be shot in low light.

If you need a 35mm print for distribution but can't afford to shoot 35mm, then super-16mm is an option. It can be enlarged, or blown up, to 35mm. Because there aren't many super-16 projectors, consider super-16 only if your goal is a 35mm print without the expense of shooting a 35mm camera negative.

Another decision that can have a financial impact on your budget is whether to shoot in color or black-and-white; 16mm black-and-white raw stock is less expensive than color, but there are fewer labs that regularly process it. One lab known to excel in black-and-white processing is Alpha Cine in Seattle. (See Appendix F for additional black-and-white laboratories.)

If you decide to shoot on video, what format should you select? The video market is changing at such a rapid rate that whatever this book recommends could quickly become obsolete. Nevertheless, here are some general suggestions. For easy portability, Hi-8 seems to be the format of choice, although some argue that Super VHS is superior. For less portable units, Beta has been considered excellent for many years. Video quality in descending order is best on one-inch tape, then Beta, three-quarter-inch tape, Hi-8, Super VHS, and finally half-inch tape. Research the cost of equipment and postproduction rental before making your decision.

Profit, Negative Cost, and Deferred Fees. *Profit* is defined as the money the production company receives after it recoups the negative cost. The negative cost is the cost of making a film or video project, from preproduction through a final print. If an individual is promised money for his or her services to be paid from the profit generated by the project, these fees are termed deferred. *Deferred* fees are not guaranteed. An individual or service company can work for no up-front money, opting to take their pay from the profits. If there are no profits, they will never see any money.

Film-developing laboratories often offer another option for payment. They sometimes agree to develop and process the negative film for no up-front money. If a laboratory has faith in your project, it might be willing to wait until you can generate enough funds to pay the bill. This type of deferment is simply a postponement of the bill.

005 Production Department

A good production manager and assistant director are worth their weight in gold, especially if the director is a novice. These people keep the production running smoothly and on budget. Experienced production and crew members can be hired for an up-front salary, a deferred salary, or a combination of the two. Inexperienced crew members might work for free merely to gain experience.

006 Crew

The size of your crew will determine a large part of your daily production costs—that is, how many people you need to pay, feed, transport, or house (if it is a distant location) while the picture is in production. It is therefore extremely important that you decide how many crew members are essential to support the demands of the script. (Refer to Chapter 6, "Crewing," for the 3–30 rule.)

The director might have certain specific requests regarding the size of the crew. She might prefer to work as light as possible, or perhaps she feels secure only with more bodies around her. Documentary crews are by nature small, but some fiction directors prefer this approach as well. There are several factors to consider when making this basic decision.

Elaborateness of the Production. In the next chapter, we list many of the important positions that are necessary for executing a well-run production. These positions represent the actual duties that must be performed on a set. Of course, not all productions are alike, but particular individuals are essential to ensure a smoothly run shoot no matter how modest the scale.

It is logical that a two-character piece shot in a small apartment will make fewer technical demands than one shot during a high school basketball game. You can double and triple up on many positions, but don't think that you can get away with less than you need for something so "seemingly easy" as the two-character piece. The success of a single shot, whether in the apartment or at the high school basketball game, requires that many technical chores be performed perfectly on every take. *The Lunch Date* had a crew of five, *Truman* was shot with a crew of 10, and *Mirror Mirror* a crew of two.

Stage versus Location. Some basic decisions will have an immediate impact on your crew requirements. The first is whether you will be shooting on a stage, in a practical location (an existing site), or both. Having to design, construct, and dress a set requires crew members whom you will not need if the entire production is shot in a practical location. (See Chapter 8, "Art Direction," for details.)

Union versus Nonunion Crew. If you can hire a union crew, you are usually guaranteed to get your money's worth. These are highly skilled and trained individuals prepared to perform under the stressful time constraints of large and small projects. Union minimum rates are available in *The Producer's Masterguide* and *Brook's Standard Rate Book* (see the Bibliography for details). It might surprise you how much even "scale" (minimum salary) is for most of the crew positions on a set. To keep this in perspective, an assistant camera operator earns a minimum of $1,111.80 a week but might work only six months out of the year.

Learn about union work regulations. Such items as meal penalties, overtime, double overtime, and golden time can greatly inflate the budget. The union code of regulations and ethics should serve as a model for your production behavior, even if you do not use union labor. These regulations were developed to protect workers from exploitation and to guarantee extra payment if they are required to work additional hours.

Nonunion crew workers range in experience from recent film school graduates to the seasoned professional. The pay scale for nonunion labor is usually based on what the market will bear and on the crew member's experience. Everything is negotiable. Many directors of photography and sound recordists work with their own equipment, so the price they quote includes labor and equipment (or, as it is sometimes called, their *kit*.)

What you can expect is a flat rate per day, per week, or for the run of the show. The rate should be based on an agreed "day" of so many hours (usually 12). Because there are no nonunion regulations defining overtime pay, there should be some agreement about compensation for extra-long days. The 12-hour cap doesn't have to be strictly adhered to, but if abused, it can cause bad feelings that won't work to your advantage in the long run. Pushing the crew too hard without giving something back is considered exploitation. In addition, if the crew is too exhausted to work effectively, you will reach the point of diminishing returns.

Credit and Experience in Lieu of Compensation (CELC). If you can find experienced crew members who want to make the jump from their current position to a more advanced position, such as a 2nd assistant director who wants to work as a 1st assistant director or a location manager who wants to try her hand as a production manager, you might obtain their services for free. The production benefits from their general experience, and they benefit by gaining specific experience in a new position.

Documentary Crew. Documentary crews are usually small and mobile. They require a director of photography and a sound recordist who can move quickly and efficiently. Assistants can be employed to help set up lights and sound equipment and to control traffic.

> I did sound on the shoots, and we always went out as a two-person crew, including on *Mirror Mirror*. We never had more than two people on location.
>
> *Jan*

When Do You Need Them? The "Producer" section of Chapter 10 contains a detailed week-by-week preproduction schedule that indicates when particular crew members should begin work. There are no absolutes in this area, but this schedule can serve as a guide.

007 Equipment

Before approaching a rental house, you need to have some idea of the size of your equipment package. The following are some of the primary factors that will influence this decision:

DIRECTOR'S VISUAL PLAN FOR THE PICTURE. The director's ideas for the project might include the use of a dolly or some other elaborate equipment such as a Steadicam®, jib arm, or crane. Eventually, you might discover that you cannot afford these items, but it is still wise to get an idea of their cost. It might be possible to negotiate a few days' rental of a dolly as part of a larger equipment package.

SIZE OF INTERIORS THAT MUST BE LIT. Your equipment package should accommodate all lighting requirements dictated by the script. You might need to scale down some of the lighting packages or else change the script to find a balance. Often, when the cost of a lighting package is examined, the all-important night scene easily can be shifted to an all-important day scene. In any case, it is a good idea to pad this area, because you don't want to get caught with too little money for grip and electric.

SPECIAL EQUIPMENT REQUIREMENTS. Identify and budget the specialty rigs that the script demands, such as car mounts (if there are many driving scenes) and zoom lens motors. Now is the time to explore different equipment options and their cost. There are imaginative ways to shoot people talking in cars without elaborate rigs and slow motor zooms.

ABILITY TO WORK WITH SMALL LIGHTING PACKAGES. The ability of the director of photography (DP) to work with small lighting packages can't be judged until you begin hiring, but it is good to know what you can afford so you can approach potential DPs with realistic expectations of the kind of equipment with which they will be working. If your DP is comfortable with the limitations of your budget and doesn't demand more lights, it is a good sign that you have hired the right person.

DEALS YOU WILL BE ABLE TO NEGOTIATE. Once you have determined the equipment required for the shoot, shop for a rental house. You can negotiate a deal at a special rate if you rent all your equipment from one source. Besides the big items like the camera, dolly, lights, and dolly track, you must allocate money for expendable items such as construction materials, bounce cards, gels, and diffusion material. (See the "Producer" section in Chapter 12, "Camera," for more about rental houses.)

It is best to price a number of equipment packages. Think of it as A, B, and C lists. The A list is the wish list, and the C list is the make-do list. The B list stands as a compromise between what you would like to have and what you can realistically afford.

008 Art Department

The art director supervises the team that is responsible for the total look of the picture. Props, wardrobe, set dressing, set construction, hair, and makeup all fall under the auspices of the art department. This catchall category also includes many items customized for your show, such as animals, special effects, and picture cars. A small-scale project might only need or be able to afford one to three people to handle this important area. Much depends on the requirements of the script and what you can make do with, given your limited budget.

A number of factors will affect how you approach the budget for this department. They include the following:

SCRIPT REQUIREMENTS. The breakdown sheets provide you with a list of the props, wardrobe, and special hair and makeup required for the picture. From this starting point, you can begin pricing these items. The script of *The Lunch Date* called for the protagonist to wear a mink stole. This means renting or borrowing one unless you are lucky enough to hire an actor who has one of her own and is willing to wear it for the show.

> I said to the wardrobe designers, "Here's $1,200. You can take out of it what you want, and pay yourself what's left over." Basically that worked. They paid themselves $400, and used $800 for the costumes.
>
> *Howard*

SETS THAT MUST BE BUILT. Set construction—renting a stage, building sets, and dressing them—is a big-ticket item. Set construction is labor-intensive work and requires building supplies like lumber, canvas, nails, and paint. There are ways to economize in this area, such as redressing already built sets, but there is no getting around the extra costs compared to working with practical locations. Because of the costs involved, the producer traditionally oversees set construction directly.

AMOUNT OF SET DRESSING REQUIRED. How a location is to be dressed doesn't usually show up in the script. The writer might describe the general look or feel of a room without going into much detail. Set dressing comprises the objects that make up the world your characters inhabit. It is different from props, which are described in the script, but is no less important. Set dressing can come from many sources, including the actors themselves. A found location might already have personal items that are suitable for your picture, or it might have to be stripped down and dressed from scratch.

THE ART DIRECTOR. How experienced and frugal your art director is will have an impact on how much you get for your money. Inexpensive building materials and frequent trips to thrift shops can save money for the production.

Although this category is budgeted before the shoot, it should be well padded. Many unanticipated changes or necessities can arise, resulting in petty cash flowing like water from a leaky bucket. There is high risk of going overbudget in the art department.

009 Location

The breakdown pages will furnish you with a list of all the location demands for the production. It's possi-

ble that one location can serve for many in your story. Perhaps one apartment can be dressed to feel like two. Although you might hope to secure most locations for free, it is best to budget as if you were going to pay for them (even if it's just $50). An exchange of money, however minimum, signifies a business transaction. It changes the relationship between you and the individual who is renting the location.

Near or Distant? Your script might indicate a location that is not available locally. Without having to scout different areas, the producer can contact local film bureaus, which have on file pictures or descriptions of available locations that suit the needs of the script. Shooting at a location more than 50 miles from your home base obliges you to transport, house, and feed the cast and crew for the duration of the shoot. This decision puts a strain on the budget but might be unavoidable given the requirements of the script. For example, if the production base is in a city and the script is set in the woods, the company might have to travel to the countryside (the exception to this example occurs if a big city park can be manipulated to look like the woods).

This budget category can become inflated with little or no warning. Locations fall through or become more expensive on the day of the shoot. A neighbor can decide that he is disturbed and needs to be paid off to remain quiet. Vehicles break down, gas prices rise, it rains, there's an earthquake!

Transportation. The movement of people and supplies to and from the shooting location is an important part of a successful production. It requires proper vehicles and responsible drivers. This budget category also includes funds for gas, tolls, and parking. Rental companies often make good deals, so it pays to shop around.

Your transportation budget should reflect three basic items:

SIZE OF EQUIPMENT PACKAGE. The size of the equipment package will define the kind and number of cars, trucks, or vans you will need to rent. Several cargo vans might be sufficient to handle a small grip and electric package.

SIZE OF CAST AND CREW. If you are shooting at a convenient location in and around your hometown, you will not need to transport cast and crew to the set. However, if you are moving the production unit to a distant location, you will need to rent enough passenger vans for the run of the show.

REQUIREMENTS OF LOCATION. If you are shooting at an exterior location without an available green room nearby for the actors (see Chapter 7, "Location"), it might be necessary to rent a large van or recreational vehicle for the actors to dress, make up, and relax in when they are not required on the set. This is especially true for cold-weather shoots.

> *Students:* Vehicle rental is an area where students looking for a really cheap deal can get burned. If one business's price for a rental vehicle seems much lower than the competition's, be wary. While you are sitting on the road waiting for a tow truck, you will discover why it was so much cheaper.

Food. Cast and crew members run on their stomachs, and they like their food to be prepared well and tasty. You can estimate your food budget by using the following formula:

> No. of days × no. of personnel × dollar amount per head = food budget

Caterers will quote how much they charge per person per meal. It might be $2.50 for lunch and $3.50 for dinner. Ask about specific menus for each meal, and have the caterer come to your office with samples.

You will usually be required to serve two meals a day: breakfast and lunch or dinner and a late snack if shooting nights. For craft services, budget for a standing table of water, juices, sodas, fruit, and whatever snacks are convenient.

> I had a friend of my mother's cater, and I paid her $100 for the week and the rest went into food. You better be prepared to spend a great deal. It is important to keep your crew happy and make sure your meals are served on time and are good. A problem people often run into is they serve good meals but not on time. With kids, especially, you have to be very regular, otherwise they are going to get upset. No matter where we were in the day, we would stop at noon and have lunch. That time was for everybody to do what they wanted until we started again.
>
>   Meals are very important. They should be adequate and nutritious. For that part of the budget, you have to plan how many paper plates you're going to buy, napkins, etc. Caterers take care of that for you, but it costs money.
>
> *Howard*

> *Students:* Feeding a cast and crew can be expensive. If you wait until the last minute and have to send out for pizza or sandwiches, the price per head will be high. Plan out in advance each meal of each shooting day, decide who is going to make it, and determine how it will arrive on the set. Heating up

a big pot of stew or cooking pasta for lunch can be a big savings. Keep a large coffeemaker on the set. This will be less expensive in the long run than sending out for individual cups of coffee.

Housing. Do not neglect the creature comforts. If you travel out of town, sleeping and traveling accommodations do not have to be first class (unless you are so obligated contractually), but if eight crew members sleeping in one hotel room means no sleep for anyone, then the next day's work will reflect their dissatisfaction and fatigue.

If you are offering to fill a number of rooms for a set period of time, hotels often make deals with production units. Remember, they're in business to rent their accommodations. They would rather have their rooms occupied than empty.

010 Film and Laboratory

Laboratories will make overall discount deals with filmmakers for processing and printing. You can calculate the lab bill based on the amount of stock you are planning to shoot. The price of stock, however, is a fixed figure. Film from Kodak or Fuji should be all from one batch; that is, the serial numbers for the film stock should be consecutive. Videotape should come from the same batch as well. This guarantees that the quality of the entire batch will be consistent from roll to roll.

The laboratory's price for film developing and printing is based on a price per foot. You can easily calculate this figure to place in the budget. Check this figure again as you get closer to production because laboratories change their prices often.

Buying old stock or short ends (film leftovers from another production) can be risky but is an excellent way to trim costs. With old stock and short ends, you need to weigh the savings against the risk that the stock might be outdated and therefore unusable. Video stock should always be new.

> We underestimated slightly the amount of film stock we needed. During the production, the last day, we had to run out and get some more. I went through a film broker. I asked a DP who I knew for short ends, but he didn't have any 16mm short ends, so he gave me 35mm short ends instead. I traded those in for 16mm black-and-white stock.
>
> *Adam*

> *Students:* Many laboratories offer a student rate. Kodak offers a discount for raw stock to registered film students.

Amount of Stock to Order. You can determine the amount of stock you will need for your show once the director and the director of photography become involved. It is possible, however, to estimate how many rolls of raw film stock to order based on a projected shooting ratio (the ratio of film shot to film developed). If you are preparing a 10-minute film and anticipate a 4:1 shooting ratio, you need to buy 40 minutes of stock (four rolls of 16mm at approximately 11 minutes per roll). This particular shooting ratio is considered lean even by professional standards and requires that the director be well prepared and economical with her shots. A more realistic shooting ratio for beginners would be somewhere between 6:1 and 10:1. It is best to budget for the larger figure as it can always be pared down with input from the director when the budget is revised.

> I budgeted myself 14 rolls of film, and that's exactly what I shot.
>
> *Howard*

Video stock is inexpensive and rarely a budgetary consideration. This is an advantage if you are producing a documentary where the shooting ratio is usually very high. A box of a dozen 30-minute Beta tapes costs around $100.

Postproduction

Postproduction overwhelms many beginners. They focus so much energy on mastering the complexities of production planning that they neglect postproduction. You are sure to encounter hidden costs and unknowns that can't be clearly understood at this stage. How long a film or video will take to edit and complete depends on many variables. (See Chapters 17 and 18 for more details.)

Strike a balance between allowing ample time to make the correct artistic choices and the amount of time that the budget can support. It is a reasonable estimate that your postproduction budget will equal your production budget. This equation is a good starting point when evaluating your numbers.

011 Editing

The main items in this category are the cost of the editor, the editing room, supplies, and the editing equipment. Here you'll notice a distinction between film and video. Whether you shoot on film or video, explore all the costs related to video editing. The off-line video edit period is equivalent to the rough film edit stage, and the on-line video edit period is comparable to film negative cutting, optical placement, and the mix.

The length of your postproduction schedule depends on these factors:

WHO EDITS? A professional editor will speed the editing process along in both film and tape. It might take a beginner months to do a job that an experienced editor can do in several weeks. If you are editing a short film or video for the first time, allow for a slow startup as the editor feels her way around the editing room or off-line facility. Beginners have been known to spend an inordinate amount of time working on a 15- to 30-minute short.

ACCESS TO EDITING ROOM. This applies mostly to students and independents on a budget. Students with full-time class schedules or jobs might only be able to work for sporadic stretches at a time. It is difficult to sustain creative momentum with this limitation. Independents with limited budgets might have to rely on low-cost facilities from local media groups that don't allow full access to the equipment. Some expensive video facilities give customers a special price if they come in on a will-bump basis or during the graveyard shift.

SHOOTING RATIO. Even for professional editors, the more film or tape they must wade through and cut, the longer it will take to shape it into a final product. Documentaries traditionally use a very high shooting ratio, especially if they are using tape. It is only during the editing process that the true shape of the documentary emerges, so it is best to budget for a long postproduction period.

RENTAL DEAL. This is a good time for striking an excellent deal on film postproduction equipment because so much media work is now being done on video. Nonlinear editing systems incorporating video and digital technology are working their way into the professional domain. Be sure to look into and price nonlinear editing systems as a legitimate option for film.

012 Postproduction Sound

The area of postproduction sound encompasses sound effects, Foley, automatic dialogue replacement (ADR), mixing, and the music track. There are a multitude of details related to these steps that involve the expenditure of money.

Sound Effects. You must consider several options in the area of sound effects, ranging from the traditional methods of creating a sound track to the new digital technology that is radically changing the way sound is treated.

> *Students:* This new digital technology is slowly working its way into film and video programs, which usually lag far behind the industry in terms of innovation. For the current generation of computer-fluent beginners, integrating the learning experience with the new technology should not be difficult.

Postproduction houses may offer the student or beginner a set price for the sound design/editing/ADR and the mix based on a flat rate per minute. However, don't be seduced by the new systems. The speed and ease you might gain may not be worth the price—at least, not for your first project.

Music. The music for your project, if needed, either will come from prerecorded sources or will have to be composed specially for the picture. One method is not inherently less expensive than the other. The rights to a few bars of a very popular song could cost far more than original music for the score of a short film or video.

It is difficult to know at this stage what role music will play in your final product. It sometimes happens that a piece of music indicated in the script has an important relationship to character, mood, or plot. If it is a popular song or recording, research the rights to the music now before it becomes a permanent fixture in the cut. Securing the rights to well-known songs can cost hundreds and even thousands of dollars, depending on when the song was released and the popularity of the recording artist. (See Appendix K for more information about music rights.)

Mix. During the mix, the entire sound track for the project comes together. Call around to various mixing facilities, and ask for prices. Most offer student or night rates for independents on a budget. This usually means having a trainee mix your film or video.

> *Students:* If your institution has an ADR, Foley, or mixing facility, it is best to work with it as much as you can. Mixing a 10- to 15-minute project professionally can add $2,000 to your budget. Make the first pass at your institution. Spend the time learning the intricacies of the mixing board without the financial pressure of the clock (at $150 to $250 an hour). If you are not happy with the result and decide to opt for a professional mixing stage, what you will have gained in experience and confidence will far make up for what you might have lost in time.

013 Laboratory Postproduction

Obtain a price list from the lab you plan to use. If you haven't decided on a lab yet, get a price list from any lab for a ballpark estimate. If your script is 15 pages long, figure that the film will be 12 minutes, or 425 feet. For postproduction lab expenses, such as the answer and release print, use the budget breakdown and simply multiply 425 times the price per foot. Make sure you include money for opticals, negative cutting, dirty dupe, reprints, tax, and so on. This budget category should be padded. You will encounter unanticipated expenses later on, so it's wise to have enough money in the budget to cover them.

014 Office Expenses

A good formula is to budget 5 percent of the below-the-line budget for your production office expenses.

015 Insurance

Do not neglect insurance. There are many companies that insure film and video shoots. Equipment and personal liability are the minimum insurance packages. You can purchase additional insurance for such items as stunt work, foreign or hazardous locations, and the negative; the latter coverage protects the film once it reaches the laboratory.

> *Students:* Some film and video programs automatically supply basic liability and equipment coverage.

016 Contingency

A contingency is a buffer between the budget and insolvency. The normal contingency figure is 10 percent of the below-the-line total. Although this number might seem high, contingency money is a key protection against cost overruns. Think of this as a slush fund for costs you cannot anticipate.

Petty Cash

One of the easiest ways to drain a budget and incur overages is to lose track of your petty cash. Petty cash is all the loose cash spent during production (not checks or prearranged expenses). During principal photography, money seems to fly out of the producer's pocket. Buy or make up petty cash envelopes. Then give each department head a fixed amount, say $100. He or she puts all receipts in the envelope and writes the expenses on the outside. When this allowance is spent, the department head turns the envelope over to the production secretary, who advances another $100. When possible, pay bills by check. Checks provide good recordkeeping for production expenses and for the government.

Animation and Video Postproduction

Because animation and video postproduction have slightly different needs, budget forms are included in Appendix D for these two categories.

BEGINNING THE BUDGET

Armed with your shooting schedule and a set of basic assumptions, you can now enter some numbers. Remember that you have stripped out from the script the items that will cost money, so refer to your breakdown pages. They will tell you to which items you will need to assign a cost. Once you have decided on the size of the crew, estimating crew costs is just a matter of multiplying the number of people by the number of days you will be shooting, including prep and wrap time.

The Budget Process

Consider this first pass at the budget as one of many drafts. The budget will go through several incarnations as more production information is funneled into the process. Your estimates will become more realistic as you hammer out deals and set locations, cast, and crew.

Put the numbers in their appropriate categories, and add up the total. It is always good to overestimate at this point. If the numbers add up to less than you expected, you have room to pad specific areas. If the total is greater than you anticipated, look at the bigger budget items and begin to trim.

Information Is Power

The more choices you have, the better prepared you are to make the most sensible decisions. As you look around for the right deals, it is important to understand that the telephone is your weapon. Be ready to use it a lot. When seeking out the best deal for a van rental or production equipment, secure a local production guide (see Appendix F) or a phone book and begin calling. Here are several important tips for phone work:

BE AGGRESSIVE. Don't wait days for your call to be returned. If vendors don't call you back within a reasonable period of time, call them again. You are competing with others who want the vendor's attention. Keep plugging away until you get it. Remember that the squeaky wheel gets the grease.

GET THE NAME OF THE PERSON WITH WHOM YOU SPEAK. Write down the complete name of whoever gives you information about a price or deal. Later, you can verify the figures by quoting the individual who gave them to you on the first call. Otherwise, another party can deny that anyone in the company ever gave you such a quote.

TAKE NOTES OF WHAT YOU ARE QUOTED ON THE PHONE. Get as much information as possible about what the vendor is offering and the price. Write it down neatly and carefully, and organize the notes in your production book so you can refer to the information. If, after you hang up, you realize you forgot to ask a specific question, call back.

BEWARE OF THE REALLY CHEAP DEAL. If you find a price that is suspiciously lower than everyone else's quote, be wary of what is being offered. Examine and test all goods. A *good* deal does not necessarily mean faulty equipment, but an incredible deal might spell disaster.

MEET THE PEOPLE WITH WHOM YOU WILL BE WORKING. This especially applies to film or video equipment rental houses, postproduction facilities, and film laboratories. You are creating a relationship not just for the duration of this particular project, but, it is hoped, for many to come. Vendors receive hundreds of phone calls a day, so be sure to help them connect your face with your voice. The personal connection will make an impression and might allow you to negotiate a better deal.

DON'T RUSH THROUGH THIS PROCESS. Take your time. Beat as many bushes as you can to find the best deals. Don't be satisfied until you have checked out every available rental company. Your legwork in preproduction might save enough money to enable you to purchase more stock or to rent the perfect location. The heat of production affords you little or no time to negotiate; production is not the time to strike deals.

EVERYTHING IS NEGOTIABLE. Don't be afraid to ask for what you want. Always start with your lowest bid for services, talent, and materials. All people can do is say "No." Enter a negotiation with a figure culled from the budget in mind, but try to get it for less. If you can secure a location or make a deal with a caterer for less, you can use the difference for a line item that costs more than you budgeted.

GET IT ON PAPER. Get all agreements confirmed in a Letter of Commitment. Verbal agreements can be forgotten.

ABOVE ALL, BE FRIENDLY. Personal relationships are the foundation on which all business is conducted in the industry. This is a given. People generally want to work with individuals they know and with whom they are comfortable.

PRODUCTION VALUE

Production value is the quality of your production efforts in relation to the money you have spent. It is dictated by how many pages are to be shot per day on average, coupled with the amount of money allotted for each day: The budget (minus postproduction costs) divided by the total number of script pages equals the cost per shooting day.

You can get a feel for what kind of quality you're likely to end up with by comparing how much money you have to spend per day with your production demands. A high-budget picture burdened with expensive sets, many special effects, and high fees might have to be shot quickly for a large amount per day. Conversely, a low-budget show with few production needs might shoot over a longer period.

It's true that money can solve most production problems. However, money is often at a premium, especially in a low-budget arena, so ingenuity must take the place of unlimited funds. No matter how large or small your budget, its total is based on the production items needed to fulfill the script.

Many film and video producers get through the shooting stage by moving money from the postproduction categories to the production categories ("robbing Peter to pay Paul"), and ultimately, they cannot complete the picture due to lack of funds. When budgeting, err on the side of too much because it is better to come in under the budget than over the budget.

> Don't let money hinder your process. If you feel like you don't have enough, don't let that be a reason not to shoot your film. If you have enough to at least get started, I suggest doing it. And if you have a lot of money, I suggest being careful of how that money is

being spent. Just because you have a lot of money doesn't necessarily mean you're going to come out with a good film.

> *Adam*

Students: These are the key production budget items for a student film:

- Stock (film or video)
- Processing (film only)
- Food
- Expendables (gels, tape, batteries, etc.)
- Transportation
- Art department

These items will be the bulk of the hard costs required to get a picture into the editing room. Students might also spend extra for special equipment that is not included in the equipment package they receive from their program, such as special lenses, dollies, and car mounts. If funds are tight, be sure that you will have enough money to get the film out of the lab (this is not an issue with video). You can use the time during postproduction to raise money to complete the project.

DIRECTOR
Shoot for the Moon

The director is not usually involved in calculating the budget. This is the domain of the producer. When asked, the director will most likely want to shoot for the moon and surround herself with as much time, equipment, and personnel as she can to achieve her goal.

However, a seasoned director can serve as a welcome consultant to the novice producer during the budgeting process by bringing her experience to play in several key areas, such as her shooting plan and her crew, equipment, and cast needs.

The budgeting process is a team effort. An experienced director can serve as a guide while the producer does the road work, making the calls and negotiating the deals. There can be a healthy dialogue between the two as the producer fleshes out the figures that represent the script's needs.

> Garth was terrific. I couldn't have made the film without him. Basically, what happened was I had all the locations locked, and then as the film got closer, I started having to worry about how I would shoot it, so I loaded all the production concerns on him, and he was great.

> *Adam*

The director can also advise the producer about her minimal needs to do the picture. There can be a "wish" version of the budget as well as a "bottom-line" version of the budget. Ultimately, the director strives to make the best picture possible with the available resources, but it is also her duty to fight for her vision. If she feels that she needs additional time or equipment, she should request it. Her goal is to shoot for the moon while understanding the constraints of the budget.

> I knew art direction in the fantasy sequences would play a big, big role. Much had to be done with the way they were dressed or the makeup effects, e.g., the arrows in the chest. It had to be lively and have a sense of fun about it . . . and I knew it was going to cost money. Nobody in film school can accomplish those effects. And you can't just wing it, or it won't have any weight to it.
>
> *Howard*

LEARNING BY DOING

To gain an idea of what things cost, work on as many productions as possible in whatever capacity you can, hopefully in some job that allows you access to the set. This entry-level job will most likely be as a production assistant, a catchall title for the person who does the grunt or "gofer" work (go for this, go for that) that isn't handled by any defined crew position. A production assistant might get coffee for the director, run errands for the producer, or help with traffic or crowd control, among other duties.

A set is a living laboratory. Soak in as much of the atmosphere as possible. Learn to identify everyone on the crew, what they do, and how they handle themselves. Get to know as many people as you can. You can't afford to be shy in these situations, although you should learn when it is acceptable to ask questions and when you should be silent. After a job is over, keep in contact with the key people you've met.

> I got a job as a production assistant and just hung around with the grips for a while and started doing grip work. There was a shot with the fence swinging open in the wind, and I was there behind the tree with a fishing line pulling the thing back and forth.
>
> *Adam*

The set is the ideal place to learn; however, working in the production office can also be educa-

tional. Aiding the production coordinator and production manager, even if it is by photocopying contact sheets, is an invaluable opportunity to experience the ebb and flow of daily production activity. Be enthusiastic about every job you are asked to do, no matter how menial it might seem. Prove yourself first on the basic tasks before bucking for the more demanding ones.

Students: Get as much experience as you can on "professional" shoots as well as your own student productions. Exposure to professional standards will invariably help your own work. You can never have too much experience. Each production has its own set of unique problems, and learning how others work through the process of solving them is an important part of your education. Through this process, you will surely learn valuable lessons that you can file away for use in similar situations on your own productions.

KEY POINTS

1. Estimate the size of the production. Will you need a big cast, lots of crew, or many locations?

2. Examine your resources and potential funding. Do not try to make an epic on a shoestring.

3. Balancing the budget and the script is a constant struggle. If money becomes too tight, the script itself can be altered to reestablish a balance.

4. Things change. Be prepared with ample contingency plans to make adjustments.

5. Establish a system of petty cash vouchers to keep track of the cash flow. The art department can be an unexpected drain on the budget.

chapter six

Crewing

The most important rule of filmmaking is to always feed your crew well.

Howard

PRODUCER

Hire the Crew

The *crew* is defined as all of the personnel, besides the actors, who are employed in the making of a film or video during principal photography. Just as important as finding the right actors to flesh out the story in front of the camera is the search for the right support group behind the camera. The crew represents the nuts and bolts of the production machine. The success of the project lies in their ability to collectively carry out the director's vision of the script. The sum of their energies and creative input is responsible for the project being produced.

The best-laid plans are only as good as the talented people who carry them out. The production hours are long and hard. Crew members who can be creative and inventive under pressure while maintaining a sense of humor are worth the search. These positions might not be romantic or showy, but they are all essential to the making of the film or video. If a production assistant doesn't control the flow of traffic, the director can't get the shot. If the assistant camera operator doesn't clean the film gate properly, a whole roll of film could be scratched. If the lens is not properly set or the lighting is inadequate, even the most brilliant performance will be out of focus or impossible to see.

WHO HIRES THE CREW?

The producer (in the role of production manager) is in charge of hiring the crew. His responsibility is to surround the director with the best creative team the project can afford. The director participates closely in this selection process, but it is the producer who negotiates with potential crew members, makes the deals, and, if necessary, does the firing. This is to ensure that the director's relationship with the crew is on a purely creative level and that any tension over business issues does not interfere with what should be a positive and supportive relationship.

WHEN DO YOU NEED A CREW?

Crew members not only need to be present for the duration of the shoot, but they also need time to prepare. This period is termed *prep time*. After the shoot, the crew requires a clean-up, or *wrap*, period to complete any work that has to be done after principal photography. The only exception to this is if a crew member is hired to perform a specialty job, such as prosthetic makeup, an explosion, or the operation of a second unit camera.

The amount of prep time needed depends on many factors. For short films and videos on tight budgets, it depends on the availability of key people to give as much time as possible without being paid. (The "Producer" section of Chapter 10, "Rehearsals," outlines a sample preproduction schedule, which indicates when particular crew members should ideally come on board. Each project has its own set of requirements, but this schedule should serve as a model.)

The director of photography did have a meeting with the assistant camera, the grip, and the gaffers, his whole crew, for an hour or so the week before the shoot. They went over what he was trying to do, how he wanted to do it, and how he was going to run his department.

Howard

HOW BIG A CREW DO YOU NEED?

Only by recognizing the script's technical needs and understanding the director's design for translating the story into images can the producer adequately crew the project. If the director's shooting plan calls for several dolly moves, as did those of *Truman* and *The Lunch Date*, there will have to be someone on the set, at least on certain days, who can handle this technical responsibility.

Documentary crews are small and compact by nature. They must be able to move quickly in and out of confined spaces. At the other end of the spectrum, a full union crew will have a size and complexity that most beginning film- and videomakers do not need and cannot afford.

It is important for you to be familiar with the many positions that exist on a film or video crew and to understand the primary responsibility of each (Figure 6.1).

The 3–30 Rule

Short film and video projects employ a crew of from three to 30 members. Like so many aspects of the breakdown process, the script and the budget dictate the type of crew members required. Your challenge, should you have less than this number of crew members, is to determine how the positions will be filled by the number of personnel employed on your shoot. For example, if the script requires 30 crew positions but you can only afford a crew of 10, each person will have to perform an average of three jobs.

SELECTING THE CREW

It is not enough just to find hard-working and talented individuals. You also need to find crew members whose personalities complement one another. Crewing is similar to the casting process for actors. The chemistry of the group is important because these people will be working closely under the stress of production. It is also valuable to know the kind of egos with which you will be working. Are these team players or prima donnas?

Talk to producers, directors, or anyone who has worked with these individuals in the past. Find out as much as you can before you decide to hire. If this is not possible, you must go with your intuition and instinct. Don't feel pressured to hire a supposedly "great" director of photography (DP) if you are uncomfortable with his attitude or arrogance. Beginners are bound to make mistakes in this area, but the more experience you acquire, the more astute a judge of character you will become.

If your choices prove to be wise ones, this project could signal the beginning of professional and creative relationships that last a long time. As a producer or director, you have to rely on dependable and talented crew members to execute your ideas. Finding people you can trust, who you enjoy working with, and who are good at what they do is a promising start of a solid creative network from which you can draw in the future. Remember that this business is built on relationships.

> The worst and best choices you will make are your people choices—in other words, the crew and the actors. Everybody you choose to work on the project is going to influence the outcome, so you really have to be very careful about whom you're choosing: Are these people going to get along? Are they going to help me? Am I choosing this guy simply because I heard he was the best director of photography around? But if he has an ego problem, you're really going to regret that decision later.
>
> You want people who like you, who like the project, and who want to be there, for obvious reasons, not somebody who's just doing you a favor. Students often throw people together just to get somebody there, and they get a person who doesn't want to be there or with whom they have a problem. The project gets made, but it becomes a very unpleasant experience, and people end up enemies. I've seen it many times.
>
> *Howard*

Attracting the Right People

How you present your project to others will have an impact on the quality of the people who are interested in working with you. If you appear to be an organized and professional person, you will attract more of the same. Create a professional-looking flier to post at film programs, media organizations, and high schools. Place advertisements in media journals, magazines, and newspapers.

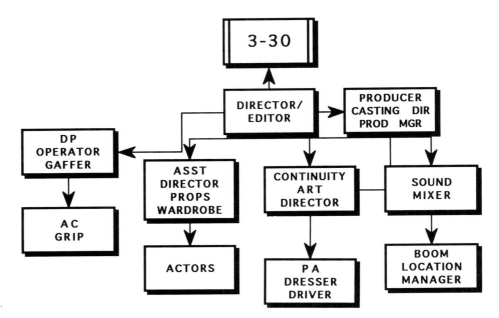

Figure 6.1 Crew flowchart.

Students: You have the benefit of being able to draw personnel from your class and your program. Because a great deal of work is being done at film and video programs around the country, you'll find many young and old professionals alike eager to work on student projects. Professionals who agree to work on student projects know that there isn't much in it for them financially. They are attracted by the opportunity to work and, most important, by the material itself. A good script attracts good people, no matter what its source. Most people would rather invest their time and energy on a project with some inherent value, something they can be proud to put on their reel as a sample of their work.

Independents: You can advertise in all the places students do. There are many eager students, hungry for experience, who are willing to put in long hours on a semiprofessional shoot. The good ones can be of great help in understanding the low-budget world because that's where they work and live.

Evaluating Credits

How do you know who did what? It can be risky hiring people that you either don't know, haven't worked with before, or both. Scrutinizing their reels and talking to producers, directors, and other crew members about them will definitely help. However, these solutions are not foolproof. Making a film or video is a collaborative endeavor. So many people can have an influence on the final product that it is often difficult to discover who really did what. Consider these examples:

- The director of photography's reel might look great, yet he might have worked with a director with a good eye or he might have had an excellent gaffer who was responsible for much of the lighting.
- A film or tape might be well edited, but the editor might have been slow, and you might not have the budget to accommodate her lack of speed.

You are on the right track if you find consistency from show to show. The fact that most of someone's work is mediocre except for one piece will tell you that someone else might have been responsible for that one piece's success. You hope to get honest answers from the people who worked on these films or videos, but this is not always the case. Who really did what might change depending on the person to whom you speak.

If you do your research well, you will reduce the risk of making a serious mistake. If things don't end up well, you always have the option to fire that individual and find another.

Negotiating the Deal

The producer negotiates a fee with each crew member. This is generally a flat daily or weekly rate, with some proviso for extra-long days. It is a good business practice to draw up a simple deal memo for each crew member. A *deal memo* is a Letter of Agreement between two parties that defines what services are to be rendered and the compensation for those services. The deal memo also either details the crew member's screen credit or contains a clause giving the producer the right to assign credits at his discretion.

If you negotiate a flat fee with the crew, they will give you the hours you need as long as you do not abuse their time and energy. If crew members are on a daily or even an hourly rate, you need to pay special attention to their schedule. For example, if you need an extra hairdresser for a short period, make an effort to allow that crew member to perform her task and then leave the set, rather than linger and accrue additional compensation.

KEY CREW MEMBERS

The first step in assembling a crew is to choose the key people who will form the creative and technical nucleus of the production. Once you have chosen the key personnel, you can assemble the support crew based on their recommendations. These pivotal crew members work with their own smaller teams on a regular basis.

The following are the key people on a crew:

- Production manager
- Assistant director
- Director of photography
- Sound recordist
- Art director
- Editor

The first five positions are discussed in this chapter. See Chapter 16, "Picture," for information on the editor's responsibilities.

Production Manager

When the producer has a lot of money at his disposal, he hires an individual who is known in the industry as a *production manager*. This individual breaks down the script and creates a schedule and a budget. Once the budget is agreed to, the production manager (with the producer's approval) begins to organize the production.

The following are the production manager's basic duties. As you can see, the position plays a pivotal role in the production process. The production manager performs these tasks:

- Coordinates, facilitates, and oversees all pre-production
- Prepares the script breakdown and preliminary shooting schedule
- Establishes and controls the budget
- Makes deals with the crew
- Makes deals for equipment
- Oversees daily cash flow
- Supervises the selection of locations
- Oversees day-to-day production decisions
- Facilitates schedule changes
- Manages all off-set logistics
- Arranges for housing and meals
- Sets up necessary insurance
- Ensures that permits are obtained
- Secures releases
- Keeps on top of all production activity to keep ahead of the director in production planning
- Completes a daily production report reflecting the status of the picture's cost

The production manager is the engine that drives the project. The importance of this position cannot be emphasized enough. It is also the least glamorous key position. It must be occupied by a well-organized person who wields power efficiently. The production manager answers to the producer.

> The first person I chose after the director of photography was the production manager. Production managers take on such an enormous role, particularly on student films. I was fortunate that I had someone who was not only my friend and a good filmmaker but who really liked the idea. Not only did he fulfill the production manager role by lining up caterers and the like, but he was involved in the story process as well. He was one of the people who sat down with me, went over the story, and got excited by it. When people get excited, they put more of themselves into it at all levels.
>
> *Howard*

The production manager hires the department heads, who, in turn, suggest personnel to make up the support teams for their departments.

> I had a production manager, an assistant director and a director of photography—they formed the core. Additionally, I had an assistant camera operator, a sound person, a boom person, and two grip/gaffers. Below that I had a runner/production assistant, a

baby-sitter, and a costume person. If you want to go even farther down the line, I had the caterer. I don't know if you really call that a complete crew, but those were the people who were involved in the shooting of the movie.

Howard

Unfortunately, a production manager is a luxury that most beginners can't afford. The producer usually assumes this important position on low-budget productions.

Support Crew

The production manager's support crew consists of the following personnel:

PRODUCTION SECRETARY. The production secretary is the liaison between the producer or production manager and the cast and crew. She is a key player at the hub of the production office. Some of her responsibilities are:

- Facilitates communication
- Disseminates information to cast and crew
- Coordinates transportation in the absence of a transportation coordinator
- Completes paperwork, cast and crew lists, call sheets, and so on

The production secretary should be a highly organized, efficient, and even-tempered individual who is accustomed to remaining calm in the middle of a storm. She is the producer's or production manager's right hand.

LOCATION MANAGER. This crew member scouts and secures locations and serves as liaison between the production company and the location. His other duties include arranging for parking and catering and obtaining permits, location contracts, and certificates of insurance. He sets up each location so that the production unit can shoot properly, and then he arranges for the cleanup.

CATERER. All crew members and actors like to eat. Shooting a film burns up calories that must be replenished. Having someone manage the food affairs of the shoot can make for a smooth ride. The craft services people set up a table with food near the set for snacks throughout the day, and they arrange for midday meals in a comfortable setting.

TRANSPORTATION CAPTAIN. If a project requires many vehicles, a key driver called the

transportation captain is responsible for transporting the production from location to location. Being able to wrap out of a location and move to the next shot with efficiency saves time and money. It takes an ever-watchful eye to keep tanks filled with gasoline and maintain the vehicles. The captain hires a team of drivers to shuttle actors and equipment to and from the set, and she makes deals for picture vehicles. This position is often filled by a production assistant.

Assistant Director

The assistant director (AD) works closely with the producer or production manager to create a shooting schedule. He also has the responsibility on set of making sure that the production sticks to the schedule. He represents the production manager on the set as well as being the director's right hand.

The assistant director must communicate with all the actors and crew members because he is the company sergeant, the ship's pilot, the traffic cop. He has the onerous task of making sure that everyone is in the right place at the right time. He must constantly remind the cast and crew members of the schedule and must perform this task with grace and tact. The assistant director watches the clock while the director of photography sets up and fine-tunes the lights, the sound recordist places microphones, the art director dresses the set, and the director rehearses the actors. Most of all, the assistant director must be totally in sync with the director.

I don't know, it was a miracle. We were never more than 25 minutes off our schedule. The AD did a great job. He was always looking at his watch, without making me nervous. He always knew where we should be and where we could make up time, which is the job of a good AD. Everything stayed fairly constant, it was like a vacuum-sealed environment— the same crew, the same people, the same location every day.

Howard

Support Crew

The assistant director's support crew consists of the following personnel:

2ND ASSISTANT DIRECTOR. The 2nd assistant director's duties include preparing the call sheets, arranging call times, and coordinating all cast and crew arrivals to the set. The assistant director is also responsible for directing the background action. The

2nd AD is the off-set person who is responsible for having the actors prepared for their calls.

3RD ASSISTANT DIRECTOR. The 3rd AD telephones the actors in coordination with the production secretary to set up the next day's shoot. If traffic or crowd control is needed, all of the ADs are involved in securing the set.

CONTINUITY (SCRIPT SUPERVISOR). The script supervisor works closely with the director to determine what coverage has been shot and what shots remain. He marks the script with a description of each shot of each scene. He takes detailed notes after each take regarding action, dialogue, gestures, lens used, costumes, makeup, and so on, to ensure continuity of all these elements from shot to shot and scene to scene. This script is then sent to the editing room so the editor has a written reference to the shoot. The script supervisor's other responsibilities include matching each actor's actions from take to take and from angle to angle. Neglecting this attention to detail can create major continuity problems in the editing room.

Director of Photography

The producer and director's concern is to hire the best DP they can afford. This is an important decision. The DP's job is to fulfill the director's visual design for the project and to participate in building the camera team. This means that before bringing on any of the camera crew, you must decide on a DP. On most small projects with a limited budget, the DP also operates the camera. So you are, in fact, looking for a DP and a camera operator in one.

The director of photography must be resourceful and able to make use of simple lighting situations or none, depending on the situation. He must be flexible and able to light and shoot on the run. If yours is a project like *Mirror Mirror*, the technical demands might be less rigorous. With only one setup in a studio situation, there was ample time to set up lights.

> One of the great things about the cinematographer was that he was able to work very quickly and improvise as well. He could work under tough situations, with no light. That was important for me, having someone I could trust doing the camera. There were a few times when I didn't even look through the camera other than to maybe say, when we were first setting up the shot, "This is perfect," or "Maybe a little tighter."
>
> *Adam*

Students: On student productions, the DP might serve not only as the camera operator, but also as the gaffer and the grip!

Evaluating Potential Directors of Photography

When deciding among potential DPs, consider these criteria:

PREVIOUS WORK. Look at the professional reel. However, you are not always looking for the quality of the work but the different kinds of lighting situations with which he has worked. A DP may be able to function with the flexibility of a set, but not be experienced or comfortable with limited lights in practical locations.

Is there something identifiable about his style that is compatible with your story? If his work is excellent but his lighting style(s) is very different from what you envisioned for your project, you may want to talk with him anyway. He may have been typecast to do a certain kind of work and may be eager to branch out and try something different.

WHAT FORMATS, CAMERAS, AND STOCKS HAS HE WORKED WITH? It might be an obvious point, but if you are looking for a DP to shoot video, he should be fluent with the specific format of video you wish to shoot. (You might lock into a specific video format because of a lucrative deal you have negotiated.) The DP must also know how to shoot and light for video. The lighting requirements for video differ from those for film.

If you're looking for a DP for film, ask about the experience candidates have had with different equipment and, more important, their experience with different film stocks in your chosen format. If a DP is shooting in 35mm or 16mm for the first time, it is appropriate to ask for tests with the equipment and stocks until you are confident that the DP is comfortable with the new format.

SPEED. How long does it take the DP to set up the camera and lights? His sample material might look terrific, but if a candidate takes a long time to set up for each shot and you are working on a tight schedule, he might not be the best person for you. You want someone who can create stunning images, but you want it fast unless, of course, you have a luxuriously long schedule.

You can research a DP's speed by talking with the producers or directors who have worked with him in the past. Often, a DP will spend the morning lighting and breeze through the afternoon. If you want to sacrifice speed for a particular look, you can offset the longer setups by planning a smaller shooting ratio of 1:2 or 1:4. Use the extra setup time to rehearse the actors more thoroughly.

DOES HE HAVE HIS OWN EQUIPMENT? Many DPs come with their own cameras and sometimes their own lights as well. The fee they quote includes their services and their equipment package. This can be an asset because not only does it simplify things, but if anything happens to the equipment, the DP is responsible. He might even have his own insurance policy. Don't assume that because a DP has his own equipment he is automatically good; the equipment is just a bonus.

COMPATIBILITY WITH DIRECTOR. The director and the DP must get along and must share a mutual vision of the piece. There should be a tight creative bond between the two. It is the producer's job to support the director within the boundaries of the budget by providing her with a DP who satisfies her creative needs.

SCHEDULE. Is the DP available and can he work on your scheduled dates? Is he booked so tightly that if your schedule fluctuates, he will not be able to accommodate you? Finally, can the DP work within your (probably tight) schedule?

Troubleshooting

The following warning signs could have an impact on your production planning and budget:

1. An inexperienced DP asks for too much high-end equipment. Watch for these items in particular: HMI lights, expensive dolly, large equipment package, Steadicam®, Luma crane, video tap, camera car. This might occur because the DP wants the opportunity to work with the fancy equipment or because he is not able to evaluate properly the technical needs of the show. Insecurity might lead the DP to order as much equipment as possible and then decide what he needs during the shoot. After doing a detailed location scout and discussing the director's visual ideas for the project, an experienced and resourceful DP should be able to give an accurate breakdown of the project's equipment needs for the entire show and know how to maximize the equipment package that you can afford. You might have room in the budget for some or all of these items, but you might not actually need them to fulfill the director's visual plan for the script. The money you save could be better spent on props, costumes, or an interesting location.

2. You have hired a seasoned DP on a student or inexperienced crew, and the DP is trying to take over the creative aspects of the shoot. This can happen when an insecure crew doesn't stand up to someone who appears to know what he is doing. The DP might have very strong ideas about how scenes should be photographed or staged that might not be in sync with the director's vision. If the DP's work is terrific, you don't want to antagonize him, but if he gets his way, the result won't be the piece that the director envisioned. This is a tough situation for beginners. As soon as this problem appears, it is best that the producer confront the DP. Remember that it is your film or video you are making, not his.

If you are working with an inexperienced or student DP, an experienced gaffer can be very helpful.

> The next important search was to find a DP; I wanted someone to go over the storyboards; I wanted someone to be involved. I found an older student, and every week we'd have a story meeting where we'd talk about the story as well as the storyboards. In those sessions, other problems became apparent. We realized we'd need a 5.9, a very wide lens. We'd need to rent a variable-speed motor. But if you need a variable-speed motor, where are you going to rent it? The production manager was there and I'd say, "Ian, can you call a few equipment houses in Rochester and find out what their rates are for the day?" which then impinges on your budget. So when you start talking to each other, you realize how interconnected the process is.
>
> *Howard*

Support Crew

Now that the DP is aboard, you can hire the support crew—camera, grip, and electric. The size of your particular crew will depend on the budget (what you can afford in the way of salary, transportation, lodging, and food), the demands of the script, the size and difficulty of lighting and filming the locations, and the director's visual plans for the material.

Does the director want a fairly static camera, long dolly moves, or both? Does she want high-key or low-key lighting? She might even be thinking of using a Steadicam for several scenes. After the director and DP finalize their overall visual plan, you will have a better idea of the crew needed to match the creative requirements of the production.

The DP will want to have around him people with whom he has worked before. In most cases, a DP's speed and effectiveness result from his support team. The support crew for this department consists of 10 positions with specific responsibilities for operating the camera, lighting for the camera, and moving the camera.

Operating the Camera

CAMERA OPERATOR. Often, the director of photography is also the camera operator. If he decides to concentrate on the lighting, he has the option (budget permitting) to hire an operator whose job will be primarily to operate the camera.

ASSISTANT CAMERA (AC). The AC's duties include changing lenses, following focus, and assisting in setting up the shots.

2ND ASSISTANT CAMERA. The 2nd AC, also called the *loader*, threads the film into the magazine and loads the magazine onto the camera. The 2nd AC slates each take and is therefore in communication with the script supervisor as to the numbering of the shots. The 2nd AC fills out the camera reports for the lab and for the editor.

STILLS. A stills person takes photographs of key sequences on the set for publicity. He usually takes still photographs during rehearsals. A professional stills photographer can shoot the actual take but only with a silent camera housing.

Lighting for the Camera

GAFFER. The gaffer serves as the DP's left hand. He is responsible for setting the lights and securing the power to illuminate them.

BEST BOY/ELECTRICIAN. The best boy is the gaffer's assistant.

SPARKS. Sparks are electricians who round out the electrical team if the DP needs more than two assistants.

Moving the Camera

KEY GRIP. The key grip serves as the DP's right hand and supervises the physical movement of the camera.

BEST BOY/DOLLY GRIP. The best boy is the key grip's assistant. This crew member, also called a *dolly grip*, is the person responsible for pushing the dolly.

GRIP. The grip is responsible for the physical movement of the camera.

Sound Recordist

Beginners usually find it easier to find a DP than a sound recordist. Recording sound is not as glamorous as recording images. Beginners and students are usually more focused on getting the best DP they can than the best sound recordist. This priority for camera is usually continued on the set as well. Time will be spent making sure the lighting is right, but many crews are hard pressed to repeat a take because of a sound problem. This attitude can result in acting that is beautifully seen but not properly heard.

This happens, in part, because it is technically possible to rerecord all the dialogue and add in other sounds in postproduction without going back to the original locations. It is far more expensive to have to reshoot a scene as a result of camera or lighting problems because the entire cast and crew have to be reassembled at the original locations.

If possible, try to record clean dialogue, or *production sound*, on the set to capture the "magic" that can happen between actors during a scene. Dialogue can be rerecorded during the postproduction period, but this kind of sound work can be time-consuming and expensive (see Chapter 17, "Sound"). In addition, some actors, especially nonprofessionals, are not adept at recreating in a dark recording studio months after principal photography the dramatic chemistry they worked hard to convey on the set.

One of the inherent problems of evaluating a sound recordist is not knowing if the dialogue in the final print was recorded on the set or in a recording studio. If it was recorded in a studio, was that because of unavoidable problems with the location that made it impossible to record clean production dialogue or because the sound recordist did a poor job? These questions can only be answered by the producer, director, or editor of the project.

> There was one guy doing sound. He was operating the Nagra and the boom, and then eventually he enlisted one of the homeless guys to help us, which turned into a disaster.
>
> *Adam*

Evaluating Potential Sound Recordists

When selecting a sound recordist, consider the following criteria:

KNOWLEDGE OF EQUIPMENT. The recordist should know the Nagra or whatever recording device you will be using. This might seem like an obvious point, but it is helpful for you to explore the candidate's technical sophistication. Most important, is the candidate experienced with a wide assortment of microphones, such as radio microphones and lavalieres?

OWN EQUIPMENT? The sound recordist who comes with his own recording equipment and microphones is very common in the industry. He is comfortable with his own rig and can rely on it. For the producer, it means that he can quote you a price that includes his services and his equipment. This figure is usually less than if you hired the sound recordist and had to rent the equipment separately. However, do not hire a recordist just because he has his own rig. Always go for the best you can find. The rig should be a bonus.

EXPERIENCE. Does the candidate have a wide range of experience working in challenging practical locations? It is less demanding to record *clean dialogue* (free of unnecessary sounds or noises) in a soundproof environment like a sound stage. You need to question how he has performed on locations that were not "sound-friendly"—that is, those with distracting or loud ambient noises that interfered with the dialogue.

TEMPERAMENT. The ideal sound recordist is easy-going but assertive on the set. He is adept at asserting himself if he feels that things are not right for sound. He might have to fight to be heard because the needs of the recordist are many times subjugated to those of the camera. The sound recordist must be sensitive to actors' needs and be able to discreetly but accurately tape a radio mike or lavaliere to an actor or to request volume adjustments. The sound recordist can be a sea of calm in the midst of chaos.

Support Crew

The boom operator comprises the support crew for the sound department. The boom operator is an important position and should not be filled by just anybody. The best sound recordist in the world can't record proper sound if the microphone is not pointed in the right direction. The sound recordist you hire will most likely recommend a boom operator with whom he likes to work. The boom operator's duties include collaborating on the placement of the microphones and positioning the boom pole during takes to best record the dialogue or ambient sounds.

Art Director

This is a very important position and one that beginners often slight. The art director is responsible for fleshing out the director's vision of the script. It is her job to create, in tandem with the DP, the world that

the characters of the script inhabit. You will most likely find promising candidates among those trained in designing for the stage. However, there are fundamental differences between designing for the stage and designing for film or video. The stage requires designing for an entire proscenium, whereas film or video requires designing only for what the camera will see. The camera might only see a wide shot of an entire room for several seconds and concentrate on a corner of the room for most of a scene.

Evaluating Potential Art Directors

Use the following criteria to select an art director:

EXPERIENCE IN FILMS AND VIDEOS. Your first choice should be an art director who has experience with cameras, not just theater, and who understands what the camera sees and how to control the visual environment. If your candidate is eager to get into motion pictures but has little experience, she should be prepared to spend time analyzing films and videos.

ABILITY TO WORK WITHIN A LOW BUDGET. The art director must be inspired to use imagination instead of money. This might mean scrounging around thrift shops for bargains or creatively rearranging an existing environment.

COMPATIBILITY WITH DIRECTOR. The art director must share the director's creative vision of the story. A creative bond should develop between the two.

Support Crew

The art director is responsible for putting together her support team, which might consist of the following positions:

- Storyboard artist
- Construction coordinator
- Set dresser
- Property master
- Costume designer
- Dresser
- Makeup artist
- Hairstylist

Depending on your budget for the project, the art director might be asked to handle many of these responsibilities, including set dressing, props, and even wardrobe.

I knew art direction in the fantasy sequences would play a big, big role. I started calling older students, which is always a great idea when you've got production problems, and I found out who had made films with heavy costume designs or heavy makeup effects. I got names, and I started calling. That's how I met Jan Fennel, a costume designer in New York who does off-Broadway, commercials, and small production stuff. For costumes and salary, I had a total budget of $1,200.

Howard

STORYBOARD ARTIST. The storyboard artist translates the director's vision of each sequence of the script into drawings or panels that represent what each shot will contain.

CONSTRUCTION COORDINATOR. A construction coordinator plans, budgets, and oversees the work when a set, set piece, ceiling piece, or new floor must be constructed.

SET DRESSER. The set dresser buys, rents, or makes set pieces and furnishings. During the shoot, the set dresser is on standby in case any of the set pieces must be adjusted or painted. The set dresser also works ahead of the company, if possible, to dress the set for the next day's photography.

PROPERTY MASTER. This crew member gathers all necessary hand and set props for the project and doles them out as needed. For example, if the actors are eating a meal on camera, it is the prop master's responsibility to keep the glasses filled and steam on the food from take to take and from angle to angle.

COSTUME DESIGNER. Everything the actors wear in the show is prepared by the costume designer. This is done in conjunction with the art director's designs and the DP's contributions.

DRESSER. On set, a dresser assists the actors in and out of their wardrobe. One dresser is employed for the men, and another for the women. If there are many actors and extras, additional dressers might be hired for big sequences.

MAKEUP ARTIST. The makeup artist designs and applies the actors' makeup and facial hair pieces. The makeup artist's responsibilities include the maintenance of continuity and script days.

HAIRSTYLIST. This crew member designs and styles the actors' hair and manages any wigs used in the production. The hairstylist also maintains the continuity of hairstyle. On a windy day, he stands by and recombs hair that has become mussed.

Production Assistant

Production assistants (PAs) can be placed in any and all departments, depending on the needs of the company; the most needy department gets help first. If the company requires another driver, another camera assistant, a grip, or a dresser, the producer can place a PA in that position.

> Students never plan for enough crew, and more importantly, they don't plan for enough PAs. You should have one or two PAs just to run around, pick up stuff, drop stuff off, and help the production manager. It's always the last person assembled in a student crew, and it's always a big mistake because then the energy starts draining away from the set; people are leaving to go buy extra quarter-inch tape, batteries, or whatever is missing at the moment. All of a sudden the crew is being cannibalized to become runners and PAs, and the set starts to fall apart. You lose a lot of time. Getting PAs for student films is always a difficult task. I was fortunate: My father was my PA. He took a week off work and ran around for me. Because he had no ego problems about doing that, it worked out really well.
>
> *Howard*

SPECIALTY CREW

There are many other crew members who cover specialty areas. These include special effects, choreography, standby painters, Steadicam operators, greens people, animal wranglers, tutors, and stunt coordinators.

Video Shoots

All the positions listed above apply to video. In single-camera video shoots, there are some differences in the way jobs are performed. The most significant difference is that narrative video shoots require slightly different lighting plans.

Because many video shoots are documentaries, another difference is the mobility of the crew. Documentarians work with a light crew so they can move freely in the field. Video cameras have microphones mounted on the camera, so technically, a video shoot can consist of one person.

> In terms of roles, I wore many hats in *Mirror Mirror*. I was the production manager, I handled the budget, I decided on stocks and ordered fill, and I spent a lot of time trying to track down appropriate and affordable mannequins to use in the set.
>
> *Jan*

Documentary Crews

What factors play an important role in hiring a crew for a documentary shoot?

> Because *Mirror Mirror* wasn't shot on location, I did think about a third crew member as a production assistant. Ordinarily, I only work with one other person, as it keeps expenses down and minimizes our presence. In this case, I was wary about the crew outnumbering the subject, and I weighed the possible benefits of having a PA against the possible impact an additional person might have on the intimacy of the interviews. With just two of us, we were both involved in primary crew roles (camera and sound), whereas a PA would be there as an audience member. I decided against it.
>
> *Jan*

Documentary crews are usually composed of the director/producer, DP, and sound recordist. They need to be small and mobile. This has to do with budgetary concerns as well as aesthetic ones. Documentaries might be shot over long periods of time, and their budgets can't support a high overhead. Crews must keep a low profile and not get in the way of the people they are photographing. They should be able to move quickly and follow the action if necessary.

It is not unusual for the documentary film- or videomaker to serve as the producer, director, writer, and DP or sound recordist. This person conceives, develops, finances, and creates the project. Producing a documentary can demand an intensive devotion over many months or possibly years of work.

> This was now my sixth film in which I worked with a two-person crew—myself on sound and a cinematographer. What's important to me as both the director and the sound person is to get the best sound possible by wearing the headphones at all times so that I can monitor what is coming off the tape. In the case of *Mirror Mirror*, it wasn't too hard because I set up a boom, so I didn't have to worry about handling the mike. Those women were in a static position—I knew they weren't going anywhere. For each interview, I would just set up the boom to an optimal position, check levels, and then I sat just to the left of the camera. The mike was far away from the camera, so we didn't have to worry about camera noise. I was just there with the Nagra, and I would ask my questions and be attentive to their responses while checking the modulometer periodically.
>
> *Jan*

DEVELOPING THE RIGHT CHEMISTRY

Preproduction is the time to shake out any potential crew problems before principal photography begins. If you hire key people early enough in the preproduction process, you will have time to get a sense of how well they will work with the director, producer, and other crew members. If you sense that potential problems are brewing, confront them immediately. Don't wait until you are so close to production that replacing a key player would create a serious dilemma. If there is tension during preproduction, you can be sure it will only escalate during production.

If you discover you have a serious problem with a crew member, air it out reasonably. If the problem cannot be resolved amicably, it is time to look for a replacement. It is up to the producer to be the heavy and do the firing. Try to break off working relations as amicably as possible. Just because a crew member is not the right choice for your current project doesn't mean he or she won't work out another time. Don't burn your bridges with anyone if you can avoid it.

Always be prepared for the eventuality that someone you hire might not work out because of schedule conflicts, health problems, creative or personal differences, or whatever. You must be able to get on the phone and find a replacement immediately. This is only possible if you have a list of backups—that is, people you didn't choose for the position initially but who were good candidates. Backups are essential for the crew as well as for the cast and locations. An efficient producer will hold onto the names and phone numbers of the rejected candidates for all positions. Approaching people you have already rejected is usually not a problem as long as you were reasonable and fair the first time around. This is an established part of the business. If your backups have been working for a while, they should be used to it.

> *Production:* If you are in the heat of production and have to fire a key player, don't fire that individual until you have found a replacement.

DIRECTOR
Hire the Crew

For the sake of harmony on the shoot, the director must be intimately involved in choosing the key people around whom the crew will form. The director will be in charge of the set, and she must trust the key people to execute her vision for the script. She looks for creative partners as well as people with whom she can work and get along. The production hours are long and hard, and the director must feel confident that those around her will come through for her when needed.

During the process of choosing the crew, the producer and director have the opportunity to develop a complementary working relationship. They need to bond as a team and to develop a strategy for dealing with all sorts of production-related issues. It is difficult to make important decisions in a vacuum. The producer represents another set of eyes and ears as the director hones in on the right people for the project.

Together, the director and producer should develop a strategy for interviewing prospective crew members. After each interview, the director and producer can discuss how they felt about the candidate. Differences of opinion can be important not only in making the right choice, but also in learning about how each other views people. The ultimate choice must rest with the director (budget pending), but by sharing impressions in an open forum, the director and producer develop a rapport and have a productive dialogue, the goal of which is to secure the best crew for the project.

Choices about the crew are only the first of many that will include decisions about the cast, locations, sets, props, costumes, hair, makeup, and so forth. The entire preproduction process involves a long string of decisions that will have a direct impact on the resulting film or video. As more of these decisions are made, the producer and director must develop into a tight-knit team, both moving to the beat of the same creative drum.

DIRECTOR'S DISEASE

There is a phenomenon in the business known as *director's disease*. It is a rash, a cold, or a headache that is directly related to the pressure under which the director puts herself. While shooting *Beauty and the Beast*, Jean Cocteau developed horrid boils that had to be lanced each evening. Miraculously, when the picture wrapped, the boils disappeared. Good health is a key factor in maintaining the rigorous pace of a shoot.

> We started shooting on a Monday—it was the Martin Luther King holiday—and that weekend, out of nowhere, I suddenly came down with a 102° temperature. It was totally psychosomatic. I didn't even think I

was going to make it to Monday. But then you just start working, and you go and you do it.

Adam

Students: We have identified several problems that are specific to student shoots. Understanding at an early stage what it means to be a professional takes time and experience.

The following guidelines should help a new director through those first projects:

MAKE IT CLEAR WHO IS IN CHARGE. There must be a leader and a decision maker on the set. The director should know what she wants and be able to communicate her desires to others. The assistant director should keep the production moving forward at a good clip without alienating the crew.

TREAT ALL CREW MEMBERS WITH RESPECT. In most cases, the crew (and cast) is working for little or no pay. Remember that they are all part of a team and that everyone on the team is important.

KNOW WHAT EVERYONE DOES. If you understand the value of every position, you can evaluate what you really need for a particular production. Know also what every piece of equipment does.

CLARIFY JOB REQUIREMENTS. If crew members hold more than one position apiece, be sure that job requirements don't conflict, and clearly establish who will do what. There shouldn't be any assumptions on the set; you don't want to hear, "I thought *he* was taking care of that." An effective crew should be able to accommodate any demands asked of it.

KEY POINTS

1. The department heads are responsible for hiring their own crews.

2. Make sure that the crew members you hire are people you want to be around for long days.

3. If certain crew members are not pulling their load, do not hesitate to terminate their employment. No one is irreplaceable.

4. Crew members often have more than one job. Define all crew responsibilities.

5. Maintain good health. The stamina needed for a shoot can be taxing.

6. Qualified people are often interested in working on a short project to build their reel or to jump into another crew position for the experience.

chapter seven

Location

I got the stage free because it was part of the university where I taught.

Jan

PRODUCER

Securing Locations

In his task of securing locations for the shoot, the producer should communicate trust and confidence. People who might grant permission to use their home, restaurant, facility, loft, office, or building must feel that the production crew will take proper care of it. This means the crew should leave the location in as good a condition as when they found it (if not better). No matter how much or how little you pay for the location, this is proper professional behavior. The producer wants to establish a good reputation in the film and video community. It also might be necessary for the company to return to the location for reshoots.

Price, proximity, schedule—the producer sees all locations with these elements in mind. He negotiates for the location once members of the key creative team have made their choice.

If the director requests a particular location that is priced out of reach of the budget, the producer should suggest an alternate or backup location. Should the director insist on a particularly expensive location, a compromise will have to be struck.

WHERE TO LOOK FOR LOCATIONS

When scouting for locations, seek the advice of professionals in the film and video business. Many cities have a film commissioner at City Hall, as well as a statewide film commission, to accommodate film and video shoots. Look in the paper for apartments for rent and inquire at local realtors. Sometimes, a house that is for sale can be rented for a short period of time. Ask friends, painters, and interior designers for leads. Put up fliers on community bulletin boards, at schools, and at local media organizations. Advertise in the local paper. These methods are especially useful for finding locations and housing when shooting at a distant location.

It's best to find locations as close to the production office as possible. When locations are 50 or more miles from the production office, the union rules governing professional actors and crew change. So, too, do the logistics, which will have an impact on the budget.

Take pictures of interesting locations with a panoramic film or take enough shots to create a 360° montage of the area. A video camera also can be handy when scouting locations.

If you are in a real bind, you can always alter the script to accommodate locations that are available.

I went looking for a restaurant, and it was difficult. I spent a few weeks going everywhere in New York, Queens, the Bronx, and Brooklyn looking for one that had a row of booths. By accident, I was walking down 43rd Street, and there was this burnt-out space, and next to it was a bar. I looked through the smoked-up windows, and I could see that it used to be an old diner. I went into the bar next door, and the guy said he would let me take a look around. The place was a disaster. There had been some sort of fire, probably an insurance fire. It was cold, water was on the floor, and the ceiling was caving in. It was also being used as a storage space for pretzel carts! But there were these booths, and it was the right style. I told him I was a student. He charged me $500 for the day, including electricity.

Adam

SCOUTING THE LOCATIONS

A location scout is begun by the location manager, although all key crew members can keep their eyes open for the best site. Once the number of potential locations has been narrowed down, the director, DP, and art director pay a visit to the prime candidate sites. When the final decision has been made, all department heads do a walk-through of the location as the director talks the crew through the shooting plan.

To evaluate a location properly, you will need to consider lighting, power, sound, and other variables, in addition to the script breakdowns. Use the following 15-point location checklist—the points that apply to your project—as a guide.

Lighting

- How will the scene be lit?
- Where is the light source?
- Where will your source light come from?
- If the location has windows, how long will the set receive direct sunlight?
- Is there ample space to place the lights in the location?
- Can you prerig or rough in any lights before the day of the shoot?
- Can you put spreaders on the ceiling without damaging the walls?
- Will you need to provide a fan to cool the room?
- For an exterior, will the sun provide adequate light for proper exposure, or will you have to supplement the sunlight? Will you need silks to even out the light?

Power

- Where is the power source?
- Does the power source have enough amperage to accommodate the lighting instruments you plan to use?
- Check the amperage available at each outlet. The gaffer will calculate whether the lighting instruments can function with the power available. If there is not enough power, you will need to either tap into nearby power or rent a generator.
- If you will need to rent a generator, do you have ample cable to run from a generator to the lamps?

Sound

- Is the location quiet?
- Can existing sounds, such as refrigerators or air conditioning units, be silenced during shooting?
- Do the neighbors have a noisy dog or child that must be quieted?
- Is there an abnormal amount of traffic outside?
- Can you use sound blankets to dull the traffic noise?
- Is the outside noise the same all day long?
- Can the shots be planned so that the microphones point away from the windows?
- Are there plans for construction nearby during the shooting period?

Green Room and Other Special Areas

- Is the green room (a holding area for the actors) far enough away from the set?
- Are there toilet facilities for the cast and crew? Is there someplace they can go to relax?
- Is there a quiet area away from the set where you can leave food out all day for the company?
- On an exterior shoot, is there a place where the company can retreat from the elements if necessary?
- Can a dressing room be rigged for the actors?
- Where will the actors apply their makeup?
- Is there an area off the set to store equipment?

Safety and Security

- Does the location require any security?
- Have you made arrangements to lock up any valuables?
- If the equipment is stored in a van and parked in a lot, is the lot bonded?
- Can the equipment be left in the location overnight?
- Do you need police from the city for traffic control?
- Are you performing any stunts or tricks that would require additional safety precautions?
- Do you have additional personnel to direct traffic or hold parking spaces?
- Do you have a fire sequence that requires a standby water truck?
- Are there stunts that require a standby nurse or ambulance?

Catering

Like an army, a production cast and crew runs on its stomach.

- Calculate a meal plan schedule for the entire shoot.
- Audition caterers by having them prepare a meal.
- Check with the cast and crew for any particular dietary needs.
- Have coffee and munchies available all day.
- Provide hot food for the midday meal if possible.
- Arrange a place where cast and crew can sit down for the midday meal and a short rest.
- Make provisions for a second dinner should the day's shooting run longer than anticipated.

Communication

- Double-check all location arrangements. Make sure you alert tenants of the production's impending arrival.
- Have a phone list of people to contact if there are problems. Who will let you in?
- Prepare maps and directions to the location for the cast and crew.
- Have the appropriate city officials been notified of your presence?
- Rent walkie-talkies for the crew if needed.

Transportation

Shooting sites, whether near or far, require that all departments, equipment, and personnel be transported to and from the set. Transportation logistics is one of the breakdowns that you must plan to maximize the time allotted for production.

- Rent vans, trucks, and cars.
- Coordinate company moves to and from each location.
- Calculate the time required for each move. Allow extra time for problems.
- Arrange for drivers.
- Make travel plans for distant locations.
- Find and secure all on-camera picture vehicles.
- Make parking plans for all production vehicles.
- Rent the proper car mounts for moving vehicles. Hire an experienced grip to set the camera. You might need to secure special insurance and permits for towing picture cars.

- Create proper signage to direct the cast and crew to the location.
- Calculate all contingency plans, including weather, gasoline rationing, disaster, and personnel problems.

During the production period, drivers are constantly out in the field picking up actors, special equipment, and supplies. Pickup times are designated on the call sheet, and adequate time should be allowed for traffic and trips to the gas pump. Drivers are responsible for the vehicles to which they are assigned.

At the end of the day, during the *wrap*, the drivers return to the production office to drop off actors, run to the laboratory to drop off film, or take the principals to screen the dailies.

Company Moves

If your project calls for several locations, it might be necessary to move the production unit during the production day. The time it takes to wrap out of one location, travel to another, and then unload and set up the equipment can monopolize a big chunk of a production day. This type of move should be avoided if possible. If it cannot be avoided, factor the time into your production schedule and remember the following:

- Create a detailed daily transportation plan.
- Assume that each move will take longer than anticipated.
- Do not leave equipment unattended in a vehicle.
- Keep the gas tanks full at all times.
- Travel time is time taken away from principal photography.

Parking

- Have arrangements been made ahead of time for parking?
- Have the appropriate permits been obtained and posted?
- Will the vehicles ever be in the way of a shot?
- Do you need parking spaces for picture vehicles?
- Does a street need to be blocked off the night before a shoot?

For Grand Central we got a permit to park near there, in a driveway, to unload. We went to the mayor's office and got a permit to park on the street.
Adam

Permits

- Have the appropriate permits been obtained for the time and place of the shoot?
- Keep the permits on the set, ready to be shown to authorities.

Insurance

- Have you obtained adequate insurance for the location?
- Does the insurance cover all the types of shooting that you are planning?
- Does the owner of the location require any special insurance?
- Have you allotted adequate time to process the insurance forms?

Location Fee

- Have you negotiated a fair price for the use of the location?
- Does the fee include the use of power at the location?

Location Contract

- Have you signed an agreement between the company and the location owner?
- Is the person signing the contract indeed the owner of the location?
- Have you been honest about the time you require?
- Have you promised in writing to return the location to "as good if not better" condition?
- Have you offered the location owner a credit in the end crawl?
- Do you have permission to use the telephone and restrooms?
- Do you have the option to return for reshoots?

I had to find out if I could shoot in Grand Central Station. I found out that Grand Central is privately owned by Metro-North. I spoke to the public relations person there, and she said, "Yes, we love to help students." I asked about the cost, and she said it was free, as long as I didn't plug in any lights. Once I used their electricity, I would have had to pay some guy $15 an hour to sit there and watch the plug.

One of the stipulations for shooting in Grand Central was that I could only shoot between rush hours, 10 a.m. to 2 p.m. each day.

Then we ran into the usual hassles. Every morning when we got to Grand Central and started unloading the equipment, the station master would come and kick us out. Because of the bureaucracy, the messages weren't coming through that we were allowed to shoot there. So we would run and find the woman in the publicity department—and get permission again!

Adam

Backups

One final word about locations: It is highly advisable to secure a backup location in case the location you have chosen suddenly becomes unavailable. Do you have a dressed location you can shift to if weather presents a problem?

DIRECTOR
Scouting Locations

As important as it is to choose the right actors for the piece, it is equally important to choose the right world, or at least the illusion of that world, for those actors to inhabit. The credibility of the story depends on it.

What does a particular environment do for the story? How can a specific locale enhance or detract from the script? Will the setting lend itself to an interesting visual background? Locations have symbolic meanings. The texture and feel of an environment can quickly and efficiently bring us into the province of a story as well as communicate exposition about the characters. It was crucial for the audience to feel that they were in a metropolitan train station for *The Lunch Date* and in a real gymnasium for *Truman*.

By seeing where and how the characters live, we learn about who they are even before being introduced to them. This is subtle information that must be communicated. Your choices should not be arbitrary.

AESTHETIC CONCERNS VERSUS PRACTICAL LIMITATIONS

When choosing a location, you must find a balance between your aesthetic concerns and your practical limitations. The aesthetics of the location are based on the dictates of the script. A "dingy bar" does not mean the Oyster Bar at the Plaza Hotel, a "suburban house" does not mean an apartment building, and a "beach" does not mean a forest. The search for the appropriate location means ensuring that what is seen on the screen is what is indicated on the page.

The practical considerations for choosing a specific site are based on what the budget can afford and the schedule will allow. A specific apartment might excite the director visually, but it might also involve inherent problems for one or more of the production departments. Balancing is the key to a final decision about where to shoot a sequence.

THE POWER OF ILLUSION

Like so many aspects of production, you can employ tricks with the location to create illusions the script requires. For example, you can create movie magic by transforming a less than exciting site into a glamorous one described in the screenplay. The art department can work miracles to redress a location to look like the required setting. If the shots are specified, the redressing need only be done for the angles the camera will see. If you avoid shooting telephone wires and cars, your local park can look like a forest. By cheating your camera angles, you can make a large loft space look like a tiny apartment.

In addition, you don't have to find your ideal location all in one place. A home can be pieced together out of many rooms in various houses that seem to fit together. Suppose, for example, that an actor walks out a door and the camera picks him up in the corridor. He walks to an elevator and gets in. We are inside the elevator with the actor. He alights into the building lobby and crosses to the front door. From outside, we see the actor come out onto the sidewalk. This could all be done at four different locations: a corridor, an elevator, a lobby, and a building exterior. The audience assumes the locations are all part of one building.

The cafeteria in *The Lunch Date* was not actually adjacent to Grand Central Station, but the audience connected the two because the filmmaker did. Adam Davidson did this with the sound. In both the station and in the cafeteria, we hear intermittently a train station announcer calling out track numbers and destinations over the public address system. Hearing the announcer in the station and in the restaurant binds the two locations together. What is amusing is that there is no public address system in Grand Central Station. The filmmakers went to Penn Station to record the announcements! It is convenient to find everything in one place, but it is not essential.

I wanted to find a restaurant that would work. I knew there was nothing in Grand Central, but I wanted it to feel as if it could be a part of Grand Central. Because of that, it's really funny, what happens. There are no train announcements in Grand Central. I went to Penn Station and picked up train announcements there. So, of course, some people watch the film, and they say, "Wait a minute. This isn't right. There are no trains that go to New Jersey from Grand Central." Well, I never said it was Grand Central.

Adam

Many concerns about location are applicable to both narrative and documentary forms. Each of the short films explored in this book are defined by the space in which they were shot. *The Lunch Date* employed New York's Grand Central Station, *Truman* was shot in a gymnasium, and *Mirror Mirror* was photographed on a soundstage (Figure 7.1).

The location became important to me early on. I saw getting a gym for a week for free and getting it near where these kids come from as a big problem. So I spent a great deal of time nailing down the gym. Then I could dream about it and mentally place my characters there. It wasn't just something I was hoping or wishing for. I knew it was there and that it was mine.

Howard

What Does the Script Require?

The script might define very specific kinds of locations, or it might describe locations so vaguely that it allows for leeway. "EXT. FIELD - DAY" gives little indication of what kind of field, how large, what kind of foliage, what time of year, and so on. "INT. OFFICE - DAY" leaves the kind of office open-ended: Is it a high-tech, ultra-modern, antiseptic office or a wood-paneled, warm, cluttered room?

IDENTIFYING THE LOCATION

Each location is broken down into four categories for identification. These are the major factors you must consider when scouting your shooting environments.

Interior or Exterior

The location you are identifying will either be interior (INT.) or exterior (EXT.): inside or outside. Both of these location settings carry with them a variety of factors to be weighed when determining a suitable background. Interiors are easier to control, but exte-

Figure 7.1 The gymnasium.

riors are less confining. Interiors can be blacked out, or tented, and shot at any time of the day, whereas the shooting schedules for exterior locations are dictated by the sun and the weather.

Day or Night

The script will indicate whether the scene is a day scene or a night scene (or dawn or dusk). Exterior day scenes mean that the source of light will be the sun. Remember that the sun has an arc, the sun may go in and out of the clouds, and daylight saving time reduces the number of daylight hours. Interior night sequences can be shot during the day if the windows are blacked out.

Stage or Practical Location

A scene will be shot either on a shooting soundstage or in a practical location. The stage is an ideal environment for controlling both light and sound, but the facility rental fee can be expensive. Practical locations look real but come with problems relating to space and control.

Stage

There are three main factors in determining whether you should use a stage:

COST. Soundstages can be expensive. Check out prices. An unused stage might be rented to a film or video crew for a limited period at a reasonable rate to make a short.

CONTROL. Soundstages exist for the sole purpose of allowing the director a soundproof, controlled environment in which to shoot. Stages provide a grid for hanging lights, which can be a major problem on a practical location. Stages come with unlimited power, heating and air conditioning, offices, dressing rooms, parking, telephones, bathrooms, and other conveniences that make the shooting process more convenient and comfortable than in a practical location.

A stage gives you the freedom to build any set and any backdrop. There is adequate room for the placement of lights, camera, and sound. This undisturbed freedom can translate into a focus on the job at hand that might not be available in a practical location. If the production team on location has to stop and start constantly due to noisy neighbors or cramped quarters, it drains the energy on the set (Figure 7.2).

I knew from the outset that I was interested in shooting it in a studio. Although I have done only location shoots in the past, with *Mirror Mirror*, I wanted to use the studio sets to make a visual state-

Figure 7.2 A set built on a soundstage.

ment and thereby enhance the themes of the film. I felt that to have a woman talking about her body while seated in front of bookshelves in her living room or at her kitchen table would make a boring talking-head film.

Jan

SETS. If sets are required, they must be constructed. A stage is an empty shell that can be outfitted with walls, rooms, facades, and backdrops. The art department will rent or build walls, ceiling pieces, furniture, rugs, ashtrays, lamps . . . the works. From an empty space to a lit set takes time. Constructing, furnishing, and striking the sets are additional costs that need to be factored into the stage rental.

Practical Location

Practical locations have two bright sides. The first is the cost. If your budget is tight, a soundstage will most likely be out of the question. Practical locations might be expensive, or they might be free. If the cost of a location is high, most likely the cost to reproduce the location on a soundstage will be higher. The second advantage of a practical location is "the look." A practical location will always appear real to the camera, whereas it is a challenge to make a set look like an actual location.

One of the main drawbacks to a practical location is the "boxed-in" feeling. Walls cannot be moved; ceilings cannot be raised. Lights must be set off camera in limited space. When the camera, lights, boom, actors, and crew are all assembled, the quarters are cramped, hot, and confining. Keep several fans on set for air circulation. In a cramped set, even the choice of lenses will be limited by the space allotted.

Near or Distant

Your location, whether it is a practical location or a stage, day or night, interior or exterior, will either be near to the production office or distant. Having to transport cast and crew to and from the location is a major budgetary concern. If you employ union actors (SAG), the definition of *near* and *distant* is very clear. On a map of the downtown area of your production, circle everything within a 50-mile radius. Any location within the circle is considered "near," and any location outside the circle is "distant." For a distant location, actors' travel time is factored into their hourly rate as if it were part of their workday. Also, a near location does not require the production company to transport the actor to and from the set.

Even if your company is a small unit with a van and several cars, traveling to and from the location uses up valuable time that might be better put into production. If a suitable location is found closer to the production office, precious time can be shaved off the production schedule.

> It had to be something, first, that I could get for a week and, second, was located near the kids. I made *Truman* in Rochester, New York, where I grew up. This helped because I was able to draw from all of my connections. I got free scaffolding from a high school friend whose father was in the construction business.
>
> *Howard*

If the location is so distant that plane or train tickets as well as hotel accommodations become necessary, your budget will need to reflect these costs. Employ a local contact person to smooth over rough edges with locals and to receive any goods or communiqués the company needs to send. There are some distinct advantages to working on a distant location. The cast and crew will bond quickly. Most distant locations see a film or video shoot as a novelty. This may translate into *cooperation* and possibly free goods.

> What jacked up the expense was shooting away from home. There are tremendous advantages to it—you have the crew at your disposal and they are there to focus only on your film and that's tremendous—but it makes for a more expensive shoot. Every location trip costs something. Getting people back and forth isn't cheap, and eating costs increase.
>
> *Howard*

WALK-THROUGHS

Once you have secured the locations, it is advisable to call for a walk-through with the key personnel. During this floating production meeting, indicate how you will place the camera for the scenes in that particular location. The DP can sketch out a lighting plan so that on the day of the shoot, the gaffers will know where to place instruments and how to locate power. All the department heads can ask questions during the walk-through. It is, in essence, a dry run of the production.

KEY POINTS

1. Scout your locations with the full crew before the shoot.
2. Try to centralize your locations.
3. Arrange for locations with written contracts.
4. Make sure you have backup locations.
5. If possible, prerig an interior location by dressing it in advance and roughing in the lights.

chapter eight

Art Direction

I let the subjects know from the preinterview stage that if they were cast in the film, I would require them to wear a mask during the interview. Because it was a peculiar request, I didn't want to spring that on them when they arrived for the shoot.

Jan

PRODUCER

Assemble Team

The producer has two major concerns with regard to the art department: hiring the best creative people for the project and creating a good look without having to pay top dollar. Production value is about balancing fiscal responsibility and respect for the artistic mandates of the script. A good producer takes pride in stretching money as far as possible. The producer's role in terms of art direction involves these five steps:

- Hiring an art director
- Establishing a visual style
- Approving the budget and the schedule
- Hiring key support people
- Supervising the preproduction/construction schedule

THE ART DEPARTMENT

The art director, also known as the *production designer*, is the head of the art department. When working on small-budget projects, the art director sometimes has to handle all the duties of a full art team. (Refer to Chapter 6, "Crewing," for full art team.)

The art director is the person ultimately responsible for the overall "look" of the picture. She must be able to work in tandem with the director, the director of photography, and the budget. She strives to fulfill the director's vision of the piece, but must do so economically. The art director scrutinizes the script carefully and, in conjunction with the director, arrives at a visual plan for the picture. Whatever the plan, the art director must come up with a comprehensive budget and a schedule to accomplish her task.

Most beginning film- and videomakers work with small budgets, forcing them to look for an art director who has experience working with limited resources. In hiring for this position, compare the candidates' flexibility, experience, and fee. Keep in mind that one art director might cost more than another but might be more inventive or a better negotiator and thus will actually save you money. (The topic of hiring the art director is discussed in more detail in Chapter 6, "Crewing.")

In many ways, money definitely makes the producer's job easier. With enough money, you can hire a comprehensive art department. If you can afford it, you can hire a hair and makeup person for the entire shoot, ensuring day-to-day consistency. An alternative is to rely on the actors to do their own hair and makeup. If you can afford standby painters, they can quickly take care of sets that need to be touched up or recolored. An alternative is to anticipate such changes and schedule around them.

No matter what the budget, someone has to make sure the crew is accountable for its work. The producer is the guardian of the budget and the schedule. He approves the budgets and production schedules devised by the key crew members and sees to it that everyone adheres to these figures and dates.

RESPONSIBILITIES OF THE ART DEPARTMENT

Sets and Locations

During preproduction, you must decide whether to shoot your story on sets, in practical locations, or both. If you face this dilemma, compare the costs of constructing and dressing sets against the location fees. (In Chapter 7, "Location," you read about the pros and cons of working on a stage or in a practical location.)

In a practical location, the art director is confined to the space at hand. She can alter and redress it, but only within the limits of the existing dimensions and only with the permission of the owner.

On a set, the world must be created from scratch. The primary benefit of shooting on a set is that it is a camera-friendly environment. A set can be designed for flexibility, ease of manipulation, and good camera angles, and it imposes none of the constraints of a "real" location. The process of creating a world from scratch follows specific steps:

1. The art director analyzes the script.
2. She engages in conceptual and practical discussions with the director, who has a vision for the piece as well as practical requests regarding the kind of coverage she plans.
3. The art director furnishes the director with ideas through sketches of set renderings and pictures. These sketches might later be modified or altered.
4. On approval of the basic design, a drafter executes blueprints. If necessary, a model of the set is constructed.
5. The art director presents budget and building schedules to the producer. Design changes might be made to reduce costs. The department heads give final approval.
6. The construction coordinator supervises the construction of the set according to the approved design.

The completion of a set must fit into the production schedule. If multiple sets have to be built, the construction schedule of each set must be timed so that the set is available when needed.

Probably the most important consideration when constructing a set is determining precisely what the camera will see. The art director must find a balance between (1) how the director envisions the scene and (2) the budget, allowing some leeway for adjustments. If the director only needs to see a bed in a corner of a room, the art director should not build a fully dressed four-walled room. Similarly, the director should not order a fully dressed four-walled room and then shoot only the bed in the corner. The entire art direction budget will be stretched during the shoot, so waste should be avoided.

However, a good art director will not build a set with just two walls and a bed. Standing by will be a third wall and maybe even a ceiling piece. If, as the director blocks the scene, she desires more room in which to shoot, additional set pieces can easily be provided if prepared in advance.

> I was thinking about painting the floor in front of the mural. I knew I wanted it to be fairly monochromatic. I didn't want color in these sets, but I don't really know why. I suppose I wanted the women to stand out from the backgrounds and for the backgrounds not to be too assertive. I had a bunch of black-and-white linoleum tiles in my garage. You know, it is funny how ideas emerge. I was really wrestling with this floor dilemma, and suddenly I thought about those tiles and how I could make an interesting design with them. So I brought them into the studio and laid them out on the floor and thought that it looked pretty striking. Audiences commented on the floor —really noticed the black and white floor that the women are standing on.
>
> *Jan*

Everything is designed for the camera. Make sure the creative team spends its time on what the camera can see, and not on anything off-frame.

Set Dressing

The locations and their details set a tone for the film. They can help tell the story and convey a great deal of information about the characters themselves. Sometimes a key detail in the frame solidifies the credibility of a scene or moment.

Set dressing is everything that is placed on the set. This includes rugs, lamps, furniture, paintings, windows, chandeliers, and cabinets as well as all of the extraneous details, such as plates in the cabinets and bulbs in the chandelier. Set dressing does not include smaller items, such as guns, canes, lighters, or rings, used specifically by the actors. These are props.

The art department is responsible for "dressing" the location according to the director's wishes. Dressing a location might be as simple as spreading a few leaves near a park bench to make it look like fall, or as complex as furnishing an entire set from scratch. If a director walks into a living room and decides it will work for the film, this might mean that the room can remain as it is, or it might mean that the room must be stripped down to the bare walls and everything, including the stains on the rug, must be "imported" from another location.

Duplicate Set Items

Each department is responsible for the manufacture or purchase of duplicates—that is, items that are to be destroyed, distressed, or consumed during the course of shooting a sequence. If a table is broken during a scene, it will need to be fixed or replaced for each take.

Props

The property master is responsible for all the props identified in the script. A prop is a movable object, used by an actor, that is integral to the story. Props include jewelry, glasses, books, and weapons.

The beauty of film and video is that something doesn't have to be real to look real to the camera. Costume jewelry, for example, looks as real to the camera as do true gems. A person cannot deceive the camera, but a thing can.

The property master provides an assortment of props based on the needs of the script. He rents, buys, or makes the props. He might also use personal props provided by the actor. Like the costumer and the set dresser, the prop master should consult with the actors concerning their preferences. If there is little or no time for prior consultation, a good prop master will have several props available from which the actors can choose.

Most property masters own a kit or box of common props. This is called a *box rental*. Instead of shopping outside for some props, the producer can rent them directly from the prop master. Spend money on props that are dramatically important or used extensively. When disposable props are involved, have an idea of how many takes and retakes might be involved. Err on the side of having too many props rather than too few.

Weapons

All weapons fall into the prop category. It is the property master's duty to ensure safety with regard to these props (Figure 8.1). He must arrange with the local police for a permit to use firearms during the production, and the weapons' firing pins must be removed. The prop master usually gives a weapon to an actor just prior to the scene. Props, especially weapons, should not be handled except during a rehearsal or take.

The use and handling of weapons is a delicate issue. Special permits and insurance must be obtained just to have a gun on the set. The prop master is responsible for the weapon before and after its use and must keep it in good shape. There is never a need to have live rounds on a set.

On an interior set, keep the prop secured until it is needed. On an exterior location, make sure everyone nearby, especially the police, is aware that a scene involving a weapon is about to be photographed. You never know when a passerby might misread the scene and return fire.

Food

If a scene requires that food be consumed, make sure it is purchased in advance and that someone can prepare it. Buy all food items in bulk if possible, and try to use wholesale clubs or discount warehouses to get the best buys.

Duplicate Props

Often props are eaten, damaged, or distressed during the shoot. The property master and director should discuss how many backups will be needed, and the property master should provide extras, just in case.

Wardrobe

The costumer, or wardrobe designer, works hand in glove with the art director. Together with the director, they develop the look for the show's wardrobe. The wardrobe department is charged with making the characters identifiable by the clothes they wear. They might decide to dress the lead actor in bright colors and the secondary characters in grays, or they might choose pastels, or specific materials—whatever they feel contributes to the overall statement of the story, the characters, and the style of the production.

> The idea of the mask was there from the very beginning, although I don't remember what prompted it. I look back at my first proposal and see that it's in there. Two years before I shot the film, I was interested in homogenizing the faces so that the viewer's attention would be deflected away from the face towards the body. People look at bodies in this culture, but they are also judgmental about a woman's face. I wanted the audience to focus their attention on the bodies of the women and not have access to their faces.
>
> *Jan*

Figure 8.1 Weapons of any kind can be dangerous. Scene from *Truman*.

What each actor wears provides worlds of information about the character he portrays. Even though we are taught that you cannot judge a book by its cover, most people form a strong first impression based on how a person is dressed. In *The Lunch Date*, the contrast of wardrobe between the woman and the man having lunch together says a great deal about their stations in life (Figure 8.2). The homeless man wears a hat with the manufacturer's tag still attached. This small detail informs us about the man and fills us in on exposition important for the scene and the character. Can you imagine the scene if the wardrobe were reversed, if the woman were dressed in rags and the homeless man were in a coat and tie?

Make sure the wardrobe doesn't look as though it just came off the rack (unless this is your intention). A garage mechanic should look like a garage mechanic, and the audience should believe he is a mechanic before he utters a line. The clothes should be aged, tattered, and stained with grease. The process of attaining this look is referred to as *distressing* the wardrobe.

Consulting the Actors

Who better understands the character than the actor who must portray him? Soliciting the actor's suggestions about style, color, and specific choices will increase his involvement in the show. If the costumer gives him an outfit that the actor feels is inappropriate, "creative differences" could result. It is best that the costumer consult with all actors or at least have

several choices from which the actors and director can choose.

> I went over the wardrobe with the actors. I had them bring down a few things, and my art director, Claudia, was there, and we discussed it together. This coat would be better than that. What was in the purse? The contents had to be identified.
>
> *Adam*

Using an actor's own wardrobe is an inexpensive way to obtain clothes that fit. If your actors offer to supply their own clothes, ask them for a number of different items from which to choose. The company should pay for the cleaning of all wardrobe pieces that are worn.

Thrift shops are another source of some very interesting costumes at reasonable prices. Remember that clothes can be altered, dyed, and borrowed.

Specialty Garb

Period pieces, of course, require period clothes. Paying attention to history is critical. Each period of dress must be carefully researched and represented accurately. Certain genres, such as film noir or science fiction, require a special look that must remain consistent throughout the picture to maintain a specific style.

Duplicate Costumes

If a scene calls for damage to the costume, the costumer will need to have doubles and triples of the same clothes. Suppose, for example, that a character

Figure 8.2 Characters are partially defined by the clothes they wear. Scene from *The Lunch Date.*

is supposed to be stabbed in the chest. A blood pack under the shirt is rigged to ooze red liquid to give the illusion that the character has been wounded. When the director calls for the second take, the dresser replaces the stained shirt with a new one.

If an actor gets wet in a scene or spills ketchup on a costume, the wardrobe department will need to have another standing by for each additional take. Stunt people who double for an actor need to have a costume that is identical to the actor's. For some shoots, this might require three or more of the same suit.

Continuity and Script Time

The costumer is responsible for maintaining the continuity of the costumes. Using the stabbing example again, some scenes involving the bloodied victim might be shot before the actual stabbing scene itself is recorded. In this case, the costumer needs to distress one of the duplicate shirts to represent a stab wound as exactly as possible. This can get very complicated. Ideally, the assistant director will schedule the shoot with this problem in mind.

Script time is the logical progression of the days in the script. Wardrobe and script supervision are the departments most responsible for script time. If a story takes place over three days and there is a different wardrobe for each day (most people change clothes every day), the wardrobe department keeps a chart of what clothes are worn in each scene. Then if the script is shot out of continuity, the character will be wearing the correct clothes throughout the filming.

Consulting the Director of Photography

The costumer consults with the director of photography regarding colors and materials. Some DPs, for instance, are adamant about not allowing actors to wear bright white clothes. White can make lighting difficult because it reflects the light.

Makeup

The glamour of Hollywood is exemplified by the bright, clean, unblemished look of movie stars. In the old days, audiences did not seem to mind that their heroes on the screen could be kicked and beaten yet still look like a million bucks. Audiences today are more sophisticated and prefer greater realism.

Men wear less makeup than women. Sometimes, actors wear no makeup at all, or a director might demand that they wear none. Usually, though, they wear at least a base, a skin-toned makeup called *pancake*, which is spread evenly over the face and hands. With a base, the makeup artist can maintain a consistent skin tone throughout the picture. In addition to a base, women generally wear lipstick, eyeliner, mascara, and powder.

There is specialty makeup for creating cuts, wounds (fresh, oozing, and recently healed), moles, bruises, and so on. Anything more elaborate than these specialty items falls under the domain of the special effects makeup department.

Special Effects

The special effects makeup department might work in conjunction with the makeup artists or as a separate unit, depending on the nature of the project. These artists work on large-scale specialty makeup jobs, such as monsters, which require major prosthetics. They might also be called on to perform more subtle tasks, such as making an actor look older or younger. Special effects makeup techniques generally employ large latex pieces to reshape the actor's face or body. Special makeup sometimes requires camera tests. Hire a stylist to design makeup for each actor, and ask the actor to be responsible for sustaining it.

Hair

Hairdressers often use hairpieces, wigs, beards, and toupees. Many balding actors have maintained a full head of hair for years with the aid of a hairpiece. Some women prefer to wear a wig when performing because they don't have to sit in a chair for hours while the hairdresser creates an elaborate hairdo. They can slip the wig on and off without worrying about destroying the style. Another advantage to hairpieces of all types is that they can be maintained at a constant length and color. Actors need to have their own hair trimmed frequently to maintain continuity.

Men can use facial hair to achieve a different type of look. Beards and mustaches have to be made and fit well in advance of principal photography to ensure enough time for alterations. In addition, several pieces must be made as backups because facial hairpieces disintegrate after several wearings.

A typical production problem involves a character who has a "change of look" in the story. She goes from long hair to short hair. This can most easily be accomplished with a short haircut and a wig. If no wig is used, the schedule must reflect this choice: Any scenes that require long hair must be shot before the performer's hair is cut.

Actors might be required to change their hairstyle or hair color or even add facial hair for a role. Experiment before committing to a particular look.

THE PRODUCER'S ROLE

QUESTION ALL REQUESTS (WITHIN REASON). During the creative discussions between the director and her art director, the producer should, within reason, question every request. The creative process involves a series of discussions in which many ideas are bandied about. The solutions to a problem can run the gamut from very expensive to inexpensive. For example, should you wish to fly a character through the air, there are several ways to accomplish this stunt, including a wire-flying rig, blue-screen photography, and imaginative framing. The difference in cost among these three choices is enormous. The director considers each idea and, with deference to the budget, makes a suggestion that will be cinematographically satisfactory. When there is a choice, it behooves the producer to opt for the less expensive solution, of course (Figure 8.3).

> I originally thought I would have the women wear different masks, and I spent a lot of money buying a variety of masks. After trying on the masks at home, I realized they were quite grotesque and not what I wanted. Finally, I found an inexpensive white kabuki-type mask in a costume store, and the minute I saw it, I knew this was the one. So I bought six of them, and I cut out the lips so the sound wouldn't be muffled.
>
> *Jan*

REVIEW BUDGETS CAREFULLY. Always expect that the art department's needs will be more expensive than anticipated. Don't be afraid to play the heavy and challenge a production request. The director needs to be cozy with her creative team, but the producer doesn't. His job is to be cozy with the budget.

KEEP TABS ON WEEKLY SPENDING. Money flows very quickly through the art department. Don't give the department the entire budget amount at once. Keep on top of the cash flow. Have each member of the department turn in receipts each week for everything bought or rented. (See "Petty Cash" in Chapter 5, "Budget.")

KEEP AN EYE ON THE CONSTRUCTION SCHEDULE. If the construction personnel promise a set will be completed by a particular date, follow their progress. When scheduling, it is prudent to allow extra time in the construction timetable. If the construction coordinator swears that the

Figure 8.3 Each of the women in *Mirror Mirror* wears a mask.

turnaround time for the next set is three days, schedule four.

DIRECTOR
Create a Look

The "look" of any film or video project has its origins in the script. Its tone, the genre, and any specific elements described by the author will impact the final product. After the director and the director of photography plan how they will photograph the script, the art department details the elements within the frame and realizes them. Once the major location decisions have been made with the producer, such as construction, distant locations or stages, the director works with the art director to shape the sets and locations.

The director must be familiar with the capabilities of all the production departments, especially her art direction team. Knowing how clever they can be in stretching the budget is instrumental to her creative decisions. It is unfair to the production to request an item that might enhance the show but would overtax the art department's time, talents, and money.

> The rental of the mannequins was too costly, so I had to be resourceful, and figure out how to get them for free. A friend of mine knew someone who worked in a large department store and he dressed the mannequins. He thought he might be able to loan me some damaged ones. So that's what I did. I went and borrowed five mannequins from this huge department store—unbeknownst to them, I think. He gave me a bunch of damaged mannequins from a back room and I was able to use them for the two-week shoot and then I returned them.
>
> *Jan*

ARCHITECT OF ILLUSION

The art director supervises a creative team that designs, builds, and dresses the sets and helps choose and dress the locations. Anything that communicates information to the audience involves a decision of some kind. Every piece of clothing, hairstyle, prop, or article within the frame tells us something about the character and the world of a story. Many aspects of art direction are also story points, such as the salad in *The Lunch Date* or the rope in *Truman*.

The art director is responsible for interpreting the director's ideas and transforming them into a visual plan. Working from the script, photographs, paintings, and other films, these two department heads create a "look" for the film or video. The art director and her team are also responsible for overseeing the continuity and consistency from scene to scene.

The art director's duties vary from project to project. The script might require designing sets or simply altering existing locations. The screenwriter strives to craft a story in which every scene and character supports the theme. The art director's job is to ensure that every article within the frame complements the story, illuminates the characters, supports the theme, and serves the director's vision.

The director chooses the actors who will portray the characters, the location or production manager secures the locations, and the cinematographer lights and frames the set. The art director is responsible for everything else. It is a key position and one that beginners frequently misunderstand, undervalue, and fail to appreciate. This is because the ability to create an illusion through art direction is like a magic trick: Everyone admires the end result, but no one realizes that it took hard work and special talent to achieve what is only an illusion.

For example, a cheap cardboard column is painted a la trompe l'oeil to look like marble, and voilà, the audience sees a stone pillar. A small off-screen wind machine blows small white polystyrene pellets at the actors, who pretend to struggle to stay afoot, and a "blizzard" is created.

Knowing how materials react to light and how they "read" on film and videotape helps the art director avoid buying unnecessarily expensive materials. A good art director knows that rayon chiffon looks exactly the same as silk chiffon on film.

Color has an emotional effect on the screen. The art director must have a comprehensive knowledge of color, color combinations, and the effect of color on an audience.

IMAGES CAN TELL A STORY

The audience must believe that the actors are the film's characters, and they must believe that the rooms they live and work in, and the clothes they wear, are true to the world of your story. Nothing in any frame of your picture should disrupt the illusion you are striving to create.

Think about the seedy hotel room Travis Bickle inhabited in the film *Taxi Driver* or the interior of the *Millennium Falcon*—the spaceship Han Solo pilots in the *Star Wars* trilogy. Each of these decorated sets gives the audience a wealth of information about the identity and idiosyncrasies of the character. The producer's job is to spend as little as possible and still achieve these effects.

Adam Davidson secured Grand Central Station for free. Using this authentic location lent great credibility to the project, and getting it for free was probably the only way he could afford it. Howard McCain was able to shoot in a gymnasium for *Truman,* thus ensuring the realism of his script. Jan Krawitz surrounded her masked women with an array of mannequins. This imaginative set inexpensively symbolized and reinforced the theme of stereotypical female physical perfection.

BREAKDOWNS—LISTEN TO THE SCRIPT

The "look" of the project has its origins in the script, and in the director's visual ideas for it. An in-depth analysis of the script affords the art director an understanding of the story, character, and theme evolving through the plot, all of which can and should be reflected by the art direction.

Consider an example:

INT. LUNCHEONETTE - AFTERNOON

The woman walks into a station luncheonette. It is a simple place—a grill, some booths, and rows of refrigerated cabinets filled with salads and sandwiches. She reaches into a glass case and removes a salad.

A COOK stands behind a white linoleum counter. He fiddles with his white paper hat and white apron.

Art department personnel breaks down this scene from *The Lunch Date* by creating lists of what they have to rent, buy, or make.

LOCATION. The scene above takes place in a luncheonette. The location needs to look like it belongs in a train station. To find the appropriate location, the art director scouts for a real train station luncheonette. The location manager attempts to secure an actual luncheonette. If a real location cannot be found, the art director either builds a set on a soundstage or redresses an existing location to give the illusion of a working luncheonette. For this scene from *The Lunch Date*, the director decided to redress an abandoned lunch counter to look like a functioning establishment.

DRESSING. Once the decision was made to use the defunct restaurant, the art department created a plan to bring the location to life. That meant cleaning, putting up signs and posters, and adding elements such as ashtrays, salt and pepper shakers, napkins, and extra salads.

PROPS. The key props for this scene included the salad, silverware, the woman's personal effects, her handbag, and change.

WARDROBE. The woman's wardrobe is the same throughout the piece. For this scene, the costumer needed to find a chef's hat and apron for the actor playing the cook.

MAKEUP AND HAIR. No special concerns.

EFFECTS. No special effects.

DEFINING THE SPACE WITH STORYBOARDS

For adequate preparations, the director should give the art director the details of each shot, either with a storyboard or verbally. Storyboarding scenes in a film or video affords the director and art director common ground from which to create a frame. What should the character's habitat look like? How much of the space needs to be art "directed"? How much does the camera need to see?

Communication is the key to a successful shoot, and storyboards are a precise way to transmit information. If you have a set with no ceiling piece and in your storyboards you indicate a low-angle shot that will include the ceiling, the art director must make appropriate arrangements beforehand. If the director decides on the day of the shoot that she now wants a low-angle shot, the budget probably won't cover the cost of constructing a ceiling that quickly.

CAMERA TESTS

Depending on the nature and design of your project, it might be wise to shoot some tests with the actors in full makeup and wardrobe. This is an added expense, but it will clarify what you will be shooting during principal photography. Camera tests also inform the director and producer of the dynamics between the cast and crew in a work environment.

KEY POINTS

1. Duplicates must be purchased, made, or rented for many items, such as food and wardrobe.

2. Unless you shoot a scene only once, the art department will need to match each take with the previous one in terms of wardrobe, makeup, and hair.

3. Much of art direction is an illusion. A piece of costume jewelry looks like the real thing to the camera.

chapter nine

Casting

One of the things I did in terms of casting the film was I worked on food lines at Grand Central every night before filming, and I saw this guy Willie the night before. He had this harmonica and this great face, and I asked him to show up.

Adam

PRODUCER
Auditions

The credibility of the project rests on proper casting. It cannot be stressed enough how important it is to find the right actors for the project. The actors are the words with which you will tell your story. They allow the audience to enter the world of your drama by bringing to life the scripted characters. No matter how slick the camera work, it will be difficult for viewers to empathize with your story if they don't believe in your characters.

The young boy in *Truman* and the woman and homeless man in *The Lunch Date* seem to inhabit their roles effortlessly. As viewers, we experience the characters, not actors playing parts. This illusion is due partly to their performances and partly to their being physically right for the characters. Had the actors' physical types not suited the characters they were supposed to play, no degree of performance could have overcome this false impression.

No matter how many people participate in the casting process, the final decisions should rest with the director. Not only must the actors fit her vision for the project, but she must feel comfortable with their working relationship. The producer's job is to ensure that the director has the widest choices of talent to review. The producer also lends support by serving as a creative sounding board when the director requires an objective opinion.

The assistant director hires the background or extra players based on the number requested by the director. The producer must balance that number against the budget. Although it is always better to have a fully peopled scene, extras are paid a negotiated fee and must be fed and transported to and from the set.

THE CASTING DIRECTOR

An important addition to the creative team is the casting director. After gaining an understanding of the director's requirements, the casting director sifts through many of the submissions so the director sees only those actors who are genuine possibilities. The casting director looks at a script and, based on her experience in the field, establishes a viable list of actors for each part. The following are some of the elements a casting director brings to a production:

- Valuable creative input
- A solid resource bank (file of actors)
- Awareness of new talent
- Good working relationship with agents and managers
- Ability to make deals with actors (understanding of SAG rules)

A good casting director does all the setup work so the director and producer need only make the decisions. If you can afford it, this is a valuable and worthwhile person to have on the production team. If you cannot afford to hire a casting director, the producer and director assume these duties.

To find a casting director, inquire of other producers and directors who work in the low-budget arena. Breakdown Service publishes a useful guide, the *Casting Director Directory for New York and Los Angeles.*

THE BASIC CASTING STEPS

Although the exact method used to cast a production varies from project to project, the following steps provide a useful overview of the basic process:

- Advertise specific roles
- Scout local theater companies
- Scout acting schools
- Organize submitted head shots and résumés
- Arrange casting calls
- Arrange callbacks
- Negotiate with selected actors
- Deal with rejected actors

Advertise Specific Roles

Use advertising to let the creative community—actors, agents, and managers—know about your project and the specific parts available. It is easiest to locate a variety of talented performers in major metropolitan areas. Actors are attracted to these areas because of the opportunities they offer for professional work. Here are some suggestions for advertising your project:

1. For a small fee, you can submit an advertisement in the appropriate trade publications, such as *Backstage* (New York City) or *Drama-Logue* (Los Angeles). (See Appendix F.) The ad should be succinct yet clearly represent your casting requirements.

2. Create a professional-looking flier (desktop publishing programs are useful here) that clearly represents your project and available parts. Post it at acting schools, schools for the performing arts, community theaters, local college theater programs, high school drama societies, and community and acting guild bulletin boards.

I put a little survey out and said I'm a filmmaker. I didn't say I'm interested in meeting women who want to be in a film because I think that can be pretty threatening and off-putting. I just said I was doing research for a film about women and body image and I was interested in talking to as large a group of women as possible about their experiences with this. They had to fill in their name, height, weight, age, and phone number. I got about . . . 65 responses that way. I wrote them all a letter and thanked them for the responses and said I'd be back in touch with them.

Jan

3. Submit your project to Breakdown Services (see Appendix F). This company is an excellent casting resource for producers. It distributes vital information about what films and videos are in the casting process and what roles are available throughout the United States. Agents and personal managers pay a weekly subscription fee for this information. You pay a small fee to submit a synopsis of your project and descriptions of your principal parts. This information is submitted to all the agents and personal managers in your area who subscribe to this service. Represent the nature of your project accurately; that is, is it a non-SAG production? Does it include violence, nudity, or sex? Interviewing actors under false pretenses wastes everyone's time and will blemish your reputation as an ethical producer.

4. Locate a copy of the *Academy Players Directory*. This huge and expensive two-volume set is put out by the Academy of Motion Picture Arts and Sciences (see Appendix F) and contains a photographic listing of practically every actor in the motion picture business along with his or her agency representation and guild affiliation. You can usually find this directory in a library. You can also purchase it directly from the Academy or at a media bookstore.

I started out with *Backstage*. I put my ad in for $27 and got a whole stack of head shots. Next I wrote to Breakdown Services, which sent me people more in line for the gym teacher. Then I contacted talent agencies, which now is a very accepted thing, but it was not at that time in New York. I just said, "I'm doing this great film. It would be a wonderful reel piece . . . will pay expenses . . . Do you have anybody?" At the time, there was something called Manhattan Kids on Stage. I saw some performances and had a few more kids audition for me.

Howard

Scout Local Theater Companies

If you live in a major metropolitan area that has small theater companies, such as New York City, Chicago, Los Angeles, Boston, or San Francisco, it can be useful for you and the director to scout out the currently running shows for new talent. These cities have many small and interesting theater groups, but don't discount the many community theaters all over the country. Don't ignore summer stock and dinner theaters either.

Check the cast lists for the specific types for which you are looking, and plan to see these actors in action. If you are impressed by an actor's performance and feel that he or she might be right for your project, go backstage after the show and introduce yourself. The actor will be flattered by the attention.

Scout Acting Schools

Many acting programs in metropolitan areas run their own theater groups, and these can be a good source of talent. Posting a flier may work, but contacting the teachers personally might be more effective. Ask them about the best ways to approach their students. They might allow you to sit in on a class.

Organize Submitted Head Shots and Résumés

When they hear that you are casting, interested actors or their representatives will submit a photograph, or *glossy*, with a résumé attached to the back. From the résumé, you can cull the following information: experience, height, weight, age, union affiliation, and the actor's contact number. A single advertisement in *Backstage* has been known to attract hundreds of 8-by-10 glossies. Organize and file the glossies according to the part.

From these head shots, look for actors you are interested in auditioning. This is a tough call because you will most likely be flooded with applicants. When choosing actors to audition, base your decision on their "look," their experience, and your gut instinct. However, be aware that a glossy may be an idealized version of what the actor really looks like.

Arrange Casting Calls

Find a space in which to hold the auditions. It should have some kind of waiting area where the actors can study the pages they will read for the audition. The audition space should be large enough to allow the director, producer, camera operator, and reader to sit comfortably and to allow the actors to move around with ease. The space you choose should also have adequate light for video.

Set up a working schedule for the day or days you plan to audition. Find out how many actors the director wants to see each day and for how long. Start with a plan for 15-minute intervals, and work from there. Call the actors or their agents to schedule appointments. If you can't reach an actor, leave a phone number where he or she can reach you or leave a message.

On the day of the audition, be sure to do the following:

- Have a production assistant log the actors in at the door.
- Be sure you have plenty of copies (at least one per actor) of the sides to be read.
- Arrange to have someone read opposite the actors. (The director should not read with the candidates because it will hinder her objectivity.)
- Have a pitcher of water and paper cups available for the actors.
- Keep the auditions as close to schedule as possible. It is impolite and unprofessional to keep actors waiting for long.

There's more information on holding auditions in the "Director" section of this chapter.

Arrange Callbacks

It is now that the casting process begins in earnest. The goal is not only to look for the best actors for the parts, but also to find the right chemistry or balance among the players. This is especially critical when casting a love story. Your two lovers must seem to be attracted to one another. To achieve the right chemistry, read actors opposite each other in different combinations. The best combinations can then be put on video. (See the "Director" section in this chapter.)

The Screen Actors Guild allows its members to attend three callbacks without a charge to the producer. After three callbacks, the producer must pay the actor to attend additional casting sessions.

Negotiate with Selected Actors

By the time you sit down with the actor you want to hire or with the actor's agent, everyone involved should already have an understanding about your budget constraints. Be honest and up-front at the beginning about how much money you have to spend.

If you have no budget for talent, your only hope to attract good actors is a well-written script with good parts that can showcase performers' talent. A video copy of the project might prove to be payment enough.

If you are working primarily with "struggling actors" who do not earn a living from their craft, you might have to work around their schedules. They usually have day jobs to pay the rent.

It is not uncommon for non-SAG talent to receive little or no compensation for work with beginning or student filmmakers. Generally, their entire compensation consists of the following:

- A screen credit
- A video copy of the completed film
- Transportation to and from the set
- Meals during the shoot
- Dry cleaning of the actor's personal wardrobe

If you are obligated to pay one of your principal actors, however, you should pay all of them (at least all the speaking parts) to avoid resentment on the set.

You can hire a nonunion player with a simple deal memo or letter of agreement that indicates the compensation (if any) and the performance dates (see Appendix D). No contract is required.

If you hire SAG actors for your project, you must deal with a SAG contract, which involves minimum payments for daily or weekly rates, or what is called *scale*. What SAG actors receive even for scale can put undue financial stress on a small budget. If you hire a union player, you must become a signatory to the SAG contract and agree to all its provisions. When negotiating with a union member, remember that unions require payments to pension and welfare funds. In addition, if you have one SAG actor in a show, the union requires that all the actors be on a union contract. There are some exceptions to this ruling. Check with your local SAG representative.

Students: In some situations, scale payment for SAG talent is deferred. Some film and video programs in the United States have worked out an agreement with the Screen Actors Guild that enables the actors' salaries to be deferred until the film is distributed. Then, the first dollars from the distribution royalties (excluding film festival prizes) go directly to pay the actors' salaries. In effect, these salaries get tacked onto the negative cost of the picture at the end of the production process. This arrangement enables first-time directors to work with professional union actors without having to pay them if the project does not make money. Note, however, that if you use SAG, Equity (stage), AGVA (variety), or AFTRA (TV) actors under this waiver and book them for your shooting dates, they are under no obligation to stay with your project if they get a paying job. This often happens, so you are advised to have backup actors.

Deal with Rejected Actors

The producer should be the "heavy" when it comes to breaking the bad news to actors who have not been cast. It is emotionally difficult to call an actor who has come in for several callbacks to tell him that he has not been cast. A courteous phone call thanking the actor for his time and enthusiasm during the casting session will be appreciated. Always strive to build good relationships with good actors. What if you rudely reject the next Dustin Hoffman?

FRINGE BENEFITS OF CASTING

The casting process offers many benefits besides finding the best talent for your project. Casting offers an excellent opportunity to audition the script as well as the actors. Hearing the lines spoken will give the director and writer a sense of what works and what doesn't. Scenes are often overwritten, and readings can expose fat that might be eliminated.

Through the casting process, the producer can get a sense of how the director works with actors. Is she comfortable? Does she put the actors at ease? The ability to find a rapport with her actors is a necessary part of the director's craft.

Finally, the casting process offers the producer and director an opportunity to meet and build relationships with talented performers. Once you have worked with an actor, if you feel that the results and relationship were successful, you might want to work with that actor again. The bond that results from the actor–director relationship is very special. It might last only for the duration of the shoot or for a lifetime.

From a selfish point of view, my documentary work has been a passport to experiences and people that otherwise would be completely off-limits. For example, when I made *Cotton Candy and Elephant Stuff*, I literally ran away with the circus for a month because I was making a film about them. Otherwise, I never would have lived with the circus for a month. And with *Little People*, I came to know a lot of dwarfs and midgets who are still in my life 12 years later.

Jan

DIRECTOR

Auditions

As a director, your relationship to the actor is extremely important. The producer is involved in casting and is ultimately responsible for hiring the cast, but it is the director–actor dynamic that breathes life into the characters that propel the story.

The director, cinematographer, and art director exercise their craft behind the camera. It doesn't matter how they look or how they feel when they work because they are not exposed to the camera's eye. The actor, though, is the very instrument through which the drama is played.

Actors must sometimes call on deep, personal feelings. Helping the actor discover the emotional life of a character is a trying, exciting, and sometimes painful process. When casting, you want to find the actors who have the craft to make truthful discoveries about the character and the talent to reveal these discoveries to others.

The life of an actor is not easy. Actors constantly audition for parts they don't get. Most work at acting intermittently. Many work at other jobs to pay their bills. When an actor auditions, he or she usually competes with dozens of other actors for a single part. To help you understand something of the actor's work process, it is recommended that you attend acting classes. This will help you discover how to draw out the best in the performer.

> I took acting classes while I was a student at Columbia University. We had a course in directing actors, but it wasn't enough, so I took some acting classes with Stella Adler. I learned you must respect actors and their process.
>
> *Adam*

CASTING

The audience attends a film or video to witness a story told through actors. If viewers do not care about the characters, then they will not care about the story. The case studies used in this book present characters in situations we care about. Will the woman in *The Lunch Date* stand up for herself and get the food she believes is hers? Will Truman climb the rope? Will the women in *Mirror Mirror* tell the truth about their bodies?

The important creative relationship between actor and director begins during the casting process.

If the film- or videomaker makes an error at this juncture, it will affect the whole production. Choose wisely. Take your time. Be objective, and remember that the casting process is not perfect. Some actors, for example, audition better than others. This does not necessarily mean that the actors who audition well are the better actors.

Casting Children

Finding talented child actors can be particularly difficult. First, there are far fewer child actors than adults. Second, even trained child actors can be difficult to control. Many children are born performers. An untrained child can often give a more spontaneous and engaging performance than a professional child actor (Figure 9.1). When casting, assess a child's energy and attention span as well as his or her talent.

> I had three casting sessions and didn't find anybody. Finding the little boy for Truman came out of sheer persistence. I told my acting teacher I was desperate and asked if he knew anyone (even his second cousin) who looked like the person I needed. He said, "Well, I met this playwright, and she had this kid with her, and he kind of looked like what you were talking about. I'll give you the number, and you can call and make your pitch." That's what I did. Once the kid walked through the door, I said, "That's Truman!"
>
> *Howard*

Audition Guidelines

For a successful audition and to make the most of the search for the best actors, we recommend following the guidelines in the next sections.

Before the Audition

The audition can be held in any quiet room. A rented rehearsal hall is an ideal place to hold an audition. The space should contain at least three chairs: one for the actor, one for the director, and one for the person who will read opposite the actor. Some additional personnel might be present at the audition, including the producer, the casting director, and a camera operator if the audition is recorded on videotape.

Beginning the Audition

Introductions. The production assistant ushers each actor into the audition space. The director should at-

Figure 9.1 Finding your lead actor
is an exciting moment.

tempt to relax the actor and put him at ease. If the director creates an atmosphere that encourages the actor to feel confident, the audition will go better. The actor will perform at his best, and the director will be able to make an informed decision.

The director should greet the actor, introduce the people in the room, and make small talk before beginning the audition. The actor will bring to the audition a recent photograph, called a *head shot* or *glossy*. Attached to the back of the photo will be the actor's résumé, which contains information about the parts the applicant has played. It also describes the actor's talents and interests and lists the teachers with whom he has studied.

This material can be used as a good place to begin small talk. For example, you might say, "I see you studied with Mira Rostova" or "Do you enjoy doing Pinter?" or "When you say here you speak French, are you fluent?"

Depending then on how much of the script the actor has read, you might briefly tell the story you plan to shoot. This will put the audition scene in context, which will be helpful to the actor. Only when the director feels the actor is ready should she begin the audition.

Types of Auditions

Sides. The most common method used to audition actors for a film or video project is to have them read a scene or part of a scene from the script. These pages are called *sides*. When the actor reads the sides for the first time at an audition, it is called a *cold reading*.

Auditions for the first call usually run at five- to 15-minute intervals. The material you prepare for the actor to read should be short. This will allow you to make the most of the meeting.

The actor will need to act with a partner the production provides. This individual should not be the director because she needs to observe and assess the performance. The reader can be the producer, a production assistant, or another actor.

The reader should make eye contact with the actor. This gives the actor someone to whom he can relate. Because the audition is for the actor, not the reader, the reader should not "act" nor read in a monotone, which would be equally distracting.

When the actor begins reading, allow him to read through the scene with no direction. This reveals the actor's interpretation of the role, which might bring a unique slant to the character, one you had not considered before.

If you like the actor, ask him to read the scene again for an emotional value different from that of the first reading. Ask him to find the humor in the scene, for instance, or the irony. This second reading is key because it gives you an idea of the actor's range and flexibility. During the audition process, it is more important to discover whether the actor can take direction than whether he already understands the character.

Take notes on your assessment of each actor. Your notes will help you decide at the end of the day which actors you would like to use or which you would like to call back.

Monologue. In addition to or instead of the cold reading, you can ask the actor to prepare a monologue for the audition or the callback. A monologue is a speech for one person from a play or film. It gives you the opportunity to witness a prepared performance. The combination of the cold reading and a prepared monologue offers that much more information on which to make casting decisions.

Improvisation. Another useful technique is to have the actor improvise a scene from the script. That is, to act like his character, spontaneously, in a situation you create. Improvisation is a specialized acting form. Some actors, especially comedians, are very adept at this type of performance. Other actors do not have this facility. It is, however, an acceptable request to make of an actor.

Evaluating the Audition

The primary goal of the audition process is to discover the actor's range of talent and his ability to take direction. If the actor reading for the part is absolutely perfect, indicate this in your notes, but never offer an actor a part during the audition. You never know who might come in later and cause you to change your mind. If the actor is not ideal but has interesting qualities, this too should be noted. After all, the ideal actor for the part might never audition. You will have to cast the role based on the talent available.

Keeping an Open Mind. The readings are an excellent opportunity to explore many different casting possibilities, and these possibilities are as varied as the actors who walk through the door. Remain flexible and open-minded as to the many ways a part can be cast.

Too often, directors have a set image of a character in mind during the audition. If an actor matching that image doesn't appear, the audition is merely an exercise. Casting against type often makes the script even more vital. Can the part be played by an African American, an Asian, or a physically disabled actor? It might be interesting to cast as the villain of your piece an actor who has the appearance of a nice guy. This will create a doubt in the viewer's mind and add a tension that wouldn't otherwise exist.

Use your imagination when casting. If a talented blond actor auditions but you see the character as a redhead, consider using a wig or asking the actor to dye his hair. The director must be aware of how the various departments can help shape an actor's look.

The audition process requires stamina and concentration. Reading actors all day with only a short lunch break can be exhausting. Be sure to give adequate consideration to the last few actors who audition. Among them could be the actor who is just right for the part. Remember, casting can make or break your project.

Notes. If you write pertinent observations on the actor's résumé or on a separate log sheet during the reading, you can later review the day's many auditions. It is also important to note the actor's schedule and availability.

> Casting *Mirror Mirror* was an interesting process. I invited 60 women who had filled out questionnaires at a local film festival to attend one of several discussion group meetings that I had. My intent was to set up informal groups where the women would feel comfortable talking about issues related to body image and I could observe how articulate they were, what stories they had, and so on. The original questionnaire didn't ask for women willing to be in a film but only to participate in discussions as part of my information gathering. I gave them a choice of six different dates and some evenings. Two women might show up, and other nights, there would be a group of eight. None of the women knew each other or me. I decided not to prerecord at these sessions as I wanted the conversation to be as uninhibited as possible. However, after the session, I would make notes about what stories each of the women shared so I could use those as aids in casting the film. I made mental notes of what they each looked like.
>
> *Jan*

Videotaping. Videotaping is an excellent way to review auditions and helps in making a casting decision. Recording the audition on video gives the creative team an opportunity to review the different combinations of actors at a later time. It also allows you to see how an actor relates to the camera. Certain actors have an affinity for the lens, and some don't. Some very talented people freeze under the scrutiny of the lights and the camera. Therefore, videotaping is best used for the second audition, or callback.

Using video during auditions is most effective with actors who have little or no exposure on film or tape. It is vital that you see them on tape before making any final decisions. A film test is ideal but is more expensive than shooting on video.

If you use a video camera during the audition, set up the equipment unobtrusively. For example, the camera might be placed in a corner, with a long lens at an angle, out of the actor's eye-line.

> *Video Operators:* Make sure there is enough light for the video camera. Shoot with lenses of several sizes. Start wide to see how the actor moves and communicates with his body. Then move in to a medium shot and finally a close-up to see the actor's face, particularly the eyes.

Callbacks

When the general auditions have been completed, the producer arranges for callbacks. A callback is another audition, but with actors who have already read for the director once and are being considered seriously for the part.

The callback can be conducted in the same fashion as the first audition, but with some modifications. The time periods are generally longer, say 15 to 30 minutes, which permits the director to work on specific details in the scene. Actors are asked to read opposite other actors who are being considered to determine whether there is the right kind of chemistry between them.

If the lead has been cast, you can ask that she read with all the candidates who might play opposite her in the film or video. This process, referred to as *mix and match*, is useful in casting family members.

If you can't find the actors you want, you might have to look beyond the normal casting arena. Leave no stone unturned.

> At the end of these informational preinterviews, I asked them all if they might be interested in appearing in the film. Every single person I preinterviewed was interested in being in the film, although the initial call was just for information gathering and discussion. Not one person said no at the end of those sessions, which I found pretty extraordinary.
>
> There were a lot of great women among those initial 50, but there was a preponderance of women between the ages of 25 and 40, and they were mostly white. I knew from the outset that I wanted the film to be multicultural and, of course, to transcend any particular ethnic or racial delineation. So I had to cast the net a little farther, and I found out about a women's spirituality group at the Unitarian Church that was specifically for older women. I got permis-

sion from the organization to pitch the idea to them. From that group I was able to cast three women who wanted to be in the film.

> *Jan*

Things to Keep in Mind

Benefits of the Casting Session. The casting session is a learning process for the director. How lines are read, how a character is interpreted, and how a scene is performed all add to the director's excitement and enthusiasm during preproduction. Although the casting session is not foolproof, it is a time-tested process that generally provides successful results (Figure 9.2).

> My experience was if someone's not busy and they're professional and they like you and they like your script, they'll do it. So I just started picking people out of the *Academy Players Directory* because there I could see their faces and head shots. And I hadn't really got anything I was satisfied with in *Backstage*. So I found this guy, Jerry Klein, and he came in, and he was terrific. He looked right. And even though the role is fairly one-dimensional, he brought something to it that made it kind of fun. . . . He's a professional actor—the Midas Muffler Man. He does all sorts of things.
>
> *Howard*

Figure 9.2 Jerry Klein, who played the coach in *Truman*, was the Midas Muffler Man.

The "Nonaudition." If you're interested in using an actor of some note, her body of work should be enough on which to base your decision. Actors like to work. They especially like to work on projects with good scripts.

> I had advertised in *Backstage* and met a lot of people, but I didn't find anybody right. I went to a talent director, and she gave me Scotty's name, but she told me I couldn't audition her because she's doing it as a favor and she is beyond auditioning. All I could do was an interview. So I met her, we talked, and it was great.
>
> *Adam*

KEY POINTS

1. Leave no stone unturned in your search for actors. Once you have cast a part, there is no turning back.

2. Watch for chemistry between actors who play opposite one another.

3. Understand the life and process of the actor. This will enable you to get the most out of an audition.

4. Be prepared to cast a backup actor in case your actor of choice must leave the production.

chapter ten

Rehearsals

This was a hard script to rehearse because it's basically all action with very, very little back-and-forth dialogue.

Howard

DIRECTOR

Work on Scenes

One of the director's primary responsibilities is to assist the actor in discovering and playing his role. The director accomplishes this through script and character analysis, staging, and postproduction editorial techniques. Once casting has been completed, the character development process begins with rehearsals.

During the rehearsal period, the following takes place:

- The director gets to know the actor. (The actors will have a chance to get to know one another during the rehearsal period.)
- The director and the actor develop a mutual trust.
- A character research method is devised.
- Scenes are shaped, beats are discovered, and business is created.
- The director and actor evolve a shorthand for communicating on set.

If possible, do not wait until the cast is assembled on the set during principal photography to rehearse. Although the scene can be rehearsed on the set, time will not allow for long rehearsals with the entire crew standing by at full pay. The crew's presence can be distracting, and their salary is a drain on the budget. A set can be cleared for rehearsal. This might cause some delay in the day's schedule, but it is better than rushing a scene.

BEFORE REHEARSALS

Getting to Know the Actor

Before rehearsals, the director can meet with the actor in a casual, nonwork setting. This is an opportunity to begin developing a rapport. There is little pressure in a meeting of two artists simply talking about their work. You might ask the actor questions like these:

- What are your work methods?
- How were you trained?
- How do you like to approach the development of a character?
- How do you see this character?
- How do you see this character in relation to the other characters and to the plot?

You might discuss the following with the actor:

- Your working method
- Your feeling about the material
- Your interpretation of the character
- Your plan for a shooting style
- Any difficulties you foresee in the production

The first goal in rehearsal was getting Truman's confidence and trust.

Howard

Developing Mutual Trust

Discussing the actor's character casually over coffee starts the process of discovery and trust in the director–actor relationship. Discovery is the process of finding things to help build the character, of seeing the character grow. Trust allows the director to be an integral part of that growth. Without trust, unfortunately, there is usually friction and miscommunication.

> The first aspect of rehearsal is actually no rehearsal at all. . . . I took Truman out for ice cream; we played video games and did "kid things." It was a way to gain his trust and make him feel comfortable.
>
> *Howard*

Researching the Character

An actor develops his own character under the director's guidance. If the actor is inexperienced, he might ask the director for her help. One way he can develop his character is by observing and studying similar characters. If his character is based on a real person, the actor can research material written about that individual and can seek out videotapes, radio broadcasts, and so forth. Every character has a history, or back story. It can be useful for the actor to write a brief biography of the character.

An actor builds a life for his character based on the text. All the information that the actor and director need to develop a character should be found in the script. The author will have indicated important physical characteristics, emotional motivation, and pertinent surroundings. The story itself is the key to the arc of the character. For example, in *Moby Dick*, Captain Ahab begins as a rational and collected character. During his journey, as revenge comes near his grasp, he starts to lose his sanity. He will do anything to kill Moby Dick, no matter what the cost. This ongoing process, which spans the course of the novel, is referred to as the *arc* of the character.

The director and the actor should be in agreement throughout the shoot on the arc of the character. Film- and videomakers rarely record the scenes in screenplay order. If you must shoot the last scene first, it is imperative that you know how the characters arrive emotionally at that point in the story. Knowing the emotional arc of the piece allows you to shape each moment so that there is an appropriate dramatic build. If the final scene is played too low-key, you will have nothing toward which to build. Conversely, if the final scene is played at a fever pitch, the actors might never be able to build truthfully to that pitch over the course of the shoot.

REHEARSALS

As in the theater, the exciting process of discovering the characters, the dramatic beats, and the rhythms in a scene takes place at rehearsals. Find a quiet room or a setting similar to your location where the actors can run through each scene. There should be no crew, no equipment, and no time pressure—just the work.

Know what you want, but don't give the actor too much instruction. Work with the actors to achieve a specific goal—that is, your vision of the piece. Have a clear idea of what you want to achieve in a scene, but remember that the director should be flexible. An actor, following the flow and inclinations of the character, might discover a completely new approach to the material. Learn to guide actors in the direction you want to explore, but do not hinder their creativity.

The British director Ronald Neame told this story during an AFI interview:

> I first learned this lesson from Alec Guinness of being completely fluid when I go on the set. . . . As a director the first film that I made with him was *The Promoter*. It was only the third film I had directed. I had got it all beautifully worked out. I had done my homework. We came on the set one morning and I said, "Alec, I thought that maybe you should do this, that, and the other thing."
>
> He said, "Well, Ronnie, I've been thinking. I'd rather like to play this scene lying on my back underneath the table."
>
> I said, "Lying on your back, underneath the table?"
>
> He said, "Yes."
>
> I said, "Well, you're out of your mind, Alec. What's that got to do with the scene?"
>
> He said, "Now wait a minute. Don't get impatient. Just bear with me a minute." Of course he suggested something in relation to the scene and it was absolutely marvelous played on his back underneath the table. That was the way that we shot it.
>
> If an actor can bring you something and wants to do it his way, provided that he is following the character accurately and he's not being absolutely stupid, then he should be encouraged to do it this way.

The goal of every actor is to have the camera capture every moment as if it were happening for the first time. There is such a thing as rehearsing too much. The director needs to be sensitive to her actors and should strive to find a balance that will allow the actors to be "fresh" during principal photography. If the actors perform for the camera as if they have been drilled, the performance will lack spontaneity; therefore, some directors do very little rehearsing. They want to save it for the camera. You will develop your own style, based on what you find works successfully for you.

Shaping the Scene

Blocking Action

When blocking a scene, don't "show and tell" the actors what to do. Instead, allow the scene to grow organically. Start the actors with no movement, perhaps seated. When it is indicated in the script or when the actors feel compelled to make a move, they should do so. Little by little, as the scene is repeated, various actions, known as *business*, will evolve, and the scene will begin to take shape. Examples of business are the lighting of a cigarette at a key moment in the scene or the jiggling of a set of keys to break a tense moment of silence.

To simulate the location, use masking tape to mark out the floor plan of the location, including the walls, windows, and prominent set pieces. Then when the actors arrive on the set or location, they will already be familiar with it.

Discovering Beats

Just as the director breaks down the scene into shots and angles, she must also help the actor break down the action into dramatic beats. This enables the actor to memorize the arc of his character moment to moment. Each scene has many small beats that together make up the major objective of the scene. When the action or objective change, so too does the beat.

The script gives the actor a situation. The actor explores with action and with dialogue how he might respond. With each change of the situation, a new beat begins. This is all apparent in the text. (For more on beats, see Chapter 3, "Director's Breakdowns.") Occasionally, the director finds that what read well on paper does not play well in action. Often, action can replace dialogue or might render words unnecessary. The luncheonette scene in *The Lunch Date* is a good example of a scene in which a few lines of dialogue and a wealth of silent business and reactions create a full conversation. The rehearsal process is an excellent opportunity to trim any fat from the script or to revise the dialogue to accommodate blocking, props, or set pieces.

During the rehearsals, directors and actors often like to improvise a scene to help identify the beats. Improvisation is a spontaneous use of invention in which the actor keeps the character and the situation but is not tied to the text. For example, suppose a scene from the script is set at a park bench. A man is attempting to break off his relationship with a woman. The director can ask the performers to improvise the scene many ways, with each performance exploring different and subtle emotional nuances within that particular situation:

- The man can't go through with his speech.
- The park is empty.
- The park is crowded.

In the middle of the improvised scene, the director might add information to the situation—for example, it begins to rain, the woman begins to cry, or a nearby musician plays "their song." During the scene, the director might whisper a direction to the actor that will further adjust the direction of the scene. For example, she might tell him, "You suddenly realize you love her" or "Try to get the ring back." Each of these whispered directions will allow the actress to react without prior knowledge of what the director desires. An interesting discovery made during an improvisation can then be used in the scene.

> Because there wasn't much dialogue for Truman's first rehearsal, we played some games. He pantomimed climbing up a rope with his eyes closed as well as various other little physical actions. Then I asked him to draw me some pictures—pictures of what he thought his character looked like and what he felt.
>
> At the third session, we brought in the gym teacher so they could get comfortable with each other. They just talked and had a hamburger. From there, we actually did some minor improvs between the two of them. I had Jerry pretend to be his father. From that I could gauge how the little boy would react to him as a figure of authority.
>
> *Howard*

Pace and Rhythm

Pace is defined as the rate of movement or progress. It is the amount of time required to bring the audience to the height of the emotions the scene requires. This is a primary responsibility of the director. During rehearsals, the director and actor determine the pace of each moment, each scene, and ultimately the entire show. The director can then instill the project with a pace, which can make or break it. If the actors peak emotionally too early or too late, the delicate fabric of the story can be torn. The director memorizes her feeling of the pace during rehearsal so she can be objective during the shooting period and remind the actor both of the pace itself and of how the pace fits into the arc of the story. Once the performances are recorded on film or tape, any further adjustments to the pace can only take place in the editing room.

Four key directorial phrases are often employed during rehearsals and when photographing a scene: louder, softer, faster, and slower. However, rather than imposing these words arbitrarily on an performer, encourage her to "use urgency" or "take your time" at a certain point of the scene, thereby allowing the pace to come out of the character.

Communicating on the Set

The director and the actors constantly refine a scene by honing beats, restructuring dialogue, and inventing business. With each adjustment, they come closer to developing a shorthand for communicating what they want to do. This is important preparation for the shoot. The next time the director and the actors will work together is on the set, where time will be a critical factor. If they can work efficiently together, problems relating to script and performance can be solved quickly.

> We spent a long time going over the script, page by page, examining each thing that would happen— where Scotty would be, what was going through the character's head, etc.—which paid off in the end because I could do things on the set like say, "This is just after you lost your wallet, and this is going to happen next," and Scotty would know where she was, in terms of the character's emotions. We didn't actually rehearse until the day we arrived on the set.
> *Adam*

Special Situations

The director is often faced with a great diversity of acting styles from the talent she employs within a scene. Some actors are trained to improvise; others are trained in a Method school of acting. The director will need to use all her wiles to meld these acting styles and special situations together so that the scene looks like everyone on screen is part of a whole.

The Method

In the early part of this century, the Russian director Konstantin Stanislavsky developed a method of acting that became known as *the Method*. In this process, the actor digs deep into the well of her own experience and finds an emotional response similar to the one called for in the script. The actor tries to relate her own experience to the character's. This acting technique is also referred to as *emotional recall*.

It might take time, but by digging into her own emotional well, the actor brings a great deal of truth to the moment, and the results can be rewarding. As the actor's goal is to make each moment truthful, finding that truth within herself makes the result seem all the more genuine. The Method creates a very "internal" kind of performance; rather than acting, the actor seems to "live" the role.

Comedy

Comic acting is based on talent, skill, and timing. Many comedians excel at improvisation; spontaneity is an integral facet of the comic actor's skill. Because timing is so critical in comedy, it often takes considerable time to work out a routine or even a moment within a scene. Chaplin was famous for rehearsing on camera. He sometimes shot a sequence a hundred times, constantly refining the routine until the only business left was his exit through a revolving door.

Comedy is serious business. Just because the crew laughs doesn't mean that the scene will play in a screening room. The director is the only audience on the set who matters. If she thinks the scene is working, she can shoot it and then move on.

Understatement

Whether the scene is dramatic or comic, understatement will always work better than overstatement. It is easy for actors to play big, broad, and loud. For one thing, it feels good to use their instrument with full broad strokes. The line or moment that is understated, though, has twice the meaning. The camera picks up the most subtle details. The director needs to watch actors who were trained for the stage carefully. Their tendency is to play a scene to a large audience. In film, less is more.

Untrained Actors

Working with untrained actors can be both reward-ing and frustrating. An untrained actor might be a "natural" for the part, but he will not be familiar or comfortable with the technical aspects of the actor's craft. Working to find a character, sustaining a per-formance, shooting out of continuity, and even hit-ting marks will be a mystery to him.

In this situation, the director must be especially patient. She should explain the process at each step, coaxing a performance out of the actor. With an un-trained actor, it is permissible to give a line reading, which means asking the actor to repeat a line just as the director delivers it. Ask the performer to think the line before saying it.

Interviews

Documentaries are based on spontaneity. The subject of a documentary is not an actor, so there is no re-hearsing for a scene. Often, the director is in the field with a camera, capturing the subjects as they go about their lives. This doesn't mean the subject is to-tally "cold." A documentary director might inform the subject before the interview what topics and questions she might introduce. This gives the subject an opportunity to think about the shoot and how she might phrase her answers.

In *Mirror Mirror*, the director interviewed her subjects using a set of questions she felt would reveal interesting material on the topic of women's bodies. From the hours of responses to her questions, she pieced together a story that captures the spirit of her subjects.

> I met these women a month before the shoot. I did not want to give them the questions in advance because I knew that if they thought too long about an answer, the responses would lose spontaneity. So when they arrived at the set, I said to them, "You're going to be seated there, and I will ask two questions. Then we'll move over here and do two more questions." I told them that any time they wanted to stop between the questions, they should let me know because I knew that the mask got hot. So I let them know that they were somewhat in control of the process.
>
> *Jan*

Sometimes the director must probe for the kind of answers she feels will best match the script she has previsualized. This approach might require ask-ing provocative questions designed to stimulate the subject.

READ-THROUGHS

If possible, assemble the entire cast and key crew members for a read-through of the script just before principal photography. This can be helpful for two reasons. First, everyone involved in the show will be-come familiar with the dramatic arc of the piece. This is particularly important because most shows are shot out of continuity. Therefore, if an actor peaks too early in a scene, negating his previous "build," everyone—particularly the director and his fellow ac-tors—will be aware of it and can work toward mak-ing adjustments.

Second, many technical functions can be ad-dressed at a read-through. Is a scene too long? If so, has the proper amount of film or tape stock been al-lotted? A scene or part of a scene that feels totally ex-traneous should be eliminated.

> We rehearsed with the whole class. I wanted every-body to meet each other before starting. We had all the kids there Saturday afternoon, and we read the script out loud—this must have been the third time —now with their participation. Then we walked through it in the gym very quickly so it didn't get bor-ing and I kind of said, "This happens and then this happens." This was more about making everybody feel comfortable with each other, feeling like they could be themselves. We did this quickly because I didn't want to lose the spontaneity.
>
> *Howard*

PRODUCER
Prepare Call Sheets

The preproduction period is one of planning, prepa-ration, organization, communication, information gathering, checking, and double-checking. The pro-ducer, who is in charge of the preproduction period, gathers and processes information from the depart-ment heads. He must consider and weigh this infor-mation when shaping the schedule and the budget.

The producer must keep the creative team fo-cused on its goal: being totally prepared for the shoot. As each week of preproduction passes and as the cast, crew, and locations are locked into place, the producer adjusts the schedule to reflect their spe-cific requirements. He and the other members of his department handle the multitude of elements that will affect the production. The production manager, the production coordinator, the location manager, and the office production assistants look at and take care of hundreds of details. (If you don't have these people working for you, then you must take of everything yourself.)

SAMPLE PREPRODUCTION SCHEDULE

To give you an idea of what the flow of activity looks like from week to week, this chapter includes a sample preproduction timeline for a 12-page script. It is difficult to predict how your project will fit into this model because each project has its own set of challenges. Your project might require devoting more effort to cast, location, or crew. The challenge of *Truman*, for example, was to find a 10-year-old boy to play the lead, children for the supporting characters, and a gym that was available for a whole week. The producer of *The Lunch Date* needed to secure Grand Central Station and a luncheonette. Jan Krawitz had to find suitable women to interview for *Mirror Mirror* to bring the issue alive.

The sample schedule assumes six shooting days. At two pages a day, this is a reasonable schedule for a student or beginning film- or videomaker. Our formula for a beginner allows one week of preproduction for each day of principal photography. This gives you six weeks to prepare for the shoot. Depending on the experience of you and your crew and on the complexity of the script, the preproduction period might be longer or shorter. This prototype will at least give you an idea of what must happen before the cameras can roll. The order and the time during which each task occurs will vary from production to production.

The schedule on the next two pages assumes you have the following:

- A finished script
- A director
- Adequate financing
- A preliminary budget
- A shoot date

PREPRODUCTION PLANNING SUGGESTIONS

1. If shooting at distant locations, have a production assistant on call at the base location to handle the dailies pickup at the airport. Film must be brought to the lab, and quarter-inch tapes must be brought to the sound transfer facility. The editor should arrange to pick up the dailies from the lab.

2. If you are putting up the cast and crew at private homes, do not house more than two to a room. You want your cast and crew to be rested and comfortable during the shoot.

3. Have one person at the lab act as your contact throughout the entire project. He or she should be able to verify over the phone that there are no problems with the dailies.

4. If editing or screening facilities are not available at or near your location, have your dailies transferred to video and shipped to you.

5. If your equipment vehicles must be driven to the location, allow enough time for a leisurely drive before the shoot.

PRODUCTION MEETING SUGGESTIONS

Production meetings are opportunities to brainstorm ideas and to solve problems. The key to running an effective production meeting is to be organized and to stick to the agenda. Maximize the time you spend with the crew. Respect all points of view, but don't linger too long on one issue with the whole crew present. Deal with a particularly thorny issue later with only the appropriate crew members. You might have to set up smaller meetings with individual department heads—art, camera, sound, wardrobe, props, hair, and makeup—to deal with specific issues in their respective areas.

Here are some additional suggestions:

1. Hold the production meeting at the same time and place each week.
2. Have refreshments available.
3. Before the meeting, make sure everyone has a copy of the script.
4. Moderate the meeting, keeping everyone focused on one topic at a time.
5. Publish and hand out a written agenda if possible.
6. Set a time limit for the meeting.
7. Deal with one department at a time.
8. At the end of the meeting, summarize the points of agreement.
9. Assign tasks to appropriate crew members.
10. Set an agenda for the next meeting.

Week 1

Producer	Director
Sets up office/furniture	Finalizes script
Buys supplies	Scouts locations
Sets up phone/answering machine	Discusses script with art director
Leases photocopier	
Buys or leases typewriter/computer	
Creates filing system to keep copies of all agreements	
Establishes company name (DBA, "doing business as")	
Buys cards/stationery	
Opens bank account	
Advertises for actors	
Advertises for crew	
Breaks down script	
Creates stripboard and schedule	
Submits script to insurance company for estimate	

Crew

Production manager
Location manager
Art director
Casting director
Production coordinator

Production Meeting 1 • Key Points

1. Introduce all crew members.
2. Set up preproduction schedule.
3. Set goals for next meeting.

Week 2

Producer	Director
Reviews budget	Scouts locations
Reviews shooting schedule	Art director presents plans, ideas
Collects, organizes head shots	Reviews head shots for actors
Signs SAG waiver or guild contract	Breaks down script
Sets up auditions	
Reviews proposed insurance package	
Orders all necessary forms (location agreements, release forms, call sheets, petty cash envelopes, etc.)	

Crew

Director of photography
Office production assistants

Production Meeting 2 • Key Points

1. Discuss art director's plans.
2. Request art budget.
3. Go over preliminary schedule and budget.

Week 3

Producer	Director
Sets up auditions	Reviews location pictures
Looks for postproduction facilities	Visits locations with DP
Advertises for editor	Holds auditions
Settles on insurance package	
Negotiates with laboratory for overall package	
Researches equipment houses, vendors	

Crew

Wardrobe
Props
Special effects (if needed)

Production Meeting 3 • Key Points

1. Approve art department budget.
2. Narrow down location choices.
3. Approve construction schedule (if appropriate).

Week 4

Producer	Director
Sets up more auditions	Holds callbacks
Finalizes locations	Finalizes locations
Forms crew	Creates floor plans, storyboards
Reviews shooting schedule, budget	Reviews wardrobe, props with Art Department
Sets up dailies, projection schedule	
Negotiates agreement with caterer (meal plan)	
Makes transportation plans	
Rents vans, recreational vehicles	
Sets up account with lab, sound transfers	

Crew

Assistant director
Makeup/hair
Transportation coordinator

Production Meeting 4 • Key Points

1. Discuss casting alternatives.
2. Settle on final crew needs.
3. Finalize transportation plan.

Week 5

Producer	Director
Finalizes cast	Begins rehearsals
Negotiates cast contracts	Finalizes shot list
Secures location contracts	Reviews script
Finalizes crew, crew deal memos	Reviews makeup, hair designs with Art Department
Publishes cast, crew contact sheet	
Secures parking permits	
Secures shooting permits	
Makes security arrangements	
Approves expendables request for all departments	
Orders complete equipment package (camera, grip, electric, sound, dolly, generator, walkie-talkies, etc.)	
Orders first-aid kit for set	
Sets up tentative postproduction schedule	

Crew
Key grip
Sound recordist
2nd assistant director

Production Meeting 5 • Key Points
1. Discuss wardrobe, props, hair, and makeup issues.
2. Discuss budget considerations.
3. Have script timed.

Week 6

Producer	Director
Checks weather report	Holds rehearsals
Finalizes budget	Makes script changes
Distributes contact sheet	Visits set construction
Finalizes schedule	Finalizes shooting script
Reconfirms locations	Does final location scout
Confirms crew	Walk-thru with Department Heads
Distributes one-liner schedule to cast, crew	
Distributes call sheets for first-day cast, crew	
Distributes maps of locations	
Purchases film, tape stock	
Orders expendables	
Obtains certificates of insurance for locations, equipment, vehicles	

Crew
Gaffer
Boom
2nd assistant director

Production Meeting 6 • Key Points
1. Go over shooting schedule, day by day, with all department heads.
2. Give general pep talk.

Week 7

Producer	Director
Picks up equipment, transportation	

Shoot Date

KEY POINTS

1. Plan your project on a week-to-week basis during preproduction.

2. The goal of the rehearsal period is to work out the beats and the business. There will be little time to do this during production.

3. The process of discovery is everything. Once you know how the piece should work, it will inform all aspects of principal photography.

4. Use the rehearsals to develop a mutual trust with the actors and a shorthand for communicating with them.

5. There is a fine line between rehearsing too much and rehearsing too little.

part two

Production

As the producer, you set the start date for production. During preproduction, this date inches closer and closer. If you are well prepared, the shooting period merely means shifting into a higher gear. If you are not prepared, you will experience problems that might be serious enough to force you to push back the start date.

The start of production is the moment when the ship has been constructed, the crew has been chosen, and the captain pulls anchor and heads out to sea. The score has been written, the musicians are assembled, and the conductor raises the baton. The director will by this time know intuitively how to influence the creative drive of the production.

Production is also called *principal photography*. This is the industry term for the period during which the first, or principal, unit completes photography. (Professional shoots sometimes employ a second unit to shoot action sequences or scenes that do not involve principal players.)

During production, you can look back on the many hours of preparation, planning, and rehearsal and be thankful you took the time to refine the production schedule, look for that unique location, and develop a positive chemistry with the actors. Your hard work in preparing the picture should free the creative team to explore all the possibilities the script, cast, and crew have to offer.

Principal photography can be an intense and trying period. Working with the same people for long hours many days in a row tests the mettle of the strongest personalities. During the shoot, you will discover firsthand how important crew selection and casting can be. You will recognize almost immediately whom you can rely on and whom you can't. If you have a problem with a crew member or an actor on the first day, you must decide whether you want to give this person time to improve or replace him or her.

There is ample time during pre- and postproduction to solve problems. During principal photography, however, time is more precious. The production unit must be flexible but be prepared to make expeditious decisions. Even though compromise is inevitable during a shoot, there is no reason to sacrifice quality and integrity.

The best way to be flexible is to maintain the flow of communication among all parties, creating a Gestalt mentality. If, during preproduction, you anticipate all possible variables of what could go wrong on any given day, these problems can be addressed or a satisfactory compromise can be found with relative ease during the shoot.

To reach this level of communication, learn everything there is to know about the production process. This part of the book is organized to familiarize you with what happens during principal photography, when hard work and creative fervor transform the words on the page into the images and sounds that will become your final product.

A film or video is put together with some degree of magic and chance. Listen to the project as if it had a voice of its own. The finest films and videos are greater than the sum of their parts.

BASIC PRINCIPLES

CLARIFY THE CHAIN OF COMMAND TO THE CREW. Make sure everyone knows who's in charge. If there is a problem on the set, every crew member must know where to turn for an answer.

AVOID DUPLICATION OF ENERGIES. It is not efficient to have two production assistants running around looking for the same prop.

KEEP THE BALL ROLLING. Focus on where you are going and what you have to achieve. Don't let a problem with cast, crew, or location slow down the momentum.

KEEP BAD NEWS FROM THE ACTORS. Actors should always be in a positive frame of mind. If

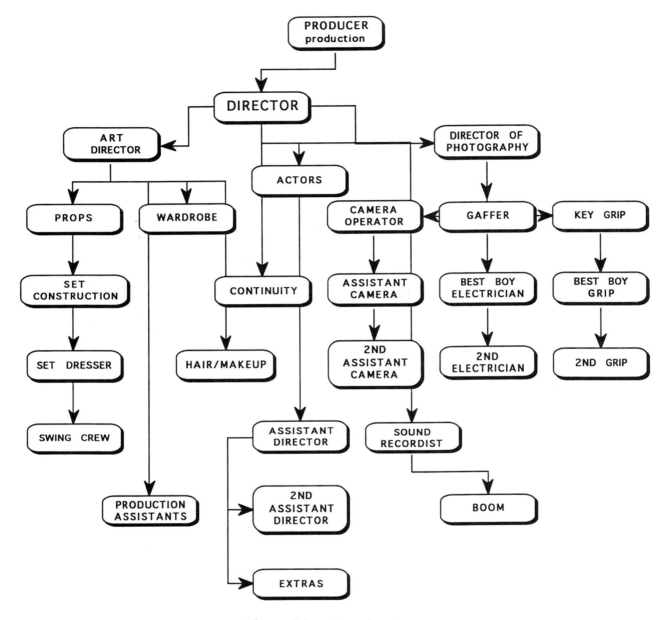

Figure II.1 Production flow chart.

there is tension on the set, relax the actors while you deal with the problem.

AVOID PASSING THE BUCK. If someone makes a mistake, don't waste time and energy placing blame. This is counterproductive. Put your energy into correcting the mistake. At one time or another, everyone will make a mistake, even professionals.

DO NOT ASSUME ANYTHING. Check and double-check all arrangements for cast, crew, transportation, meals, and locations.

DELEGATE RESPONSIBILITY. Don't take on more than you can handle. Spreading yourself too thin usually means that nothing gets done properly.

DOUBLE THE TIME ALLOTTED FOR ANYTHING OUT OF THE ORDINARY. Stunts, special effects, fire effects, car mounts, and even special effects lighting always take longer than you anticipate. The phrase "hurry up and wait" was created for the picture business.

KEEP MURPHY'S LAW IN MIND. Be prepared for the worst, but accept the best. Don't keep waiting for the other shoe to drop because it just might not.

STAY HEALTHY. You are no good to anyone if you are sick, especially during the shoot when there is no downtime to rest.

REMEMBER TO HAVE FUN!

chapter eleven

Set Procedures

They told me, "Don't worry. Everything's fine. He's all set; he knows what he's doing." So the actors took their places, and we started, rolled sound, rolled camera. I called action, did the shot, called cut. It was great. Then, I suddenly notice there's a commotion going on next to me. I look over, and there's yards of magnetic tape spewing out of the Nagra, and the homeless guy, who was trying to help, now has his hands over his face. We quickly went back to the original way of the sound man operating the recorder by himself.

Adam

DIRECTOR

Control

RUNNING THE SET

The hierarchy of the crew is a pyramid, with the director on top. Her goal for production is to shoot the script within the schedule and to walk away with enough shots to tell the story adequately. Achieving this task depends on the director's ability to communicate her vision confidently to the cast and technical support personnel who will execute her ideas. A strong director creates a tone, attitude, and pace on the set that allows the team to respond to whatever problems and challenges arise. An insecure director, on the other hand, brings down morale and slows the natural pace of a well-oiled and capable crew.

On the set the director's word is law. Her talent, intelligence, and drive are applied to the script and the resources available to her. Her choices and swift decisions are able to be made because she's spent hours and hours of formulating and interpreting the script in her mind. A director often seems to function by intuition. Her decisions might be right or they might be wrong, but they are for her to make. She is free to consult whomever she chooses, and she can

always change her plan for a scene. Ultimately, however, the vision of the piece is in her head. It is the director's job to impart that vision succinctly and successfully to the cast and crew through her words and performance.

A TYPICAL DAY

This is what happens on a typical day during production.

CAST AND CREW ARRIVE ON THE SET. The director often arrives at the location before the cast or crew begins to arrive. It is a good idea to walk around the set to get a feel for the location. It might be the first time you have been on the fully dressed set.

The call time, indicated on the call sheet, tells each cast and crew member when to arrive. If a particular department needs lead time, the call times can be staggered. For example, if an actor has to undergo a lengthy makeup application, the location manager, makeup artist, and actor will be called before the rest of the crew. The assistant director makes these arrangements. Call times should be arranged so that when the actor is ready, the crew has arrived and he need not wait to begin rehearsal.

SHOT IS BLOCKED FOR THE CAMERA. As soon as the actors arrive, it is customary for the director to conduct a short run-through rehearsal of the first scene scheduled for the day. A "director's viewfinder" allows the director to "see" what the camera lens sees. It simulates many camera lens sizes and can inform the communication between the director and the director of photography (DP) about camera placement and framing. The director and DP then make a plan for the day's photography, based on the storyboards or floor plans as well as information gleaned from the rehearsal.

> The scenes in the cafeteria I diagrammed from an overhead floor plan—the camera here, her walking this way and that. And the scenes in Grand Central I designed with storyboards. But you've got to get to the camera; you've got to look through the camera; you've got to see.
>
> *Adam*

As the director and DP talk over the shooting plan for the day, they decide on the first setup and where the camera will be placed. On the basis of the rehearsal, the director might decide to shoot the scene differently than originally planned. Seeing the completed set or dressed location might inspire her to reveal the environment or characters in another way. This is the time to discuss any changes.

MARKS ARE PLACED ON THE FLOOR FOR THE ACTORS AND CAMERA. If the blocking of the actors or camera is complicated, the key grip will put tape on the floor to mark the actors' and camera's positions. Any camera move, such as a dolly, is rehearsed for smoothness.

> The camera was on a dolly, so we could put tape on the floor to mark the exact position of the camera for both setups. The positions had to be precise from one interview to the next in order to ensure a jump-cut aesthetic. We were a little off on some of them. If you look closely, you can see the composition shift just a tad, but it's not something anyone really notices.
>
> *Jan*

THE FOCUS MARKS ARE SET. The assistant camera operator sets the focus for the actors' movements. Each time the camera and/or actor moves, the operator adjusts the footage ring on the lens to maintain focus.

THE SET IS LIT. The DP directs the gaffer to set the lights and the grip crew to set the camera. As the lights are being positioned, turned on, and aimed, the DP moves around with his light meter, checking light readings from each unit. Once the lights are in place, a stand-in sits or stands where the actor will eventually be placed so the camera team can reestablish focus, lens size, and lighting. During these technical rehearsals, the gaffer tries to keep the lighting instruments out of the shot and tries to block, or *flag*, any glare from hitting the camera lens.

The time it takes the camera team to light the set to the director's satisfaction is critical for meeting the daily schedule. The director's estimate of the number of scenes or shots for a day is based on the DP's projected setup time at each location. The DP bases his setup time on the location scouts and final walkthroughs. It is the assistant director's job to monitor the DP's schedule. If it appears that the lighting team will fall behind on their projected schedule, adjustments to the shot list might be required.

ACTORS ARE DRESSED AND MADE UP. While the set is being prepared, the actors are sent to the makeup area and then fitted in their wardrobe.

A RUN-THROUGH IS HELD FOR THE ACTORS AND CAMERA. Once the technical aspects of the shot have been finalized, the actors are brought back to the set for a final dress rehearsal.

ADJUSTMENTS ARE MADE FOR THE ACTORS AND CAMERA. Between the rehearsal and the lighting period, technical adjustments or new creative ideas might require altered or additional blocking for the actors and camera.

THE SCENE IS SHOT. When the director determines that everything is ready, she shoots the scene. Each time the scene is shot from a particular angle with a specific lens, it is referred to as a *take*. The director shoots as many takes of each shot as she feels are necessary. Between takes, the DP walks into the shot and checks the light to see if the readings are correct.

A word of advice: Don't act as though the production company can return to a location should the footage be incomplete. Get it right while you are there.

> I didn't think I had everything by the end of the production. I thought, "Oh, my God, there are shots that I don't have." By the time I put the rough cut together, it occurred to me I could go back and get those shots, but the cost would have been too great.
>
> *Adam*

The director might request a retake for any number of reasons: The director or an actor wants adjustments in the performance, technical problems occurred with the camera or lights, an actor flubbed or misread a line, an actor doesn't hit his or her focus mark, the dolly doesn't hit its mark, a microphone dips into the frame, the boom shadow enters the frame, a light bulb pops during a take, or an airplane or loud noise buries the sound.

Even if the director is satisfied with the first take, it is wise to take each shot at least twice, with one of the takes acting as a safety. Unforeseen mishaps often necessitate a safety shot being used in the editing room to get around a problem.

THE CAMERA IS MOVED FOR THE NEXT SET-UP OR SEQUENCE. When the director is satisfied that all of the required takes from a particular camera angle have been shot, she requests that the camera be moved to the next camera position. In this way, the director works her way through the script.

> Sometimes in shooting observational footage, I don't know exactly what I'm getting because I'm not actually behind the camera and there's little time to confer once a scene begins. There are always a lot of surprises—not big surprises because I'm on the shoot doing the sound, but I won't know exactly what the framing looks like. *Mirror Mirror* was different. We discussed each setup, and I looked through the camera beforehand because it was an entirely controlled shooting situation.
>
> *Jan*

CAMERA MOVES

If the shot must be terminated because of a technical error from the cast or the crew, the script supervisor marks the shot as a false start. Out of ten takes, there might be only two complete takes.

Every time you decide to use a moving camera, even for a small pan or tilt, you'll need time to rehearse the camera and the actors. Each member of the camera team has a particular function that must be performed properly. In a long dolly, crane, or Steadicam® shot, the DP must light the entire area the actors or camera travel along and must make sure that everything is in focus. These moving shots often require that precision moves by the dolly grip or Steadicam operator be repeated exactly for each take. This increases the chance of something going wrong.

Static shots, where the camera does not move, are generally easier to set up and less risky to shoot than dolly or Steadicam shots. They also require less rehearsal time.

> *Students:* Do attempt elaborate camera moves, but consider adopting an alternate plan if you face too many technical hurdles in getting a satisfactory shot. Don't give up unless it becomes obvious that time is being wasted. If the dolly shot you are attempting is taking too long, consider breaking the scene down into pieces or basic coverage. Your goal is to get into the editing room with something to cut.

VIDEO TAP

Many directors use a video tap. This feed line from the film camera to a video monitor gives the director and others on the set an opportunity to see the take as it happens. The video tap can be recorded, enabling the take to be studied immediately afterward. This is especially useful for continuity when staging a complicated camera move.

Video tap is also extremely helpful when the director is acting. Being objective while acting is difficult. After the take, the director can watch the playback on the video monitor and judge for herself whether to move on or shoot another take.

The problem with video tap is that those who are watching often become instant critics. As mentioned earlier, the only audience during principal photography should be the director.

> I personally don't like video tap. It's a good way for producers to look at your dailies while you're on the set.
>
> *Adam*

SLATES

In film, it is necessary to identify each sync sound take with a clapboard. Written on the clapboard, or slate, is pertinent information about the take for the editing process (Figure 11.1). When the sound and the developed film arrive in the editing room, the assistant editor matches the clap of the slate on the sound track to its corresponding film image. This is called syncing up the footage. This ensures that all the sound will be perfectly in sync with the picture. The editor must be able to read the material on the slate so she can relate her log books to the script supervisor's notes.

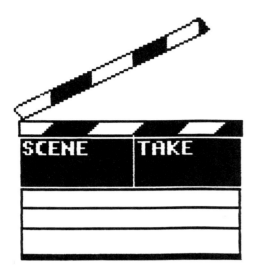

Figure 11.1 A slate contains information for the editor.

Slating Procedure

On the set, when the assistant director calls for the slate, the assistant camera operator holds the slate up in front of the lens with the clapper open. The AD then calls for the sound person to "roll sound." The sound recordist turns on the Nagra, and when the tape is rolling at 15 inches per second (ips), he calls out loudly, "Speed!" The AD then calls out,

"Roll camera!" at which point the camera operator turns on the camera. When the camera speed reaches 24 frames per second (fps), he calls out, "Rolling!"

At this cue, the assistant camera operator, or whoever is holding the slate, reads the information off the clapboard: "Scene 49 apple, take 2." When the assistant camera operator has called out the slate information, he slaps down the upper bar onto the slate, which makes a sharp "clap" sound (Figure 11.2). The assistant camera operator hustles behind the camera position, crouches, and waits patiently and is very still until the take is completed.

When shooting the slate, the goal is to be able to read all the information clearly in the editing room. The slate must have ample light on it, be held steady when it claps, and be close enough to the camera to enable the editor to read the small print. In a low light situation, the AC may shine a flashlight on the slate. A slate held far from a camera may require the operator to zoom in to shoot the slate and then zoom back out for the shot.

I would start the Nagra, then slate the shot with a clapper, and then return to my seat and start the interview. Normally, when we're on location shooting observational footage, because there's not a third person, we use a bloop slate or a mike tap rather than a clapper.

Jan

Figure 11.2 Assistant Director David Hamlin holds a slate to mark the beginning of a take on the set of *Truman*.

The person who holds the clapboard should be sensitive to the actors and not clap the slate in their faces. The "clap" sound doesn't have to be loud. If need be, use a tail slate.

Slate Lights

Another slating device is alled a *slate light*. This is a trigger connected to the recorder that, when pushed, flashes a small light and produces an audible beep. This system often is used in documentary film-making.

Smart Slates

As some films are being shot with the intention of transferring immediately to video dailies, a slate with a time code LED readout has been introduced to allow the recording devices to be locked up to the slate, thereby identifying the time code visually. This slate has clap sticks with the time-code display imbedded in them. Time code is fed to both the Smart Slate and audio tape and the laboratory can use these numbers to quickly and electronically sync the dailies in telecine.

Informal Slates

If you do not have a slate, you will still need some distinct event that can be clearly seen in the picture and heard on the track. You can make do by holding up fingers to indicate the take number, and then clap your hands together sharply. Another informal slate is called a *mike slate*. Hold the microphone up to the camera lens and tap it. The number of taps is the number of the take. This makes a sharp "bump" sound on the track by which the editor can sync up the material.

Tail Slates

When an opening slate would be impractical or inconvenient, a tail slate can be used. For example, the opening shot might have a very tight frame and then pull out to a wide one. In this case, slating the scene at the head of the take might prove difficult. It would be easier to start the scene without a slate, and when the director calls "cut," keep the camera and Nagra rolling and slate the take at the end, or *tail*, of the shot. The slating procedure is the same.

Video Slates

Slating is used in video for identification purposes only. There is no need to create a "clap," as the sound is recorded directly onto the tape stock. It is wise to log each shot into a notebook to keep track of what you have photographed.

> *Students*: If you have a limited amount of film stock, you can conserve a few feet of film on each take by having the AD call for the camera to roll as the slate is being read. Then when the reading is completed, the DP calls, "Mark it!" and the slate is "clapped" with the take information recorded on quarter-inch tape.

Action! Cut!

After the slate has been clapped and only when the director feels that everything is ready, she calls, "Action!" The scene plays as long as the director deems necessary, and then she calls, "Cut!" The director will ask for as many takes as needed or as time allows to get the best material in the can. The cast and crew make adjustments after each take. Hair, makeup, and continuity must be maintained from take to take.

SCRIPT SUPERVISION

The script supervisor keeps track of the slates, maintains the continuity within each scene and from scene to scene, and makes notes in her script about each shot. Besides taking notes about each shot, her duty is to ensure that the material delivered to the editing room can be cut together. The script supervisor bears the responsibility of making sure that the action is matched from one shot to the next. For example, an actor crosses to a chair, sits down, and crosses his legs. Did he put the left leg over the right, or vice versa? The script supervisor's tools include an instant camera (to record continuity) and a stopwatch (to time the shots).

The script supervisor's book contains shooting notes and a lined script for the show like the one in Figure 11.3. Her notes include the following:

- At what point in a scene an actor does what
- Length of each shot
- Lens used
- Director's comments
- DP's comments
- Brief description of what happened during the take

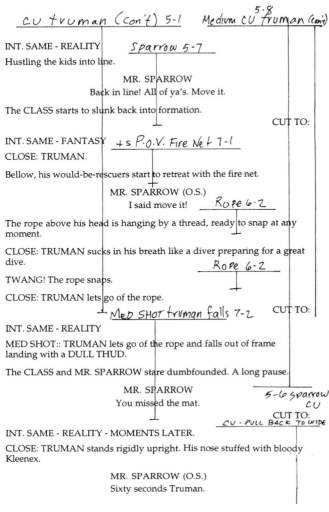

Figure 11.3 A lined script.

The lined script has a series of vertical lines on it that indicate from which angle and in which take each part of the script was shot. If, at the end of production, a part of a scene does not have a line through it, it probably was not photographed. A precise record of what was shot is an important guide for the editor.

PRODUCER

Organize

The producer's responsibility is to ensure that from the beginning of the shoot, everyone has a precise idea of what they are supposed to be doing and when and where they are supposed to be doing it. This requires the following:

- Clear chain of command
- Realistic budget
- Day-out-of-day schedule
- Enough crew to carry out the director's visual plan
- Secure locations
- Call sheets
- Daily meal plans
- Transportation schedule

Unless the producer is also serving on the crew as the assistant director, there is no traditional position for him on the set. The director is in charge of production, and it is up to the assistant director to keep the production unit moving in accordance with the agreed-upon schedule. This allows the producer the freedom to deal with the problems that inevitably arise during the course of any shoot. (Murphy's Law applies to every aspect of the picture-making process.) The producer becomes involved with set operations only in special situations, such as these:

- The production unit starts to go over schedule.
- The producer is needed as a troubleshooter.
- He has to alleviate tension between the director and the DP.
- He has to reassure an actor.

During production, the producer keeps a daily watch on both the budget and the material that is shot. This requires that he oversee all aspects of the production. During the shoot, the producer does the following:

- Keeps on top of daily cash flow
- Finalizes location arrangements, transportation plans, and meal plans
- Deals with schedule changes
- Completes daily production reports

GUIDELINES

Each shoot presents unique challenges and obstacles. The producer must be ready to deal with each as they arise. The following guidelines should help the novice understand the producer's basic priorities that can be applied to any production.

Keep Morale Up

As the producer, you are the head cheerleader and support person. You should remain positive and unflappable even under the most trying circumstances. Keep a "happy face," no matter what you are thinking or feeling.

Support the Director and the Creative Team

Support the director and the crew by creating a comfortable work environment that includes good food to eat. Production is stressful and physically demanding work. If the crew performs well, show your appreciation. Don't take the crew for granted; the success of your project rests on their shoulders. If you treat crew members well, they will be more likely to go that extra mile for you.

Watch the Budget

The budget dictates what the director can do. You must know from day to day if the production is on, over, or under budget. To do this, you must approve of and account for all expenditures and keep track of the daily cash flow—that is, the money being paid to vendors for food, supplies, or expendables. Keep a complete itemization of every expenditure and a thorough collection of receipts and bills.

Act as Coordinator

During principal photography, you must see to it that arrangements for locations, transportation, and food are confirmed and reconfirmed. (Never assume anything.) This includes establishing a regular system of getting the exposed film stock to the lab. (This is not an issue with video.) You must always keep ahead of the production unit to ensure that each day will go as planned. During this time, you should also be confirming the postproduction arrangements, such as editing space.

If exteriors are planned for the week, keep on top of the weather forecast. If the forecast is for rain, either have a cover set ready or assemble proper gear for shooting in the rain, such as umbrellas and parkas. The actors will need a dry and comfortable place close to the set.

Keep the Production Moving Ahead

Always keep the production unit focused on moving ahead. Don't let problems interfere with the momentum on the set or with the schedule. Keep problems away from the cast and crew if possible.

Be a Troubleshooter

You will need to find creative ways to solve problems if you don't have the money to do so. There is often a great deal of satisfaction in "saving the day" and allowing the creative team to complete photography by solving a difficult problem with your head rather than with cash. Some of the potential problem areas are:

SCHEDULE. The key to making the daily schedule is to get the first shot by a specific time. The department heads agree to this time beforehand. If the crew does not complete the shot per this plan, it not only pushes them back for that day, it inevitably pushes them back for the entire shoot. They must make up the lost time either that day or squeeze it into another day. If the crew is pushed to make up the time, it infringes on proper turnaround, pushes the next day back, and so forth.

There are several ways to get the crew back on schedule so that one bad day doesn't throw off the whole shoot:

- Cut scenes or pages
- Cut shots
- Collapse several shots into one

All these options must be considered and agreed to in a timely and calm manner.

It is the producer's job to serve as a stabilizing influence on what could be tough decisions for the director and DP. Compromise is an unfortunate but necessary part of the process. Having to make changes in the original plan doesn't necessarily mean that the original idea is compromised. Sometimes, the best ideas emerge from economic necessity.

On the basis of your experience with the crew's pace during the first few days, you might have to adjust the schedule. If the crew picks up speed along the way, so much the better.

CREW. During the first days, it will become clear whether you have hired the correct number of crew members. The effective people will stand out; the slackers will be revealed. It is good to cut the deadwood from the crew quickly so as not to slow down shooting. Finding replacements should not be too difficult if you kept a list of available crew people.

DEPARTMENT HEADS. The most problematic position on the crew is the director of photography. There must be a creative bond between the DP and the director. If there is tension, it can affect the entire crew. The director sets the tone and the pace of the production, and if she is unhappy, dissatisfied, or angry, it will have a ripple effect on everyone around her. Working on the set is difficult enough under the most ideal circumstances. Stress and tension between the key players can drain the energy and enthusiasm from the best of crews.

If there is a problem with the DP-director relationship or with any of the department heads, the producer serves as the mediator For example, a strong, experienced DP might take over the set and override an inexperienced director's designs. If the DP is slow, you may need to replace him, even if the material looks terrific. If you have a suitable replacement, you might decide to fire the DP. Some personality conflicts you must live with; others you must confront. Use your best judgment to resolve the situation quickly.

LOCATION. Losing a location can throw a monkey wrench into the best-laid plans. If you are prepared with backups, the loss will be only momentarily disruptive.

TRANSPORTATION. You must carefully monitor and coordinate key moves from set to set.

SAFETY ON THE SET

Safety and security are two of the producer's main concerns during principal photography. Equipment and personal items on the set are covered by the company's umbrella insurance policy, but these policies come with large deductibles. Follow these guidelines to reduce the risk of loss or injury:

- Do not leave equipment or valuables on the set or in a vehicle unattended.
- Do not place lighting instruments near pictures, drapes, or other items that are sensitive to heat.
- Lighting units must be secured and properly weighted down with sandbags.
- Keep electric cables away from sound cables and water.

PROPER WRAP-OUT

Make sure you leave each location in as good or better shape than when you arrived. One way to alleviate a major cleanup is to lay down plastic or butcher paper where the crew will be working. If objects, furniture, lights, pictures, or knickknacks have to be moved or put away before the crew can shoot, someone (usually a set dresser) should make careful notes of where these items were, arrange to have them

stored properly, and then return them to the correct place when wrapping out of the location. It is helpful to record the original layout by taking instant photos.

This is proper professional behavior. Keep in mind that you might need to come back to the location for additional work or reshoots. Even if you will never see the owners again, think of each location as if it were your home. Someone should be assigned to keep an eye on what is happening to the location during the shoot. Here are a couple things to watch out for:

PLACEMENT OF GAFFER'S TAPE. This tape has a tendency to peel paint off walls. Remove it carefully.

GARBAGE DISPOSAL. A crew can generate a lot of garbage. Make sure it is packed up and disposed of regularly.

On leaving a location, arrange to have the area cleaned and, if need be, repainted.

DAILIES

While the company shoots, the assistant editor syncs up the material shot the previous day. At wrap, the editor takes this material to the screening room. There she meets the producer, director, DP, and department heads, and they screen the footage. During the screening, important decisions can be made about the progress of the project. Should an actor's hair be changed? Does the lighting match? Should a costume be more distressed?

During dailies screening, the director makes comments to the editor about the different shots. For example, she might instruct the editor to use the head of one take and the tail of another, to start it tight and reveal the master shot farther into the scene, or to use a specific take because of performance. Video dailies are instantly available for viewing and discussion.

KEY POINTS

1. The director has the final say on the set.
2. Move the camera to the next setup position only after you are confident that you will not have to return to that position.
3. Give the art department ample lead time to dress and strike the set.
4. Put safety first.
5. Wrap out carefully.

chapter twelve

Camera

It was very hot. The conditions were definitely not very pleasant because there were these lights . . . and it was summer in Texas!

Jan

DIRECTOR
Collaborate

All the planning, storyboarding, and previsualization that occurs during preproduction is translated into a finished product during production by the camera. The camera is the tool through which the director realizes the script. The use of this tool is limited only by the imagination of the film- or videomaker.

Cinematography is an illusion—a magic trick. It is 24 still frames projected each second to create the illusion of a moving image. The illusions the director can create through cinema are boundless. Almost every aspect of film and video can employ a cinematic trick, perhaps a computer-generated optical effect, a miniature set, or the use of paste jewels in place of real gems.

STYLE

When choosing a style for a project or when developing a personal style of her own, the director should look first to the history of the medium. She needs to know what has come before so that she can help originate what will come after. The language of film is a relatively new vernacular (about a hundred years old), but it is rich in tradition and ripe for innovation.

A personal style comes only after acquiring a thorough knowledge of the craft and by much experience. By thoroughly understanding her craft, the director can respond to and meet each situation of the mediamaking with confidence. Why a director makes a decision, alters a shot, or adjusts a performance is based as much on her intuition as on her knowledge. In fact, in the heat of principal photography, it is often an improvised moment, a jury-rigged set, or an accident that makes for exciting dramatic moments.

Personal identity with the form and the subject is what makes for a strong visual style. Jean Luc Godard said, "Style is just the outside of content, and content the inside of style, like the outside and inside of the human body—both go together, they can't be separated."

Documentary styles include interviews ("talking heads"), voice-overs with visuals to illustrate the text, or cinema verité. Some documentaries include elements of all three styles. One of the keys to a good documentary style is flexibility.

COLLABORATION WITH THE CAMERA DEPARTMENT

The camera department consists of the director of photography (DP), camera operator, 1st assistant camera operator, loader/clapper, and stills photographer. The gaffing department lights the scene. Under the direction of the director of photography, electricians move lighting instruments that will illuminate the set or location. Grips are in charge of moving the camera. If the director calls for a complicated shot, the grips will find a way to maneuver the camera to best advantage. Grips do not like to compromise.

Given enough time, they will find a solution to almost any problem.

Described in this section are a few helpful ideas for collaborating with the camera department. Note that these suggestions should be carried out during preproduction.

Consult with the Director of Photography

The camera crew executes the director's visual ideas for each scene. The individual responsible for translating those ideas into concrete decisions is the DP. The director is responsible for camera placement and for what the camera sees. The DP heads the camera team and is ultimately responsible for keeping the image in focus and illuminating and framing it properly. A good working relationship between the DP and the director is key to a successful shoot. Their relationship is like a marriage; there has to be a productive synergy between them.

The DP should be thoroughly versed with the storyboards and the floor plans developed during preproduction. These will help him translate the director's ideas efficiently into shots that ultimately realize her vision for the script.

There are many ways to approach a scene visually, and ideas can come from anywhere. A good director taps the creative resources around her. As with all good teamwork, there must be a balance between the contributions of the individual members. The DP should be allowed to choose some, but not all, of the shots. He should be permitted to express his creativity on the set, but he must not be allowed to take over the show. On the other hand, a dominating director will reduce the DP to a mere technician. This might cause resentment and affect his overall performance on the picture. Remember that the DP sees himself as a visual artist, a painter with light. To get the most out of this individual, encourage him to believe he is making an important contribution to the "look" of the picture. In practical terms, you want the best he has to offer. Any decisions, however, must ultimately reflect your overall vision for the show.

Until the film is processed, there is no sure way of knowing whether all the ideas created in preproduction and during the shoot were executed properly. This is one advantage of working with videotape, where, for better or for worse, you see the results immediately.

Do Your Homework

The success of principal photography depends on proper preparation before and during preproduction. The director brings weeks of work and preparation to the set. The director's "homework" gives her a thorough understanding of what she wants to see at each moment of the story, how she wants to manipulate the audience with sights and sounds, and how she plans to effect her vision.

During preproduction, the director creates a plan on paper in the form of storyboards and floor plans. She might videotape some scenes to evaluate their cinematic qualities. She balances her shot list with the planned schedule and determines at this point that, barring catastrophe, she will be able to realize her vision successfully.

> *Directors:* The breakdowns prepared during preproduction distill the script into breakdown sheets, a schedule, a budget, storyboards, and finally a shot list. Although you will carry the script and all of these breakdowns with you onto the set, it's a good idea to write down the shots that you plan for each day on a three-by-five index card, perhaps putting a bright-colored asterisk on those of highest priority. Keep these cards in your pocket, and as the shots are completed, tick them off one by one. At the end of the day, all of the shot cards should have a check on them.

Introduce the Camera during Preproduction

It is recommended that you work with the camera during your preproduction rehearsals. The frame is as much a part of the scene as are the actors. What is included in the frame, what happens there, and how it moves are all part of visual storytelling.

With a film camera, the rehearsals are for framing and blocking only. Do not actually roll the camera. However, with video, you have the option to shoot the rehearsals for study purposes.

TEN BASIC DECISIONS ABOUT THE SHOT

The writer uses words and sentences to convey thoughts and ideas. Shots are the basic element of the director's visual vocabulary. She uses the camera to express ideas and to tell the story by combining shots. How the audience perceives these shots involves them in the story.

If every frame, every shot, and every scene have a visual dynamic, you will maximize their potential for impact on your audience. How you imbue each shot of a scene with energy and momentum is part of your plan. Consider the following when you compose a shot:

- Camera placement
- Composition of shot
- Size of shot
- Lighting
- Camera movement
- Editing
- Coverage
- Continuity
- Shot perspectives
- Specialty shots

Camera Placement

The director is responsible for placing the camera. To determine where the camera is placed, ask yourself, "From whose point of view is the scene experienced? Who is doing the seeing here?" Is it a main character's point of view or that of an unknown bystander or the omniscient storyteller? The point of view can shift back and forth within a scene, but you should always know from whose vantage point the scene is unfolding.

You should also know whether the shot is objective or subjective. Distant shots tend to be objective and are well suited for the storyteller's point of view. The closer the shot, the more subjective it becomes. The dramatic tension within a scene can best be achieved by bouncing the camera between these two extremes. Characters speaking to one another with the camera directly over one character's shoulder creates an extremely subjective point of view. Techniques for playing a scene along this axis, or *eye-line*, are discussed later in this chapter (Figure 12.1).

The camera is normally placed at eye level. This is the position at which an audience sees the world. Altering this perspective creates very definite emotional responses from the audience. A camera placed high, looking down on a character, gives the audience a "god's eye view." A camera placed low, looking up to a character, makes that character seem powerful. If the camera is positioned to look down slightly on one character, it makes the other characters seem superior.

In placing the camera, the director or DP will ask, "Is the camera in the right place to tell the story properly? Are we seeing what we want to see?" All other camera decisions, including size and composition of the frame, derive from this basic judgment.

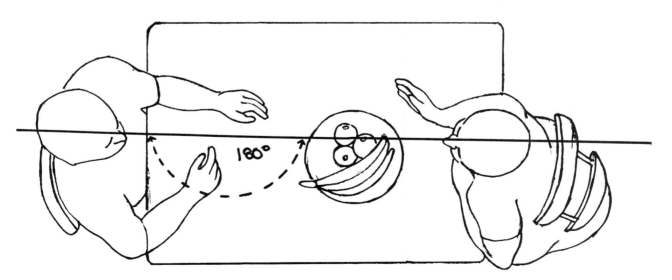

Figure 12.1 The eye-line is this side of the 180° axis. For correct eye-line match, the camera over the first actor's left shoulder should match the angle of the camera over the other actor's right shoulder.

Composition of Shot

Think of the frame as a picture frame surrounding a painting. Make the elements in that picture move, and then make the frame itself move. This is the magic of the camera, and it is orchestrated by the director. Composing a shot takes into account many factors, including the confinement of the set or location, the limitations of the equipment, the time allotted for setup of the shot, the outcome of the rehearsal, and the ability of the production team to solve problems successfully and quickly.

Drawing the Viewer's Eye

The director places people in the frame. She places objects in the frame. She moves the frame. All this cinematic construction is not arbitrary. Composition within a frame, even a still one, has more or less dramatic tension depending on how the director juxtaposes all the elements.

The key is to draw the audience's eye to what you want them to see. In motion pictures, sounds, as well as images, are used to direct the eye. A blacksmith hammering a horseshoe in the upper right background of the frame becomes more prominent if the only sound heard is the clanging of hammer on metal.

The director can further encourage the audience to focus on the blacksmith's work if a portion of the foreground frame is obscured by something, such as the hanging branch of a tree. The partially obscured frame forces viewers to look at the blacksmith.

Depth

To create dramatic tension, the director can manipulate the foreground and the background. Although the frame is two-dimensional, the audience experiences the illusion that there is great depth within the frame. For example, in *The Lunch Date*, Adam Davidson placed a woman by herself in the distance of a huge train station lobby, giving the audience a feeling of isolation. In Howard McCain's film, when we see Truman in a close-up with his peers in the background sneering at him, a feeling of tension and compassion is created.

Extending the Frame

The director can even design (and control) the space beyond the frame. Incorporating off-screen elements through the audience's imagination is called *extending the frame*. For example, a beautifully composed landscape devoid of characters holds the audience's attention for several beats. A voice and a bell heard off screen pique the audience's interest. The voice and bell get closer and closer, and finally a man and a cow enter the frame.

Size of Shot

The composition of the frame is directly related to the size of the shot. The frame size is dictated by the size of the lens placed on the camera body. Lenses come in a variety of sizes (Figure 12.2). A long lens (250mm) can shoot a close-up of a lion at 100 yards. A wide-angle lens (10mm) can shoot the entire British royal family on the steps of Buckingham Palace from 10 yards.

The size of the lens is a factor in determining how much information can be placed in the frame. If the scene looks too empty, use a tighter lens or move

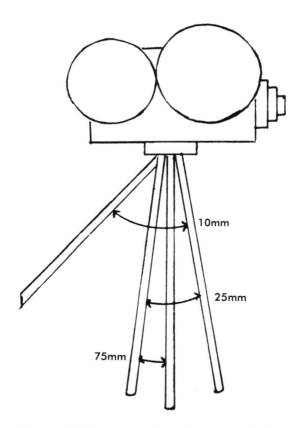

Figure 12.2 As opposed to the human eye, which has wide peripheral vision, the 10mm wide-angle lens has a margin of 54°. The 25mm standard lens is 23° wide, and the 75mm telephoto (long) lens has a margin of only 7.8°.

the camera closer to the subjects. Conversely, if the frame is too tightly packed with people or objects, move the camera back or switch to a wider lens.

Camera lenses are an important area of study. Certain lenses are commonly used for close-ups. Long lenses compress the image, whereas wide-angle lenses distort the image. The choice of the lens becomes integral to achieving the director's vision.

Lighting

The most significant addition to the composition of the frame is the use of light. Photographers have known this for years, which is why they describe their work as "painting with light." It should be the script that dictates the mood and amount of light. A chase sequence at night needs to be full of mystery: pools of light, areas of shadow. A comedy, on the other hand, is usually brightly lit.

Based on the script, the director and the DP determine a look for the staging, photographic, and lighting style for the project. This look can be either naturalistic or stylized. Once a style has been determined, it should remain consistent throughout the shoot. The three case studies used in this book are good examples of a consistent look and style. *Truman*, a comedy, is evenly and brightly lit. *Mirror Mirror* has a glossy "studio" look. *The Lunch Date*, inspired by the black-and-white photography of

Alfred Stieglitz, maintains a look that is consistent with that style (Figure 12.3).

There are two basic artificial lights: hard light and soft light. *Hard light* has a single or point source, such as a candle, a bulb, or the sun; whereas *soft light* has a broad, or diffused, source. Hard lights include incandescent, quartz, ellipsoidal, and Fresnel instruments. The sun is considered to be a hard light. Soft lighting instruments include scoops, strips, and banks. Hard lights have a longer throw than soft lights and are more contrasty. Hard lights create shadows; soft lights fill in the shadows.

Classic three-point lighting uses three lights: key, fill, and back. *Key light* provides the main source of illumination on the set or subject. *Fill light* provides detail within the shadows and softens the impact of the source light. *Back light* outlines the subject, separating it from the background. From this basic setup, both naturalistic and stylized lighting designs can be produced, depending on the angle, distance, and intensity of the light from these three positions.

Lighting should generally be motivated (i.e., we should know the source of the light). Sunlight or moonlight shining through a window can be the source, or key, light. Other lights can fill in the rest of the set to reduce contrast. Contrast should not be so pronounced that the part of the actor's face in the key light is well exposed, but the other side of the face is dark.

Figure 12.3 For *The Lunch Date*, studying the light at the location meant scheduling a shot for a particular time of day to obtain the desired effect.

To develop a comprehensive and effective lighting plan, the director should consider the following questions:

- What is the mood you want to convey?
- Do you want high-key (Whistler, Degas) or low-key (Rembrandt, Caravaggio) lighting?
- Do you want high or low contrast?
- Is the scene intended to have natural or artificial light?
- Do the shadows have hard or soft edges?
- Is the key light at a high angle, at eye level, or at a low angle?
- Is the lighting setup frontal, broad, narrow, or backlit?
- What are the practicals (real lamps) in the scene?
- What is the source light?
- What is the time of day?
- Must any practical lights be replaced?
- What is the intensity of the light?
- What is the direction of the light?
- What is the quality of the light?
- How can continuity of light quality be maintained from shot to shot?

The human eye is more sensitive than film. Use a contrast viewing filter to see what light really exists on the set?

Lighting for Exteriors

Shooting outdoors can be tricky if the production relies only on the sun for illumination. The sun's arc in the sky causes the direction of the light, the shadows, and even the intensity of the light to change constantly. In addition, the sun is often obscured. Should you wait for the sun to come out from behind the clouds? A good trick is to look at the sky in the reflection of your sunglasses. The sun will appear as a bright ball behind the clouds, and you can estimate when it might emerge from behind them.

There are several methods for overcoming the powerful influence of the sun. One is to erect large translucent squares called *silks*, which can act as a filter for the sun. With silks, a soft constant light can be maintained all day. If the sun goes behind clouds, electric lights can be pumped into the silk to maintain a consistent f-stop (see "Exposure" on page 140). Silks work only for medium and close shots. In a wide shot, they might appear in the frame. Try to grab the wide shot when the light on the set is appropriate for the scene.

Reflectors, or *bounce cards*, are commonly used in the field for fill light. When placed just off camera, these shiny or white surfaces reflect the sun's light (or any light source) onto the actors' faces. They produce additional light that separates the actor from the background.

When shooting outdoors, the company is at the mercy of the light and the weather. "Chasing the sun" is a common exterior location occupation. You cannot shoot until the sun has risen, and when it falls, the fading light will not be strong enough to light the scene.

Lighting for Interiors

Interior lighting comes with a different set of problems. Although day interiors can rely on the sun, it is easier to maintain a consistent look with artificial lights placed outside the windows. Study your location. From where does the light come? What are the practicals doing? In most cases, it is a matter of taking existing source light and enhancing it to obtain the desired f-stop.

The biggest hurdle to overcome with interior lighting is space. In a practical location, the combination of the lights, the set pieces, the crew, and the actors allows little room to maneuver. It is recommended that you use spreaders to create a grid from which to hang the lights.

> There were light problems: This gym was lit with fluorescent lights. I didn't have the time or money to gel all those fluorescent lights. There were over 120 of them, so we had to do all our lighting with the fluorescents, which meant we had to find an equipment house nearby that rented fluorescent fills.
>
> *Howard*

Lighting for Documentaries

A documentary production company travels with little equipment. A few lighting instruments and a bounce card are usually sufficient to light a set for an interview. Outside, a sun-gun that runs off a battery belt will help fill in dark areas; there's no need to run the light to a power source. This gives the documentary crew freedom to be anywhere for filming. This is imperative when shooting cinema verité style.

> As an aesthetic, I prefer exterior interviews. In documentaries I made about drive-in movie theaters and a traveling tent circus, it enabled me to use the exterior environment creatively in the interview setup. I like to avoid lights and usually just set up a flex-fill [bounce card] in an exterior location. I know that this is

somewhat unorthodox because most documentarians put their subjects in offices or living rooms where they have complete control over the light. A major liability of exterior interviews is the sound. Documentary subjects always seem to live near a major airport!

Jan

Lighting for Video

In the past, heavy video cameras on pedestals in a three-camera setup required copious amounts of light. This is still true of any multiple-camera setup. To capture an image from several positions at the same time, there must be a flood of light on any set. As the look of video steadily began to approach that of film, the lighting schemes also became similar.

Even today, the look of video is unlike that of film because the light sensitivities of film emulsion and videotape stock differ. This results in different depths of field and different contrast ratios. Film can hold an average f-stop of 8 to 11 in a situation where the light goes from an f-stop of 22 to 2.8, but video cannot. The contrast ratio of video is approximately 40:1, equivalent to five stops. Film has a contrast ratio of 128:1, or approximately seven stops.

The video image holds up well in close-ups, but the image begins to break apart in very wide shots. This is significant because one of the primary distinctions between these two media is projection. Video projection is limited, so most of what we see is geared for the television screen. This frame size also is good for close-ups, but it is difficult to hold wide shots, as the elements in the frame are less distinct.

When shooting video, avoid white backdrops and red costumes. The white tends to "blow out" the frame, and red may bleed. Never shoot into the sun. A film camera can be adjusted to shoot at the sun, but direct sunlight can damage sensitive components in a video camera.

In low light, some video cameras can produce a ghost, or comet-tail image, on the screen when the camera pans or tilts. These lasting impressions of highlights in the scene appear as slowly fading streaks. Only by pumping in additional light can this problem be resolved.

Most video cameras are programmed with an automatic iris. This means that if the camera is recording a scene in a room and then pans toward a window, the light from the sun in the window will force the aperture to adjust quickly. The adjustment, which is visible, is a dead giveaway that the image was produced by a video camera. To avoid this problem, use the manual iris override.

Ultimately, video production is tied to broadcast standards. Using a waveform monitor while recording allows the videographer to determine how much light is needed to create a signal on the monitor that conforms to broadcast standards. In some cases, lighting that is meant to set a mood will prove unacceptable. The solution is more light.

To illustrate this point, consider video distribution. Suppose that a film with many night scenes is scheduled to be released on video. It is transferred from its 35mm negative to a one-inch low-contrast video master. Half-inch videotapes are then "struck" for marketing. By this stage, the night scenes are so dark and muddy that it is difficult for the viewer to see what is happening. As a result of this problem, many buyers for the video market, especially the foreign market, do not want films with too many dark, moody, or night sequences.

Camera Movement

When choosing a cinematographic style for your piece, you should consider whether the camera will be static or moving, and why. Like lighting, camera movement should be motivated. Movement can come from within the frame, the motion of the frame itself, or a combination of the two. The camera can be stationary, with the action in front of the lens choreographed, or staged, to its angle. Actors then move toward the camera into a close-up or away from the camera into a long shot.

In dialogue sequences, the actors are often in a stationary position. The fixed angle on a close-up or over-the-shoulder shot allows the editor to bounce back and forth between takes, creating the illusion that the characters are speaking to one another. It is easy to place actors in one position to simplify the job of covering the scene. Will the scene ultimately look stiff? Do people in this situation actually stand in one place and talk to one another, or do they move in the space, sit down, open a window, and so on?

To give her film an interesting pace, the director can use the camera to bring energy into a scene by moving the frame. A pan, tilt, dolly, zoom, or crane shot adds tremendous vitality to the images. For example, suppose that two characters are eating dinner in a restaurant. A waiter walks through the kitchen door and places their order on the table. You can use the waiter to motivate the pan or dolly through the restaurant to the table. In a dialogue sequence that is photographed with a slow, constantly moving dolly, the movement is not motivated by any action but will add mystery and tension.

Balance

Excessive camera movement can distract the audience from the flow of the story. The director must find a way to motivate the camera and to keep the movements subtle enough so that there is a balance between the storytelling and the energy from the camera. If the script calls for a bold camera action, such as a snap zoom or a fast dolly, the director should not hesitate to use all the facilities at her fingertips, within the confines of the budget and the schedule. A shot with a lot of energy that cuts to a static shot has a particular kind of effect, as does a high-energy shot, such as a fast-moving dolly, that cuts to another high-energy shot, like a moving crane.

One Long Take

Choreographing the camera, lights, and actors in a single shot is an ideal way to maintain the energy within a scene. It allows the actors to develop the beats within the scene organically. Using the dynamics of these elements of photography in one shot is the height of cinema aesthetics. However, staging a single-shot scene is time-consuming. If you find that the shot becomes too difficult to execute, you can resort to covering the scene in several different shots.

A single-shot scene photographed in a single take is unusable unless it has the correct pace and rhythm. Therefore, when you design a sequence to be taken all in one shot, shoot some inserts to give yourself an "out" in the editing room. Often, to save a single-take scene, the editor can use the beginning of a scene, cut to a matching insert or close-up, and then return to the single-take scene, using a different but better take.

Creating Camera Movement

There are several ways to move the camera:

- Pan
- Tilt
- Pan/tilt combination
- Zoom (cheap dolly)
- Dolly (with or without tracks)
- Steadicam
- Hand-held camera work
- Crane
- Car, helicopter, boat (traveling shots)

These methods can be used in different combinations. (There is more on these tools later in this chapter.)

Editing

Think ahead to the editing room and consider editorial techniques when choreographing camera movements. Learn to think like an editor. Ask yourself these questions:

- What will the shot about to be taken cut from?
- What will the shot about to be taken cut to?

Create a visual flow that disguises any editorial technique unless used for dramatic effect, such as a smash cut, a wipe, or a flip.

Some of the best directors have years of editing room experience. Editors quickly develop a sense of what works well cut together and what does not. All directors, DPs, and script supervisors should be aware of how a scene that is being shot will ultimately cut together.

Coverage

A scene is photographed, or *covered*, from a variety of angles and points of view. When pieced together in the editing room, these angles should represent the director's visual plan (Figure 12.4).

> When they were sitting at the table, I covered the scene in a standard way. I did a medium wide shot, both of them in frame, and then came in for close-ups. Then I got insert coverage of the plates.
> *Adam*

One of the director's main duties is to deliver proper coverage to the editing room. *Coverage* is the sum of all of the shots that go into the making of a sequence. There might be 20 shots that make up or cover a one-minute scene or one shot that covers a five-minute scene.

A key to adequate coverage is to shoot the important elements of each scene from more than one angle. The scene with multiple shots—perhaps a combination of a master shot, two-shots, close-ups, and dollies—is picked apart in the editing room, taking 10 frames from one angle, 20 feet from another, and so on, until the scene has the desired pace and rhythm.

> Making a student short film must be different from making a professional short film. Certainly, as a

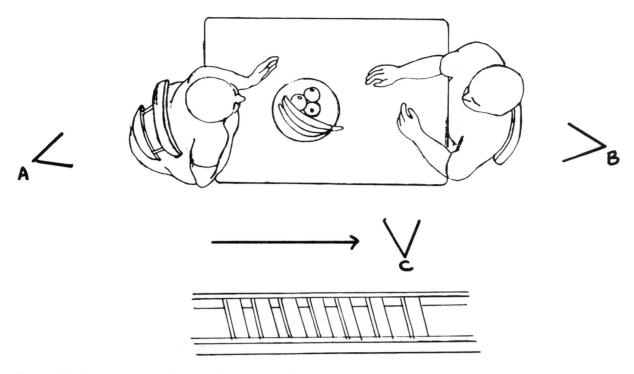

Figure 12.4 The camera angle on the left is a mirror of the angle on the right. A third position is added when camera angle C moves on the dolly from left to right. (Floor plan from *The Lunch Date*.)

student, you are going to encounter a lot of problems with just getting the film made: getting equipment, getting a good crew—that's always difficult—dealing with a school's bureaucracy. And you're never going to have a perfect shoot. You're never going to have a perfect piece. Nothing is going to go as planned.

Adam

Students: Many students plan too many shots. Experience will show you how to plan a day. A good rule is to aim for five well-executed shots rather than 10 sloppy ones.

Documentaries

For some documentaries, you might need cutaways and a reverse to the interviewer. These shots are usually mandatory so that the editor can keep the text flowing without a jump cut on the speaker. Besides learning from personal experience, the best way to learn coverage is to study great narrative and documentary film sequences. Count the number of shots and observe the variety of angles and how they cut together. On what line or movement is the edit made?

Continuity

Editors want to make a seamless picture, and this can only be accomplished with the proper coverage. The best way to guarantee a seamless cut is to maintain the continuity within a scene and to overlap action.

Continuity is the maintenance of the same action throughout a scene. If a character smokes a cigarette, it should get progressively shorter as the scene unfolds. If you shoot out of sequence, which is often the case, maintain the cigarette at a length that will match the real time of the scene.

Overlapping Action

Cutting on an action produces a smooth transition from one shot to the next. Suppose a character sits down in a wide shot. The next camera position is a medium shot of the character in the chair. On "Action," the director should have the actor "sit into" the shot. Having the action of sitting from both angles will enable the editor to find a perfect place in the action to make the cut.

180° Rule

One of the more confusing areas of coverage has to do with the 180° rule. Although not inviolable (many directors have disregarded this rule), cutting from one character who is speaking to another character can look odd if the rule is not followed.

The *eye-line*, or where a character is looking, relates to screen direction. Viewers must be able to follow the eye-line from the character's eyes to what the character sees. The camera operator needs to be sure of the match so that the cut will work in the editing room.

Refer back to Figure 12.1. If the director never crosses the 180° line, a character will always appear to be looking at the person to whom he is speaking. If the director crosses the line, it might appear as though the character is looking away from the person to whom he is speaking.

If character A looks at character B from screen left to screen right, character B must look at character A from screen right to screen left if the audience is to believe that they are speaking face to face. For an over-the-shoulder shot, the camera should be placed over character A's right shoulder. The complementary, or reverse, angle would have the camera placed over character B's left shoulder. With this setup, the characters will appear on screen to have eye contact with one another.

For a close-up of character A, the camera is placed where character B was sitting, or even a little closer, and the actor is asked to look to camera right. The off-camera actor can put his face right next to the lens. This gives the on-camera actor the correct eye-line. If the confines of the set do not allow the character B actor to stand next to the camera, he must deliver his lines from elsewhere. To ensure correct eye-line, the camera operator can place a piece of white tape on the right side of the lens and ask the actor to speak to the tape.

When shooting a dialogue scene in which the camera swings around to shoot the reverse angle, the director and script supervisor can easily become confused as to which direction the character should look. Should he look screen left or screen right? Rather than take a chance, shoot it both ways. This gives the editor an opportunity to choose the correct position in the editing room.

Keeping Score

The director risks losing the audience's attention if they are confused about technical points such as who

is speaking to whom or where the characters are placed spatially in relation to one another. Both of these problems can easily occur, such as when a scene is shot exclusively in close-ups. The audience needs reference points, such as a master shot that defines the space.

Screen Direction in Movement

Suppose that a character walks from screen right to screen left. If the next shot is a continuation of the walking shot, the character should maintain the same screen direction. If another character walks in the opposite direction and is intercut with the first character for parallel action, the audience will assume that

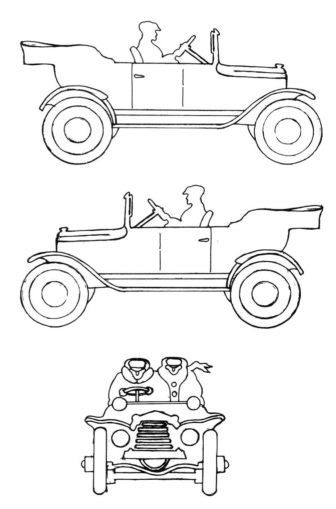

Figure 12.5 Vehicles should maintain a consistent direction. One way to change direction is to have the vehicle come toward the camera.

they are walking toward each other and might eventually meet.

A moving vehicle traveling screen left to right should always maintain that direction unless the director wants to change the direction of the vehicle. She can execute this change by having the vehicle move directly toward or away from the camera. The director can then change the screen direction on the next shot (Figure 12.5).

Crossing the Line

You can cross the 180° line with a dolly move or an insert. By changing the audience's viewpoint, you establish a new 180° line. Make it clear to the audience where the scene is taking place. If, in a master shot, the director has clearly indicated where the characters are positioned and what the set pieces look like, it makes it easier to move the characters and the camera in this space to maintain clarity.

Shot Perspectives

A shot can be taken from several different perspectives. The director informs the audience of the point of view, whether it be that of the character, the director, or a "god's eye" view.

The Fourth Wall

In the theater, the audience often looks at a proscenium stage. The two side walls and the rear of the stage make up the set. The wall on which the curtain is drawn is called the *fourth wall*. This is the invisible window through which the audience witnesses the events of the play.

In film and video, the camera lens is the fourth wall. If a character speaks directly to the audience—that is, if he speaks directly to the camera—he "breaks" the fourth wall (Figure 12.6). Because this can be disturbing to the audience, it is done for dramatic or comic effect only. If the character looks just to the right or left of the lens or over or under it, the result does not betray the drama.

Point-of-View Shot

An effective way of using the fourth wall and taking full advantage of the "voyeur" aspects of cinema is to use the point-of-view shot. The camera (usually hand-held) can become the character by moving with an empty foreground, as when a character stomps through the woods, the camera unsteady and the breathing heavy.

The "Reveal"

The "reveal" is a rich piece of film language. In this technique, the scene starts with a pan, dolly, or zoom shot that stops on a character, prop, or location that reveals something about the story.

In the cafeteria, I knew there would be a couple of dolly shots to have her walk down the aisle, to have

Figure 12.6 Looking directly at the camera lens breaks the fourth wall. Scene from *Mirror Mirror*.

him revealed. And then I figured out, I would like to do a pan to reveal that she sat down at the wrong place.

Adam

Specialty Shots

Confer with your DP and consult the *American Cinematographer's Handbook* to determine the best way to shoot special situations, such as variable speeds, shooting off the television, day for night, matte shots, miniatures, split screens, blue screens, and underwater photography.

EQUIPMENT

As a director, you need not have a complete technical knowledge of the camera or other equipment, but you should be acquainted with its capabilities and uses. The director can better convey her vision if she is familiar with camera techniques. You should to be completely familiar with the tools with which you will manipulate the content and ambience of the frame.

Camera and Related Equipment

Camera

A motion picture camera is a lightproof mechanical device through which the unexposed film or tape stock travels. A film camera contains the following components:

- The film chamber is a lightproof compartment that holds the film.
- The drive mechanism is the power source for the operation of the camera.
- The claw pulls the stock down into the film gate, which holds it steady for proper exposure.
- The shutter blocks light from the stock as it moves between successive exposures.
- The viewfinder allows the camera operator to see what the camera sees.
- The lens mount is an attachment to the camera body for lenses.

A video camera works on the same principle as the film camera, but with magnetic tape instead of film stock. The video camera has an optical-electrical system that converts images into video signals that can be stored on magnetic tape.

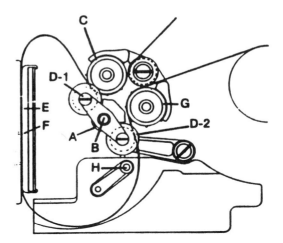

Figure 12.7 Threading diagram. (Courtesy of Arriflex.)

Magazine

If the film stock comes on a very large roll (400 to 1,000 feet), it is placed in a magazine, which in turn is attached to the camera body for threading the film past the lens aperture. One side of the magazine is the supply reel. The film passes behind the lens for exposure and is spooled on the take-up side of the magazine (Figure 12.7).

Aperture

The plate between the lens and the film is the aperture plate. The aperture itself is a rectangle cut out of the plate through which light from the lens shines. The base of the film rests on the other half of the gate, which is called the *pressure plate.*

Shutter

Once the film claw has moved a frame through the film gate, the shutter opens to allow light to hit the film. The film comes to a complete halt before the shutter opens again for the next exposure.

Exposure

The amount of light that passes through the lens and the duration of time to create an image is called the *exposure.* Changes in the amount of light are measured in stops. On the lens is a ring that can open or close down the stops. Changes in exposure can also affect the depth of field.

Light Meter

The exposure of an object on film or tape is related to the amount of light falling on the subject, which is known as *incident light*. An incident light meter measures the amount of light falling on the subject from all angles. The total amount of light on the subject can also be determined by measuring the light reflected off the subject. This reflected light is measured with a reflectance light meter. Whereas the incident light meter is pointed from the subject toward the camera to read the light, the reflectance light meter is pointed at the subject. The meter reading tells the camera operator which stop to set the lens to in order to obtain the desired results.

Lenses

Lenses are interchangeable. The lens placed on the front of a camera is determined by the needs of the shot. One shot might require a long lens (250mm), whereas the next shot might call for a wide-angle lens (5.7mm). "Super"-speed lenses can be helpful in low-light situations.

> Because it wasn't a thesis, I wasn't allowed to use a lot of equipment at Columbia. I basically got the dregs. I knew there were a couple of things we had to rent. I rented high-speed lenses for the stuff in Grand Central, which economically worked out better than renting the many lights it would have taken to get exposure.
>
> *Adam*

Although a wide variety of lenses is available in a camera package, most lenses fall into three basic categories:

WIDE-ANGLE LENSES. These lenses (5.9–12mm) are used to capture a lot of information, or *picture*, in the frame. They take advantage of low-light situations, hold a large depth of field, absorb camera motion, and can be used to distort the image.

NORMAL LENSES. Normal lenses (16–75mm) are used to gain a "normal" perspective on a scene or character. They hold a considerable depth of field.

TELEPHOTO, OR LONG, LENSES. These lenses (75–250mm) are used to shoot beyond unwanted foreground detail, to flatten and compress the perspective, or to create a dramatic visual statement.

Zoom Lens

A popular lens is the zoom, which allows the director of photography to change frame sizes quickly merely by "racking" through the rings of the zoom lens. Hard, or fixed, lenses, especially high-speed lenses, can expose film with less light than is needed for a zoom lens. Most video cameras use zoom lenses exclusively.

Filters

Filters, diopters, and gels can be placed directly in front of the lens to obtain a correct color balance or an interesting effect, to reduce light entering the camera, or as a polarizer.

Eyepiece

The camera eyepiece, which allows the director and the DP to see exactly what the lens sees, has a series of thin black frame lines that show what is inside the frame, on the edge of the frame, or outside the frame lines. This is especially helpful when determining how close the microphone can come to the actor without actually appearing in the frame.

These black lines also allow the camera operator to determine what will appear in the television frame if it differs from the aspect ratio chosen for the shoot. The television frame is smaller than the aspect ratio for film. If the action occurs within these lines, it is referred to as being *in TV safe*.

Tests

Many elements (film or video stock, lens size, filters, lighting, and f-stop), combined with the director's aesthetic design for the shot, are calibrated to cause a specific result. If the result the director wants is complicated or out of the ordinary in any way, it is recommended that tests be made in preproduction to determine how the desired results can be achieved.

Grip Package

The grip package brought to the set includes all the elements needed to move the camera, including tripods, heads, a dolly, and track. Heavy rigging equipment, such as rope and clamps, rides with the grips. The grips are also responsible for the apple boxes, which are used to raise the height of set pieces, actors, or camera operators.

Head

To keep its movement fluid, the camera is placed on a *head*, which allows for smooth pans and tilts. The head can be placed on a dolly or crane so that the pans and tilts can be accompanied by the physical movement of the camera.

Tripod

For static shots, tilts, and pans, the head is placed on a tripod, or *sticks*. For low-angle shots or if the sticks are too tall, the head is placed on a plywood base, on a high-hat, or even directly onto sandbags.

Dolly

A dolly is a moving tripod system, usually with attached chairs for the camera operator and the director. If the surface on which you wish to dolly is smooth, you might not need to lay track. Track must be laid on rough surfaces, however. The dolly is placed on the rails, and it glides smoothly along the track.

To extend the camera off the dolly, an additional piece of equipment, called a *jib arm*, is placed perpendicular to the post. The head is put on the end of the jib arm.

Crane

A crane is a dolly that has a movable extension arm. The camera is placed on this arm, which moves parallel to the ground and can lift the camera to great heights. Cranes are cumbersome, expensive, and unwieldy, but crane shots add a great deal of energy to a scene, especially one in which the director wants to move from a close shot to a very wide perspective, or vice versa.

Car, Helicopter, Boat

The ultimate in dynamic camera work is to shoot with your camera moving on a fast vehicle. Slow-moving cars are sometimes used as an alternative to a dolly. If you plan a shot from a car, it useful to let some air out of the tires. This adds smoothness to the shot. Shooting into a car or from a car, helicopter, or boat requires special mounts. You can also rent a camera car, which is a truck equipped with camera mounts in several places for specific kinds of shots.

Hand-held Camera Work

Hand-held camera work brings a special dynamism to a scene. A slight movement in the camera, especially if the angle is from a character's point of view, adds both realism and tension to a shot. Be advised, however, that too much movement in a shot disorients viewers. Hand-held camera work is most often used to give a documentary, or "realistic," feeling to a shot.

From a practical point of view, if you are pressed for time, shooting from a hand-held camera position saves considerable setup time. Use wide lenses if possible to stabilize the image.

Steadicam

The Steadicam® is used today to provide a steady, interesting movement shot in films and videos. In this system, a gyro-balanced camera is placed on a rig that enables the operator to go where a dolly cannot go and obtain a smooth tracking shot. For example, a Steadicam operator can go up a stairway, through a crowd, or from a walking position to a seated position on a crane.

Lighting Package

The lighting package consists of all the instruments and globes the DP requires, plus lengths of cable for moving the lighting instruments some distance from the power source.

TRICKS

Over the course of your career in the film and video business, you will be forced to devise unique solutions to problems, and these solutions will become part of your personal bag of tricks. Some common camera tricks you might someday need to employ are described in the following sections.

Poor Man's Process

To shoot a scene with characters in a vehicle at night can be expensive and time-consuming. At night, the rear window looks black. Shoot the vehicle in a stationary position, either inside or outside, and add these three elements:

1. Have two crew members sit on the rear bumper and gently bounce the vehicle to simulate movement.
2. Strafe the back window with a light at intermittent intervals. This simulates passing cars.
3. In postproduction, add the sound of an engine.

Simple Mattes

Using a hard line in the frame, such as the horizon, black out the sky at the top of the frame and photograph the action in the bottom of the frame. Rewind the camera, black out the lower part of the frame, and reexpose the film with an image that will now be the "sky" part of the frame. This eliminates a costly painting and lab fee.

Night for Day

You will often run out of sunlight as you try to meet the day's schedule. For tight shots, HMI lights simulate the color temperature of the sun. Therefore, even when the sun has set, you can still shoot as if it were day, and the material should match. Use this technique in emergencies only. Do not attempt to shoot all day and then all night just because you can get the exposure.

PRODUCER
Support

The producer's goal is to keep the operation running smoothly with minimum personal involvement. The director runs the show during production, and the producer should not interfere unless he is needed. He should feel confident in his choice of director and allow her to complete her task.

RESPONSIBILITIES OF THE PRODUCER

Laboratory

The producer should establish a contact person at the laboratory who will serve as a liaison through production and postproduction. During the shoot, the liaison at the lab should report daily to the DP about the quality of the footage.

Equipment

The producer must make sure that the equipment package is kept up-to-date. Any equipment that is not being used should be returned.

Rental House

It is the producer's job to negotiate with the film or video equipment rental house. This can be an intimidating experience, but it is possible, even for the beginner, to work out a very reasonable deal and to turn the process into a learning experience.

Treat rental houses as more than just a place to pick up equipment. Go there with all your equipment questions before you decide what you want. This is the first step in being a more informed consumer.

Negotiate with an equipment house for the best values just as you would deal with a car or stereo salesperson. The rental house has expensive equipment on the shelves, and they would rather rent it for a fraction of the full cost than let it sit there. This means you can shop around to different equipment rental houses looking for the best value and use one bidder against another to get the best price.

The producer and the DP need to determine what lights, camera, and grip equipment actually are required. Visit the equipment house and ask to be shown around. Establishing an in-person relationship will make it easier for you to negotiate. A tour will also give you the opportunity to see if the rental house is an impressive establishment or is a two-bit operation.

The most expensive way to rent a piece of equipment is by the day. If you need the equipment for a week, you can get up to half off the aggregate daily price. Ask what kind of discount you can get for a set period of time. This is easier, of course, if you have done business with the company in the past and have established your credibility.

The following are other well-known ways to get discounts:

- Weekends count as one day. If you pick your equipment up on a Friday and bring it back on Monday morning, you pay for only one day.
- Travel days and holidays often are not charged.
- Use cash as an incentive. After you have negotiated a deal, offer to pay cash up front. This might get you an additional 10 to 15 percent off the one-day price.

Equipment houses make money charging for accessories that you thought were included in the package. Get a complete list of what you need, and make sure the price you are quoted covers everything.

The rental house will need to see proof of insurance. They won't let their equipment out without it. If you are not covered by a policy through your film or video program or are an independent who cannot afford private insurance, you will have to pay the rental house's rate. Most houses offer some kind of in-house coverage, which might cost up to 10 percent of the rental fee for the equipment.

Students and independents: Being a student or an independent on a low budget is not necessarily a liability. Tell those with whom you deal that you must try to get the best price you can because you simply don't have the cash. This predicament might get you sympathy *and* a better deal.

TECHNICAL CONSIDERATIONS
Power

If a shoot needs more power or a different power source than that provided at the location, it is necessary to supply a generator to power the lights. Generators can be noisy, so be prepared to run extra cable to move the generator as far away from the set as possible.

Be prepared to change fuses on location if you are using the power from wall sockets. If you know how much power each instrument draws and you know how much amperage is available from each socket, you can plug in all your instruments without blowing a fuse. Ideally, the director of photography or the gaffer should gather this information during a preproduction location scout.

Lights

Lighting instruments are placed on heavy-duty legs called *light stands*. These supports can be lowered or raised to position the instrument at a specific height. Sandbags are placed on the base of the stands for security. Flags, cookies, or tree branches are often placed directly in front of a lamp to create effects or to prevent the light from falling directly onto the camera lens, creating a flare.

The greater the light that illuminates the scene, the greater the detail that will be exposed onto the film. Less light, less detail. Areas of the scene that are lit will be exposed; unlit areas will "fall away."

> When you're in the field, you've got to trust the cinematographer because you don't want to interrupt the interview. I see the scene in a wide shot because of where I sit as a sound person. If you film in someone's living room and position your subject on a couch, I'm not sure they feel very comfortable because all of a sudden, their living room has been transformed into a film set. There are lights and cables running everywhere. I prefer the naturalness of exterior interviews for that reason and have used them quite extensively in all of my films prior to *Mirror Mirror*.
> *Jan*

Fans

In a tight location, it very quickly becomes warm under the lights. Be prepared to ventilate the room, and turn the lights on only when necessary.

> It was very hot. The conditions were definitely not very pleasant because there were these lights, and the actors were wearing masks.
> *Jan*

KEY POINTS

1. Use camera language to shape the frame. This includes lights, camera positions, and lenses.
2. What you shoot determines what can be edited, so shoot ample coverage.
3. Plan your transitions from shot to shot and from scene to scene. Shoot overlaps.
4. Blocking means that you can move the camera, the actors, or both.

chapter thirteen

Sound

There was a problem we weren't prepared for: the hum of the fluorescent lights.

Howard

DIRECTOR

Record Clean Tracks

During the past 20 years, the processing and transmission of sound to film audiences has undergone a radical evolution. Today, projection sound systems like THX®, Dolby®, Domino®, and Surround Sound® have heightened the aural dynamic of the film experience. Digital sound reproduction is drastically changing the way that audiences hear sound tracks in theaters. However, with everything that can now be done in postproduction to process and deliver a complex and exciting sound track, the most important step in this chain is still the first one: the recording of good clean sounds during principal photography.

PRODUCTION SOUND

The sound recorded on the set, called *production sound*, is an extremely important aspect of your short film or video, and it should be examined, recorded, and mixed with the same care and enthusiasm given to the visuals. Production sound consists of dialogue, the natural sounds associated with each scene, and any other sounds that might be of value during the postproduction process. The person responsible for recording production sound is the sound recordist. This individual is also known as the *production mixer* because he controls, or *mixes*, the levels of the dialogue spoken on the set. Equally important is the boom operator, who positions the microphone for optimum recording levels.

Although all sounds, including dialogue, can be recreated during the postproduction process, it is economically and aesthetically best to record as much of the dialogue and natural ambience as possible at the location during principal photography.

Dialogue can be replaced during postproduction with a process called *automatic dialogue replacement* (ADR), but ADR can be time-consuming, costly, and problematic, especially for the beginner. It requires that the actors report to a studio months after the shoot to duplicate their original performances line by line. Even having to duplicate unique sounds from a particular location can be a problem.

Aesthetically, the dialogue recorded on the set is usually the best representation of each scene. There might be interference, of course. Unavoidable noises from traffic or airplanes might make it impossible to record clean dialogue.

In the long run, the sound recordist can save the production time and money by delivering an accurate rendition of the production dialogue. A little extra time setting up a microphone or baffling an annoying sound can save hundreds, even thousands, of dollars in postproduction.

This emphasis on location sound recording is all the more critical in 16mm. The 35mm format has better sound-reproduction capabilities. With 16mm, any problems with sound quality on the set are compounded later in postproduction.

Along with a mastery of his craft, the sound recordist should have a thorough understanding of the postproduction process—that is, what happens to the sounds after they are recorded in production. Being aware of what can be accomplished in postproduction gives the recordist a proper context for judging the work he must do and for properly evaluating the sounds he must sometimes fight to record clearly (Figure 13.1).

The sound recordist must also have a clear understanding of all the crafts that interact with his, such as camera, lighting, and grip. He needs to find a way to achieve the best sound possible within the limitations of each lens choice, camera move, or lighting setup.

SOUND PREPARATION

Just as the director and the director of photography (DP) previsualize the picture, the director and the sound person "preaudiolize" the sounds. This requires reading and breaking down the script from the sound perspective: how much dialogue, how many characters, the nature of the locations, any extra sounds that must be recorded. The script usually reveals many of the challenges for the sound recordist. Often, a bit of business or a joke relies on the presence of a sound, or at least the cue of a sound that will be added to the picture in postproduction, such as a gunshot, a doorbell, or the sound of screeching brakes.

> We sat down and made a list of wild sound before the shoot, e.g., the sound of a squishing sole, a ball hitting the court, a hand on the rope. . . . We had a list of sounds that took about an hour to get once the shoot was over.
>
> *Howard*

Playback

When examining the script, the sound recordist looks for any situation that might require unusual equipment such as radio microphones or a playback machine. The latter is necessary when actors must sing, dance, or otherwise respond on the set to previously recorded music. Because this music will be used later in the film or video, it must be recorded with a reference or pilot tone (SMPTE time code for video) so it can be synchronized with the picture. In addition, the recordist will need a second Nagra to play the source material on set. Unless the sound person is familiar with handling playback duties, he may need to bring in a specialist on days when playback is required.

Location Scout

Having "preaudiolized" the project's sound requirements, the sound recordist should visit the locations next if possible. Walking through the actual spaces in advance will reveal any inherent sound problems that the sound recordist must deal with before the start of principal photography. The one location choice that has no inherent sound problems is a stage, which is a soundproof environment. The only noises you should hear there are the actors' voices.

When visiting a site, the sound recordist needs to consider the following:

- How large is the space?
- What are the acoustics of the space? (Hard surfaces reflect sound.)

Figure 13.1 It is important to pick up wild sounds on location. Photo from the filming of *Truman.*

- Can a loud refrigerator or air conditioning system be shut down?
- Can neighbors be controlled?
- Are key windows right above traffic noise?
- If the location is near an airport, what are the air traffic patterns?
- Will sound blankets solve the noise problems?
- What time of day will the shooting occur?

Production teams often scout locations on weekends when it is quiet and peaceful. Then the crew shows up to shoot on a Monday, and the street activity makes the noise level inside impossible for sound recording. Therefore, it is advised that you scout the location on the day of the week and at the approximate time that you'll want to shoot.

The location manager can research any street maintenance scheduled to take place in and around your location during the time of the shoot. Many unfortunate crews have found their supposedly quiet neighborhood suddenly invaded by a team of construction workers and their equipment. Once they get started, there is nothing you can do about the noise.

Be sure to listen for planes. If a location is on a flight path, the sound recordist will be hard-pressed to record clean sound.

If recording clean dialogue in a particular location appears to be impossible, the production manager should be notified about the problem and asked if it's possible to look for another location that is more "sound-friendly." If the location is locked, the mixer will have to do the best he can.

> We scouted the gym and listened for noise. There weren't any classes because the school was closed, but the bell was still working on a timer and scheduled to go off every 45 minutes. We had the janitor dismantle the bell so it wouldn't go off in the middle of the shot.
>
> *Howard*

It's possible that the sound recordist might walk onto the set for the first time on the first day of principal photography, whereas the director has visited it many times. In this case, the recordist must play catch-up.

RESPONSIBILITIES OF THE SOUND TEAM

The following are the basic responsibilities of the film sound team:

- Record "clean" dialogue
- Match sound perspective with camera angle
- Record sound effects to accompany the shot
- Record room tone
- Record additional sounds
- Record the scene so it will cut smoothly (sound continuity)
- Take accurate sound notes

Dialogue

The sound recordist's primary responsibility is to record all the dialogue spoken on the set *clean*—that is, unencumbered by any other ambient sounds connected with the shot. Just as the DP is responsible for focus and proper exposure, the sound recordist strives to record dialogue at consistent levels that can be replayed clearly. A great effort is expended to create magic on the set, and it should be recorded properly. You can't duplicate a magical performance in a sound studio.

If it is impossible to record the dialogue clean, the sound team records it *dirty*—that is, cluttered with the overbearing sounds of airplanes, cars, or ocean surf in the background. Although unusable as the final product, this recording is used as a reference, or guide track, in the editing room for both cutting and ADR work.

Perspective

An important goal of recording dialogue is that it should be consistent with the point of view of the camera and from the perspective of the lens used for the shot. If the camera sees the action from across a room, the sound should approximate that visual perspective and should sound somewhat distant. In a close-up, the sound should have an intimate, almost overbearing presence. Ideally, viewers should hear the sound from the same point of view from which they see the visuals. Of course, there are times when it's necessary to sacrifice perspective, especially if proper perspective means that the dialogue will not be heard.

There are times when the camera is so far away from the action that performers can only be recorded if their voices are transmitted to a receiver from microphones concealed in their clothing. An example of this is a scene shot with a long lens of a couple walking along a beach. The audience sees the couple from a distance but hears them as if they were right there. To help correct this "unnatural" perspective, sound effects of waves, seabirds, and wind can be added during postproduction.

Sound Effects

The sound recordist should capture during production as many of the ambient sounds and live effects connected with the shot as possible. Examples are footsteps, rustling clothes, and slamming doors. These extra sounds should be properly slated and labeled for future reference. They will be mixed in separately during postproduction.

For example, in a bar scene, after the principal photography is completed or before the extras are dismissed, the sound recordist should ask the assistant director for a short recording session in which the crowd chats, drinks, sings, and cheers as though it were in a real bar. Two minutes of this sound will furnish the sound effects editor with ample material to create a full bar atmosphere. Because the main dialogue is recorded while the crowd is silent, the editor will have the dialogue and the background sounds on two different tracks, giving her complete control over volume levels.

Room Tone

If you stand on a set and ask everyone to be still and quiet, the silence you will hear is *room tone*. The sound team should record 60 seconds of room tone from each set before leaving the location. The tone should be recorded with the lights on and the full cast and crew on the set, just as if dialogue were being recorded. The AD will ask everyone to freeze in their place for one minute. These 60 seconds of tone can then be copied and used in postproduction to fill in holes and smooth out the dialogue tracks when preparing for the mix. If it is difficult to get the cast and crew to stand around at the end of a sequence, record the room tone before the first take of the day.

It is also suggested that you record the hum of a refrigerator, fluorescent lights, or other equipment separately. This gives the editor freedom to add that ambient sound during the editing process.

Additional Sounds

Supplementary sound effects should be recorded and delivered to the editing room. If the crew is shooting in an interesting location, especially if it is distant, the sound team should record any particular sound that is unique to that area. It saves time and money

to record additional sounds during the shoot, rather than having to come back later. During the shoot, for example, if the sound recordist knows that a school is near the location, he might go to the school yard and record children at play.

These sounds might be used for background ambience, or they might not. Regardless, they give the sound editor a variety of choices and might even stimulate other sound ideas during postproduction.

> The sound recordist tried to record everything, which I think was a smart move on his part.
>
> *Adam*

Sound Continuity

It is important to create sound continuity from shot to shot. This involves recording strong and consistent sound levels and not changing microphones for similar angles in a scene. Sound recorded with different microphones will seem unbalanced when cut together. The goal is to create sound takes that will cut together smoothly and not demand a lot of equalization from shot to shot.

Notes

The sound recordist should take clear and comprehensive notes of the dialogue recorded on the set and the "wild sounds" recorded on or off the set. He should confer with the script supervisor or assistant camera operator for the scene numbers and the director's comments. These notes, called a *sound report*, will later serve as a reference for the editor (Figure 13.2).

> Every night during a location shoot, as exhausted as I am, I will listen to all the sound recorded that day and do my sound log. It keeps me familiar with what I have, and it enforces that discipline of keeping my material organized and not assuming that I have something on tape and finding out that I don't.
>
> *Jan*

SET PROCEDURE

On the day of the shoot, the first step for the sound recordist is to decide where to place the recorder. It is best to be on the edge of the set, close enough to see and hear what is happening, but away from the traffic of lights and grip equipment. Careful attention must be paid to positioning the microphone cables. At no time should an electric cable and a microphone cable be parallel to one another. Electric current can

SOUND REPORT

Order #:_____   Date:_____

Production title:_____ Transfer studio:_____

Episode:_____   Recordist:_____

Recorder:_____   Stock type:_____   Line-up tone level:_____
                                                                  #/coat
# of tracks:____ Speed (IPS):____ Sound Roll #:____ X/fer to:_____stripe

Instructions for transfer:_____

Sound#	Sequence	Take	Sync/wild	Mike	Remarks

Note: Please keep the original of this report with the 1/4" tape
and attach the carbon copy to the transfers for pick-up.

Figure 13.2 Sound report sheet.

induce hum into the signal in the microphone cable, making it impossible to record clean sound.

The next step is to decide how many microphones to use, what specific kinds to use, and where to place them. A recordist is only as good as the sound coming from his microphones. Choosing the type of microphone to use and where to place it is an important part of clean dialogue recording.

Much of sound recording involves "riding levels," which means leveling out the extremes of performance and balancing multiple characters. For example, the recordist might have to handle dialogue between one actor who speaks softly and another who bellows.

Balancing these two performances is part of the art of mixing. It also requires maintaining consistent sound among the different takes of the same scene. If you have already shot the master of a scene and the background ambience is clean but a plane flies over when you shoot the close-up, you should redo the close-up to match the background of the long shot.

There are many variables in recording, and before making any decisions, the sound recordist must watch a rehearsal of the scene. Knowing where actors will be positioned and how they will move allows the sound recordist to make informed decisions.

Once the microphones are positioned, there should be a final rehearsal to enable the sound recordist to adjust for proper recording levels. Actors should speak at the level they will be projecting during the actual take. Now the recordist is ready for the take. (See Chapter 11, "Set Procedure," for slating techniques.)

Basic Attitude on the Set

The sound recordist's ability to record the best sound possible in any situation depends on his ability to communicate properly with the DP and the director. He must know when to fight for another take and when to let it go. The recordist should be assertive regarding his needs but must not be too aggressive.

In addition, the recordist must be sensitive to the needs of the actors. He must use the utmost tact and grace when placing microphones on the performers. Working with actors who mumble or shout can also be problematic. If this is the case, the recordist should request the director to ask the actor to speak softer or louder.

Finally, the recordist and the boom operator should develop a shorthand communication that enables them to work quietly and efficiently together.

APPROACHES TO RECORDING SOUND

The sound recordist has four tools with which to record sound:

- Boom
- Plant
- Lavaliere
- Radio microphone

Boom

Using a boom is, in most cases, the best way to record dialogue. *Boom* is a generic term for any long pole with a microphone attached to the end of it that is used to record dialogue. It might be a complicated unit called a *Fisher boom*, which uses a pulley system to expand and contract, or a variable-length pole called a *fishpole*, with the microphone attached to a movable "shock mount" at the end. The latter is what most beginners use.

Fishpoles usually run from 12 to 18 feet in length and are rigid enough not to bend at full extension. (You don't want the microphone to dip into the shot.) The boom is used to position the microphone close to the scene to record dialogue between several actors simultaneously. The mount allows the boom operator to manipulate the microphone from one actor to another during the scene, depending on who is delivering lines. Because it is a mobile unit, the boom operator can follow moving action at a safe distance from the camera and still be close enough to pick up a clean signal from the actors.

The boom is usually held still and secure above the scene and has a directional microphone pointed down at the actors. (Microphones can be angled up toward the actor's mouth as well.) Boom movement should be practiced during rehearsals not only for sound quality, but also to avoid having the microphone interfere visually with the camera's frame line or to create unwanted shadows as it passes under lights.

During exterior shoots, a blimp-type windscreen is required to reduce the wind sounds the microphone picks up. Even when shooting interiors, it is recommended that you use a slip-on foam windscreen because some microphones are sensitive to even the most minute air movements.

The boom operator should use a set of headphones to monitor what is being recorded. The recordist can give direction and speak to the boom operator through the headphones. This way, the recordist doesn't have to shout to the boom operator.

A cable operator might be required if the shot calls for camera movement. This crew member keeps the microphone cables clear of the camera, grip, and electric equipment while the boom operator concentrates on following the action. The movement of the microphone cable might cause a rustling noise on the track, so it must be handled carefully.

Documentary sound crews usually do not have a separate boom operator. The recordist acts as a self-contained sound recording unit. He does not have to be positioned far from the action and can easily handle the levels and position the microphone at the same time (Figure 13.3).

> The sound recordist had done some documentary work, so he was used to both operating the Nagra and doing the boom at the same time. It was just luck. I don't remember thinking ahead, "Oh, we should get a guy from a documentary because I'm going to shoot this guerrilla style."
>
> *Adam*

Plants

Plants are microphones that are not mobile; they are "planted" in a fixed location for the duration of the scene. For example, they might be used to pick up the voice of an actor who is too far away from the boom. They need to be hidden from the view of the camera. They can be taped or mounted in doorways, on bed headboards, behind pictures, under chairs, in flower pots, and so on.

Lavaliere

This small, lightweight, omnidirectional microphone is pinned under an actor's clothing or taped to the body. It must be carefully placed so as not to pick up the rustle of clothing as the actor moves. and it must be

Figure 13.3 The sound recordist needs to be quick in a real location. Photo from the filming of *The Lunch Date*.

rechecked constantly in case it becomes dislodged as a result of constant movement or moisture (if taped).

Lavalieres are effective microphones if the actor remains fairly stationary during a take, but if the actor is required to walk, dragging the microphone cable might be awkward. A radio microphone might be needed in this case. Lavalieres are often used when interviewing subjects for documentaries.

Radio Microphones

Radio microphones are used to cover hard-to-reach areas, such as a wide shot of a couple talking on a beach. If the actors are far from the reach of a boom, a plant, or a lavaliere, a radio microphone might be your only option. These microphones are attached to the body like a lavaliere, but they transmit the signal from a radio transmitter to a receiver. The basic problem with radio microphones is that they are apt to pick up other frequencies, such as police car or taxi transmissions, that interfere with your sound. They are expensive to rent and have the same inherent problems as lavalieres.

> The only problem that we had—and one that wasn't immediately obvious—was the noise. Most people, if they see a highway outside their window, understand they're going to get car noise in the background or they choose another location. But in this case, it was an unseen thing that got us.
>
> Near the school, about 400 yards away, was a high-powered radio station antenna that broadcast country music. Surprisingly, the boom pole was acting as a receiver, and country music was being picked up at certain times and transmitted into the Nagra and recorded onto the tape. We discovered that on the first day of shooting and were horrified. We realized very quickly that the microphone had to be placed precisely and not moved. If you moved the boom slightly, it came back into frequency. So only after we had the microphone set up—and it took several tries—we could shoot.
>
> *Howard*

VARIABLES FOR PLACING MICROPHONES

The placement and use of the different microphones depend on the many variables of a particular scene. Evaluate the scene first, and then work with the following considerations:

THE DIRECTOR'S VISION. Who and what does the director want to hear in the shot? Start with this as the basic premise of every decision.

PLACEMENT AND BLOCKING OF ACTORS. How much does an actor move in the shot? An actor pacing in the frame must be microphoned differently than one sitting still. A boom or two separate microphones might be necessary to record the sequence.

PLACEMENT OF CAMERA. How far away is the camera from the action of the scene? This defines how close you can get with a microphone. If even the most directional microphone is unrealistic, must lavalieres or radio microphones be used, and will they create a false sound perspective for the scene?

SIZE AND COMPOSITION OF SHOT. What is the lens seeing? This affects a number of things. How close to the actor can the microphone on the boom be positioned without slipping into the frame line? The boom operator must be keenly aware of the frame line at all times. He should rehearse with the camera operator before the final rehearsal with the actors. Both the camera operator and the boom operator must be consistent in their moves.

The size of the shot also affects the visibility of a lavaliere or radio microphone. A very tight shot of an actor will require that the microphone be more carefully disguised than in a long shot.

LIGHTING OF SHOT. The lighting plan can cause problems if the sound boom creates a shadow that can be seen in the frame. During the lighting setup, any boom shadows should be dealt with before the lights are fixed. During the shoot, the elimination of boom shadows must be a coordinated effort between the boom and camera operators.

MOVEMENT OF SHOT. If a dolly is used for a shot, the boom operator must rehearse her actions around those of the dolly. A production assistant or cable operator might be needed to keep the microphone cable free from the path of the dolly and clear of the electric cables.

ACOUSTICS AT LOCATION. The recordist might need to position the microphone away from disruptive sounds to minimize their presence on the track. Common troublemakers are refrigerators, air conditioners, traffic noise from the windows, and natural echoes in the location. Sound blankets might also be required to eliminate or at least lessen the problem.

Sound blankets can be used in a variety of ways to deaden the sound of "live" rooms by baffling the reflective sound echoes caused by hard floors, ceilings, walls, and windows. Sound blankets are heavy moving blankets, preferably with a white side and a dark gray or black side and grommets for hanging.

They can be taped to walls, hung from C-stands, or even draped over refrigerators and air conditioning units to create a quieter environment.

> We weren't prepared for the hum of the fluorescent lights. When you were standing in the gym, you didn't notice it, but it came out loud and clear on the sound track.
>
> *Howard*

CAMERA NOISE. Although 16mm sync cameras are designed to run quietly, sometimes a camera leaks noise during a take. This is most noticeable when shooting interiors in a confined space. *Blimping*, or creating a soundproof housing for the camera, might reduce the noise that emanates from the lens mount, magazine, or body of the camera. (This is the AC's job.) This muffling can be accomplished with a *blimp* or *barney*, which is a jacket that is specially designed for the camera. You can create your own blimp with anything that will deaden the camera noise, such as a changing bag, foam rubber, or a coat or jacket.

One way of cutting down on camera noise is to position the camera as far away from the microphone as possible during the take. A small amount of camera noise can usually be camouflaged by the other sounds or music that will inevitably be mixed in during postproduction. This is a good example of why the sound recordist must understand what happens during postproduction to be able to effectively evaluate the sounds recorded on the set.

> There was one guy doing sound. He was operating the Nagra and the boom. Then he enlisted one of the homeless guys to help us, which turned into a disaster. . . . I looked over at one point and there is the sound guy standing next to me, and he doesn't have his headset on. And I look over, and there is one of the young guys I had met from the homeless line the night before, sitting with the headphones on, by the Nagra, operating it. He looked confident.
>
> I said, "What's going on here? Does he know what he's doing?" "Oh yeah, he knows what he's doing." And I said, "OK." I wasn't going to worry myself because I had this next shot to do. They told me, "Don't worry, everything's fine. He's all set. He knows what he's doing."
>
> So the actors took their places, and we started. Roll sound, roll camera, action, do the shot, cut. It was great. Suddenly I notice there's a commotion going on next to me. I look over, and there are yards of audio tape spewing out of the Nagra. Now the

homeless guy with the headset has a weird look on his face. We quickly went back to the original way of the sound man operating both the Nagra and the boom by himself.

Adam

RECORDING CONCERNS

One of the differences between how sound and film images are recorded is that you can immediately hear a sound take played back on the set. Video has this advantage as well, but film must be sent to a lab to be processed. With the sound, if there is any question of quality, the director can listen to a take with the headphones on to decide whether she wants to do the shot over for sound or performance.

The director will ask whether a take is good for camera and whether it is good for sound. Camera will be first on the list. Asking for another take because of sound problems is a judgment call the director makes after listening to the track. Most sound problems can be addressed in postproduction, whereas picture problems must always be addressed on the set.

Pickups

If only a small section of a take is ruined because of extraneous sounds, it might not be necessary to do the complete take again. You might be able to "pick up" the section of the take that was spoiled. In a pinch, the sound can be also taken "wild" (audio recording only) and matched to the picture in postproduction.

If the day has been fraught with sound problems, holding a makeshift ADR session in a quiet room after the day's work can save a lot of money. If it is impossible to do it right after the scene is shot, have the actors come to the quiet area when they get out of makeup and costume. After the actors listen to their performance on headphones, they repeat the original dialogue for the sound recordist. This material will most likely match well with the actors' lips in the editing room. If it does not, with some minor adjusting (stretching and shrinking), the new material can be made to fit.

Keeping It Clean

Be aware of actors who step on one another's lines. This is called *overlapping*. If two sounds are already blended on the track, they can never be controlled separately. They will be married forever. Record dialogue that can later be controlled in the editing room. In a single shot in which an off-camera actor has lines, he should make sure there is a pause between the on-camera actor's line and his own line. Recorded separately, or with a pause, lines can be manipulated in the editing room to create overlaps, but the editor will be able to control each voice.

If the director wants the lines overlapped for dramatic purpose, the off-camera dialogue should be microphoned as well. If the scene is a wide shot, overlapping lines may be an integral part of the drama.

Difficult Situations

The sound recordist might not be able to achieve clean sound on a difficult set or location. Some locations, such as Grand Central Station, are too busy to control. Ambience must be taken and used as background for the lines that will inevitably be recorded later.

Planes traveling overhead will destroy a sound take. If the company is on a flight path where waiting for good sound translates to little or no photography, the director will have to bite the bullet and plan for ADR work.

Crowd Scenes

To record clean sound in a crowded bar sequence, the assistant director instructs the background extras to mime speech and the clinking of glasses. This means that during the take, the background actors move their lips, but utter no sound. They raise their glasses, but do not let the glasses touch. They dance to a predetermined rhythm, but there is no music playing. These sounds are added later.

This allows the dialogue recorded on the set to be "clean." It will not have any dirty crowd noise to fight the dialogue. To maintain the illusion, the speaking actors must project their voices as if they were fighting the din of the crowd and the music. (To help the actors with this, it is good to rehearse the scene with the full-blown background noise.) This way, when the three sound tracks—dialogue, music, and background noise—are married in the mix, the volume of each track can be controlled separately. The scene will sound as natural as possible, and the dialogue will come through so that the audience can understand it.

VIDEO SOUND

Video sound crews vary according to the complexity of the production (how many characters have to be recorded in a sequence) and whether it is a location shoot or a studio shoot. A single-camera setup in the field might need only a one-person crew to operate the videotape recorder, mix the incoming microphone levels, and hold the boom. A scene with many characters requires a boom operator and a sound recordist with a mixing unit that has anywhere from two to 12 inputs. A studio shoot with multiple cameras for one scene might use a mixing console of up to 18 tracks.

Documentary crews are small and mobile. The sound recordist and boom operator are usually the same person. She must be adept at booming, mixing (if additional microphones are used), and operating the recorder simultaneously.

> I always wear the headphones because I think you get in trouble if you simply trust the needle and assume that you are getting decent sound. I think the trade-off of looking a little odd is incidental. It does remind your subjects that they're being recorded, but so does all the other equipment. What's important to me as both the director and the sound person is to get the best sound, and the only way to assure that is to be monitoring what's coming off the tape, not what I'm hearing in the environment.
>
> *Jan*

PRODUCER
Control Environment

Because one of the producer's major concerns is managing the budget, anything that contributes to saving time and money will get his attention. In the area of sound recording, hiring a skilled sound recordist and boom operator is the first step. Be sure the sound recordist knows that his main concern is recording clean production dialogue.

Other than this, the following are the areas the producer must focus on:

- Ensuring that the equipment needs of the production are fulfilled (recording devices, microphones, sound tape, etc.)
- Getting the best deals possible on the rental equipment

- Ensuring that all locations are "sound-friendly"
- Asking the sound recordist to capture sufficient ambient and interesting sounds from each location
- Ensuring proper care of the equipment

EQUIPMENT NEEDS FOR THE SHOOT

Once he understands the demands of the script and the locations, the sound recordist can develop an accurate list of his equipment needs. These might include some of the following tools:

Nagra	Shock mounts
Digital audiotape recorder	Slip-on windscreen
Mixing console	Sound blankets
Assorted microphones	Blimp-type windscreen
Headphones (2 or 3 sets)	Boom pole
Microphone cables	Mounting clips
Extra batteries	Gaffer's tape
Tape stock	

Sound Recorder

A key piece of equipment for recording sound for film or video is the Nagra tape recorder. This machine was invented in Switzerland in the early sixties by Polish inventor Stephan Kudelski. The word *Nagra* means "it will record" in Polish. The Nagra records all the sounds during the shoot onto quarter-inch tape. To record sound that can be synchronized with the picture later, a 60-Hz sync pulse is recorded onto the center of the tape while the live sound is being recorded. Meanwhile, the camera is running, through a crystal motor, at a speed of precisely 24 frames per second (fps). When the quarter-inch tape is later transferred to 16mm magnetic track, the sound is resolved to run at precisely 24 fps, allowing the sound and picture to be joined in unison for perfect sync.

The Nagra is the most popular choice for documentary as well as narrative filmmaking. For voice-only recordings, the documentarian can use either the Nagra or any other high-quality tape recorder in either quarter-inch or cassette format.

Although the Nagra continues to be the standard recording device throughout the world for the portable tape recording of sync dialogue, the digital audiotape (DAT) recorder is now a viable alternative. DAT recorders employ a technology that duplicates a "clean" sound devoid of hiss or sound buildup.

There is no generation loss with digital sound as long as it is duplicated onto other digital machines.

However, DAT recorders are not as dependable as the Nagra under difficult and diverse conditions. The Nagra is a workhorse that is able to maintain its high level of quality with minimum maintenance. The following are some of the Nagra's other advantages:

- Confidence head monitoring. The Nagra has three heads—erase, record, and playback. You can listen to what you just recorded to ensure that you recorded what you wanted to record. Only the higher-end DAT players have this capability.
- Excellent microphone pre-amps.
- Long-play battery life. The Nagra runs for days on one set of D batteries. The battery life for most DAT recorders is only an hour or two.

Nagra is now offering a DAT recorder of its own, the Nagra D.

Microphones

Microphones are delicate instruments that convert sound waves into electric signals. The sound recordist must have a thorough knowledge of microphones and how they can be used effectively to capture sound under a wide variety of conditions. He must be able to identify the right microphone for each situation.

CARE OF EQUIPMENT

Proper care and maintenance of sound equipment is very important. Treat it with respect.

- Keep dust and dirt away from the tape; they can impair sound quality. Do not touch the tape.
- Keep the tape in its box, and protect it from temperature extremes.
- Keep the lid of the tape deck closed as much as possible.
- Do not smoke, drink, or eat around sound equipment—food and ashes have a way of winding up on the tape.
- Use alcohol-soaked cotton swabs regularly to clean the parts of the machine that touch the tape, including the heads, rollers, guides, and capstans.
- Clean the empty take-up reel each time it is used. Inspect it for warpage or rough edges. A damaged reel can tear or warp the edges of the tape and affect sound quality.
- Do not rewind the tape after recording or playback—leave it "tails out." Rewinding can cause a sound bleed-through.

KEY POINTS

1. The sound recordist should know what happens to sound in postproduction.
2. Scout the location at the time of day or night for which the shoot is planned.
3. During rehearsals, find the best places for the microphones and the boom. The boom operator should work out boom shadows and frame lines with the grips and the camera operator.
4. Record room tone, wild sounds, and possibly even replacement dialogue at the end of the day.

chapter fourteen

Art

I think, as much as possible, it's important to visit your locations beforehand as many times as the budget and your schedule will allow.

Jan

DIRECTOR
Guide

In the process of creating a motion picture, the art director and the art department truly are magicians, often creating something out of nothing and making things appear from out of nowhere.

There is nothing like the feeling of walking on a dressed set for the first time: experiencing the culmination of weeks, maybe months, of preparation and planning by the director, the producer, the art department, and the director of photography (DP). A great deal of imagination and hard work has transformed the words on the page into the world of the characters through the choice of sets, dressing, costumes, props, and furniture.

SET PROCEDURES

The day starts early for the art department. Finishing touches are applied to the set to allow the electrical department time to set up the lights. Other members of the art department are already working on the next set in anticipation of the company's next move. During the shooting day, the art department is constantly on standby to adjust the set, dressings, and props for the camera.

Let's look at an excerpt from *The Lunch Date* as an example of how the art department approaches a scene.

The duties of the art department for the scene on the next page are as follows:

LOCATION. The location is secured during pre-production. If a location falls through, the art department must be part of the plan to move to an alternate location.

SET DRESSING. Sometime before shooting the scene, the set dresser, cleanup crew, and painters "dress" the set to match the description in the script and any drawings, paintings, or photos given to the dresser. During the shooting, the set dresser readjusts any set pieces that have been moved for camera framing continuity. If the shoot is going well, the set dresser can leave the shoot and move to the next location to begin preparing it.

PROPS. The props are gathered prior to the shoot. When the set is ready, the property master places the food on the counter. He prepares the woman's handbag with the appropriate change. When the performer is called to the set, he hands her the handbag and her packages. He places some napkins nearby for the cook.

WARDROBE. When the actors arrive on the location, they are sent to change clothes after a brief rehearsal. The costumer dresses both actors in the costumes defined by the script. She asks the cook to keep the apron and paper hat neat and clean so they will match for each take. At wrap, the costumer helps the actors undress. She puts the costumes away neatly to be used another day. If they need washing, she takes them with her to be cleaned after the wrap.

MAKEUP AND HAIR. After the actors are dressed, they move on to the makeup and hair department. Here, their makeup is applied and their hair coiffed to match a previous scene or the art director's design. When this job is completed, the makeup and hair people stand by off set to make adjustments between takes. At the end of the day, they assist the actors in removing their makeup and any hairpieces.

INT. LUNCHEONETTE - AFTERNOON

The woman walks into a station luncheonette. It is a simple place—a grill, some booths, and rows of refrigerated cabinets filled with salads and sandwiches. She reaches into a glass case and removes a salad.

A COOK stands behind a white linoleum counter. He fiddles with his white paper hat and white apron.

WOMAN
How much is this salad?

COOK
Two dollars.

She puts the salad on the counter. She rustles through her pocket book.

WOMAN
Well, I'm not sure that I have that much.

The woman empties a dollar and some change on the counter.

WOMAN
One dollar . . . here's some.

The cook fingers through the change.

COOK
A dollar fifty . . . two dollars. Here ya go lady.

She grabs the salad plate and her bundles.

WOMAN
Napkin.

The cook hands her a napkin. She walks toward the booths.

SET DRESSING

The set dresser decorates the set according to the art director's specific designs. This crew member is responsible for renting, buying, or making all the "dressing" that occupies the set—everything from the rugs on the floors to the magnets on the refrigerator.

The set dresser should confer with the actor whose character "lives" in the location, and together they will create the character's environment.

The set dresser works in tandem with other departments, such as lighting. If the gaffer has lit the set brightly, a 100-watt bulb in a "practical" will not register on film or video stock. An electrician might need to replace the bulb with a special 500-watt lamp to balance light temperature correctly.

The set dresser is sometimes called on to assist other departments. The assistant DP might need help pulling up a rug during a take to get it out from under the dolly's wheels. Someone might be needed just off camera to jerk a curtain with monofilament wire (fishing line) to simulate the wind. These specialty positions often fall to the set dresser.

Not all set pieces are easy to find. If the director has a specific look in mind for a set piece, the art director and set dresser must make this item to the director's specifications if it cannot be found (Figure 14.1).

My dad put up the rope. He was my PA. We found a rope in another school and took it down. We built a special iron clamp because there wasn't one on the particular ceiling. My dad had a friend who was a metallurgist; he designed a specific clamp so that we could fasten the rope to the ceiling and support a person.

One very difficult prop—so difficult that we didn't find it until two days before the shoot—was the fireman's net. They haven't been used since the 1930s. They're very dangerous and very heavy. The reason they're not being used was that people would hit them and bounce out. They really didn't save many lives. The one we used we found in some guy's barn under a bale of hay. It was classic. The guy's father had been a fireman, and he let us take it out. It was very dirty and very, very heavy.

During the shot, the production manager was underneath the net, which weighed 400 pounds. The kids really couldn't lift it themselves, so he hid under it on his hands and knees, resting it on his back.

Howard

Continuity

The set is maintained by the set dresser to match the uninterrupted succession of the script's scenes. If there is a fight scene, for example, the set is cleaned after each take, and all the broken set pieces are replaced. The duplicated set is matched each time to the script supervisor's snapshots of the original set.

Figure 14.1 It's one thing to type the words *Fireman's Net* into the script and another to locate one for the shoot. Scene from *Truman*.

Duplicates

The set dresser should have duplicates of key items featured on the set in case they become damaged. Duplicates should also be provided for breakaway items. Breakaway chairs, for instance, are made of pieces of balsa wood that have been loosely glued together. A performer does not sit on this chair, but on the real chair. She is photographed as she stands up, and then the real chair is replaced with the breakaway chair. The character can then pick up the breakaway chair and heave it at another actor or stunt person. In the final product, this action will look real, but it is actually harmless. With the addition of sound effects, the audience viewing this footage will believe that the chair is hard.

PROPS

> Because I had so few, I basically handled the props. It sounds kind of silly, but as a director you get very, very particular about certain props. I even went so far as to worry about what kind of kick ball was used. It was important that it was one of those red, standard playground balls because that's what I grew up with. Gathering together those bows and arrows was also tough, as was getting permission to fire them in the gym.
>
> *Howard*

Continuity

The prop department is responsible for maintaining continuity of props from shot to shot. If a scene requires the actor to eat a meal, for example, the level of the milk in the glass, the steam on the food, and the exact placement of the cutlery must be maintained. If it looks as though the production will run out of a food item, a production assistant is sent to the local store to purchase more.

Duplicates

If a scene calls for a watch to be smashed, the watch might have to be destroyed many times in the course of covering the scene. The prop master must have enough watches standing by to allow the director to shoot the scene to her satisfaction. If it is decided in preproduction that the character will wear a special watch, it might prove difficult to duplicate. The director should ask herself whether a more common watch, which can be easily and inexpensively duplicated, will compromise the story.

Food that will be consumed on the set must also be provided in duplicate. In a dining scene, the property master is responsible for all the food a character has to eat during the scene. If the script calls for the character to eat a salad, several complete salads should be standing by for each take.

The salad—we were not prepared for that: how much salad we would need for the whole day. If you're going to do the take over, the salad has to look the same all day.

Adam

Personal Effects

The property master might be responsible for safeguarding the actor's personal belongings during the shoot. He might accept her valuables when he gives her the character's personal props, trading them back at the end of the day.

Improvisation

What if the production has run out of milk and the stores are closed? What if the location is in the middle of nowhere? The director might take the scene over and over to capture the best performance, and the props must be there each time. Even if the director tells the property master in preproduction how many takes she thinks she will need, the crew must be prepared with extra props.

The art department might have to improvise with the milk, keeping in mind that the actor actually has to consume the substitute on camera. Perhaps some creamer substitute mixed with water will match the color of the milk from previous takes. Tricks of the prop master's trade include using iced tea to simulate scotch, nontobacco cigarettes for nonsmokers,

breakaway chairs for fights, sugar-glass tumblers for breaking, and soup for vomit (Figure 14.2).

The makeup was another issue. We had to get a guy to make some fake vomit. When we were trying to get [Truman] to do the throw-up scene from on top of the scaffolding, he was really repulsed by the sight of the fake vomit and refused to get near the stuff. We wanted to put a little around his lips so after he had thrown up you could see the residue. Well, he refused to do it. At first, he laughed nervously, and then he actually started to cry. He went through a whole range of emotions. He just did not want to do this thing. I finally put some around my lips to show, "Hey, it's not bad. It's nothing but soup. Don't worry." That kind of calmed him down, and we made some jokes. About an hour and a half later—for something that was supposed to take only 15 minutes—we actually did it. That was the most difficult constraint, having to deal with the limitations of an eight-year-old boy. He did a great job. You have to remember, he was under a great deal of pressure, and I think he held up remarkably well.

Howard

WARDROBE

The company travels with all the costumes required for the show, including duplicate costumes for everyone and any sundry garb for the extras. It is important that the wardrobe be consistent with the setting.

Figure 14.2 Someone had to make the vomit. Photograph from the shooting of *Truman*.

In an exterior winter scene, for instance, everyone in the shot must wear a heavy coat to indicate the cold. This scene can be shot in hot weather, of course, because the audience knows the temperature only by what they see or hear.

Special Rigs

Special technical equipment is sometimes integrated into the costume, such as a radio microphone or a jerk harness. (When a character is shot with a big gun, he is jerked off the set by a wire attached to this harness.) The costumer works with the department responsible for the technical hardware to conceal it in the costume so that the audience will not be aware of the rigging device.

The costumer uses her bag of tricks during production. Quick changes and clothes that have to be removed during a take require special attachments. There is no question that the costumer's life became easier with the invention of Velcro™.

MAKEUP

Continuity

After applying makeup to the cast, the makeup artist spends the remainder of the day on the set helping the actors maintain a consistent look. Under the hot lights, actors perspire and must be powdered or tissued down to avoid a shiny complexion. With prosthetics work, touch-ups might require applying entirely new latex pieces, which could be just as time-consuming as the original application that morning.

Positive Reinforcement

The makeup artist is usually the last person to work with the actors before they begin a scene. Actors might be in the makeup trailer for some time, so the individual who works with them there helps the director by doing whatever she can to sustain the actors in an agreeable frame of mind. A makeup artist with a pleasant personality can help an actor maintain a positive mood.

Special Effects

Prosthetics work is very time-consuming. It is not uncommon for an actor and the makeup artist to arrive on the set several hours before the crew call time to prepare and apply the makeup.

HAIR

The hairdresser works in tandem with the makeup artist. The look of hair and makeup must be coordinated, as must their application.

Continuity

The maintenance of hairstyle continuity is very important. The hairdresser takes instant photographs of each hairstyle. These photographs are kept on a large ring for easy reference, providing a convenient method for matching hair from scene to scene. This technique works well for all departments.

Hair gets mussed easily and therefore might not match a previous take, especially when shooting in a windy exterior location. Sustaining a consistent look can take a great deal of work. If an actress chooses not to have her hair touched up between takes because it disturbs her concentration, you might find in the editing room that the cuts do not match. The hairdresser has to be discreet in this situation. If the hair is passable, the hairdresser should not say a word, but if it will cause an obvious continuity error, the hairdresser should inform the script supervisor, the director of photography, or even the director to correct the match.

ADDITIONAL CREW

Depending on the nature of the shoot, the art department might also employ a standby painter, a special effects team, or a greens person (for on-set vegetation). In the production of a short film or video project, all these roles might be performed by only one or two talented people.

PRODUCER

Construction

The producer oversees any set construction. The location manager and the production manager can coordinate all practical locations, but sets need the supervision of the producer.

The producer carefully monitors the schedule and the budget and how the art department is keeping to their part of it. Sets take longer to build and things inevitably cost more than estimated. This shouldn't be a problem if the art department budget is padded. However, if this area begins to go over budget, creative compromises may have to be made or the money must either come from another department or from postproduction funds.

> A woman who was a former student helped me with the art direction. She helped me get the murals together and dress the sets.
>
> *Jan*

SETS

If set construction is required, the art director works with a drafter and a construction coordinator to realize the set. On the basis of the director's storyboards, the art director arrives at a design for the set. After approval from both the producer and the director, the drafter turns the designs into blueprints. It is from these blueprints that the set is constructed (Figure 14.3).

Considerations in building a set include the following:

- Cost
- Construction and strike time
- Removable, or *flying*, walls
- Well-braced doors (so the set doesn't shake when a door is closed)

- Ceiling pieces
- Realistic painted scenes, or *backdrops*, outside windows

> I wanted to achieve the effect of a Greek chorus, so the natural corollary was to situate them in some kind of artificial set, which I had never done. It was completely unnatural for me, but it was a very conscious aesthetic choice that I thought would service the film. I came up with the idea of two different sets within a single studio (one for sitting, one for standing) and then had to define what they should look like.
>
> *Jan*

Weather can play a factor in any film or video shoot, unless of course the shoot is entirely indoors. The safest procedure is to schedule exterior scenes first. Then when you move inside to shoot the interiors, the weather will not affect production. If circumstances require that you shoot interiors first, you will be vulnerable to weather conditions when you move outdoors.

One way to protect the production is to maintain a cover set. This is an interior location the company can move to in case of inclement weather. Cover sets should be simple and require few actors. A true cover set is dressed and ready at all times during the production.

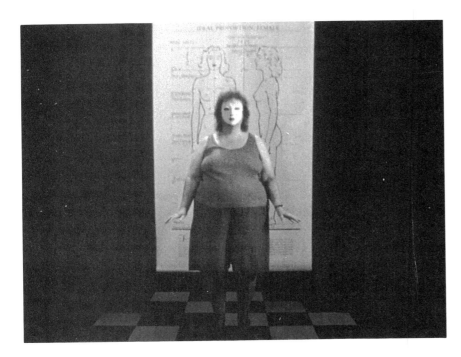

Figure 14.3 The set allows for greater control. Scene from *Mirror Mirror*.

When the photography of a sequence is completed, it is customary for the art department to wait one day before disassembling the set. They wait to receive word from the editing room that the dailies are not damaged. If the footage is damaged and it becomes necessary to reshoot the scene, the set can be used again. Once the art director has been given the word that the dailies are good technically, the set is struck (taken apart and returned if rented or destroyed if constructed).

> There was no opportunity for reshoots, which was pretty scary. I had to strike that set the minute we finished, so I didn't even get the film back to find out if there was a scratched roll or any technical problems. To reconstruct the set would have been impossible. The mannequins had to be returned, and the cinematographer had to fly back to Boston.
>
> *Jan*

KEY POINTS

1. Have adequate duplicates to maintain continuity.

2. Consult actors when choosing props, wardrobe, and even set dressing.

3. Create a cover set, if possible, in case of weather problems.

4. Allow time for predressing and striking. Do not strike a set until you have seen the dailies unless it's unavoidable.

chapter fifteen

Cast

She's a great actress, so I was very lucky.
Adam

DIRECTOR

Direct

Actors are the director's primary storytelling vehicles. A good actor can breathe life into a character and a script. Aiding and guiding the actors through the production is the director's job.

The relationship between a director and an actor is an important one. Many intangible elements must come together in front of the camera when the director calls, "Action." These elements include emotional tone, pace, projection, and the arc of the characters.

The director should know what the actor is capable of in any given situation. Casting and rehearsals will give the director a strong indication of the actor's talent and range, but the critical point comes when the cameras roll.

A primary goal for the director is to create an environment that is conducive to good work. The actors will be able to focus on their work if the atmosphere that is created by the director and her crew is relaxed and cooperative. If there is bickering and general chaos, it will be difficult for the actors to concentrate.

THE PROCESS

There is a set order to the process of shooting a short film or video. The director needs to follow that order so that everyone on set knows what is happening at each moment. To this end, it is essential that the director know what she wants from the actor and how to get it.

Call Time

The actor arrives on the set at his appointed call time and checks in with the assistant director. The first order of business is to conduct a brief run-through of the scene. Once the scene has been loosely blocked to the director's and director of photography's (DP) liking, the actor is sent to makeup. After makeup, the actor goes to wardrobe to put on his costume. After another stop at makeup and hair for touch-ups, he is ready for the camera.

If the assistant director has scheduled the actor's arrival correctly, he will have very little time to wait before he is called to the set for his scene. Do not call the actor to the set until the set is ready. On the other hand, make sure the actor doesn't keep the entire crew waiting.

Makeup and Hair

The director should be keenly aware of the personalities on the makeup and hair team. These crew members see the actor just prior to his arrival on the set. If they do not understand how to help the actor get into the right mood for a scene, they can destroy his concentration. Talented makeup and hair people who are friendly and supportive are priceless. They can ease the actor's tensions and put him in a positive mood.

Stand-ins

To free the actor from the set until his work begins, it is advisable to employ a stand-in. When preparing a scene, many time-consuming camera functions require that a live body be standing or moving in the actor's blocked positions. To flag and focus the lights and to practice camera movements, any body of roughly the same size will do as a stand-in for the actor.

On Call

An important consideration for the production unit is how the actor is treated while he is on call. Although this is primarily the responsibility of the assistant director, all principal parties must be aware of the actor's schedule and working environment.

For the actor, the emotional rhythm of a typical day is like a roller coaster ride. The actor might have to wait for long periods while the crew prepares and lights the sequence. Once the camera begins to roll, he must be able to find his peak energy level. To ensure that he has the opportunity to perform at his best, the production must provide food, a comfortable place to rest, and a call time that does not abuse his energies.

Consider the alternative: You are shooting in a freezing exterior location. The actor waits outdoors for the set to be dressed and lit. He is tired, hungry, and irritable. When you ask him to get in front of the camera, even the most disciplined actor might have difficulty "getting up" for his part. His poor performance will be reflected in the dailies and ultimately in the final product.

Final Staging

After the crew completes the time-consuming work of preparing for a scene, shooting or taping begins. The director will conduct a final staging rehearsal, during which last-minute technical adjustments are made. On the set, actors might discover moments that were not part of the rehearsal process. Props, set pieces, or a painting on the wall might be just the thing to make a scene work better. If the technical adjustments are major (a total relighting of the set, for example), the actors should be excused and encouraged to return to the green room, makeup room, or rest area.

> We knew if we didn't have all the kids in the shot, we could send the others off to the playroom. We made a playroom for the kids with a baby-sitter.
>
> *Howard*

Gaffers and set decorators will make subtle adjustments, or "tweak" a set, until they are told to stop. As soon as the director feels that the set is ready, she should get to work shooting and covering the scene. The assistant director is helpful here in determining the preparedness of the set and being aware of the director's schedule.

The actors sometimes meet for the first time on the day their scene is to be shot. In this situation, the director should conduct off-set rehearsals and discussions to allow them to warm up.

> I didn't have my two actors, Scotty and Clebert, together until the first day of shooting. In fact, the whole interaction with the salad, the orchestration of her sitting down and what she would say, him sitting at the table, getting up and getting the pepper, and putting that on the table—that took five minutes in between setting up the shots. I sat down with them, and we quickly figured out a little routine to do.
>
> *Adam*

Technical Requirements

The technical requirements for the actor are a large part of film and video acting. The head must be tilted just the right way to catch the light. The eyes must be directed at what the character is supposed to see. The raised hand must be placed so as not to block an actor who is framed in the background. Stage and nonprofessional actors who are unfamiliar with technical aspects of film and video might cause the director problems. It might be exciting to find someone who is a "natural" for the part, but if he can't be "natural" and adhere to the technical requirements at the same time, the director's schedule might fly out the window.

Lenses

Generally, actors should be conscious of what lens is being used and how many cameras are rolling. Inform your actor if you plan a tight close-up, for example, so he will be aware of the frame size and won't exaggerate his movement or bob in and out of the frame. In a wider shot, if the actor shakes his head violently, he should be instructed to compromise the movement to match the lens size. Conversely, if the camera angle is very wide, the actor should know that subtle actions on his part will not be seen.

Eye-line is another technical area in which the actor must be concerned about his relationship to the lens. An actor might have to look just to the right or left of the lens to give the illusion that he is speaking to another character. If the actor to whom he is speaking cannot put his face in the correct position for the eye-line, the camera operator might put a piece of tape on the lens in the correct position, challenging the performer to act to a piece of tape.

The director should be aware of any obstacles in the way of the actor's eye-line. If in the distance, just off set, people are watching the shoot within the actor's line of vision, he might not be able to concentrate. In this case, have the assistant director clear the actor's eye-line (Figure 15.1).

> When we were doing the shot where she loses her wallet, we covered it from a few angles. One of the angles I wanted was a dolly shot through Grand Central, right through the main hall. No tracks, but we had a dolly with wheels. It would cover Scotty after she looks at the boards and starts walking, and suddenly Bernard Johnson would enter the frame as she's walking, as we're dollying, bump into her, and then we'd cover it.
>
> Because I wanted to leave it ambiguous as to where she actually lost the wallet, I had to have her lose the wallet somewhere in the shot without giving it away how she lost it. We start off in a tight shot, Scotty takes out the wallet, she looks up, we start dollying, she starts moving. As she was walking, she was going to drop the wallet so you wouldn't notice it.
>
> People say New Yorkers don't care. Well, every time we did this shot, somebody inevitably would yell out, "Hey, lady, you dropped your wallet." And one woman even was so bold as to see the wallet being dropped, not pick it up, but turn and yell to Scotty that she had dropped her wallet, and when Scotty didn't respond, she ran over to her and hit her on the shoulder while the camera was rolling!
>
> So that shot eventually was preceded by my assistant director yelling out, "This is a movie. This lady is going to drop her wallet. Please don't pick it up!"
>
> *Adam*

Hitting Marks

It is often awkward for an actor to move in such a way as to play to the camera. Besides performing, the actor might be required to walk and stop at a particular point, called a *mark*. If the actor overshoots his mark, he might go out of the frame or out of focus. Grips sometimes place sandbags at the actor's final stopping position. This enables the actor to walk to his mark, feel the bag with his feet, and not have to look down.

> In terms of position, that was the AD's job. He was just watching to make sure people hit the same marks, looked in the same way, that the screen directions were right. And he had no problem doing that because his basic function was just to make sure we were on schedule, that we were moving on to the next shot, that the kids were either there or not there as they should be, and that was it.
>
> *Howard*

Figure 15.1 Controlling the people in Grand Central Station was next to impossible. Scene from *The Lunch Date.*

Apple Boxes

A common actor-to-lens adjustment is for height. An actor who is much shorter than his partner might need to be raised slightly in a two-shot or over-the-shoulder shot. Apple boxes, which are wooden boxes of various heights, enable the DP to put an actor at the required level so he can be in the same frame as the other performers (Figure 15.2).

Locations

An actor working on a complete set or in a location knows where he is and how his character would use the space. The art department works its miracles to make a set look the way the script says it should. However, the art department only takes care of the area that the camera will see.

> Our last shooting day was in the restaurant. The first thing in the morning, we were setting up the equipment, and Scotty comes in. She looks around and sees the pushcarts and the things hanging from the ceiling. She sees the whole messy room. She comes over and says, "Adam, I have to talk to you." She has a very concerned look on her face. I say, "Scotty, what's wrong?" She says, "I've been trying, but I just don't see how my character would eat in a place like this!" I said, "Don't worry, you're only going to see the clean part in the shot."
>
> *Adam*

The Director as Audience

In the theater, the rapport between the audience and the performer has a profound effect on the energy level and direction of the performance. In a film or video, the actor plays for the director. She alone knows how all the little bits and pieces will come together in the editing room, and she evaluates the performance.

DIRECTING ACTORS

Novice directors often give actors too much direction. You cannot request that the actor be angry, compassionate, and ironic at the same time. A good suggestion is to rehearse the scene first for anger, and then rehearse again, letting the actor add any other emotions that the scene requires. The beats of a scene are built like this: little by little, layer by layer.

As she directs, the director must take into consideration the technical aspects of the performance. At a certain point in the scene, the actor must hit a specific place on the set where a particular light will illuminate his face. Again, build the sequence beat by beat. This allows the actor to memorize the specific beats, the camera requirements, and the order in which they come.

The Director's Tools

The director can use camera, lights, and editing to help shape a performance. The camera can magnify a performance in a close-up, or it can distance the audience with an extreme long shot. Unlike the theater,

Figure 15.2 Apple boxes have many uses, including adding height to actors.

film and video acting requires little or no projection, and the camera is very unkind to overacting. If the director is dissatisfied with an actor's interpretation of his character, she might opt to shoot the actor from a distance and avoid close-ups in difficult acting scenes, even if she had planned close-ups in her storyboards.

Lighting can also be employed to disguise a weak performance. Imagine a scene where the actor is in a shadow. The audience's imagination will fill in a great deal of information that the actor does not provide. The director can control the performance even more by having the character to whom the actor is speaking well lit, so that the audience concentrates on that character's reaction to the dialogue.

Types of Characters

There are three types of script characters with which the director must be concerned: background, secondary, and primary characters.

Background Characters

Background characters, also referred to as *extras* or *atmosphere*, are the characters that fill out and populate the frame but have no direct relationship to the main players. Background characters "people" the sequence and represent the world of the story.

The presence or absence of background players contributes to the story. Imagine *The Lunch Date* without Grand Central Station teeming with people from all walks of life. What would the luncheonette scene in *The Lunch Date* be like with customers at every table?

Imagine, for example, that a scene takes place in a crowded bar:

INT. BAR - NIGHT

Joe enters the bar. He sees the love of his life, Amy, sitting at a table across the room. The bar is smoky and crowded. Joe winds his way through the crowd toward Amy's table.

It would be difficult to stage this scene as written without people to fill the barroom. If staged with only the main characters, this scene would say something very different from what the scriptwriter intended, and it would project a surreal quality.

The type of people in the background will tell the audience a lot about the bar. Is it in a large urban setting or in a small Midwestern town? Does it cater to an upscale, middle-class, or lower-class clientele? Are the patrons working people or retirees? These decisions are important.

The extras, who are traditionally directed by the assistant director, must create the illusion that they are chatting (or whatever) without making any noise. Nothing should interfere with the dialogue of the foreground action. Therefore, they must act in silence. The extras mime their noisy actions. They clap without clapping, clink glasses in a toast without allowing the glasses to touch, and throw their heads back in a laugh without making any noise. Later, in postproduction, the sound editor will add the sound of clapping, glasses clinking, and belly laughs.

If the scene requires the extras to dance, the sound recordist can play some appropriate music before the take and then shut it off before the director calls for action. This way, the extras share the same rhythm and appear to be dancing to the same beat.

Extras must maintain continuity within a scene. If, when Amy rises from her stool to greet Joe in the bar, a dancing couple stops to return to their table, they must do so in every take from every angle. The assistant director often calls, "Roll sound . . . roll camera . . . background action." Then when the director is ready, she calls, "Action." The assistant director and the script supervisor watch the extras closely to ensure that they perform consistently throughout the sequence.

Secondary Characters

Secondary characters are those characters who have several scenes, one scene, one line, or even only an interaction with the main characters. Unlike the background players, who are usually instructed by the assistant director merely to stop and go on cue, the secondary players need specific instruction from the director.

INT. BAR - NIGHT

Joe enters the bar. He sees the love of his life, Amy, sitting at a table across the room. The bar is smoky and crowded. Joe winds his way through the crowd toward Amy's table.

Joe passes by a co-worker who shakes his hand and whispers something that makes Joe laugh. Another person at the table, Sam, pulls Joe aside.

SAM
Watch out for Amy. She's pretty angry.

In this scene, the co-worker and Sam are not extras, but secondary characters. In the luncheonette scene in *The Lunch Date*, the cook is also a secondary character (Figure 15.3).

Primary Characters

The director's main job is to work with the primary characters who motivate and act out the plot. The audience should care about their lives. There are many different acting styles and it behooves the director to blend them all into a convincing whole.

If the project is well cast, the director might expect the cast to perform with a minimum of direction. If working with less talented or less experienced actors, the director might have to rehearse the actors both off and on the set until the dramatic points of the scene are clear and solid. She might have to shoot many takes and work with the actors to improve each take before moving on to the next setup.

> I could do things on the set, like say, "This is just after you lost your wallet, and this is going to happen." And Scotty would know where she was in terms of the character's emotions, but she'd also be able to divert from things and stay open. It was interesting. One time I was going over that shot where she is crying, after losing her wallet, and I said, "How did you find that? What were you going through?" And she said, "It was easy for me because the location gave me everything." She didn't have to draw something out of a bad childhood experience. She

just was in the moment there. She's a great actress, so I was very lucky.

> *Adam*

Interviewing for Documentaries

In a documentary, the performance comes from either the subject's actions in life or from her responses to the director's questions. Interviewing is an art form. Here are some suggestions for obtaining the best and most informative responses from the subject:

- Create a mood or setting that makes the subject feel at ease.
- Get the subject talking. The words will be edited at a later stage.
- Ask questions about the subject's personal experience, rather than questions of a general nature.
- Ask questions in an order that will lead the subject to reveal herself.
- Don't put words in the subject's mouth.
- Be patient.

> I let the women informally talk during the preliminary group meetings. I took notes after each session so that I could elicit those same responses again. You figure out the questions you need to ask to catalyze the stories and sentiments you may have heard in a preinterview. In *Little People*, we met people a year before the shoot. In the interview, we could say, "When we were here last year, I remember

Figure 15.3 In this scene from *The Lunch Date*, the cook is a secondary character.

you saying things about how you felt your parents felt guilty that you were born a dwarf. Could you talk about that?" And generally, they would discuss the same things we heard a year earlier. We all have our repertoire. It's reassuring to know that you can get a story again by asking the right question, but it's also important to be open to new and unheard responses.

It was different with *Mirror Mirror* because here I had the four set questions, which is different from the way I usually interview. I generally allow the conversation to flow in directions that might not be preordained. I think it's important not to get too locked into your agenda. You want to remain open to a digression that could be fruitful for the project.

You have to really listen to the person and gently guide the direction of the interview. You can't be sitting there worrying about your next question or how much film is running through the camera and how long they're taking to answer each question. You really have to listen because it's in those moments that you might hear something that causes you to ask something completely different from what you thought your next question would be.

Jan

If you have researched your subject thoroughly, you should be able to adjust your questions during the interview to ensure stimulating responses.

Continuity

An extremely important aspect of the shoot is maintaining continuity. Continuity is the uninterrupted succession of events. On the screen, a character appears to be moving from scene A to scene B to scene C, and so on. However, the norm is to shoot out of continuity: first B, then A, then C.

I tried to stick close to continuity, but where things like locations became important, we would go away from continuity. For example, as I mentioned before, we were only allowed to shoot on the platforms [at Grand Central Station] when the supervisor came down. So suddenly in the middle of the day, we would have to stop and do that.

Adam

In scene A, the actor has on a blue shirt. In scene B, she changes clothes and puts on a yellow dress. Scene C finds her in the same yellow dress. This is the progression in the script. The progression of the shoot requires you to shoot scene B first, with

the actor in the yellow dress. If the next scene is A, to sustain script continuity, the actor must change to the blue shirt. The wardrobe designer or dresser maintains the continuity of the costumes the actors wear. This is accomplished with the aid of script notes, breakdown sheets, and snapshots of the actors in their various outfits.

Continuity was the AD's department. I felt the film was so well scheduled that the production manager, the AD, and the DP all understood what was supposed to happened each moment. It was fixed in our minds that each of us could have caught the other in a major continuity mistake. Thus, the AD, besides running the set, was handling the continuity. It would have been nice to have a continuity person, but it wasn't necessary. Except for the fantasy costumes, the kids were always in the same dumpy gym clothes, including the same socks with their names on them, so we knew they were getting the same costumes.

Howard

Here is another example of continuity: The shooting schedule calls for a shot in which the actor crosses his legs when he sits in a chair. Later that day, the director shoots a wide shot in which the actor walks into the room, sits down on the chair, and crosses his legs. Which leg did he cross in the previous shot? Will the two actions match in the editing room?

Script supervisors watch constantly for the matching of liquid in glasses, hand movements, lengths of cigarettes, eye-line, and any action. Actors need constant reminders of how to repeat the actions of a preceding take and at what point in the scene these actions happen. If there is no continuity person on the set, it becomes the duty of all parties to watch for this critical aspect of the shoot.

Overlapping Action

When possible, the director should watch for places to overlap action. Action makes for a very smooth cut because the audience is concentrating on the character's movement in the frame. A cut from movement to movement is less obvious than a cut from a static frame to a static frame. For example, suppose that an actor sits down in a medium shot. When the director calls cut and moves the camera in for the close-up shot, she should have the actor "sit into" the shot in case she or her editor wants to make a cut on the action.

Special Situations

Children and Animals

If your script calls for a child or a pet or wild animal, you will face unique production problems (Figure 15.4). Children come with parents; animals come with trainers.

Working with small children and animals can be time-consuming. Allow a grace period in your schedule for these tricky performers. Be prepared to simplify or cut. An uncooperative dog can be shot so that it is out of the frame. The actors' reaction and the sound of a barking, panting dog will give the illusion that the dog is in the scene.

> Our single most difficult problem—besides the kids' stamina and interest—was the boy who played Truman. It wasn't an ego problem; it was an age and maturity problem. He was an eight-year-old boy, kind of hyperactive, who didn't want to be an actor. He got shanghaied into this because it sounded like fun. He looked right, and I convinced his parents.
>
> He had never been away from home. His first night on location, he cried for an hour on the phone to his mom; he was frightened. He was also embarrassed to have to stand in front of all these people and pretend to be something he really wasn't. His natural reaction in dealing with pressure and insecurity was to giggle or to smile. Even though he had been to rehearsals, this was different. It was no longer just him and me, but a group of people with the camera rolling, everybody staring. He would smile or giggle or lose his composure halfway through the take. We were burning up so much film we had to buy extra.
>
> *Howard*

Stunts and Nudity

Actors will do almost anything you ask of them with the exception of stunts and nudity. Although some actors can perform their own stunts, it is imperative to employ a stunt double for dangerous sequences. If an actor is injured while performing a stunt, you might have to shut down production. Besides performing stunts, stuntpeople often can inform the DP about the best angles for recording the stunt.

Nudity is a delicate issue. If the story requires a nude scene, feel free to ask the actor to perform in it. If he agrees, understand that actors often balk just before the shot. Do not panic. This is why there are body doubles. Simply redesign your shots to use the actor as much as you can, and then use the body double for long, shadowy, or close shots in which the character's face is not visible.

Tips for Directing

- Novice directors sometimes feel uncomfortable working with actors for the first time. Their language and work methods can be intimidating. Be honest and up-front with your talent. Do not try to sound as if you know what you are doing if you do not. Keep your direction simple and to the point. The actors will most likely help you.
- Make all the actors feel they are important, no matter how small or large their part. Regardless of their screen time, each character is integral to the whole. After you call "cut" at the end of a shot, do not ignore the actors or seem dissatisfied with their work.

Figure 15.4 Working with children can be quite challenging. Scene from *Truman*.

- Shoot a scene as many times as you feel is necessary. If the scene is not working, shake things up: Shoot from another angle, change the blocking, shoot reactions, or break for lunch and come back to the scene later.
- Shoot the rehearsal. Often the best take is the first because it is fresh and spontaneous.
- Half your battle will be won if you cast well.

PRODUCER
Accommodate

As long as the work is going well and the actors are comfortable, the producer is not involved in directing the actors. However, he does become involved as a mediator if a problem arises.

SOCIALIZING

The director and crew are busy all day long, but the producer has the opportunity to socialize with the cast and make them feel comfortable. He can lift their morale if they are feeling low and cue them on their lines. The time spent with the actors between scenes can be productive if their spirits are buoyed by the interaction.

CONTRACTS AND DEAL MEMOS

Even if the talent is working for free, a simple contract or deal memo between the production company and the artist is standard operating procedure. The following information should be included in this document:

- The amount or rate you will pay or any alternate compensation such as deferred money or a copy of the film or tape
- The "on or about" dates to lock the actor into your schedule
- Any unusual requests such as nudity or stunts

On or about is a legal term that allows the production company a grace period of two or three days on either side of the start date. If you are scheduled to start shooting on May 10 but for some reason do not start until May 13, the contract with the actor is still valid. If you postpone until June 15, though, the contact is void and will have to be renegotiated.

A release is required of everyone who performs in your project. The deal memo or letter acts as your release. It gives you permission to use the actor's picture and voice in your project. The release is a very important document. If not handled properly, it might adversely affect your ability to secure distribution for the picture. (See Chapter 19, "Distribution," for more information.)

As long as you honor the terms outlined in the deal memo, the actor should be content. If you try to violate the conditions detailed in the memo or exploit the artist, you will have problems. For example, if you ask an actor to play a scene in the nude without having discussed the scene with him or written the request into the deal memo, the actor has every right to balk.

Consider the following questions when preparing a deal memo:

- Are there any production dates that conflict with the actor's personal schedule?
- Should you ask the actor to provide her own wardrobe? Will you dry-clean the garments after production?
- If you will supply meals, does the actor have special dietary requirements?
- Are you obligated to provide the actor with a video copy on completion?

Firing Talent

After hiring and rehearsing the actors, it might seem strange to consider firing them, and in fact, actors are rarely fired once shooting has begun. Everyone behind the camera can be replaced at a moment's notice, but to fire an actor means reshooting all the shots in which he appears. Firing someone has catastrophic implications on the budget and on morale. Still, if a casting mistake has been made, it is better to face it and replace the actor as soon as possible. Actors cannot be changed in the editing room.

KEY POINTS

1. Respect the actors.
2. Do not call them to the set until you are ready for them.
3. If a scene or shot is not working, rehearse it until it is right.
4. After each take, acknowledge the actors' effort in a positive way.

part three

Postproduction

Your film or video is now shot, or "in the can." The task of assembling and polishing the final product can now begin. During postproduction, the pictures and sounds that have been recorded are shaped to tell your story.

DIRECTOR

During preproduction, the director translates the screenplay into storyboards and the storyboards into a shot list. During principal photography stage of a project, she transforms the shot list into dailies. This material is now ready to be delivered to the editing room for assembly.

Postproduction is an exciting time. It is certainly a more relaxed phase than principal photography. Shaping the material one-on-one with an editor is an intense and exhilarating adventure for the director. She comes to the editing room filled with the enthusiasm and experiences of the shoot.

The final picture will only be as good as the dailies with which the editor works. A finished print can be made only from in-focus, well-exposed shots; it is not created from ideas, wishes, cut lines, or the big shot that got away. Guided by the director's vision of the story, the editor's role is to make a seamless series of cuts so that the picture flows from one shot to the next. The goal is to produce the best picture possible.

If there is one rule of thumb for the director at this stage, it is to become ruthlessly objective with the footage as quickly as possible. It is natural to fall in love with the footage, making it difficult to cut anything out. However, to give the film or video a pace, the raw material must be shaped and trimmed. It is all right to hold onto footage for a while, but there comes a time when the editor must eliminate anything that does not propel the story forward.

PRODUCER

Much of what an audience perceives on the screen is created during the postproduction process when the raw material accumulated during the shoot is transformed into a product. This final phase involves thousands of details, a multitude of decisions, and many complex technical steps. Fortunately, it doesn't involve nearly as many people as production, so the overhead is manageable. However, it does demand a detailed plan and schedule.

Time is still money, and though the daily rates are lower now, postproduction might seem to take forever. If the production phase is akin to a sprint, postproduction is more like a marathon. Each project has many variables, so it is difficult to estimate how long a project will take to edit.

The importance of sound and music to a picture should not be ignored. Having been brought up in a predominantly visual environment, the novice film- or videomaker can distinguish a wonderful camera move or visual effect more readily than an effective sound or piece of music. Easily seduced by illusion, many novices do not spent enough time deconstructing all the elements of a film or video, and the contribution of aural elements eludes them. After the pictures and dialogue are cut, however, a tremendously important level of information is communicated by sound and music.

THE POSTPRODUCTION PROCESS

All films go through certain basic postproduction steps (Figure III.1). Video projects go through the same artistic process, but with some technical variations. If you are shooting on film but are interested in completing part or all of the postproduction process on video, you'll find the procedure discussed in Chapter 18.

Film	Video
1. Set up editing room	Linear or nonlinear
2. Sync dailies	Digitize (for nonlinear)
3. Code and log dailies	Affix time code and log
4. Screen dailies, selected takes	
5. Assembly	The paper cut (edit on paper)
6. Rough cut	
7. Paper cut	
8. Reshoots, stock footage	
9. Second cut	
10. Temporary music	
11. Fine cut	
12. Sound design	
13. Score	
14. Mix	
15. Shoot opticals, title	On-line
16. Cut negative	On-line
17. Timing	On-line
18. Mute print (optional)	
19. First trial	Transfer to film (optional)
20. Answer print	

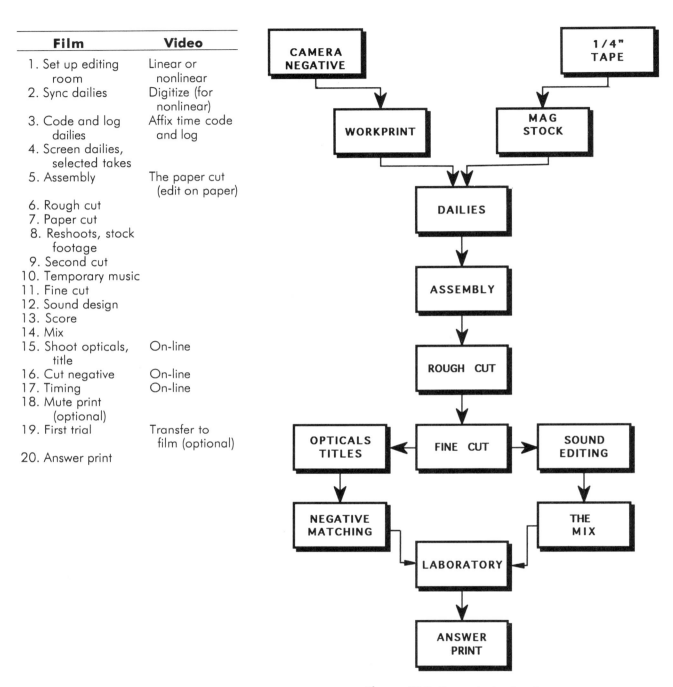

Figure III.1 Postproduction flowchart.

chapter sixteen

Picture Postproduction

Don't force the film into pre-conceived notions. Let the film find itself. The same thing goes for narrative. Sometimes the script doesn't work.

Jan

DIRECTOR

Edit

Much of the editing process is trial and error. Success is usually attributed to 10 percent inspiration and 90 percent perspiration. It is only through perseverance and patience that the project will come together.

> There were two moments that I felt some satisfaction, which both had to do with the salad sequence. When I started shooting the salad sequence, and then when I started editing it together, I felt, "There's something here, I don't know what it is, but something is working here."
>
> *Adam*

SYNCING DAILIES

Film

The first step in the editorial process takes place during the production period. An editing room is set up to sync up the material shot each day. A film editing room needs the following:

1. Flatbed editing table (Moviola, Steenbeck, or Kem)
   - Stand-up Moviola (optional)
2. Editing bench with:
   - Synchronizer
   - Squawk box
   - Headphones
   - Rewinds
   - Reel clamps
   - Spacers
   - Film splicer (sound splicer optional)
   - Split reels
3. Supplies
   - Film editing tape
   - Sound editing tape
   - Paper tape
   - Sharpies (pens)
   - Sound fill
   - Sound and picture leader
   - Grease pencils
   - Notebooks and pencils

The second step in the editing process is to synchronize the sound and picture so that they can be played simultaneously, broken up, and then put back together again. It is extremely important that this be done accurately. Sound and picture must be in perfect unison. If even a few frames are out of sync, it can be spotted on the screen. This step also will be completed during production.

Slates

The film is developed at the laboratory and a work print is struck from the negative. The quarter-inch magnetic sound tape is transferred to a sprocket mag, now referred to as the *track*. The editorial assistant will sync the picture and sound. This involves finding each scene's slate, locating and marking the "clap" frame, and then repeating that process on the magnetic track. Once the clap point has been found on both the picture and the track, the two strips of sprocket film are lined up, labeled, evened out, and built onto larger rolls of dailies.

Video

Material shot on video bypasses the development and syncing process, as the sound and picture are imprinted directly onto the video for immediate playback.

Videotape comes out of the box "blank." When shot, it has both a video and a time-code signal placed or "striped" onto it. The time code is a number that identifies each frame of video picture and sound. To prepare the videotape for editing, a time code is visually burned in on the tape. Time code takes this format: hours, minutes, seconds, and frames—for example, 02:45:31:06. These numbers can be logged into a notebook so that the machines can access the specific frames identified as the place for a shot to begin or end.

To prepare blank three-quarter-inch tape for editing, it must first be "blacked." This tape is also referred to as a "basic" tape. A black image and time code are striped onto the tape so that the tape upon which you build the show contains the appropriate codes to remain frame-accurate.

The next step is to place color bars at the head of the tape. This multicolored image allows the video editing machines to set the color and luminance levels. These balances are read on a vectorscope and are standard worldwide.

The visual time code numbers generally must be logged by hand to facilitate the retrieval process during editing. In newer computerized systems, however, logging is done automatically.

Video editing begins in an off-line room or edit bay. This is where the show is built onto videotape. Later, to complete the process, the tape may be re-edited in an on-line room.

Film to Video

Projects shot on film but edited on video need to be transferred at the laboratory from film onto tape to create *video dailies*. Instead of a film workprint, a videotape is struck from the negative. The quarter-inch magnetic sound tape can be matched to the dailies so that sync is maintained.

Film projects to be edited on a nonlinear system must have all the video dailies or selected takes digitized. This can be done by the laboratory or by the editor.

Video technology changes rapidly. Explore available options to determine the type of editing you can afford. Your choices include linear or nonlinear, analog or digital, and composite or component.

CODING AND LOGGING DAILIES

Once in sync, film dailies are coded with a numbering system that is stamped on every foot of film and on the corresponding magnetic sound track. The coding provides continuous reference points for synchronization. If the editor needs to match a particular piece of picture with its original sound, she can do so by matching the numbers. Do not confuse the edge *code* with the permanent latent edge *numbers* that are photographed onto the emulsion of the film (Figure 16.1). No matter how much the film and sound are cut up and moved, the edge code ensures that sync can always be reestablished. Coding is inexpensive (a few cents per foot) but is a critical part of the process.

Code the Film and Magnetic Track

Create a numbering sequence that begins with AA 0000. At intervals of 16 frames for 16mm film (one foot for 35mm film), the code numbers will change—AA 0001, AA 0002, and so forth—allowing you to code almost 10,000 feet of film with this system. Start the next roll with AB 0000.

> *Editors:* By not splicing the work print, you reduce the chances of the print breaking in the coding machine.

Log the Footage

Logging the footage creates a guide that will become important when you need to retrieve, or *pull*, the original negative for reprints or opticals (dissolves, freeze frames, or blowups) and to execute the negative cut.

The log consists of the following information:

- Camera roll number
- Slate number
- Start key number
- End key number
- Start code number
- End code number
- Scene number

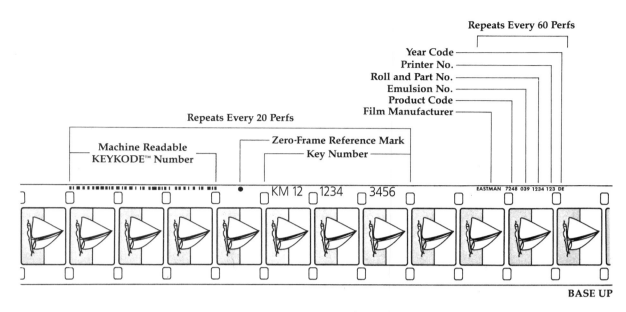

Figure 16.1 Latent edge numbers, also called key numbers, are printed on the film. Code numbers are stamped on after the syncing process. (Courtesy of Eastman Kodak Motion Picture Films, Rochester, NY. © Eastman Kodak Company 1990.)

- Take number
- Description
- Date of shoot

The log enables the editor to locate and identify any piece of negative. This becomes critical when you need to cut the negative to strike an answer print. (Negative cutting and printing are discussed in Chapter 18, "Laboratory/On-line.")

Organize the Dailies According to Scene Numbers

After coding and logging the work print, the footage is broken down and then filed away into boxes that are clearly marked with the scene or sequence number. The editor must have all the footage of each scene at her fingertips. When she is finished working with a particular scene, all the footage that was not cut into the film should be filed back in its original boxes. These pieces are referred to as *trims*. Very short trims should be taped into a notebook, called a *snip book*, and organized by code number.

Editors: If you cut out a piece of film without an edge code number on it, mark the uncoded piece of film with a grease pencil. Draw an arrow pointing to where the next number starts. Do not throw anything away!

Video material, like film, must be logged for access and reference. The time code at the head and tail of each shot, especially of the selected takes, should be written down in a log book. The log can be fed into a database, which will be useful when telling the machine what material to pull to build a sequence.

Set up the Editor's Library

The lined script, the continuity notes, the camera reports, and the sound reports together form the foundation on which the editor bases her understanding of what happened on the set. They tell her what she actually has in the editing room. These four documents are placed in four clearly marked binders and are a part of the editor's library.

Before choosing selected takes for the assembly, the editor reviews the continuity script. This "lined" copy of the script is prepared by the continuity person during the shoot. The lines on the script reflect the actual coverage of each scene and the number of each take (see Figure 11.3).

The lined script enables the editor, assistant editor, and director to "read" the footage without having to screen it. This process saves considerable time in the editing room. For example, suppose the director wants to cut to a close-up of an actor delivering a particular line of dialogue, but the line was not covered in a close-up. The lined script reveals this information, saving the editor and director from sifting through all the footage trying to locate a shot that does not exist.

SCREENING THE DAILIES

At the end of the second day of principal photography, film directors screen the first day's dailies to choose selected takes. It usually takes a day to process and print the film. More time might be required if the laboratory is far away or if it develops your type of stock only when there is ample material to justify filling a bath. (Film is developed by placing the negative in a bath of photographic chemicals.) Video dailies, on the other hand, can be screened immediately because they do not require chemical development.

The editor participates in the screening of the dailies. This initial session allows the director to offer immediate feedback about how she would like to approach the first cut of the film, which moments to use, and which to avoid.

VIDEO OFF-LINE EDITING

Although the principles are the same, there are technical differences between film and video editing. Video editing is becoming so popular that many films are being transferred to video to take advantage of the ease and speed of off-line and on-line editing.

Off-line and on-line are videotape editing processes that can be compared to editing the work print and cutting the negative. *Off-line* is the editorial session in which the editor creates an edit decision list (EDL). This list of frame numbers is taken to an on-line editing room, where the show is finalized via a computerized "assembling" process.

Your original material, whether film or video, can be transferred to three-quarter-inch videotape with visual time code—a frame-accurate numbering system that is burned into the bottom of each frame.

SMPTE time code, either an audio tone or an address track, is placed on one of the two audio tracks available on the video signal. This tone enables the video machines to "read" the time code to "search and find" any frame on the tape.

The video editor begins by "off-lining" the project. An off-line edit is comparable to a film rough edit. Using two three-quarter-inch video decks, the editor identifies one as the master and uses the other for dailies. Transferring the material from the dailies deck to the master deck, the editor "builds" the show shot by shot, sound byte by sound byte.

Each time the editor makes a pass on the cut or needs to make changes, he builds a new master tape. This means that each cut loses a generation of quality. New editing machines, driven by computers, allow the video editor to work in a nonlinear mode. This process is more akin to film editing, and each cut can be made on the same generation of material.

Linear and Nonlinear

Cutting on video can be done by one of two methods: linear or nonlinear. To understand the difference between them, consider this example. You are putting together an actor's reel, a composite of five of his best performances, to show to agents and producers. From the five original scenes, on five different tapes, you place his performances in this order on the master tape:

1. *Hamlet*
2. *Oleanna*
3. *Wuthering Heights*
4. *Forrest Gump*
5. *Naked*

You view the cut, and it becomes obvious that it would be to the actor's advantage to begin the tape with his scene from *Forrest Gump*. In a linear editing session, you would start from the beginning and re-record, or lay down on a new tape, all five scenes, starting with scene 4. On a nonlinear system, you would simply program the machine to make the change, and it would be done instantaneously.

Analog and Digital

Both types of tape are linear (in a line). Even the digital tape, though high quality, is still linear. To find a particular shot, you have to run the tape to that spot and then lift it or copy it onto a master.

The Tape

Until recently, all videotape was analog, which means that a magnetic signal read by a magnetic head shaped the tape to conform to the image recorded by the camera. Digital tape has a binary system (zeros and ones) encoded on the actual stock. This series of zeros and ones is told by the video signal how to conform the image on the tape to what the camera sees.

The Equipment

Analog tape is cut on a linear editing system. When the tape deck finds the frames identified by the time code, it stops and transfers them to the master deck.

A nonlinear video editing system transfers the original material, whether film, analog tape, or digital tape, onto a computer's hard drive. This is done through a process called *digitizing the image*. Digital editing on a nonlinear system means that the information can be retrieved instantaneously. The director and the editor can preview many different cuts in a short period of time.

A major factor in the digital technology revolution is the use of compression. Shrinking the data to ever-smaller size allows the machines to be faster and more efficient and to hold more information on the hard drive. In the world of desktop video editing, it will not be long before the compressed digital component image can be passed along the fiber optics of the director's phone line to enable her to edit at home on her laptop computer!

In the nonlinear editing session, the show is built by numbers, but it only exists in the computer's memory. It is not until the on-line session or negative cut that the original materials are conformed to the EDL produced during the off-line session.

Nonlinear systems, such as those by Avid, Light-Works, EMC^2, Montage, The Cube, and ProMedia 100, allow you to build your show with computer software and view it on a computer monitor, but the picture consists only of digitized images on a hard drive. Ultimately, the original material will be conformed to your cut in the on-line session. Today compression of the video signal is so advanced that the digitized image is broadcast-quality, as good as the original. This means the off- and on-line sessions are completed on one machine.

Is all this new technology a good thing? The answer probably is yes, but producers, directors, and editors do have some concerns about all these new systems:

- Editing is faster, but the deadlines are the same—editors have more time to "tinker" than before.
- Why go so fast? Humans need time to absorb the material and think through a cut. No computer system has yet been given a "creative" chip.
- Analog has a warmer sound and a warmer look. Is the coldness of digital merely a part of this technological transition?
- Fabulous editing equipment does not an editor make.

ASSEMBLING THE FIRST CUT

The Loose Cut

First, the story is put together in the order indicated by the script. This loose cut sometimes includes only the master shots pieced together one after the other. It allows the editor, director, and producer to experience the flow of the story and gain a sense of the direction the film is taking. Some directors opt to skip this step and move right to a rough cut.

In video, this first step can be achieved on paper. By previewing your tapes before you enter the off-line edit room, you save time and money. Prescreening and logging selected takes makes it faster to put the correct takes onto the master videotape. The paper edit, complete with time code written down for the beginning (in) and ending (out) of each shot, makes the first assembly a mechanical one.

The Rough Cut

The rough cut is an attempt to view the picture as a whole with traditional editorial techniques. It includes shots to establish location, close-ups to provide emphasis, insert shots to orchestrate the story, and dissolves to show the passage of time. This cut is a difficult one to view because it shows the story, yet lacks music, sound effects, and overlapping dialogue. In short, the entire sound design will not be present to assist the viewer in appreciating the full impact and flow of the film. The rough cut is strictly a visual cut with key dialogue.

If the picture requires any opticals or reshoots, the editor places a piece of black film, or *slug*, in the appropriate spaces, and the viewer sees nothing on the screen. Therefore, imagination is a vital element in viewing a rough cut.

The rough cut should follow exactly the continuity of the script. There should be no deviations, even though obvious changes might be required. One of the primary goals of this first cut is to evaluate whether the structure of the original script works. Revelations that affect the rest of the editing process will come from viewing this cut.

There is an analogy to this process in scriptwriting. The axiom "Writing is rewriting" can be applied to editing as well. You are, in fact, writing your film with celluloid or videotape. The script will soon be history. What will bloom as your film or video is growing from the material you exposed on the set.

> I did a shot where I thought I needed to build up more to the character's anxiety about being in this unfamiliar world. So I shot a quick little scene where Scotty, the actress, goes into the women's bathroom at Grand Central. I don't know if you've ever seen what that's like, but it's horrible. I did a shot where she walks in and then backs out two seconds later. But by the time I got to putting together the film, the scene was unnecessary.
>
> *Adam*

Guidelines for the First Cut

- Take out any extraneous sounds on the track that will be distracting, such as the director saying "Action" or "Cut."
- Use straight edits when cutting dialogue. Do not begin to overlap dialogue yet. It is not necessary.
- Do not insert sound from other takes.
- Do not waste time fine-tuning scenes until they are seen in the context of the whole. You must have a sense of the rhythm and tempo of the complete piece before adjusting each scene.

Each stage is about discovering the story because you have what you think is the film on paper, in your script, and suddenly, as soon as you start casting it, as soon as you pick a location, suddenly what's on the paper gets more specific, so it starts changing. Then you start editing the film, and it starts changing once again. What I originally thought would be the film was nothing like what it turned out to be. Yet, I think you accept that. You don't accept necessarily the end result, but you accept the process. I think it's an interesting process. If you keep yourself open to it, you can make interesting discoveries.

Adam

Speed in Editing

Editing a scene means using the images to create a rhythm that tells the story of the scene properly. Each scene forms a unit that, when joined with the other scenes, creates the rhythm of the entire film. The process of editing demands that the editor get into a rhythm of cutting. It is a visceral experience as much as an intellectual one. There is a direct relationship between the speed with which you cut and your ability to get in touch with and properly interpret the appropriate rhythm of any scene. You can't really know if a cut will work until you make it.

When in doubt, make the cut and move on. It is only film or tape. You can do it over if it doesn't work. There is no point agonizing over each cut—excessive thought about it is counterproductive; it only slows you down. Work quickly, and trust your judgment. The quicker one cut is made, the quicker you can move on to the next one. This is especially important at this stage, when subtlety is secondary to seeing a first cut of the film.

> It's hard to give it up, to know when you're done. I think the same thing probably happens in every process. Certainly with writing, you always feel like you can redo one scene, get a better line here, or whatever. Certainly, when you're shooting, there were more things you felt like you wanted to get. But with editing, you can tinker and tinker and tinker and tinker.
>
> *Adam*

EVOLUTION OF THE EDIT

An actor slips on a line, stutters, or fumbles but finally gets back on track with the dialogue. In the editing room, the director might decide that this human foible is perfect behavior to help the audience understand the character. After all, the actor was "in character," so it might very well have been a slip on the part of the character rather than the actor. Furthermore, the director might decide at dailies that the stutter should be maintained throughout the entire production to distinguish the character's actions.

In *The Lunch Date*, homeless people are integral to the story line. However, it was difficult to keep the real homeless people who congregate in Grand Central Station from looking into the lens, breaking the fourth wall, and therefore spoiling shots.

> I worked on food lines at Grand Central every night before filming, and I asked some of the homeless men to show up when we were shooting. I saw Willie the night before, and he had this harmonica and a great face, so I asked him to show up too. I didn't even think he heard me. But we had a shooting schedule,

Figure 16.2 What seemed like a problem on the set turned into a bit of gold in the editing room.

so at about the time we needed to shoot this shot of Scotty reentering the station, we started looking around for Willie. We did a couple of takes with her just looking around for somebody. Then we did a couple of takes of her entering the station and being upset just by herself.

Then I looked over, and I saw Willie! I approached him and said, "Willie, I want you to play the harmonica when I tell you." And he said, "Ah, OK, OK." I told Scotty that I didn't know what was going to happen, but just to go with it, to stick to her basic motivation, which was to be upset, and we'll see what happens. We rolled the camera, I cued Scotty, I cued Willie, and he entered. He did that number with the harmonica, looking almost straight at the camera, and then he walked off. I yelled "Cut," and my crew looked at me like I was crazy. I thought that it probably was a mistake. Willie walked off somewhere, so I couldn't get him back. I decided to go with a couple of different takes of Scotty by herself.

But when I got into the editing room, there was something I liked about the shot. I knew it was a little dangerous because he looked in the camera, but it didn't bother me enough not to use it because there was something that was real about it that I liked.

Adam

The director chose to use several of these shots in the final cut of the film because they give viewers a documentary feeling, the sensation that they are there with the character at the station (Figure 16.2).

A director must be open to all elements that come into play during production that might affect the project, including mistakes and accidents. Never forget that accidents (both good and bad) that happened during principal photography—tones, moods, and emphasis that shifted, and new ideas—all become part of this editorial phase.

Shifts in Tone

The main character in the script of *The Lunch Date* delivers the line, "Get a job," to a homeless person at the end of the script. This line was cut because the tone of the film had shifted between the writing of the screenplay and the editing process. The reaction of the woman to the man eating her salad was less hostile than originally envisioned, and this reaction to her mistake made for a lighter and happier tone than in the original script. Therefore, for her to walk out into the station and deliver such a line, deliberately telling the audience that the character gained nothing from her encounter with her "lunch date," went against the grain of what the film had evolved into, and the line was therefore easily cut. The director was not aware of this shift until he arrived in the editing room.

Adam saw that to try and force the line into the film, just because it was in the script, would have been a mistake. The director must "listen" to the film. When screening various cuts of the film, the director must become as objective as the audience that views the film for the first time.

After the woman discovers that she sat at the wrong place, she goes and gets her bag and comes back into the station. I saw the film ending with her getting back on the train. I wanted to make a statement that people don't change. She certainly didn't change. When I shot it, I had a man begging for money. All my takes, I had her saying something to him. Basically, it was harsh—"Get a job," or "Get lost," or "Don't bother me"—because I thought this is true, this is what would happen. But while editing the film, I discovered that it was too harsh because something was working in the sequence with the salad. It just felt like a different movie, to have this sequence of her telling the guy to get a job. I like to believe that that was the film speaking to me.

Adam

When a shipbuilder puts a plan down on paper, like the script, it is not written in stone. As the ship is being built, as the film or video is being made, the work becomes three-dimensional. This growth is the creative process. It should be nurtured. This process can constantly change the shape and even the very nature of the work.

A good example of shifting tone is the approach the director takes with a documentary. The final script for a documentary is made during the editorial phase, not during preproduction. The director initially does her research and approaches her subject with an idea of what she would like to accomplish.

Along the way, however, the idea for the documentary might change. The chosen subject sometimes turns out to be less interesting than some other aspect of the narrative that begins to unfold to the director.

I think the editing is half of making the film in documentary. Much of the creation of structure and themes occurs at the editorial stage.

Jan

Analyzing the Rough Cut

You and the producer have just seen the rough cut, the first complete cut, of your film. Many feelings are evident in the room. You might feel depressed or exhilarated or something in between. You might even be in shock and ready to give up. Why? In this premiere screening, you might make many discoveries:

- Do you have a story? Does it work?
- If you have a story, does the current structure work?

- If the story doesn't work, what can you do about it?
- Do you need to shoot more footage (if you can) to make the story work?
- Does the existing structure need to be severely edited?
- Do you need to come up with a new structure?

I think I was ill when I saw my first cut. I thought it would never come together. I wondered how anybody could make a film out of all these bits and pieces of celluloid that didn't seem to add up to anything.

I remember thinking after the rough cut that it was not funny, that it was slow, and that it would never have any grace. It was really difficult to go in there the next day. I thought I had seen something that was unsavable and never going to work.

Howard

At this stage of the process, you can put away the script. The film has now taken on a life of its own. Unless you can do more shooting, you must deal with the footage at hand.

By the end of the film, you've forgotten what you originally intended.

Howard

RESTRUCTURING THE PICTURE

An efficient way to preview what a different scene order might look like is to try it out on paper first. Reduce each scene to one line of description (similar to the one-liner in the scheduling process), and write down the order in which the scenes now appear in this version. You can also perform this paper cut with index cards taped to a wall. With this written overview, the creative team discusses possible variations before actually making another cut.

Paper edits can be used effectively at any time you have a structural problem during the editing process. It is an efficient and time-saving device for previsualizing different structures without having to cut the film or tape.

I did a paper edit. I cut up the transcriptions and highlighted what I thought were the important phrases, so I had pages and pages with highlighted lines. Then I xeroxed it, so I had a master, and then I cut out the lines that looked good. I started doing a flowchart with them. I hung them on the wall and I would move them around, and I would read them out loud. If I cut from so and so saying, "I really hate my hips," to "My hips are the greatest thing since sliced bread," I could read them out loud and see what it would sound like before I actually made the cut.

Jan

Adding Reshoots, Reprints, and Stock Footage

At this stage, any new material (other than opticals) can be cut into the picture. Reshoots, reprints, and stock footage take the place of any "scene missing" slugs. There are many companies that supply film- and videomakers with stock footage. This footage covers a wide variety of events taken over many years, including news, sports, nature, history, person-alities, and distant locations. Images of almost any person, place, or thing can be found and used in your film or video. Most of the available footage was pho-tographed in 16mm or 35mm film and is sold by the foot. *Mirror Mirror* incorporated stock footage very effectively from newsreels of a beauty contest during the twenties and shots of women on antiquated exer-cise machines from the thirties (Figure 16.3).

My idea was to show how the tyranny of the ideal has existed over time and is still with us. In editing, the contemporary footage shot in gyms didn't work, so I had no problem throwing it out. You need to try things. You can't second guess completely what will work and what won't work. Ultimately, I went with stock footage only.

Jan

Before spending money on reshoots, reprints, or stock footage (it's expensive), wait until your film or video has found its proper structure so you can eval-uate your needs.

It is difficult to obtain footage from the Library of Congress because they're more there for research than for reprinting, but the National Archives is a completely separate building. It's in a different place. It's where Nixon's tapes are. They have a motion pic-ture and record administration, and they have all the government footage that is public domain, and some protected material as well, such as NASA footage.

Jan

Many things change during the editing process. Other than inserting stock footage, editing might

Figure 16.3 Stock footage can evoke the past.

reveal the need for additional footage to tell the story properly. Putting in a single shot can sometimes make the difference between a scene working or not. "Connectors" that are often needed at this point include

- Transitions between scenes
- An important close-up of a character to punctuate a moment
- An insert shot of an object to make a story point clear

SCREENING THE SECOND CUT

Screen a cut of the new structure. If the new version still doesn't work, the restructuring should have given you a clearer sense of what you need to try next. From this point, how long it will take to achieve a fine cut and picture lock will depend on a number of variables:

- How much productive time the editor can spend in the editing room
- Whether there are restrictions on money and the editor's availability
- How quickly the changes can be made after you've had a major screening and discussion

As in the first cut, prepare to be brutal with your cutting decisions. Avoid attachment to your footage. Don't worry about minor continuity problems. If you keep the story moving, no one will notice them. So what if there is a slight boom shadow? Only film professionals notice them, not the general audience— as long as they are engrossed in the story. Always cut for the performance.

Keep your eyes and ears open. Suggestions can come from anywhere. Include a fresh audience whenever you screen a cut. Listen to what new viewers have to say, and take notes. Their ideas might not be on the money, but their perspective will stimulate your thinking about the story. Invite key experienced people to the screening to serve as consultants. If you are just learning, you will require assistance.

> I had many screenings of the film which were very helpful. However, the best screenings were the ones in which I had collective feedback; they turned out to be like the scriptwriting process. You turn out drafts of your script to a select group of people who care about you, care about the work, and are really into it. So I had similar sessions on the Steenbeck with half a

dozen people at various stages. We'd go over a scene very carefully, talk about what worked and what didn't, and possible changes, and then I'd execute them. A week later, I'd show it again. So it was like the writing process, just writing in the cutting room.
> *Howard*

EDITING TECHNIQUES

There are editing techniques you can use to smooth over rough spots, make transitions flow, and even perform miracles with a scene that refuses to work. These tricks range from standard editing techniques to less conventional solutions to editing problems. The film or video experience is an illusion. You might need to use a little smoke and mirrors once in a while to make the illusion complete.

In the end, all that matters is telling the story as best you can. Do not force the footage into what you would like it to be. Create the best from what you have, and build on that. The more you edit, the more confident you will become and the more you will trust your instincts. There can be great joy and satisfaction in solving a problem and in seeing your film or video come together, moment by moment and scene by scene, through hard work and perseverance.

> Editing can be very discouraging. You're by yourself, and that makes it very hard. If you can surround yourself with good people who will help you out, it will make the process easier, but you've got to stop falling in love with the film, and just sit down and do it. Treat the editing process like work.
> *Howard*

The following are some editing and transition principles to keep in mind and experiment with as you refine your story:

DIALOGUE OVERLAPS. A common device, when attempting to duplicate the normal speech patterns of people talking to one another, is to overlap dialogue and picture. This requires the use of the reaction shot—that is, showing the person who the speaker is addressing, rather than the speaker. This way, we hear the dialogue while witnessing (and sharing) a reaction with the nonspeaking character.

Some editors prefer to cut two dialogue tracks from the beginning of the editing process. Most, however, wait until the picture is locked to begin separating the dialogue tracks. Although cutting two tracks is more time-consuming, the editor who cuts in this fashion can find the natural rhythms of a scene at an earlier stage of the edit. Overlapping dialogue, even having two characters speak at once as if they have interrupted each other, can be achieved early in the editing if the editor is cutting two dialogue tracks.

CUTTING ON MOVEMENT. Cuts work well when they are made on a movement of some kind. For example, a cut made as a character sits down makes for a very smooth transition between shots. Even shots that have no logical connection with one another (and no continuity of space and time) can be cut smoothly with some movement in each shot to "mask" the cut—for example, the match cut of a cloud passing by the moon to a razor slicing a human eyeball.

CONTINUITY. Do not be a slave to continuity. If you can't find the right reaction shot for a key dramatic moment in a sequence, look to another part of the scene for a shot you can "steal." It might be out of continuity, but as long as it works, why not use it? It might even be possible to steal a shot from an entirely different scene as long as it was filmed in a similar location with matching light. If you are looking for a quiet reaction shot, try stealing a close-up of an actor the moment after the slate is pulled and the director calls "Action."

DISSOLVES. A *dissolve* is a cross-fading of two scenes to overlap images for dramatic or emotional effect. Dissolves can be short (eight to 16 frames) and called *soft cuts*, or long (24 to 96 frames) and called *lap dissolves*. The length of the dissolve is fixed by the lab.

FADES. A *fade* is a gradual picture transition from or to blackness. Fades can smooth out the transition from one scene to another.

SOUND TAKES. For off-camera dialogue, look for the best line readings. It might be possible to combine parts of different readings of the same line as long as they are from the same aural perspective. That is, the background sounds should be the same. Moving bits and pieces of sound around can solve many editing problems.

NEW LINES. The addition of a line or phrase often adds a piece of exposition that wasn't clear in the script. A line can be added to the beginning or end of a speech while the actor is either turned away from or completely off-camera. For example, sup-

pose the character says, "In my life, I have made no mistakes." The director can add to the line, ". . . except when I fell in love with you." If this tag line is recorded by the same actor and added to a shot where his back is toward the camera, the director can significantly change the meaning of the scene.

SOUNDS. Work with or preview as many sounds as you can before locking the picture. If a particular sound effect will be used as an important tension-building device in a scene, transfer the sound and use it while you cut your picture.

A specific sound might change the way you look at a sequence. Perhaps the original scene was designed without a phone ringing. Now, in the editing room, you get the idea of adding this sound effect, even though the character does not answer or even acknowledge it. The sound effect might shift the meaning of the scene and even the entire story. The addition of the phone ring, if it works, would require the editor to lengthen the shot to allow viewers to ask themselves why the character doesn't answer the phone.

VOICE-OVERS. Any voice-over indicated in the script or created during the editing process should be recorded (even if it is a scratch track) and refined during picture editing to ensure proper timing before manufacturing the final sound track.

As you edit, keep these points in mind:

- Ask yourself, Does this cut work? This is the only criterion for leaving a shot in the picture. It doesn't matter if it is a cheat (trick).
- Just make the cut! A cut won't happen by itself. You can't know if it will work or not until you try it.
- Cut as tight as you can. There is no reason to keep scenes loose. You can always put back what you've taken out. The sooner you see the potential of the piece, the better.

Temporary Music

To ensure that the story has a flow and pace that will satisfy an audience, include a temporary music track, even in the rough cut screenings. Always have temporary music added when screening important cuts in front of an audience. Even a seasoned filmmaker might have difficulty watching a silent sequence that normally requires music or sound. Previewing different kinds of "temp" music will shape the director's ideas about what she eventually will want for the sound track.

Temp music is a wonderful opportunity to experiment with different kinds of themes and tempos for your picture. If you are going to be working with a composer, previewing a variety of pieces helps illustrate the kind of music you want. If you use preexisting music, be careful not to fall in love with a popular piece that might be out of your financial reach. If your goal is to distribute the project commercially, you must secure the rights to your music selections in advance. The rights to a small portion of a well-known tune might cost thousands of dollars. Even if you are only planning to screen your piece noncommercially at festivals and exhibitions, limited or "festival rights" must be secured.

Screenings

Preview different cuts of the film in a screening room or small theater as well as in the editing room. It is exciting to see your picture on a big screen once in a while. There is so much you miss when you see it on the picture head of an editing machine. More important, screening it in a large room will help you evaluate the film's true rhythm and pacing.

LOCKING THE PICTURE

Finally, the picture is screened, cut, trimmed, and shaped to the liking of everyone on the creative team. The picture is now considered to be *locked*, and the product is known as the *fine cut*. Locking the picture means that the timing of each scene is fixed, and no more picture changes should be made. At this point, sound work can begin. Sound is either handled by the editor or farmed out to a specialist known as a *sound designer* or *sound effects editor*. A composer must now be selected if the choice hasn't already been made.

PRODUCER
Advise

One of the producer's major responsibilities is to be one step ahead of what is happening. During preproduction, he assembles a well-run production unit, which allows the members of the creative team to function at their optimum ability. Once production is

in full swing and, it is hoped, on schedule, the producer's next job is to prepare for postproduction. This is the time for the transition from producer as production manager to producer as postproduction supervisor.

Think of postproduction as a separate period with its own unique set of challenges and problems. Unfortunately, many novice film- and videomakers tend to resist beginning this part of the process. Much of their hesitation is due to their disappointment with the rushes. What was captured on film or tape might not have lived up to their expectations of the script. Each viewing during postproduction might revive some of the nightmare of production. This negativity must be replaced with the excitement and anticipation of being able to sit down and solve all the problems.

The producer can play an invaluable role in helping the director get over this psychological hurdle and get back on track. Even though editing can be downright frustrating, it should be an exciting experience. There might not be troublesome weather or temperamental actors to deal with, but there are still many creative challenges to face.

EDITING ROOM

It is the producer's job to see that the editing room is properly equipped and that enough money is budgeted for supplies to last the entire postproduction period. Generally, the editor or assistant editor makes the order, and the producer negotiates the deal with the editing facility or vendor that supplies the editing suite or supplies.

POSTPRODUCTION SCHEDULE

With the mix date as your goal, create a schedule, relying on the steps outlined in this chapter. This schedule will undoubtedly go through changes. How long it takes to arrive at the fine cut of your project depends not only on the structural challenges of the picture, but also on how much time it takes to complete the changes for each cut. For students and independents, the availability of editing facilities will have an impact on postproduction progress. Fine-cutting a 10-minute project might take a professional several weeks, but for a beginner, it might take several months.

These various steps serve as benchmarks of your progress through the postproduction period. A convenient aid for staying on schedule is a large calendar board. This larger-than-life visual representation of your postproduction schedule will help the creative team stay focused on its goals as each level is achieved.

THE EDITOR

The editor is a craftsperson, technician, and artist who has the patience and facility to create order out of thousands of images. Beginning directors can learn much about the craft of editing and storytelling from an experienced editor. The editor's manipulation of sounds and images is often needed to realize the creative potential of the material. The script might be recorded on the set, but the film or video is built in the cutting room.

For many directors, the craft of editing has been an effective stepping-stone. Robert Wise edited *Citizen Kane* before he went on to direct *The Set-Up*, *West Side Story*, and *The Sound of Music*. David Lean, director of *Lawrence of Arabia* and *Passage to India*, was one of England's premier editors before being hired to codirect *In Which We Serve* with Noel Coward. Hal Ashby was one of Hollywood's better-known editors before being given the chance to direct a small picture called *The Landlord*. He went on to direct *Harold and Maude*, *Coming Home*, and *Being There*. George Lucas, a talented director, now prefers to work solely in postproduction. These outstanding filmmakers spent years practicing the art and craft of storytelling while fixing the mistakes of the directors with whom they worked. They learned about rhythm and pacing and how to control it—all the tools a director must master.

Finding an Editor

Good material is the most effective selling tool for attracting creative people. Make an interesting film or video, and people will want to be associated with it. How much you have to pay for their services (if anything at all) depends on what you can negotiate. It is a given that you do not have much to spend. However, any compensation will create a business relationship and give you some leverage when asking for a 100-percent commitment.

Independents: Advertise through the local media organizations and the editor's guild. You might be able to find a professional assistant editor who works on features, documentaries, or industrials and is looking for projects to expand his reel and gain experience as an editor. It takes a while for an assistant editor to work his way up the union ladder to become a full editor. Short projects offer assistant editors an opportunity to express themselves creatively, and they provide valuable credits. Alternatively, you might find a commercial editor who is looking for narrative or documentary work or a video editor who is looking for film work.

Students: Ask around and advertise. Put together and post a professional-looking flier for your project. Search for talented students who are interested in pursuing editing as a career. They will be looking for projects like yours to gain valuable experience and expand their professional reels.

Evaluating Prospective Editors

Evaluating an editor's contribution to another film or video requires more than just judging the work. You will need to talk to the director and producer and anyone else involved in the editorial process to find out exactly what the editor's contribution was to the postproduction process. To what extent was the editor responsible for creating the rhythm and pace of the piece? How active a role did the director play in the editing process? Did she stand next to the editor and suggest cuts, or did she stay away from the editing room? Other questions to ask: Was another editor involved? Did the director have to take over? Who was ultimately responsible for the final product?

SPEED. How fast did the editor put together a first cut, and how closely did that first cut resemble the final product? How long did the editing process take, and how many assistants worked with the editor?

FOOTAGE. What kind of footage did the editor have to work with? Was the coverage terrific? Did it "cut like butter"? Or did the editor have to perform miracles in the editing room to salvage a piece that was not coming together easily?

RANGE OF TALENT. Can the editor serve as a sound editor as well? An editor with this flexibility can save you money and time.

FORMATS AND EQUIPMENT. Does the editor have extensive experience in the format and gauge in which you are working (film: 35mm, 16mm; video: Beta, three-quarter-inch, half-inch, Hi-8)?

RESPONSE TO THE MATERIAL. The director does not want to work with someone who sees the project as just a job. An editor should be inspired by the material and want to spend weeks or months shaping it into a final product.

COMPATIBILITY WITH THE DIRECTOR. The editor-director relationship is important because the two of them will probably have to spend hours together in a small dark room, debating the progress of the project. If the director develops a good working relationship with an editor, she will probably want to continue working with him. They will develop a shorthand communication. The editor develops a feeling for how the director works, and vice versa.

TEMPERAMENT. In the editing room, all the mistakes of production are played over again and again. The editor must be sensitive to the director's ego.

SUPPORT CREW. Budget permitting, it is helpful for the editor to have an assistant with whom to work. The editor will know an assistant to bring on board.

The Director as Editor

Most beginning directors cut their own projects. This is only natural. They feel attached to the footage and want to shape the final product themselves. This is also the best way to learn how to edit. However, it does present some inherent problems. Directors can exhibit a possessiveness that will hinder their ability to be objective about the raw material. This condition is exacerbated if they have written the piece. Being emotionally attached to the project can impair the director's ability to "see the forest for the trees" and make tough editing decisions.

> The advantage to editing the film myself was that I was learning the process. The disadvantage was that I found myself losing myself, my perspective on the film, . . . because I started concentrating on each specific cut rather than on the whole picture. You start fiddling around with a frame here, a frame there, which becomes insignificant compared to whether the sequence is moving.
>
> *Adam*

The director need not personally edit her own film or video to put her creative stamp on the material. Many first-time directors get bogged down by the mechanics of editing and organization. It inhibits their creative drive and has a negative impact on the

outcome of the project. An editor can bring objectivity to the process. The editor's skills and creative input free the director to concentrate on aesthetic concerns. The editor is the technical guide who implements the director's ideas.

On the other hand, there is much the director can learn about storytelling and scriptwriting if she edits her own piece. Even if the director discovers she doesn't like editing, it is an important learning experience for her to edit at least one project herself. Physically joining the shots to tell a story can be very enlightening.

It is during the more relaxed postproduction period that the director learns whether her coverage was adequate to tell the story. Does she have enough shots? Do these shots cut together? Proper coverage gives the editor choices in case he needs to strengthen a moment, enhance a performance, or telescope the story. By reflecting on how each scene is approached visually, the director can learn what worked, what didn't, and why. She can apply this awareness to her next project.

Equally valuable to the writer-director is how the structure of the script holds up as the first cut comes together. She might discover that certain moments were overstated and that others were not stated at all. Seeing ideas realized on film is an important part of learning dramatic and visual writing.

If the director edits, it is advisable that someone else participate in the process, such as an assistant editor. This might not be practical or financially feasible, but it is highly recommended. Editing involves a great deal of organizational work that can slow down the creative drive. In film, the unused takes must be regularly organized and stored. (If you can't find a shot, you can't make the cut.) A first-time editor can become overwhelmed by the logistics. It is also helpful to have someone working with the director-editor for feedback. The producer will not be there all the time. If you can't afford an assistant editor, at least have someone who has experience or who wants to learn prepare the film or video for editing.

To summarize, there are several reasons for having someone else do the grunt work. First, the director is usually exhausted after the film is wrapped. The last thing she wants to do is run into an editing room and sync up or log the footage. There is no reason to slow things down while the director recuperates. Second, the director needs to step away from the material to gain some objectivity before she begins to edit. If possible, delay editing for several weeks.

STEPPING BACK AND LOOKING AHEAD

The person who is most responsible for spearheading the editorial process is the director. At this point in time, the producer steps aside and lets the director concentrate on shaping her vision of the film. The director might not want the producer anywhere near the editing room during this period. This gives the producer an objective point of view for the screening of the director's first cut.

While the editing is proceeding, the producer looks ahead and begins setting up the final leg of the postproduction process. An organized producer has already made a deal with a laboratory for all work on the film, from dailies through release prints. Now he must begin looking around for the best deals for the postproduction facilities and personnel who are going to be intricately involved with transforming the work print into a finished film. The postproduction personnel will be responsible for the following:

- Sound design
- ADR/Foley
- Music score
- Mix
- Optical track
- Titles/opticals
- Negative cutting
- Timing
- Answer print
- On-line editing for video

Finding the right people and the right facilities for this last leg of the production involves research, phone calls, and bids. The more you know, the better prepared you will be to secure the best deals without jeopardizing the creative integrity of the project.

Students: Many schools have their own mixing, ADR, and Foley stages and transfer rooms. Major metropolitan areas like New York, Los Angeles, Chicago, and San Francisco have postproduction houses that are willing to give excellent deals to students and independent filmmakers on tight budgets. In New York City, for example, postproduction facilities allow students to mix at night for reduced rates with mixers in training. However, students are advised to take advantage of whatever facility their program offers. It will save them money and enable them to take their time.

KEY POINTS

1. Follow the steps described in this chapter in the proper order.
2. Be ruthlessly objective in the editing room.
3. Cut a film or a video together based only on the material in the editing room. The final product might be different from what you intended. Listen to the material.

chapter seventeen

Sound Postproduction

I often go to see films that use really bombastic film music, and I'm completely distracted by it. I'm offended as a viewer when the music tells me what to feel. It usually indicates a failure of the footage to do its job. I frankly think fiction film is more guilty of this than documentary, although every once in a while you see it happening in a documentary, where music will underscore an interviewer's words. I'm much more into a minimalist approach.

Jan

DIRECTOR
Build Tracks

Sound pictures in the thirties and forties relied mostly on production sound—that is, all the dialogue and extra sounds recorded live on the set. Soundstages were quiet, controllable environments for recording not only "clean" dialogue, but also footsteps, door slams, or other sounds necessary for the scene. Very little, if anything, was added to the final track other than music. Audiences didn't care if a sound was missing here or there.

By the middle of the forties, film production began to move to natural locations. Because of the inherent problems of distracting ambient noises, the sound recordist's priority became the recording of clean dialogue. The studios developed sound departments, which filled in the rest of the track in postproduction.

Since then, the sounds that accompany the moving image have become increasingly sophisticated. Audiences now have greater expectations of what they will hear as well as see when experiencing a film or videotape. Technological advances like digitized sound and Surround Sound have elevated the craft of sound design to an art.

For the beginner, the process of creating the final sound track can seem overwhelming. When the picture is cut, it feels finished. At this stage, however, the sound track usually contains only the dialogue recorded on the set. The recording levels are uneven, the quality of the sound ranges from good to unusable, and there are many dead spots, or *holes*, on the track. A few sound effects might have been recorded with the production dialogue, but these might have to be replaced by cleaner or more impressive effects.

In truth, your film or video is only halfway there. Much work must still be done to create the sounds related to the world of your picture. Separate sound effects and music tracks must be organized, built, and eventually mixed together to form your sound track. Think of this stage as the final opportunity to polish and refine your picture by adding an exciting dimension of sound to complement and enhance the visual story.

RESPECT FOR SOUND

In every environment there exists a rich and densely varied world of sound. However, most of the information we derive from the world around us comes to us visually. We do not consciously hear. Thus, it might come as a surprise that there is really no such thing as silence. On a peaceful farm on a summer day, for example, you might hear several different kinds of birds, crickets, bees, a flowing stream, wind through the trees and fields, animal noises, a creaking barn, and so on.

If you wish to gain an appreciation for the inherent sounds of any space, try this simple but effective experiment. All you need is a blindfold and a partner you trust. Put on the blindfold, and have your partner lead you around the streets of your town or city. As your brain shifts from processing information from the eyes to processing information from the ears, you will begin to hear every sound around you. This exercise should be an aural awakening for you: You will realize how selective your hearing is. You will begin to see things because of what they sound like rather than what they look like. Cars will pass by, and you will be able to track their physical relationship to you solely from their sound perspective. A supposedly quiet afternoon will be transformed into a cacophony of sounds. If you try this experiment at home, you will discover the many subtle sounds that fill your apparently quiet room.

Your sound track need not include all the sounds that exist in a space at any given time. A sound track can easily become indistinguishable with too many simultaneous sounds. You should select sounds for inclusion on your track, basing your decisions on the criteria discussed in this chapter. Your choices will have a profound impact on the audience's response to the world your characters inhabit.

Sound Equals Space

The sounds you choose will complete the film and video experience because they bring reality to the illusion of the image. We need to hear sounds that match the images on the screen: traffic on the street corner, birds chirping in a garden, or waves breaking on the shore. These natural elements bring us closer to the drama because they make us believe that what we are seeing is real. The bottom line is that we do not believe it unless we hear it. An actor knocking on a door with no sound is not really a knock.

Sounds can indicate a world outside the frame—a world the audience need not see. Imagine, for example, that a couple is having a quiet dinner at home

when a rock band begins to practice next door. We need only hear the band to believe that it is there.

Sound can connect objects in space that have no inherent relationship to one another. Different shots of city streets can be unified with the addition of a bell tower chiming. If we hear the chimes while seeing the different city shots, we will believe that these streets are all part of the same town. The cafeteria in *The Lunch Date* seems to be a part of Grand Central Station, though shot blocks away, because of the simple train announcements in the background.

A sound can subtly affect how we respond to a scene emotionally. Imagine a scene with a couple in the woods at night, with the sound of crickets and an owl in the background. If, after a while, you add the sound of a howling wolf, it will give the scene a very different feeling. The wolf signals fear; the owl, comfort.

> The whole element of sound—both music and sound effects—was a rediscovery for me of what the story was. My first idea behind making the film was to tell a story visually, silently. So in the beginning I cut the film together without sound. I wanted to see if it worked. By first doing the images, then doing the sound—suddenly I could think of the story as being a whole set of sounds as well: the train station, the track boards flipping, salad crunching.
> *Adam*

Sound Equals Production Value

Building the sound track for your project not only is creative and exciting, but it can be cost-effective too. A well-placed sound or noise brings much to a picture for relatively little expense. You do not have to shoot a rock band to include them in your project. The audience need only hear them. Police cars, fire trucks, or a parade can pass by your character's window without ever being seen.

THE DESIGN OF SOUND

The following is a partial list of the many people who are involved in creating a sound track:

- Sound designer
- Supervising sound editor
- Dialogue editor
- Foley artist

- Foley mixer/editor
- Effects editor
- Automatic dialogue replacement (ADR) supervisor
- ADR recordist
- Various assistants

For low-budget projects, the duties of many of these positions are handled by one or two people. If your editor will cut the sound on your project, she might also serve as the dialogue, effects, ADR, and Foley editor and might perform many of the Foleys herself. (See the discussion of Foley effects on page 198.)

Let's look at the responsibilities of each position in more detail.

SOUND DESIGNER. The sound designer is responsible for the development and design of all sound track materials. He oversees the entire production and might fulfill his duties by supervising the sound editor. This relatively new position arose out of the need for an overall style for many projects.

> I owe a lot to the sound designer because one thing was that he got me to stop fiddling around with cutting the picture. The other was that we started discovering the story again. I basically became his assistant. I went to Grand Central again, getting more ambience, getting more sound. I went with a Nagra from school. I went to Penn Station and got train announcements. I did all the Foleys: the salad crunching and things like that. Then we started working on putting the tracks together, and it was a very interesting process.
>
> *Adam*

SUPERVISING SOUND EDITOR. This person handles the creation of the dialogue and effects tracks, either working alone or supervising others.

DIALOGUE EDITOR. The dialogue editor is responsible for all technically good dialogue tracks. She prepares the tracks to be mixed properly and cuts in all ADR and voice-overs.

FOLEY ARTIST. The Foley artist creates sounds for a picture in a studio using his body and a variety of gadgets, hand props, and tools. These sounds must sync up precisely with the action on the screen.

FOLEY MIXER/EDITOR. This individual records all the studio-made sound effects. The Foley editor cues all the effects needed, and supervises the Foley artist for correct sound of effect and sync.

EFFECTS EDITOR. The effects editor provides all the required sounds for the picture—everything from birds chirping to cars screeching to doors slamming. These sounds come from sound effects libraries or live recordings on the set or are created by the effects editor. He is responsible for editing all sound effects and for their placement in the sound track in order to facilitate the final mix.

ADR SUPERVISOR. This individual programs each line that must be replaced by ADR. He aids the director in determining the proper sync.

ADR RECORDIST. This sound person operates the ADR recording machine. He is responsible for microphone placement for perspective and matching of original dialogue.

VARIOUS ASSISTANTS. Among other things, assistant editors collect and log tracks, file trims, build reels, and keep the editing rooms organized and running efficiently.

The following are some of the tools the sound team uses:

- Flatbed editing table
- ADR stage
- Synchronizer
- Foley stage
- Squawk box
- Nagra
- Sound splicer
- Microphones
- Cue sheets
- Trim bins

Do You Need a Sound Designer?

A short picture, 5 to 10 minutes in length, might end up with 5 to 10 tracks of dialogue, music, and effects. For a novice editor or director-editor, this is a manageable number. With more ambitious projects of 15 to 30 minutes, many beginners and students decide to work with a sound designer. Having just learned picture editing, they tend to be overwhelmed by the prospect of sound work. They know it is necessary, but are intimidated by this completely new technical challenge. If they can afford it, they bring in someone who will take them through the process, providing a valuable learning experience at the same time.

Working on a short film or video offers novice sound editors an opportunity to gain experience and build their sample reels. They might be drawn to your project because it offers a particular challenge or an opportunity to work with interesting material. If a salary is involved, it is probably below the norm for seasoned professionals.

Working with a sound designer has obvious benefits. Take advantage of the learning experience. Ask to be involved in all the sound design steps for your picture. Share your ideas, express your concept of sound, but give the sound designer the creative space to explore other interesting sound possibilities. A sound person who has been in the business for even a short time will not only have access to sound libraries, but will have built up his own "library." Give the sound editor accurate sound reports and continuity notes because he will need to get to the original quarter-inch master.

> The film came together because of the sound editor. He was the one who came in and said, "Listen, you've got to define this opening. Here's how we're going to use music and sound effects to do it, and what you're going to do is intersperse the titles," which really gave the opening a sense of focus. If you had the titles before the montage, it would seem very repetitive: titles, montage, and then Truman. By breaking up the montage with the titles, which was the sound editor's idea, and using the music the way we did, it gave an unexpected energy and a drive to that moment when we come down the rope and see Truman and the film officially starts.
>
> *Howard*

PREPARING FOR THE MIX

All the work fleshing out the sound track is done to prepare for the mix, or, as it is called on the West Coast, the *dub*. The mix is the last opportunity you'll have to clarify your artistic goals for the piece. It is during this process that the picture is seamlessly married to the three basic sounds: dialogue, music, and effects.

To mix these elements together effectively, the tracks containing them are organized in such a way as to allow the mixer to set levels and equalization between sound cuts. The success of the mix relies as much on well-prepared tracks as it does on the skill of the individual who operates the board. To prepare properly for the mix, it is vital to understand what happens during the mix. Beginners should sit in on as many mixing sessions as possible and should talk to

sound editors about what is required before the mix can take place.

Sound work should begin while the picture is still being cut. The sounds recorded on the set or researched through sound libraries should be collected, labeled, transferred, and logged. If you preview some sounds against the picture while you edit, by the time you are ready to build the tracks, you will have made some key decisions. For example, if sirens are to be heard during a scene, cut with those sounds already on the second track because they will affect the rhythm of how the scene is cut.

It might be necessary for the editor to go out to the field to record a specialized sound with a Nagra or DAT recording machine. If you are looking for the sound of a revving 1967 Volkswagen Beetle, you might have to find the car and record it yourself. Creating and previewing many of the sounds before locking the picture will ease the crunch during the final postproduction phase.

Once the picture is locked, the job of sound design begins in earnest. Only when the picture length has been finalized can the sound editor know the exact timing required for dialogue or effects tracks. If the picture is constantly changing, all the tracks and the mix cue sheets will have to be adjusted accordingly. All picture changes after the lock must be announced to the sound designer so that he can adjust the timing to keep the sound track frame-accurate.

SPOTTING

Once the picture has been locked, the director is ready to sit down with the sound team and decide what is needed to flesh out the sound track of her film or video. This process is called *spotting* the picture. The director, sound designer, and editor look at the picture in a precise and deliberate way, scene by scene, and indicate which sounds are appropriate at any given moment.

During the spotting session, they discuss the following:

ON-SCREEN SOUNDS. These are sounds you can see being made in the frame, such as footsteps and door slams.

AMBIENT SOUNDS. These sounds are associated with the natural ambience of a space—for example, birds chirping, wind blowing, and traffic.

OFF-SCREEN SOUNDS. Off-screen sounds occur outside the frame. Examples are neighbors arguing in the hallway and a television blaring in the next room.

UNUSUAL SOUNDS. These sounds are not associated with the scene either on or off screen. If the director is planning a stylistic approach to sound, she might use surreal or manufactured sounds (the electronic buzz of the light sabers in *Star Wars*, for example) or ordinary sounds used out of context. An example of this is the climactic fight sequence of Martin Scorsese's *Raging Bull*, which features sounds that are not normally found in a boxing ring, such as wind blowing and animal growls.

PRODUCTION DIALOGUE. The spotting session is an opportunity to review the quality of the production dialogue. The film editor should be able to point out the tracks that are good and those that might have to be replaced with new lines recorded with ADR. Hearing the production dialogue in a projection room with a good sound system will enable the editor to confirm any questionable tracks.

A general rule when spotting sounds is: If you can see it, you should hear it. On the other hand, too many sounds might interfere with the dialogue, the mood of the scene, or the music the director is planning to use. The director should keep in mind how she plans to blend effects and music in a scene. (The use of music is discussed later in this chapter.) However, most effects editors approach each project as if there will be no music, and they give the director enough sounds to create a full and rich track without it because sound effects often can stir audiences' emotions in a way similar to the impact of music.

DIALOGUE TRACKS

Unless the piece has no dialogue, your first responsibility is to make sure the audience can hear the dialogue. This includes words spoken by actors on screen, off screen, and in voice-overs. Analyze the production tracks and decide which ones are acceptable and which ones might have to be replaced. Replacements can be confirmed during the spotting session. The "clean" tracks and the "dirty" tracks should be obvious. Ask for advice with the questionable ones.

Students: The analysis of dialogue tracks should ideally be done in a projection room with a good sound system. If you must use a flatbed editing machine, wear headphones to analyze the quality of dialogue tracks.

Much can be done in the mixing stage to clean up a line of dialogue. Inappropriate sounds like camera noise or floor squeaks can be covered. The question is how much background noise can be tolerated. You don't want the audience to strain to hear the words. Background noise will become even more of an issue when the mixed magnetic track is transferred to the final optical track. Because some parts of the sound spectrum are eliminated on the optical track, you might need to have a professional sound editor or a mixer analyze certain tracks. You might be forced to replace some or all of the "dirty" lines using ADR.

The editor now separates or splits the lines of dialogue onto enough tracks to enable the mixer to easily blend and equalize the dialogue. Some situations require separate dialogue tracks:

CONTROL LEVELS. A piece of dialogue must be separated if it requires its own sound level in the scene. It is very difficult for a mixer to make radical adjustments between different lines of dialogue on the same track. If character A, meant to be played softly, is immediately followed by character B, whose delivery is meant to be loud, the mixer will not have time to set a new level for the incoming sound if it is on the same track. With separate tracks, the mixer can preset the appropriate levels.

BACKGROUND CHANGES. Different camera setups sometimes involve different background ambiences. For example, a scene with two people talking on a street corner might have one background on the traffic side (loud traffic noises) and one on the sidewalk side (people walking). These two setups require two different levels.

CAMERA PERSPECTIVES. Different camera angles (wide, medium, and close) of the same scene have different sound perspectives. The lines for these camera angles might have to be put on different tracks to enable the mixer to set the appropriate levels. Sound perspectives ideally should match camera perspectives. Cutting between the different perspectives in the same scene will require separate sound adjustments so that the cutting seems more natural.

OVERLAPPING DIALOGUE. If an on-camera character speaks and is interrupted by an off-camera character, the editor can overlap the two pieces of dialogue. Speech is overlapped in real life. Splitting tracks allows the editor to simulate this reality and allows the mixer to control properly the blending of the two voices on the final track.

TELEPHONE CONVERSATIONS. Tracks are also split to enable cutting between two characters who are having a phone conversation. The editor will cut between a clean sound and one with "futz" (the sound of a voice filtered through a phone line). Even though most of the conversation will be heard this way, it should be recorded clean on the set. Any sound that is to be deliberately distorted through bad speakers or behind doors should always be recorded clean on the set to give the dialogue editor and mixer complete freedom to control the nature of the sound.

MIXING DIFFERENT CONVERSATIONS. Imagine a character walking through a busy party. She hears snippets of different conversations as she passes from one group to another. Each conversation must be separated on a different track to enable the mixer to control the tone as well as the changing perspective of each voice as the main character approaches and moves farther away.

Cutting Dialogue

Much of dialogue editing consists of evening out the background ambience or room tone of each scene and replacing the holes, or empty spots, in the track. Room tone taken on the set can be cut into tracks or run as a loop throughout the whole scene.

Another way the mixer blends together different shots with different backgrounds is by creating what are called *dialogue extensions*. This requires adding extra room tone (preferably from the existing take) to the head of one dialogue track and the tail of another so the mixer can do a quick sound dissolve fade, or segue, between the two. The result is a softening of the "sound bump" that might be heard when cutting between two different sound backgrounds.

Automatic Dialogue Replacement

What happens if the sound was not recorded well? What if there was a helicopter buzzing overhead during the take you want to use in the scene? What if you shot a scene by the ocean, and the rhythmic pounding of the surf does not match from cut to cut?

Mixers are miracle workers. They can sometimes dial out a low hum or even an airplane in the background, but dirty tracks are dirty tracks. The only way to fix a badly recorded track is to replace the dialogue. This is done by looping a line with ADR. In this electronic process, the actor stands in a soundproof studio in front of a screen and wears headphones. The scene is projected on the screen. The actor sees and hears the way the line was spoken and practices matching its cadence. When ready for a take, the actor waits for a visual or aural cue and repeats the line into a microphone. He might get it right on the first try, or he might have to repeat the line a number of times before achieving proper sync and performance. In cases of lengthy lines or even speeches, he might have to pick the speech apart line by line or even word by word.

Some actors are adept at this process, and some are not. Some are intimidated by having to duplicate in a dark and sterile room what was created in the cozy environment of the set.

The editor then cuts the rerecorded line into a new dialogue track. If the actor has made a good match, the editor can simply drop in the new material. More often, the editor has to play with the line, cutting a frame here, adding a frame there, until sync is achieved.

The ADR editor has many functions, including these:

- Programming ADR lines
- Selecting the exact footage and the exact line to be rerecorded
- Creating ADR cue sheets
- Helping actors with sync
- Cutting lines into the film or tape

ADR is recorded onto a magnetic tape with four tracks, so alternate takes can easily be saved. In fact, some directors use ADR not because of the quality of the sound, but because they want to improve or change the nature of a performance. Having the budget to accomplish this is a luxury for most beginners, who usually can't afford ADR at all.

Proper preparation for the ADR session plays an important role in its success. Paying for a studio and the engineer's labor is expensive. You do not want to waste any time in confusion over what needs to be recorded.

There are ways of creating effective ADR lines without going into a studio. You can create your own soundproof environment at home or in the editing room and perform many of these tasks there. With looping techniques and a portable cassette player, it is possible to have the actor listen to a line reading a number of times and repeat that line in a clean environment. It is not necessary to repeat long speeches. They can be broken up one line at a time.

> *Directors:* If you are shooting a scene that will obviously need to be looped, take the actors and the sound recordist off to a quiet room immediately upon completion of the scene. Have the actors listen to their lines on headphones and repeat them into a microphone and another tape recorder. This new dialogue can save you a trip to the ADR room. The actors are fresh from the scene and might be able to duplicate their tone and cadence perfectly. The lines might not be exactly in sync, but a good dialogue editor should be able to shift them into place easily.

ADR Spotting

It is sometimes easier to replace an entire scene with ADR than to replace a few lines. It is certainly easier to re-do a whole line rather than try to replace a word. Trying to match a line spoken on the set with one recorded in the soundproof environment of a studio is difficult. The sound editor must "dirty" the words with background ambience and other sounds. The mixer also has ways to help match the two. However, there always remains a perceptible difference between the tone and ambience of ADR and production dialogue, no matter what magic is performed to blend them together.

On the other hand, rerecording an entire scene allows the editor to create a consistent background ambience throughout the scene. Viewers accept the ADR and the background as natural because they are not comparing it to dialogue that was recorded on the set.

Adding and Altering Lines with ADR

During picture cutting, the director might realize that she needs to add off-camera lines that were not in the script. ADR offers an opportunity to add characters to a scene without visuals. They can exist outside the frame through sound as long as there is some logic behind their presence. In *The Lunch Date*, the audience could have heard the voices of a couple arguing in another booth. While the woman wandered through Grand Central Station, she could have heard bits and pieces of the conversations around her.

It is also possible to alter dialogue spoken on screen. For example, if a character turns his head in the middle of a line and the director decides that she wants him to say something else, the new line can be dubbed in. The head turn distracts viewers from noticing that the mouth and the lines do not exactly match. It is possible to change a line without a physical distraction, although it is a little harder. The farther away the lips are from the camera, the easier it is to fudge the dialogue. Suppose the director wants the character to say, "I want to go to Miami" instead of the recorded line, "I need to get a new pair of shoes." Here are three ways to make this change:

- Dub the new line in as the character turns away.
- Match the new line to a reaction shot of the character to whom the line is addressed.
- Dub the new line in over a long shot in which the character's lips are not visible.

These simple manipulations can have a profound effect on the outcome of your story. The alteration of one line can change the dramatic content of an entire scene. The possibilities of postproduction ADR give the director other storytelling devices that can enhance and complement what she achieved on the set. These manipulations might seem like tricks, but remember that making a film or video involves illusion. It is best to make these decisions before locking the picture because these types of alterations affect picture as well as sound.

Walla Walla

Walla Walla is a specialized form of dialogue: the sound of generic voices that were not recorded on the set. These sounds flesh out the background, providing verbal atmosphere for a busy bar or restaurant, a party, or any space with people talking or murmuring.

If the sound recordist was unable to record wild atmosphere on the set, the sound effects editor can program a Walla Walla recording session. Some experts in the industry have a special talent for looking at a scene and improvising general noise and whatever specific comments the scene requires.

The special voice-over groups or "Loop Groups" that perform Walla Walla can also duplicate major characters who are not available for ADR postproduction work. If an actor is busy when you schedule the ADR sessions, rather than wait for her schedule to free up, you might employ a "voice alike" to impersonate her.

Voice-Overs

A voice-over is a separate voice that is not in sync with the picture. It could represent, among other things, the main character commenting on or narrating the story. Some scripts start off with a voice-over built into the structure of the story. Even stories without this script device sometimes end up with some sort of voice-over in the final product. In the course of editing, the director might discover that she needs something to bind the audience more closely to the main character or narrative. Key exposition might be missing, the story might lack a focus, or it might not engage the audience sufficiently. Voice-over can help blend the images into a cohesive story.

If the story needs a unifying point of view, voice-over can do this very simply. It allows the audience to enter the world of the story through a particular perspective.

- It has the power to bind together shots or scenes that have no apparent logic to them.
- It can communicate important exposition that is not clear in the narrative.
- It can strengthen the main character's point of view and thus the audience's emotional connection to that character by personalizing what viewers see.

Do not use voice-over to tell viewers what they are seeing. This would be redundant (unless you intend it to be for comic or ironic purposes). Think of voice-over as a device to broaden understanding of the story, the characters, and/or the conflict.

It is necessary to work with a temporary voice-over track while editing the picture in order to cut the picture to a specific length. A rough recording by the director or editor will do, just to get an idea. A polished recording with the actor will be made in a studio.

SOUND EFFECTS TRACKS

Sound effects add a whole new dimension to a picture. The most important consideration should be what you specifically want to hear in a scene. The first step is to isolate the sounds viewers can visually identify such as footsteps or someone knocking on a door. The next step is to choose the sounds that are identified with a particular environment. In *The Lunch Date*, these are the sounds of Grand Central Station. From this point, the editor begins to assemble sounds that will enlarge the world of your project and add a level of information that doesn't exist in the picture.

Once the picture is spotted, the sound designer begins to accumulate the sounds needed to flesh out the director's ideas. These sounds come from many places:

- Wild sounds recorded on the set
- Sounds manufactured live on location
- Wild sounds recorded after principal photography
- Prerecorded effects from sound effects libraries
- Electronically manufactured sound effects
- Effects manufactured in a studio (Foley effects)

All these sounds must be dubbed from their original format to either 16mm or 35mm magnetic track for film or three-quarter-inch cassette or digital sound for video. Let's look at each of these sources in more detail.

WILD SOUNDS RECORDED ON THE SET. *Wild sound* refers to any recorded sound that is not in sync with the picture. In addition to recording dialogue and room tone, during principal photography the sound recordist should capture any wild sounds that might be used in the editing room. These include the pounding surf, frogs, wind in the trees, and any distinctive ambient sounds that are unique to a specific location.

SOUNDS MANUFACTURED LIVE ON LOCATION. The sound recordist sometimes records live sounds that accompany a shot—that is, sounds that happen within the frame, such as footsteps or door slams. The editor cuts these in later.

WILD SOUNDS RECORDED AFTER PRINCIPAL PHOTOGRAPHY. The sound effects editor must sometimes record certain effects that are not available in a library and were not recorded on the set. This involves going out into the field with a Nagra or DAT recording device and picking up or creating unique sounds and aural effects. For example, the sound effects editor might need the sound of a broken lawnmower on a hot summer's day or the rumble of an old pickup truck.

PRERECORDED ELEMENTS FROM SOUND EFFECTS LIBRARIES. Many compact discs (CDs), tapes, and records with sound effects are available. They offer a wide range of backgrounds and specific sounds such as birds, crickets, traffic, gunshots, tire squeals, or car noises.

ELECTRONICALLY MANUFACTURED SOUND EFFECTS. Some sound effects can be manufactured on a synthesizer. Various live sounds can be recorded and then layered electronically one on top of another to create interesting and unique effects.

EFFECTS MANUFACTURED IN A STUDIO (FOLEY EFFECTS). Sounds that must sync up precisely with the picture can be created on a Foley stage. This includes all types of body movement, such as footsteps, or eating sounds. The specialists who perform these sounds are called Foley artists. The term comes from Jack Foley, the sound editor who pioneered this process.

> I didn't go into the ADR studio at all. I didn't rerecord any of the dialogue. It was all there. The only material I had to add was some of the smaller sounds, which I Foleyed myself.
>
> *Adam*

A Foley stage has many different kinds of floor surfaces that characters might walk on in the course of a scene, such as cement, hardwood, sand, and earth. It also includes an oddball selection of hand props and tools that can be used to create a wide range of noises. On a Foley stage, you might find wind machines, buzzers, door latches, all kinds of bells, drinking glasses, nuts and bolts, mallets, and so forth.

The key to this process is that the sounds themselves do not have to be created with the exact objects or movements seen on the screen. All that matters is that the sounds appear to match the visuals. A Foley artist chomping on an apple can imitate the effect of a branch breaking. When shaken, a belt buckle will sound like a horse's bridle.

Before starting sound work, the student or beginner is urged to visit a Foley stage and watch the process in action. Foley artists are talented mimics. They can watch a person on the screen walk down a hall once and, upon playback, can duplicate perfectly the rhythm and cadence of the actor's unique walk.

However, Foley rooms and Foley artists can be expensive. You can achieve excellent results from taping sessions at home while screening a video copy of the project. If the recording is not in perfect sync,

some effort in the editing room moving the sounds back and forth should make the material effective.

> We knew we were going to have to buy two hours of Foley time. We booked two hours, and that's all we used. We were very specific about what we were going to get. We didn't go after everything. We were going to go after footsteps and that was it. Footsteps in the gym. The other ADRs I did myself—the ones that didn't have to be in sync but could be slugged in. We could slug them into the track and get them into sync ourselves.
>
> The actual ADR sounds were done by a Foley artist, which student films don't normally use. In the gym where we filmed, the sound of real footsteps was nonexistent. I wanted all the sneaker squeaks, how they resounded and how they echoed. We didn't hear them at all because of the way the floor was waxed. I thought the footsteps in the gym said something about this place, and I knew I had to recreate them, and a student really can't do that. You can't really cut several thousand footsteps into sync; you don't have time to do that. Those things had to be done by a Foley artist; they had to be put on 35 full coat and had to stay in sync.
>
> I also had some other ideas. I wanted Truman to have his own specific set of footsteps. I wanted them to have their own character and their own sound. So we got a very old pair of sneakers, put a sponge in them, and filled them with water. The Foley artists walked with wet sloppy sneakers on, and then we modified it so it had these squishy sounds. . . . All of his footsteps sounded like that.
>
> We spent the last two weeks of our five-week postproduction schedule putting effect sounds into place—adding the arrow sounds, adding the rope breaking (which was really the sound of a whip slowed way, way down), doing the ADR, bringing in my own ADR, taking sound effects off the CDs, and putting it all together.
>
> *Howard*

Unique Sounds

For some reason, you might need to create an unusual sound for your picture. You might need to manufacture or invent something new. This is what sound designers are paid to do. If you are doing the sound on your own, look for ways to fabricate strange and interesting sounds from simple ideas. Natural sounds can be altered to resemble something completely different. The amplified and distorted sound of a person breathing can be terrifying, for example. Sounds can also be layered to create effects that are more interesting than any individual sound.

When designing your sounds for film, keep in mind that an optical track has a limited capacity to reproduce certain parts of the sound spectrum. Sounds at the higher and lower range will not translate well. A low rumble or a high-pitched wail might sound different on the optical track than on the magnetic track.

Cue Sheets

A convenient way of roughing out your sound ideas is to use mixing cue sheets as a visual guide (Figure 17.1). Each column on the sheet represents a single track; your short project might use anywhere from five to 20 tracks. Each track contains any number of specific sounds, which are laid out according to the exact number of feet and frames necessary to match the picture. (The synchronizer is a very important piece of equipment in this process.) The need for accuracy becomes apparent when you remember that the mixer sits in front of a console, facing a screen with a large digital footage counter at the base of it. This footage counter tells the mixer when to expect a sound cue to come up. The counter and the cue sheets are the mixer's only references. They must be frame-accurate.

A large part of sound editing is precision and accuracy. It is not only about what kind of sound to use, but also where it should be placed. In the developmental stage, however, you need only rough out sounds on the cue sheets to get an idea of the grand design for your picture. These rough ideas will serve as a preliminary chart of what will eventually become your sound track.

As you break down and flesh out the sounds for each scene, deal with one sound at a time. One of the problems with sound editing is that you can't hear all the sounds together until you are in the mixing studio. You can only preview one or two sounds at a time (depending on the number of sound heads on your editing machine). For this reason, it's a good idea to have an interlock screening of the picture, with all the tracks running, before the final mix to see how well you are prepared.

As you accumulate and organize your sounds, you will fill up your cue sheets. They will resemble a checkerboard, with different sounds and bits of dialogue spread out over the tracks, allowing the mixer to set exact levels for each sound, dialogue, and music cue.

Laying in sound effects requires the time-consuming process of making sure each sound comes in and out in precisely the right relationship to the picture. Sounds can be marked on a flatbed editing table, but they should also be lined up with the picture on a synchronizer.

Tracks and Sound Fill

Once you have completed the cue sheets and confirmed the exact footage for each sound cut, the tracks can be built. All sounds should now be transferred to magnetic stock and laid into their appropriate tracks. Because each sound reel must be the same size as the corresponding picture reel, the extra space between sound cues is taken up with what is called *sound fill*. Sound fill is usually made up of discarded single-perf prints of movies or television shows. This stock is quite durable, so there is little chance of a track breaking during the mix. As each sound cue is added to a track, sound fill is slugged in until the next sound cue on that particular reel is ready to be added. The synchronizer keeps everything in sync as you roll down to each cut, feeding from left to right.

The sounds for a short picture are laid down on what might end up being three to five tracks of effects and two to three tracks of dialogue. There might also be one or two tracks of music. The footage count for each sound cut is critical, and all tracks should be played against the picture to correct any sync problems. There are many things to consider while cutting and laying in sound. If you are doing this yourself, seek the advice of editors or mixers. A short film or tape with five to eight tracks will serve as an excellent introduction to the process and won't tax the beginner.

Digital Workstations

The most radical change in picture-making is in the integration of digital technology with film and video production. If you have a CD player at home, you have experienced the consistent clarity and power of digitally recorded music. It is now possible to do most of the work we have been describing in this chapter on compact digital workstations. These workstations offer up to 24-track capability, random access, and previewing of the complete sound track before the mix.

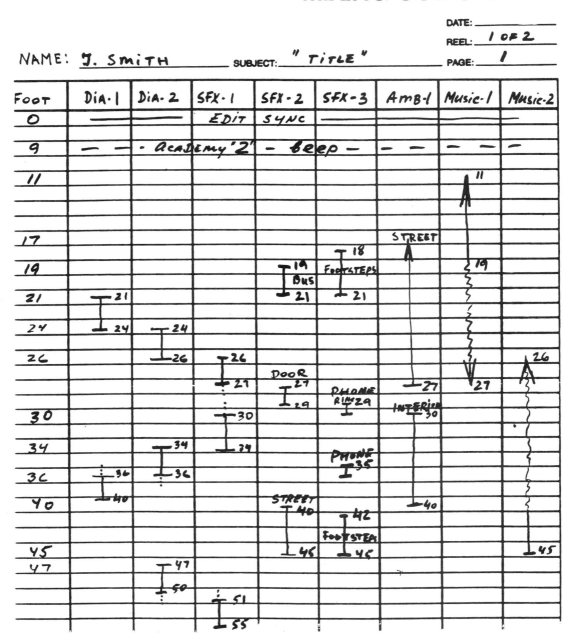

Figure 17.1 Sample cue sheet.

ADR, Foley, and effects cutting can all be done on these systems. The process hasn't changed, but the technology has. Picture-makers with basic computer skills will have no problem adapting to the new tech-nology as long as they have a fundamental under-standing of the role sound plays in a film or video. Digital workstations offer the creative person a more direct route from inspiration to execution. In the near future, sprocket mixing will be replaced by digital technology.

MUSIC TRACKS

The final major creative element attached to the picture is music. The impact of music on your project cannot be underestimated. Music can ignite strong emotions very quickly. A well-chosen and well-placed melody can take your piece to a higher emotional level. On the other hand, inappropriate or excessive music can overwhelm the delicate fabric of your story.

What does music do?

- It binds a picture together, particularly cuts and sequences. It connects shots that might not have apparent connections.
- It triggers emotional responses from the audience.
- It can drive a sequence, instilling it with energy and purpose.
- It complements or underscores the drama on the screen, either by enhancement or counterpoint.
- It strengthens a character's presence through theme. If viewers can identify a character's theme, music can place the character in a scene without his presence.
- It has the ability to transport the audience to another time and place. A single instrument can be associated with an entire culture. When we hear bagpipes, we think of Scotland. The music of any time period has the power to carry us back in time immediately.
- It creates an expectation about the story. Wistful music denotes a sad or melancholy piece. A light and bubbly melody over the same footage sets the audience up for an entirely different story.

Music has the power to manipulate how we feel about what we are seeing in a way we take for granted. To get an understanding of this power, try this experiment. Screen a montage sequence from a well-known film or video that already has music on it. Then find a piece of music with a very different mood or feel. If the original piece of music is light and airy, choose a piece that is suspenseful or dark. Play the sequence again, substituting the new piece of music for the original sound track. You will discover that music has the power to alter completely how we perceive a series of images. Respect the power of music when choosing a selection for your short piece.

The Music Team

Despite music's strong influence on the film and video experience, the composer is one of the last creative voices to become involved in a picture. It is very unusual for the composer to be called in at the script stage.

A complete music team consists of the following individuals:

COMPOSER. The composer is responsible for writing the original score. He might also arrange; orchestrate, and conduct the music.

ARRANGER/ORCHESTRATOR. The arranger adapts a piece of previously written music or the composer's basic musical ideas for the score and arranges it for the orchestrator, who creates parts and assigns them to various instruments.

COPYIST. The copyist extracts the parts for the individual instruments from the score for use by the musicians and the conductor.

MUSIC SUPERVISOR/PRODUCER. This person, a representative of the studio or production company, is responsible for overseeing the business, practical, and creative aspects of scoring the film or video.

MUSIC EDITOR. The music editor handles all the details regarding synchronization of the score with the picture.

MUSIC CONTRACTOR. The music contractor hires musicians, books the studio, and coordinates all business and financial activities for the recording sessions.

MUSICIANS. Musicians perform their parts during the recording of the score. The number of players required depends on the nature of the arrangement.

CONDUCTOR. The conductor interprets the score and directs the orchestra to play on cue.

MIXING ENGINEER. The mixing engineer is responsible for mixing the various musical sounds into the recorded composite version.

The music in a film or video can serve as either an underscore or a source. *Underscore* refers to music that plays under the action. There is no visible or implied source within the frame for this kind of music. On the other hand, *source* refers to music that emanates from a visible or implied source within the frame, such as a radio, a live band, or a tape player. The audience doesn't necessarily have to see the source of a piece of music to accept its presence. A radio might be turned on in another room, or a band might be playing in the next apartment.

The Original Score

Music for a picture can come from two sources. It might be either an original score written and orchestrated specifically for your project or prerecorded existing music.

Finding the right composer for your project is important. Your goal is to find someone who is sensitive to your story. Not all composers are right for all pictures. Some directors work with young composers who are interested in building their reels and gaining valuable experience. They need you as much as you need them. When working with a composer, you should provide him with a video copy of your fine cut (either shot or transferred off the editing table). The composer will use this to develop musical ideas.

Finding a Composer

It is much easier than you can imagine to find a composer for a short project. Composers who want to make the move into the film and video market are eager for experience and are willing to work either for free or for very little. As for all crew positions, you must advertise and ask around. If you see a short film or video with an impressive musical score, get in touch with the director and producer. Ask about their experience working with the composer. Then contact the composer and ask to hear more of his work.

You might want to let the composer hear the temp music you have cut to the picture. The risk of this method is that the composer might try to duplicate the temp music rather than come up with new musical ideas. The other method is to let the composer come up with his own ideas in response to the material. Give the composer the space to be inspired by the material.

There are several advantages in using a temp score when developing a relationship with a composer. It can give the composer insight into the director's musical ideas and serve as a point of departure from which they can discuss musical ideas for the film or video. The danger of a temp score is that the director might fall in love with music the composer cannot top and that is unavailable because it is too expensive.

Music Spotting

Once you have settled on a composer, you can begin spotting the picture in earnest. With the composer, review the entire picture, scene by scene, to discuss the *music cues*—that is, the moments that are appropriate for music. When working with film, spotting should be done on a flatbed editing table so that you can go slowly back and forth over the material.

Speaking the language of music can be frustrating if you aren't musically literate. In the absence of a temp track, you can give the composer an idea of what you are striving for by playing themes, instrumental pieces, and tempos you think are appropriate and talking about different genres of music.

The composer can help bridge this potential communication gap by bringing in selected music cues to play against the picture. This will help the composer get a clearer understanding of what the director wants. Music expresses emotion. It bypasses the brain and works directly on the heart. Yet what might be right for the composer might be wrong for the director or producer.

The addition of music will greatly enhance the film or video experience, but so will the sound effects. Do not let these two elements fight each other for dominance on the sound track. During the spotting session, if you know that you want a loud effect, have the composer keep the music gentle or use no music at all during that section of the film. One way to approach the spotting session is to let the composer go off with a video copy of your piece and spot it without your feedback. Allow the composer the freedom to respond to the material alone.

The Music Editor

After the director and composer agree on where music should be placed and on a musical style that is appropriate for the piece, the composer has two challenges: (1) to write music that enhances the visual imagery effectively and (2) to make the music fit precisely into exact music cues. It has traditionally been the music editor's role to break down each music cue into a series of beats by employing "click tracks." A *click track* is a synchronous metronome that is locked to the picture. It allows the composer to write a melody or musical riff that will stay in sync with the picture. The beats can be altered to satisfy any rhythmic changes, from slow and easy to fast and frantic. The important thing is for the composer to create a piece of music that can later be laid perfectly against the picture.

Today, there are computer programs that can calculate absolute times, allowing the composer to work at home. It is now customary for film and video composers to work with the Musical Instrument Digital Interface (MIDI) standard. With a MIDI-compatible synthesizer, contemporary composers can create an entire score in the privacy of their home or studio.

In the traditional method of composing for film, the composer writes the score, an orchestrator arranges the score for instruments, the copyist copies the different parts, and the composer-conductor scores the picture in a large scoring stage with the picture running.

This method is still sometimes used, but more and more composers prefer to work on a score in a layered fashion with synthesizers and a video copy of the picture. The video has SMPTE time code burned in, showing the exact footage and times. When the composer works with a synthesizer, the director can preview the composer's work in progress in a more complete form than with the traditional method, in which the composer could only play themes on a piano.

Working with a Composer

A good working relationship with the composer is an important part of getting the best score for your project. It might be necessary to preview musical ideas from time to time to see whether the composer is on the right track. Do not let the composer complete an entire score without having heard at least his general approach. Scoring a picture can be an emotionally draining experience for both the director and the composer because so much is expected of music and so much depends on how it works. Allow the composer the time and space to work at his own pace.

Finding a language to communicate with the composer is imperative. Even musically inclined people must find some way of expressing their ideas about the score to the composer. Here are several methods to help you steer the composer in the right direction:

- Play existing music that appeals to you. The temp music you played with the picture for screening purposes will give the composer an idea of your musical designs.

- Explain to the composer the emotional values you are interested in expressing through the music. Is it a sad scene requiring sad music, or would you prefer the counterpoint of a calliope or banjo?
- Identify specific instruments and themes for characters. Listen to *Peter and the Wolf*, which was designed with a different instrument for each character. In many scores, the main character is identified by a theme played on a specific instrument.
- Study the work of the great film composers. Watch how they work their musical themes against the picture.
- When you spot the picture with the composer, make sure to point out any possible conflicts. If there is dialogue or a specific effect you want the audience to hear, don't let it fight with the score. The composer can request quiet music for these moments, but to rely on less volume in the final mix is a mistake.
- Look for places where music can also be an effect. If a glass falls and breaks on camera, do you want the sound of a breaking glass or perhaps a cymbal crash?

After the score has been completed and the music cues are ready to be cut into the film, there is a time of fine adjustment. A cue might have to be edited slightly or shifted to fit the exact requirements of the film. The only other change that can be made is to drop cues from the film during the mix. This is often done because directors usually ask in the spotting session for more music than required. The extra music allows some flexibility in the mix. It is better to have too much than too little. By the time you are involved in the mix, it is too late to ask for new music.

Preexisting Music

Preexisting music has some advantages. The audience knows the music or is familiar with it. Popular songs and music can make your piece accessible. To say that using preexisting music is less expensive than working with a composer is not always true. Of course, a piece of music that is in the public domain costs you nothing. However, don't fall in love with a Sinatra ballad or a Beatles tune because the price tag for popular and current music is probably out of your price range. If you must use preexisting music, try to obtain music from a group that is not very well known and might relish the opportunity to have its work showcased in your project. (See Appendix K for more information on music rights.)

A special type of preexisting music is *canned music*, which is created to be sold and used in bits and pieces. This generic music can be purchased from a music stock house or from sound effects records. At a stock house, you buy a piece of music by dropping the needle onto the record (or beginning the tape or CD) and then lifting the needle when you have the amount of music you need. This is referred to as a *needle-drop* purchase.

Playback is another form of source music. This is prerecorded music, with or without lyrics, played back on the set during principle photography. The music is used to give dancers a tempo or for singers to lip-sync a song. The material is played back on the set on a Nagra, and recorded on a second Nagra as a scratch track. In the editing room, the original music is used, and the sequence is cut to that track.

> *Students:* The temptation to flood the screen with music often stems from an insecurity with the material. Some stories require music from end to end ("wall to wall"), whereas others need none at all. You must have the courage to do the right thing for your project.

THE MIX

When the tracks have been lined up against the picture and the cue sheets have been filled out to reflect the exact position of the various sounds on the multiple tracks, it's time to take your picture to a mixing studio. There, you'll place it in the hands of the re-recording sound mixer, who is responsible for mixing the narration, dialogue, music, and effects. The sound mixer will work with the following tools:

- Mixing (dubbing) studio
- 35mm full coat
- 16mm full coat
- Prepared cue sheets
- Prepared tracks

The producer should have arranged the mix date far in advance. The number of hours needed for the mix is determined by the length of the film and the number of tracks to be mixed.

It is during the mix that the total aural experience of your picture is created. The elements of dialogue, sound, and music are recorded and blended together to become a seamless unit. During the mixing procedure, the director and other members of the creative team can make significant artistic decisions about the relative balance between tracks, equalization, the amount of echo, the use of this track or the other, the amount of music to use, and so on.

Even though the final track will be transferred to 35mm or 16mm film or married to video, the mix will be done to 35mm four-track full coat. The tracks are divided up into narration, dialogue, music, and effects. If any of these elements must be changed later, such as substituting a foreign language track for the English dialogue, it can be done without affecting the other tracks.

The success of the mix depends as much on the preparation of the tracks as on the ability of the mixer to blend them together into an organic whole. The prepared tracks represent your major creative decisions. You should have determined the specific sound effects, music, and dialogue you want to use before you walk into the mixing studio. These tracks should not only properly reflect your creative choices, but also meet the highest technical standards to maximize your time with the mixer.

Many mixing facilities provide written material that gives beginners a thorough explanation regarding how to prepare properly for the mix. This can save embarrassing, time-consuming, and costly delays in what is already an expensive part of the postproduction process.

To make sure you are totally prepared for the mixing session, arrange for an interlock screening of your film with the mixer you intend to use. *Interlock* means running the picture with all the tracks at the same time. This should be done far enough ahead of time to enable you to make any necessary changes. The interlock screening will give you a feel for the mixing environment, but more important, it will allow you to determine whether you have prepared the tracks adequately.

The work print is sent to the laboratory to make a *dirty dupe* or *slop print*—a direct, one-to-one black-and-white or color print of your work print. This is done for the mix, Foley, and ADR sessions to guarantee that the film will not break in the projector. These sessions involve a great deal of starting and stopping, which leads to wear and tear that your color work print might not stand up to, even if it has been double-spliced. It is not mandatory to strike a dirty dupe, but you should weigh the chances of breakage in the mix and the subsequent repair time against the dupe's cost.

The director's job during the mix is to inform the mixer about the levels at which the sounds should be recorded in relation to each other. Dialogue comes first, meaning that it is in the foreground. The audience should not have to strain to hear the dialogue. The balance between sound effects and music is an aesthetic choice the director should make in the editing room to avoid too much trial and error during the mix. Most mixers will offer advice about levels, based on their experience.

Rhythm of the Mix

Beginners should sit in on as many mixes as possible before their session to get a feel for the rhythm and pace. Mixing sessions involve a lot of waiting around. The mixer first runs through the entire show with all the tracks "full up" to get a sense of the material. You will, of course, be anxious to start because every minute costs money. However, you must give the mixer time to become familiar with both the picture and the tracks. Remember that you have spent months with your show and know it inside out. The mixer sees it for the first time that day, unless she has already done an interlock or premix. She has only the cue sheets as a guide and must slowly feel her way through the film, scene by scene.

You might have very specific ideas about how each scene should sound and how the entire piece should resonate. Communicate these ideas to the mixer, but also listen to his creative input. Don't relegate the mixer to the role of technician. You want to get his best work from him. Listen to what he has to say. At the same time, if you are not happy with what you hear, don't be afraid to ask him to do it again, even if you have to go over one moment many times.

Mixing is a methodical, time-consuming process. You can go back and forth over the same few feet of film or tape time and again before it is right. It can be a delicate balancing act as you juggle all the sounds and music until it is just right.

The mix will sound great in a sound studio with professional speakers. Ask the mixer to play back the film through small speakers. When the film is trans-ferred to video or onto optical or projected on a dubious projection facility like a drive-in theater, the sound track will not sound as rich as when heard through professional speakers.

With a complete mix, the full coat mix master is converted into an optical sound negative. This negative is later used with the picture negative to make a positive composite print.

Video

The video sound process is similar to that of film, but it is done either in the off-line and on-line edit bays or in a 24-track mixing studio. The video mixer must respect the balance between the same three types of sounds: dialogue, effects, and music. The sounds must be manufactured or found and ultimately placed in their proper positions on the tape.

Like nonlinear digital picture editing, the digital sound mixing of a video has become a smooth and fast operation. In the on-line room or on a nonlinear editing machine, once all the tracks are prepared, the editor blends them together on the two tracks of space available on the tape. One track can be for dialogue, with the other for music and effects, or you can make one track left and the other right for stereo. On Beta tapes, two additional FM bands are married to the picture. This is the best place to put the dialogue unless you plan to have the tape dubbed into a foreign language.

PRODUCER
Set Up Mix

The producer keeps on top of all expenses incurred during the postproduction period. He sees that everyone adheres to the budget and that all additional expenses can be covered with the money that is left. However, films and videos do go over budget, and what usually suffers is postproduction. Sometimes, all work on a project is suspended until further money is raised. This is not an uncommon situation for students and beginners. Projects go over budget for several reasons:

UNEXPECTED PRODUCTION EXPENSES. This is a common but unavoidable predicament, even for professional productions. Expenses that arise in the "heat" of principal photography must be covered if production is to be completed. You shoot more stock than anticipated or spend more on art direction, food, or transportation. With beginners especially, the original budget might not have been realistic. It is easy to say that you can "take it out of post" because postproduction seems to be a long way off when you are in a distant location and your van has broken down. With the entire cast and crew on payroll, spending the extra money to get a scene right seems justified.

UNEXPECTED RESHOOT EXPENSES. Additional filming might be needed if the production unit did not shoot all the planned coverage or if it becomes evident after extensive editing that there must be more shots to tell the story properly. This expense usually comes out of the budget contingency unless, along with other overages, the contingency has already been exhausted.

HIDDEN POSTPRODUCTION COSTS. Beware of the hidden costs that surface during postproduction. These costs often cannot be predicted because so much of postproduction is trial and error. For example, different pieces of music might be tested against the picture during cutting. The original music is transferred to magnetic stock each time the director wants to preview the music or cut it to the picture. This requires transfer time, additional magnetic track, and possibly coding, all of which cost money. Students might get free transfer time, but they must still purchase the magnetic stock.

EXTENDED POSTPRODUCTION PERIOD. It is not uncommon for the student or beginner to run beyond the planned postproduction schedule. There is no way to know definitively how long it will take, and many variables can influence the creative process. (Some of these are discussed in Chapter 16, "Picture Postproduction.") Students might have limited access to their program's facilities, and independents on a limited budget might be able to edit only during the evenings because of job conflicts.

The following situations are equally difficult to predict:

- The editor needs to use the same shot twice during the film and thus has to make a new negative.
- The director decides she wants some unusual optical effects.
- The mix goes over the schedule.

- The lab has problems printing an acceptable answer print of the film, and there are a number of passes before the lab gets it right.

These are just some of the situations that will cost money that might occur in the course of postproduction. However, all these extra expenses spring from the desire to make the best film or video possible.

Howard McCain designed the end of *Truman* around an optical effect called an *iris*. As Truman is suspended over the class holding onto the rope, the image closes in on him, or *irises*, until all we see is Truman before fading completely to black. This effect isolates Truman at the end of the film. It is an effective use of the optical but was more expensive than a simple fade to black.

The following is a partial list of postproduction items to look out for (many are not very costly by themselves but will add up over the long run):

- Screenings
- Scratch or temp mixes
- Opticals
- Special effects
- Sound fill
- Picture and sound leader
- Academy leader
- Elaborate title sequences
- Magnetic track
- Transfer time
- Extra coding
- Reprints
- Transfer to video

All these additional expenses can hold up the postproduction process. Once the budget has been depleted, you might have to stop work at whatever stage you have reached. Perhaps you were ready to mix, cut negative, or on-line your show. You must now look for more financing to complete the picture. You have an advantage when raising money at this juncture that you lacked in the early fund-raising stage. You now have a picture. Having something concrete to show will help you attract potential investors who perhaps were not interested in your project at the idea stage.

You can now organize fund-raising screenings of the work in progress. Keep in mind that for these screenings, the film or video should sound as polished as possible. Most audiences are not used to hearing an incomplete sound track. You might need to add a few effects and music and make a temp, or scratch, mix. This rough mix does not reflect what the piece will eventually sound like, but at least it gives the picture a professional feel and covers up the obvious sound gaps. The goal is to have your project in the best possible condition for the screening.

You might find other opportunities for additional funds, such as postproduction grants or finishing funds, now that you have something tangible to show. Look into local, national, and university grants. Many film and television programs make funds available on a competitive basis for students with projects in the postproduction stage.

NEW TECHNOLOGY

Many beginners and students are seduced by technology and think it will save them money. Many shoot on film and edit on video. Although this procedure might save them time, they will need to convert back to film and go through most of the same steps again unless they are satisfied with a video print. The new nonlinear editing systems promote speed and access, but at the present time, they cost just as much in the long run. Analyze thoroughly the financial ramifications of any new technology. Beware of what *seems* like the better deal.

For sound work, postproduction houses offer package deals that even students can afford. These deals might involve a price per minute of film or tape that includes all sound effects, ADR, and music cutting as well as a final mix. They can offer good deals to students and beginners on a budget because these companies will do the work in their off-time. Therefore, don't expect a deal if you are on a tight schedule. As long as you are not in a rush, though, it is possible to get value for your dollar.

Because the equipment and prices change more readily than for film, video postproduction might seem attractive at first, but it could cost more in the end. The editing suites are so expensive that if you find you need additional time to edit, the cost will be considerably higher than film editing.

THE MORAL

When it is all over, make sure that you benefit from the lessons you've learned about the "real costs" of postproduction so you can be better prepared the next time. Your subsequent postproduction budgets should reflect the insight and experience of your pre-

vious project. Keep extensive records and receipts to document what happened on the entire shoot, and keep an accurate time log of the postproduction period so you will have a clearer idea of what has to happen, and when, the next time around.

KEY POINTS

1. Sound design involves dialogue, effects, and music, with dialogue being the most important element.

2. Effects can be in-sync, ambient, or "Foleyed."

3. Once it is locked, spot the picture for effects and music cues. The footage marks for these cues should never change.

4. Do not forget to record room tone when you are on the set. This material will be used extensively during the sound design process.

5. Take the time to develop a communication link with the composer. Consider how you can best express your ideas to the composer.

6. Avoid mixing using your work print. If it breaks during the mix, you will waste time repairing the print. If possible, make a black-and-white dupe.

chapter eighteen

Laboratory/On-line

You've got to be very, very careful when cutting the negative; most students aren't that careful, not even with their own material. Everybody I know hired a negative cutter. To find a negative cutter, you call other students, see who they use, and find a good price. Prices do vary greatly, anywhere from $4 a cut to $1.50 a cut; it makes a big difference. There were 198 edits in Truman. That's a lot of cuts for a 10-minute film.

Howard

DIRECTOR

Time

The laboratory plays an important role throughout the filmmaking process. (With video, the laboratory is not involved; instead, the work is finished and fine-tuned in an on-line editing suite.) Strive to maintain a good relationship with the lab from the outset. The success of your film depends on the work the lab does. The lab is responsible for taking care of the negative and creating a final product that represents the best your film can be.

A laboratory representative should be assigned to your project from the beginning. During the production and postproduction process, direct any questions, problems, or concerns to this individual. It is proper and professional to meet the lab representative in person to become acquainted. Visit the lab, and ask to be taken around to see the facilities. Remember that representatives talk to hundreds of people a day on the phone. By being more than just another voice, you will be certain to get better results.

Treat the relationship you develop with the lab as the beginning of a long, fruitful "partnership" that will carry you through many films. If you are a stu-

dent or beginner and plan to continue making films, the lab will hope to keep you as a customer, especially with so many filmmakers turning to video.

Students: Act like a professional, and you will be treated like one.

The laboratory is involved in the following steps in the filmmaking process:

- During principal photography, the laboratory develops and processes your film. The lab provides you with a work print (timed or one-light), which is what the editor cuts. The negative is kept for you in a vault at the laboratory.
- During the editing of the film, the laboratory reprints any dailies that have become lost or too scratched to use.
- While the sound is being designed, the laboratory develops your titles and opticals.
- The laboratory can provide you with a black-and-white copy of your work print to use in the ADR, Foley, and mix sessions.
- During the mixing of the sound, the laboratory can arrange for your negative to be cut (including the titles and opticals) and matched to your work print.

- During the sound mix, the director, DP, or both color-correct, or *time*, the film with the timer at the lab.
- Once the mix is completed, the magnetic three-stripe is shot onto an optical track, and the laboratory marries the printed film to the sound track.
- During the printing of the A and B rolls of 16mm negative, the laboratory can perform simple fades and dissolves if you request. The lab then strikes your first answer print.

OPTICALS

The process of creating opticals for 16mm is different than for 35mm. All 35mm optical effects must be designed and shot beforehand at an special effects house and developed at the lab. This involves making a new negative. The nature of 16mm negative cutting allows the laboratory to create dissolves and fades during the printing process itself. (See the next section for information on A and B rolls.) The editor merely marks the work print with a white grease pencil to indicate the length of the fade or dissolve.

An important technical consideration is having enough film on either side of the dissolve so that the two shots can cross-fade with each other. Spend some time talking with the negative cutter before designing any opticals.

Any opticals other than simple fades and dissolves must be shot by a company that specializes in visual optical effects. (The lab you are using might have a division that does this.) This is a time-consuming and costly process that sometimes requires trial and error. The optical house might not achieve the results you want the first time around. For example, the image that you want "blown up" is shot, and the new negative is sent to the lab to be developed and printed. You preview a work print of the new optical to be used in the film, but it doesn't work. It must then be shot and developed again, costing yet more money.

> I wanted a crawl at the end and I wanted an iris effect, so I knew there was going to be an optical in both cases. To get those, you have to shop around, just like for a caterer or for anything else. Again, by looking at other students' work, you can tell which work you like and which work you don't.
>
> *Howard*

The following are some of the opticals that require a wedge test and must be run separately from the final printing:

SUPERIMPOSITION. Superimposition is placing two or more images over one another.

LAP DISSOLVE. Especially long dissolves, usually over 96 frames, are referred to as lap (as in overlap) dissolves.

STEP PRINTING. The film can be slowed down or sped up by printing more or fewer frames than exist on the negative.

BLOWUP. An image can be enlarged to eliminate a boom pole or other unwanted element in the frame. Blowups are a last resort for solving an image problem because when you reprint a shot, the grain on the film gets larger and thus creates a mismatch to the grain size of the shots before and after the blowup.

TITLES. You might want to superimpose your main or end titles over images from the picture or create some special visual effect with your main title.

END CREDITS. You might want the credits to scroll up or "crawl" continously over black or over images for the end credits.

REPRINTS. If you need to duplicate a scene several times in the picture but have only one take of it, you will need a duplicate negative, or *dupe*, created from the original negative of the scene.

SPECIAL VISUAL TRANSITIONS. Wipes and irises are examples of special visual transitions (Figure 18.1).

Optical work is expensive. If you have your heart set on a special visual effect, it is best to find out what it will cost before editing a sequence around it. This applies also to fancy title sequences.

> *Students:* To create a title and end credit sequence cheaply, shoot it yourself using computer-generated titles and a Kodilith. With a hundred feet of high-contrast film, several lights, a camera, and a tripod, you can generate something that is simple but looks professional.

CUTTING THE NEGATIVE

During the mix, when the filmmaker is positive there will be no more changes in the picture, the editor

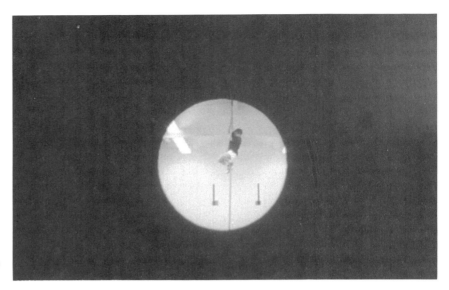

Figure 18.1 *Truman* ends with an optical: an iris-out.

sends a prepared work print to a negative cutter to have it cut, spliced, and prepared for printing. The director or editor can set up a clean room in which to cut the negative, but this is a somewhat tedious and critical part of the postproduction process. A mistake here could lead to disaster. A negative that is not cut or spliced properly could break apart in the printing process, permanently damaging part of your film.

It is best to consult the negative cutter for specific guidelines on preparing the work print to be cut. Unintentional splices, dissolves, fades, and title ins and outs must normally be marked when working in 16mm. The cutter will also require a detailed log sheet, which should have been prepared when the footage was initially coded.

The processes for cutting 16mm and 35mm negative are fundamentally different. Cutting the original negative in 16mm and 35mm requires that a part of the emulsion of one frame be scraped off and laid on top of the next frame. These are glued together and sealed with a heated splicer, creating a *hot splice*. The heat enables the splice to seal properly. Scraping off a frame of 16mm film exposes part of the frame line, which will then print through as a white line. Because of the density of 35mm film, frame lines are not a problem.

To avoid having this visible splice, the original 16mm negative is never cut with another piece of original negative. Instead, a shot is cut to a piece of black leader (the A roll), and the next shot is attached to a second roll (the B roll). The use of two separate rolls creates a checkerboard pattern called *A and B rolls*. This prevents one piece of original negative from being cut with another and makes it possible for the lab to print fades and dissolves (Figure 18.2).

TIMING

At the laboratory, a technician called a *timer* consults with the director of photography (DP) to create a visual continuity for the film. This means giving each scene a consistent color and tone as well as giving the whole film a specific look, whether it be cool (tending toward the blues), normal, or warm (tending toward the oranges).

It is not unusual for shots within a scene to be warmer or colder in color or lighter or darker in tone. They might have been shot at a different time of day or with a different batch of film stock. The timer tries to smooth out these inconsistencies in color film. She does this with a Hazeltine machine, which tells the printer how many light bulbs— "lights" of green, red, or blue—are required in the final printing of each sequence. Color film is broken down into these three dyes. The balance of these three colors creates accurate skin tones. The timer

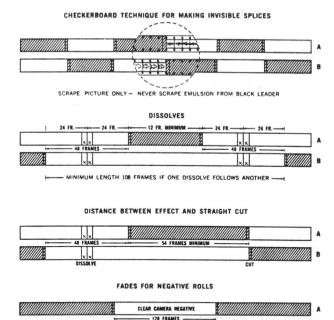

CHECKERBOARD TECHNIQUE FOR MAKING INVISIBLE SPLICES

SCRAPE PICTURE ONLY — NEVER SCRAPE EMULSION FROM BLACK LEADER

DISSOLVES

24 FR. — 24 FR. — 12 FR. MINIMUM — 24 FR. — 24 FR.

48 FRAMES — 48 FRAMES

MINIMUM LENGTH 108 FRAMES IF ONE DISSOLVE FOLLOWS ANOTHER

DISTANCE BETWEEN EFFECT AND STRAIGHT CUT

48 FRAMES — 54 FRAMES MINIMUM

DISSOLVE — CUT

FADES FOR NEGATIVE ROLLS

CLEAR CAMERA NEGATIVE

120 FRAMES

NEGATIVE SCENE — NEGATIVE SCENE

48 FR. FADE — 48 FR. FADE

Figure 18.2 A and B rolls. Used with permission from the American Society of Cinematographers.

sets the number of lights per color to make the flesh tones match the character.

The director and DP sit with the timer and make special requests if they want something other than "normal" printing. Suppose, for example, that a sequence was shot so that the dailies are bright and well saturated with color, but the director wants a dark and moody feel to the scene. The timer can instruct the printer to bleed some of the color from the scene and to make it less bright. If the timer has a lot of latitude, she can make some adjustments to the look of a scene. This requires that the negative be well exposed, or *dense*. There is not much a timer can do with a "thin" negative. The Hazeltine is not a magical instrument.

It is important to note that the timer cannot alter the color balance or flesh tones of only a part of the frame. Every adjustment, however minor, affects the entire image. The director can change the color scheme but must live with how it affects the characters' flesh tones.

Black-and-white film goes through a similar timing process, although the visual concerns are differ-

ent. The timer works with a gray scale and black-and-white contrast ratios. She strives to smooth out the inconsistencies of lighting, to enrich the blacks, and to create a consistent tone for each scene and for the entire picture.

> I went to get the answer print, and I called up the cinematographer, and we watched it together. I brought him there specifically to make sure they were printing it with enough richness and stuff. We went for a second printing and darkened it a little bit, just in some areas.
>
> *Adam*

TYPES OF PRINTS

The first print struck from the negative is a work print (or video, if you choose video dailies). The material is either timed scene-by-scene to correct for proper flesh tones, or developed by one-light, which is an overall timing of one setting for the entire roll. When the negative is cut, you will begin to strike prints for screening purposes. The following sections describe the types of prints the laboratory can provide.

Mute Print

Before the mix is married to the optical track, the laboratory sometimes prepares a mute print. This is a picture-only print from the negative, which the director, editor, and DP can examine for color corrections or optical errors before an answer print is made.

> The timer looked at the work print to get a sense of the film. It was really an odd film to time because the backgrounds had to look completely consistent, so the flesh tones become subordinate to the backgrounds. I'm sure if he had timed every shot according to flesh tones, he would have come up with quite a different timing. But you know, you can't have the gradation of the black-and-white floor changing or the mannequins' flesh tone jumping around from shot to shot.
>
> *Jan*

First Trial

When the optical track is married to the print, the laboratory screens this print, called the *first trial*, for the production team to review for final corrections.

Answer Print

When all the corrections have been made, the next print the laboratory strikes is called the *answer print*. Once the answer print has been approved, additional prints can be struck.

Release Print

The next step depends on the number of prints you will eventually need (a distribution issue). The general rule is that the less you run your original negative (A and B rolls) through the printing process, the better. Too much wear and tear could damage the film or break the splices. Therefore, if you are planning to make more than a couple of release prints, it is best to strike an interpositive (IP) and then an internegative (IN). An *internegative* is a single strand of negative that can be run through the printer many times with no risk (it has no splices).

Video Copy

You will want video copies of your picture for cast and crew members, festivals, promotion, distributors, and so on. The print should be transferred to a master that will serve as your original, and dubs will be made from this. Today, Beta SP is the format of choice for the master. Make sure the sound used in the transfer is from the original mix. The sound quality is superior to the optical track on your print.

VIDEO ON-LINE

When the show is "built" on three-quarter-inch videotape or on a computer's hard drive, the original materials are taken to an on-line edit room to be completed. Here, all picture and sound elements are conformed to the cut made on the off-line master. A new on-line master is made, and it becomes the final product.

The goal of on-line is to complete the off-line decisions with effects, color correction, titles, and audio sweetening. On-line rooms, although expensive, provide the director with opportunities for elaborate and exciting opticals and titles.

The edit decision list (EDL), made from the off-line edit, can be fed into the on-line computer to tell it where what images and what sounds should be placed on the master tape. The videotape masters used on-line are typically one-inch, Betacam, or digital videotapes. Copies can be struck from the master tapes for distribution.

PRODUCER
Makes Prints

The producer plays a pivotal role during this final stretch of the postproduction process. He serves as creative partner, negotiator, deal maker, troubleshooter, independent eye, and promoter. The producer can do the following:

- Negotiate the overall deal with the lab. This should be done in preproduction. If possible, it is good to stay with one lab for the entire project because generally the lab's price for the entire job might be a better deal than if you have only your dailies or your final printing done there.
- Negotiate a deal with an optical house if necessary.
- Review the bills for all postproduction expenses (lab, ADR, Foley, mix, off-line, on-line, optical house) to check that they are consistent with the work done.
- Serve as an independent eye for the director throughout the timing process. Review color-corrected prints for quality control.
- Help organize the names and the design for the end credit sequence. Thanking the appropriate people and organizing the names in order of priority can be a big job.
- Troubleshoot if there are problems with the lab or the postproduction facilities. This process might go smoothly, or it might be a struggle. There might be sync problems with the optical track or color problems the lab says cannot be fixed. Remember that these jobs are done by humans who sometimes make mistakes. Unfortunately, they are not always willing to acknowledge them. It might be just a small project to the lab, but it is *your* film. Be prepared to fight for what you want.

LOOKING AHEAD

It is now time to begin planning what must be done once the film is finished. Here is a list of tasks the producer must handle as the physical process of creating the project winds down:

- Set up screenings for the cast, crew, and investors.
- Organize the press kit for festivals and distributors.
- Check the deadlines for key festivals.
- Decide how many video copies are required and who needs them.
- Prepare a list of potential distributors to contact.
- Write thank-you letters to vendors, volunteers, and the key people who helped in making it all happen. Thanking people for their hard work is easy to do and can go a long way in creating goodwill and support for your next project.

KEY POINTS

1. Wait as long as possible to cut the negative. Once the negative is cut, it cannot be reconfigured.
2. Except for simple fades and dissolves, have a wedge test run on every optical shot.
3. The timer cannot change the negative, but she can alter the brightness and color.

chapter nineteen

Distribution

I think the short is as healthy as ever. I think we are seeing a proliferation of film and video festivals that welcome the short form, whether fiction or documentary.

Jan

PRODUCER

Make a Deal

There is nothing like the feeling of having produced a creative work. What might have begun as a simple notion or image is now a completed film or video. You should congratulate yourself and all those who helped in the realization of this project.

The question now is, What are you going to do with it? Let's go back to the beginning for a moment to examine the reasons why you took on this project in the first place. It might have been to create something to advance your career as a producer or director. Perhaps you sought a learning experience, or maybe the picture is rooted in your fascination with the subject matter or your desire to say something profound with the visual medium. The project might have been financed by a sponsor to serve a specific corporate or educational purpose of the organization. In any case, you have done your job and are ready for the next project.

Truman got me some professional recognition, which is what I originally wanted. Besides being entertaining, I wanted Truman to be something I could put on a résumé reel. I wanted it to say, "I can make a movie, I can direct, I can put the camera in the right place, and I can do something fun." It did well for me. I got a manager and an agent out of the blue, so I was thrilled. In terms of its goal and its aspirations, I think Truman more than fulfilled them. It also got distributed. It put me on a professional path.

It's making a little money now, and all of this for 10 minutes.

Howard

You might have thought that there was a predetermined audience, or market, for your project that would eventually lead to financial remuneration. This might not have been the sole reason for your effort, but you probably want people to see your work, and it would be nice if they paid for the privilege. A project that is not seen by an audience is like a tree that falls in the woods: Does it make a sound?

Looking for financial gain does not taint or undermine your serious or "artistic" intentions. If people pay to see your project, it is a tribute to its power. In addition, it will make it easier for you to raise money to make more projects. Remember that there are now investors with whom you have a business relationship. They might not have expected a return from your first project, but repayment of the debt will foster goodwill and perhaps lead to future investments.

All film- and videomakers want their vision and ideas to be experienced by as many people as possible. All artists want their work to be displayed, but there is a different relationship between the work and the audience in film and video. Most art is experienced on a one-to-one basis. Our relationship to a book, poem, or painting is a private one. Although many viewers might have similar reactions to a painting and appreciate its artistic merit, they do so as a result of an individual, not a group, experience.

A unique aspect of film and video is that much of their power stems from the dynamic of being experienced by a group. The impact of a piece resonates with an audience. A film or video viewed by a large audience offers a group catharsis. This is most evident while watching a comedy. Laughter is contagious. The consensus of the group grants the audience permission to express not only laughter, but also the myriad emotions that play throughout the piece.

The exhibition of motion pictures and videos in front of an audience is a vital component of their existence. If your goal is to expose the piece to the audience it deserves, you will need a calculated way to reach that audience—in other words, a coordinated marketing and distribution plan.

DISTRIBUTION OPTIONS

One option is to distribute the film yourself.

> I approached SAG because the film was going to be commercial, and you have to do this. I paid the actors their wages. Then I purchased the music rights, and so I own it now. I distribute the film myself. I like knowing where it's going. I like to give the film away free to hear feedback because I get a lot of requests from institutions. There wasn't a distributor that really interested me.
>
> *Adam*

Alternatively, you can place the project with a distributor.

> Because *Mirror Mirror* focused on women's issues, I contacted Women Make Movies as a possible distributor. I sent them a tape, and they were very interested, as was a second distributor. I decided to go with Women Make Movies because I felt that the subject matter fit their catalog and that it might find a larger audience through their mailing list.
>
> I negotiated for a one-sheet flier for *Mirror Mirror* that they would send out as a special mailing at their expense. I signed with them in the fall of 1990 and gave them nontheatrical rights. In the winter of 1992, I placed the film with Jane Balfour Films in London for international nontheatrical and foreign TV.
>
> Since I retained domestic television rights, I entered *Mirror Mirror* in the PBS series, "POV," which showcases independent documentaries. It was accepted and was broadcast in the summer of 1991. It was clustered with four other short films into a 90-minute program. The license agreement with "POV" was the standard PBS exclusive: four broadcasts in three years. Unfortunately, after the initial broadcast, it will not be aired again, but I am prevented from marketing it further until the license agreement expires later this year.
>
> I think it has done well in nontheatrical distribution. I'm not ready to retire off of the royalties, but they have probably sold about 80 video copies in three years, and the rentals are four times that amount. It has an active rental life in both film and video, which I like.
>
> *Jan*

Self-distribution is a full-time job. You will need to buy mailing lists and lots of stamps. The loss of the product in the mail can reduce profits. Although a distributor takes care of these things for you, the distributor can charge a steep price.

THE MARKETS

There are five basic markets:

- Theatrical
- Nontheatrical
- Exhibition
- Television (pay and network)
- Video

The first part of this chapter is devoted only to the United States and Canada, which is known as the *domestic market*. Foreign distribution is discussed briefly on page 219.

Theatrical

There are few possibilities for short films to be released in theaters. At one time, feature films were preceded by a short film, an animated cartoon, and newsreels in addition to previews for coming attractions. Commercials and previews now dominate this period.

Some people have tried to distribute a collection of short films in the form of a feature. This has been successful when combining award-winning animated short subjects into longer programs (Tour de Animation), but it hasn't been as successful when it comes to combining narrative shorts. There have also been several occasions when feature-length films have been deliberately constructed from three or four short pieces (*New York Stories, Dreams, ARIA*); these are referred to as *anthology films*.

Nontheatrical

The most substantial domestic market and potentially the most lucrative one available to the short film or video is nontheatrical. This is primarily an educational market for the following:

- Schools
- Universities
- Libraries
- Churches
- Hospitals
- Summer camps
- Government organizations
- Homes
- Focus groups
- Businesses

Nontheatrical distributors supply fictional and nonfictional films and videos: narrative, documentary, animated, and experimental. The basic criterion for a successful film in this market is subject matter that can serve some kind of educational need. This covers a broad spectrum of interests. The best way to discover whether your project fits into this market is to submit it for consideration to one or all of the nontheatrical distributors that interest you (see Appendix J).

> If you want to get distributed, you must have something a library or school would want to buy because they are the major purchasers of short films in this country. The short film market is about education. Can I sell this to a library or school? If your film is a wonderful art film, in all likelihood it just isn't going to be distributed. There are distributors who will pick it up, but it will probably sit there. Sometimes, the overseas market is a little different because the short film life is longer, they have a wider appreciation for it, and they can sell the film to foreign television.
>
> Now I'm making money off of *Truman*. Someday, I might make all the money back—maybe 20 years down the road. But I'm starting to see $500 here, $500 there, which is great. I did not expect it. Schools and libraries have limited budgets. If they can go out and buy *The Wizard of Oz,* with Judy Garland, at $19 a copy, what would possibly motivate them to pay $75 for a 10-minute copy

of *Truman?* That's what the educational market is running into: There are very limited resources, and Hollywood is dumping tremendous amounts of videotape on the market at very, very cheap prices.
> *Howard*

Short films and videos sell in schools because the classroom period is approximately 45 minutes long. Teachers want at least 10 to 15 minutes of material to screen before generating a discussion among the students.

Documentaries have obvious educational appeal because they are factual explorations of real events. They can serve as both historical and behavioral models. Documentaries form a large part of the nontheatrical market.

Fiction work, which is either narrative, animated, or experimental, doesn't fall automatically into any educational niche. There must be something in the subject matter that can be used in an educational context. The story must provoke some moral or ethical discussion. Narrative stories, whether they are live action or animated, can offer strong metaphors for human behavior. If your story explores the nature of human relationships in a poignant way that could serve as an educational model, it might have a continued life in the nontheatrical marketplace.

Exhibition

Exhibition is a broad term that represents the many opportunities film- and videomakers have to screen their work in front of an audience. These are some of the venues that fit under this category:

- National festivals (domestic and foreign)
- Museum showings
- Ethnic societies
- Film school festivals
- School and community groups

Exhibition opportunities serve a number of purposes. They give the film- or videomaker an audience response to the picture, public acknowledgment for excellent work, the potential for financial reward, and valuable exposure.

National Festivals

It seems as though new festivals sprout up every year. Listed in Appendix E are important and historically well-attended festivals. Also included are recommended readings and a book listing all the current festivals and their vital information. Remember that each festival requires a print or cassette of your film or video. Ultimately, you need to compare the benefits of a particular festival to the costs of submitting your work. The entrance fees, although not expensive individually, can add up.

> I think film festivals are springing up all over the place. We have a new one in San Jose. I recently went to the Rocky Mountain Women's Film Festival in Colorado Springs, which was in its fifth year. I'm going to Louisville in a couple of months to judge their festival. I think there's a lot of people with initiative who are starting film festivals in small communities and providing a forum for this work to be shown, and I think that will continue.
>
> *Jan*

The valuable exposure you receive after winning awards at various festivals can elevate your status in the industry, not only for the purpose of finding work as a producer or director, but also for building an impressive portfolio. This portfolio will come in handy when you are raising money or applying for grants for future productions.

> The "festival game" is expensive. You've got to be selective, and the way to be selective is to look in the magazine, *The Independent*, which lists all festivals throughout the world and what kinds of films these festivals are looking for, what they're interested in.
>
> *Howard*

Museum Screenings

Museums regularly screen the work of emerging film and video artists. This type of screening is highly prestigious and an excellent opportunity to have your work seen by a potential distributor or buyer.

Ethnic Societies

If your film or video deals with ethnic issues or concerns, research organizations that are seeking a visual device as a springboard for discussions.

Film School Festivals

All film and video programs hold an annual screening of their students' work. These festivals provide an opportunity to be recognized by your institution and to be seen by the industry. If your film or television program is located in a major urban area, it is likely that distributors, agents, and industry professionals will attend to become familiar with the new talent.

School and Community Groups

This category includes church groups, union organizations, local institutes, corporations, and youth programs.

> What's most satisfying out of all the things that have happened with *The Lunch Date* is the requests I get from schools and other instructional institutions and groups like the Girl Scouts, asking for the film because they're using it to discuss race relations. That, for me, is what I had set out to say with the picture. So that's been very rewarding for me: that the film is being used for instructional purposes.
>
> *Adam*

Television

Television might seem to be a natural conduit for the short subject, but this market is in transition. In the past, local access channels and cable networks like HBO, Showtime, A&E, Bravo, and MTV offered the short film airtime. A&E has since dropped its "Short Subjects" programming, but there are other opportunities. Nickelodeon developed an animation department that offers young and innovative animators a chance to develop unique styles and story lines.

The medium is constantly evolving. The development of fiber optics is revolutionizing the industry. The blossoming of the cable industry with an anticipated 500 channels offers unlimited possibilities. There will no doubt be a real need for original programming. However, there is no way to predict what role short films or videos will play in this evolving scenario.

> The other myth is, "I'll sell my film to cable television. There's a lot of money in cable television." Well, it's become increasingly harder to sell films to HBO, Showtime, or A&E. They've all dropped their short tapes programs. If they do buy, they pay very, very little. There is no market for a short film in television— what are you going to do with a 10-minute piece? It's not long enough to program any commercials around; it doesn't draw any names. It's not worth anything in terms of advertising time, so stations will basically use it as fill. The market has definitely decreased all the way around for short films.
>
> *Howard*

Video

It is rare to be able to find short films on video at your neighborhood video rental outlet. You will have more luck in the larger cities at the more eclectic video stores. These videos are usually self-distributed. The film- or videomakers pay for the tapes, transfers, artwork, and promotion themselves and literally peddle the tapes from store to store.

> Once you have a one-inch video master, you can make dubs very cheaply. If you have a distributor, you'll get a nice cover for your video box, but be forewarned—the dubs and artwork will be charged back against the profits you make.
>
> *Howard*

Foreign Markets

The short film is considered more of an art form in Europe and around the world than it is in the United States. For films made in the United States or Canada to have an appeal in the foreign or European market, the film's basic narrative must come through in the visuals. It must be driven by image, not dialogue. Comedies do not necessarily travel well because humor sometimes reflects national sensibilities.

What is clear about foreign markets is that they are generally much more creative from a programming perspective. The BBC programs short dramatic pieces in the afternoon so that a school class can turn them on and watch. After the piece is finished, the class uses the short film as a tool to deal with language skills, social studies, group dynamics, or whatever the strength of the piece is. The BBC puts together study guides to go along with the short pieces so they can be used within a proper educational context. This approach has been so successful that the BBC has programmed these short films during the evening prime-time slot as well.

Foreign distribution plans must also consider issues related to subtitles. Some distributors arrange for subtitles to be shot locally. Others put into your contract a requirement that you must deliver a print with subtitles already burned in. In either case, the producer is required to supply a complete transcript of the project.

APPROACHING A DISTRIBUTOR

Many distributors specialize in the short form in both the domestic and foreign markets. Ask for catalogs from the distributors that interest you, and study them thoroughly before approaching anyone.

> Rather than run out and find a distributor first thing, I did what I always do, which is to show it at a couple

of festivals and see how people respond. It's easier to get a distributor if you have a product that other people have conferred recognition on. It becomes more marketable.
>
> *Jan*

One way to find out whether a particular distributor is right for you is to set up a meeting and ask the following questions:

General Distribution

1. What kinds of markets does your company target?
   - Nontheatrical
   - Theatrical
   - Video
   - Television
   - Foreign or domestic
2. With which markets have you had the most success?
3. How has current technology affected the marketplace?
4. What are some examples of successful shorts from your catalog?
5. Do you work with a publicist? Do producers have approval or input over marketing and distribution plans?
6. What kind of subject matter is easiest to market and sell? Is there any type of picture you are specifically looking for now?
   - Narrative
   - Documentary
   - Animation
   - How-to
   - Sports
   - Fine arts
   - Business and industry
   - Health sciences
   - General interest
7. What lengths or running times have been most successful for you? Is there a relationship between the length of a project and its success in the marketplace? Is there an ideal length for any particular market?
8. Do you handle the nontheatrical and television rights for most of your clients?
9. Is there much potential revenue in the television market?

10. Do you use film festivals to promote your new products? Which festivals in particular do you feel are the most important?

11. How do you use preview copies?

12. Are you ever approached by filmmakers with an idea for a new project? How do you respond? Do you offer advice about the chances of that particular idea for distribution?

13. What do you offer to a film- or videomaker that your competitors do not?

14. Do you cover the costs of the internegative, one-inch, and other related costs?

15. Do you use a tiered royalty scale based on the market of a film? Is this a gross or net point? Is it based on the cost of the film rental and sales?

16. Do you give advances?

17. For how long do you usually commit to distribute a short work?

18. Does it matter if a product is on film or video? Which formats do you prefer?

19. What materials do you require from a film- or videomaker?

Foreign Distribution

1. Do you handle foreign rights for any of your films or videos?

2. How familiar are you with the foreign markets: theatrical, nontheatrical, television, video?

3. On which markets do you focus?

4. Which film festivals are most important overseas?

5. Which film markets do you attend (Cannes or Berlin)?

6. Does your company use sales agents or sub-distributors abroad?

7. What are the strongest foreign markets for the short today?

The responses to these questions will assist you in deciding which distributor to employ. When all is said and done, most distribution contracts are similar. Your decision will most likely be based on the people who run the company, their track record with works of a similar nature, and your gut response.

Show the contract the distributor offers you to an entertainment attorney. You will need to understand the difference between gross and net points, deferments, and the various positions for recoupment. A lawyer can help you understand the difference between a profit and a nonprofit company. The bibliography at the end of this book lists several books to assist you with contracts.

MARKETING YOUR SHORT FILM OR VIDEO

It is up to your distributor to sell your film or video project, so ask prospective distributors about how they would market it. *Marketing* mean promoting what is best about your work, giving buyers a reason to want to own or rent it. Any ideas you have about how and what to promote will help the distributor devise a successful marketing campaign. You'll need a good marketing plan to make your venture into the marketplace a fruitful one.

The Press Kit

You can promote yourself and your product by creating a press kit. A press kit presents your project to the public and to prospective distributors and entices them to screen it. The kit should contain at least the following:

Cover
- Title
- Length and type of film or video (comedy, drama)
- Your name
- Contact number and address

Inside
- Black-and-white production still
- Still from the show
- Your résumé and telephone number
- Details about the production
- Reviews and clippings
- Awards (if any)
- Credit list
- Transcript for foreign markets

DIRECTOR
Publicity

There is no better person than the director to publicize the short picture or to build an audience for it. The best sales tool is the picture itself. Favorable word of mouth, festival prizes, and ultimately distribution are based on the quality and salability of the final product.

> Students put a lot of time and energy into production values, and the film may look like a million bucks but have no center. I think that's why *The Lunch Date* did so well. It's a simple film. Technically, it doesn't have a lot of bells and whistles, but it's got a great story, and the story is really well told in a filmic way.
>
> *Jan*

We end this chapter with the extraordinary festival and distribution stories of *Truman, Mirror Mirror*, and *The Lunch Date*, as told by the filmmakers themselves.

TRUMAN

Truman did well in the festivals, but the "festival game" is expensive. It's $25 to $50 a shot, and you have to put out for the tapes, which you don't think of. This is one of the nice things about distribution: Once a distributor makes you a one-inch video master, and they have it, they can make dubs for you very cheaply, and they just charge it back to whatever profits you make. So it's a nice way to get dubs and a nice cover for your video copies.

The magazine *The Independent* lists all festivals throughout the world and what kinds of films these festivals are looking for, what they're interested in. You have to be careful, but even if you're careful, you can still pick twenty-five festivals for the year. The festivals I submitted to were recommended to me by my distributor, Direct Cinema, and they said it would help enhance the market for the film in terms of the educational market. The film won the Princess Grace Fellowship, a Warner Bros. Film Fellowship, was a Regional Finalist—Student Academy Awards; it screened at Sundance Film Festival, was voted one of the top ten best children's films of 1992 [American Library Association], and is one of the highest-grossing children's films of 1992.

It was really a learning process, going through this negotiation process for a short film, because a short film is not like another kind of contract. The whole means of supply and return is different; the market is different. The first thing that came as quite a shock is that when you get your film distributed, they have to make it an interpositive so they're not striking prints from your original negative. Well, guess who pays for the interpositive? You do, because it's yours; you own it. This is a huge expense, even for

a ten-minute film. It was around $3,000 for the interpositive. So whatever money you make for the first year or so goes into paying off this interpositive you bought and/or whatever video, whatever dubs, you get struck for yourself.

It's been several years now, and I've only started to make money, even though the film has drawn astronomically well for [the distributor]. For a ten-minute film, it has done very well. In fact, a year ago, I think it was one of the top ten children's films in the USA—short films. But, again, now I'm just starting to see money. I never expect to make all my money back. . . . The only film market that really exists for short films is the educational market. Now, I never imagined my film would be considered educational, but [middle schools] often buy it as a way to entertain kids on a rainy day, which is always how I imagined it, so it's turned out well.

It's only ten minutes long, so it's really a diversion for kids at school, and because it's what's called an evergreen film, that's part of what's attractive about it. *Evergreen* means that it is always in season. There is nothing about this film that will date it. It is what it is: kids in a gym with sneakers. I mean, the themes in it, what it's about, will never get old. So it's attractive to schools even though it's not directly educational. If they have this film in their library, they can always pull it out for another twenty years to show the students, and it will always be of interest. That's really what a film distributor looks for because the short film market is about education. Can I sell this to a library or school?

I heard a story about my film that tickled me a little bit and surprised me because I didn't know what had happened. Apparently, when the film was done and it did well at the NYU screenings, it began to circulate. Copies get out that even you don't know about. People make dubs of dubs, and they start circulating the picture. I met this friend two years later who had another friend who was a West Coast junior agent for a while. He was talking to his friend, and his friend said, "There's this film that's the hot thing in Hollywood right now. Everybody's trying to get it, and there are very few copies available. Everybody wants to see this film, and I can't get a copy of it. I think it's an NYU student. Have you heard about it? It's about this kid climbing this rope."

This all went on unbeknownst to me. All of a sudden, without my knowing it, my film was a hot thing in Hollywood, and everybody wanted to get their hands on it, and there weren't enough copies to go around. That was two years ago, and I found out about it a year later. So if your film finds a certain niche, people will start talking about it, people will hear about it, and it will get around. Which is how I guess my agent found me. He must have been one of those people who had seen the tape, and he just called me out of the blue.

Howard

MIRROR MIRROR

The first real public screening of *Mirror Mirror* was at the Margaret Mead Film Festival, which I had entered the previous spring with a videotape because the film wasn't completed at the time I entered it. People liked the film at Margaret Mead, and they started asking questions about this statement versus cross-cultural perceptions of body type. The kinds of questions you get at festivals are like that, which was fine. And then the film started doing very well. The next good thing that happened was it won the best documentary at the New York Film Expo. It won the director's choice at Black Maria Film Festival, and a Jury Award at the Big Muddy Film Festival. It won best documentary at the Humbolt International Festival and was the Judge's Choice winner at Louisville Film and Video Festival. It was shown in London at the London International Film Festival. It didn't get into Sundance, although the director wrote me a note and said it came very close. So it wasn't a total flat-out rejection.

For distribution, I contacted Women Make Movies. I sent them a tape, and they were very interested. I felt comfortable about putting the film with them because if people don't know about this film but they're teaching a "Media and Women" course at Podunk U. and trying to find a film, it seemed to me that they would look up the Women Make Movies catalog first. If they called around and asked if there is a distributor who distributes films about women, that's where they would end up.

I did negotiate for them to do a one-sheet flyer just on this film, which to me meant a lot because it meant they would target this film—and direct it to a mailing list that was appropriate and so on—at their expense. So I signed with them in the fall of 1990. I only gave them nontheatrical; I retained domestic TV rights for myself, and I retained international, which eventually went to Jane Balfour Films in the winter of '92.

In terms of domestic TV, because I had retained it for myself, I entered it in "POV," and it got in. It was broadcast in the summer of '91. I received all the revenue since I was the one who had made the deal. Now they have an exclusive. I can't do anything with it, cable or PBS, for three years. That's their deal. Because it is a PBS contract, it has been on two other PBS series. First was the "Territory" series that comes out of Houston, so it's been shown down on Texas public television independently of "POV," on this other series in Houston, Corpus Christi, and Austin. So I got some more money for that. And then it's also been on the "Through the Lens" series, which I think is on WYBE. It's a public station in Philadelphia. They put together a program of independents, unbeknownst to me—they actually went through Women Make Movies to get it—so it was on there. And now actually it's showing this month in the "What's Happening" series at MOMA.

I think it's done well. I'm not getting rich off it, but when I look at the statements—I don't know how it's done compared to the distributor's other films—but I think it's really getting out there.

Jan

THE LUNCH DATE

The first three festivals I sent *The Lunch Date* to didn't accept the film. I found this very discouraging. I think the first festival to accept it was San Francisco, and then suddenly every festival I applied to, it got into. I believe the film took on a life of its own. Once you're done with a film, it's out of your hands. There's nothing you can do. It has its own life, and who knows what that's going to be. I got very lucky: first in Atlanta and Houston—it won prizes there—and then AFI, which was noncompetitive. The only one I went to out of all of those was the AFI because it was an excuse to go home. For all those who I'm sure are wondering how the hell it got into Cannes, I can tell you it was just a fluke of luck.

Cannes

Around the time I finished the film, I screened it for my professor, Vojtech Jasny. After showing it to him, he told me two things. One was that I should submit the film to Cannes, which I thought was completely crazy. He said, "Submit it; the festival is coming soon." I didn't act on that right away. I delayed. Eventually, I sent the film to Cannes.

The other thing Vojtech told me was that he had a friend who was a casting director, Diane Crittenden, who was in New York casting a film, and she was looking for an intern, an unpaid intern, to run a video camera during the casting of her next movie, and would I be interested? And I said, "Sure." I always like to work, and casting was part of the process I had not gotten to see. I was working part-time doing the same kind of thing at a commercial house, but I was interested to see how different it was for a movie. So I spoke to Diane, and she said she had heard from Vojtech that my movie was good, and would I send her a tape? She was going to Los Angeles, but she would call when she got back.

I sent her the tape, and a few weeks went by. We eventually got in touch again, and she said that she didn't need anybody anymore, but that she had seen my film and she liked it. We had a little talk on the phone, and she suggested I come down to meet with her, just to talk. We set up a date.

I ran all the way over from Fifth Avenue to Eleventh Avenue where her office was, and for some reason it didn't connect with me what she might be doing. I went up in the office, and there were all these signs for *Green Card*, and I thought that was her casting company or something. I got upstairs and saw it was a film production, and I realized, "Oh, this is *Green Card*, Peter Weir's film." So I went into the office, and I asked someone if they could show me to Diane Crittenden, my name is Adam Davidson. The receptionist said, "Oh, you're the person who made that short film, the one that takes place in Grand Central?" And I said, "Yeah, yeah." Then she said, "Diane's been showing everyone that film, and we all love it." I said, "Really?!"

I went down into her office and met Diane, and she said yes, she had been showing it to everyone. In fact, she had shown it to Peter Weir, who loved it and had taken the tape home to show Gerard Depardieu. Then she said, "Do you mind that I gave the tape out?" I was flabbergasted.

Then I got a call at work which I thought was a joke: "Hi, my name's Andy. I'm Peter Weir's assistant. I just wanted to tell you that Gerard Depardieu has recommended your film to Cannes, and he has given me this number that he wants you to call to contact Cannes." And I thought, "What! This is unbelievable." I called this number, and it was a French film office in New York. They said, "We got a call from Gerard Depardieu, and we would like to see your film." And I said, "Well, I submitted it about three months ago on my own. You have it. It's in France." "We have it?" "Yes, yes." "OK, we'll get back to you."

About a week later, the French woman from the Cannes office called, saying, "Your film has just been accepted at Cannes." It was amazing, absolutely amazing. I went over to Cannes. It was interesting.

First of all, I went there with these very naive film-school fantasies of what Cannes would be like. I figured, it's the oldest film festival, it's France, the last bastion of where film is considered an art. I could walk down the street and see Akira Kurosawa and say, "Hey, Akira, let's go get a cup of coffee and talk about film and talk about cinema." Of course, it's nothing like that. It's a market. Now there's the festival there, and there's also the Cannes film

market. There are these beautiful châteaus there, and these beautiful hotels, covered with giant Schwarzenegger posters and giant Stallone posters. It's a zoo, and I hated getting in a tux.

It was incredible because when I was going there, they were showing the new films of my heroes. Kurosawa was there with *Dreams*. Goddard was there with *Nouveau Vague*. Fellini was there with his film *La Volce de la Luna*. So I was happy to have a chance to see these movies.

Supposedly, I could get into any film, but I had to report to this one office every day. It was always the same story. I'd go in, and I'd have this list, and I'd say, "I'd like to see this at this time, and this at this time." I tried to only see the films during the day because going at night meant getting in a tux. There was only one way to enter the theater. You have to enter down the red carpet where people have gathered the whole day to get a glimpse of whoever was in the movie. So there I would be—alone—walking down, just feeling like the biggest loser in the world. I tried to go during the day when the press was going.

But every time when I went to get tickets, it was always the same answer. *"Non, monsieur, c'est complet. Je suis désolée.* I'm very sorry, but we're all filled." And then I'd sit there. I don't know why it is, it seems with the French, their first answer is no. Because then you sit there and ask, "Don't you have one, just any ticket?" And they say, "Oh, let me check." Then she'd open the door beside her, and she'd say, "Oh, I do have one." So I'd get my one ticket. So the screening of films came about.

There are *all* these shorts. In Cannes, the short category can be anything as long as it's short—under 15 minutes. So there were, in my category, a few animated films and something that resembled a documentary. Most of them were 35mm. Most of them were color. After seeing that screening, I was convinced that I didn't have a chance. It didn't matter. I was glad to just be there.

I was convinced the film wasn't going to win, and the day of the awards . . . I hadn't received anything about if I should go, where I should go. And I went down to the office to speak to the same woman and said, "What am I supposed to do?" And she said, "You're supposed to get a ticket." "Well, do you have one?" *"Non, monsieur, je suis désolée. C'est complet."* I siad, "Are you sure?" She opens up the drawer, and there is one.

So I go to the awards thing, and they seat me. It was in the front row! And I'm sitting between two guys who are in the short film category. One guy turns to me and says, "Is my hair OK?" And I say, "Yeah, it looks fine." And he says, "Good. This is my third time here." I said, "Great. Congratulations."

The show starts, and it's strange. It's like a mixture of "The Dating Game" and something else. It goes by very fast. It's not like the Academy Awards, where they stop to do numbers and things like that. The host came out, the back door opened up, and—like "The Dating Game"—the eight jurors come out on this sliding platform, sitting on stools. Bernardo Bertolucci was the head of the jury that year. They're going through the different categories, and with my French, I'm picking up some of it. And then they get to the short film. They announce the award for the short film, and the two guys sitting next to me both get up at the same time and go up. And I thought, "Whoa, what a relief. It's over. The anxiety is over. I don't have to worry anymore." And these guys go off.

Then Bertolucci starts speaking again because he gives the award as the head of the jury. He starts talking about short film again. And he says, the Palme d'Or, which is the grand prize in Cannes . . . goes to Adam Davidson. I went up on stage. He handed me what looked like a diploma thing, and I didn't know what the hell to do.

The next thing I know, I'm standing before this microphone, and I just wanted to make sure that I had thanked people. Well, as I'm speaking—and I was very nervous—I hear the emcee, who is a Johnny Carson type guy, start speaking too. And I was convinced (because I wasn't really listening) that this guy was saying, "What the hell is the stupid American doing? We don't want to hear it. It's just a short film. Get on with it." What I didn't know was that he was trying to translate. I just looked over at him and just kind of said, "That's it."

The whole thing with Cannes was a fluke. If it wasn't for the chance that Depardieu had seen it accidentally, I don't think it would have gotten in, even though I had sent it out there.

Academy Awards

I submitted the film on my own to the Student Academy Awards. It won in the category there. I was informed that since my film won there, it qualified for submission to the Academy Awards. I'd had enough of awards and things, so I said, "No thanks." After

the urgings of a few people, family, and agents and at the insistence of Rich Miller, the head of the Student Academy Awards, I said I would submit it. It was nominated. So I went to Los Angeles for the awards ceremony.

I decided to bring Scotty [the lead actress in the film] as my guest, but she doesn't fly, so like her character, she took a train all the way out to Los Angeles. She telephoned me the day of the ceremony and said, "What time is the limo coming by to pick us up?" I said, "Well, the Volkswagen will be by at such and such a time." We went together. We were seated in the middle of the row. You know how a mind works: I figured, "Obviously, this whole show is rigged, and they seat the people who they know are going to win by the aisles so they can get out easily. So at least I don't have to worry about that."

And then I saw my mother, and she came and sat down behind me. It was pretty quiet in that theater, in that space, and she leans over and not too quietly says, "Adam, do you have enough room so you can get out?" And everybody—all the other nominees—just turns to look at me scornfully.

The category came up, and the film was announced. It didn't hit me. The name was said, and I heard this primal yell. It was my father, who was touching the roof of the theater. I got up—and I was just hoping I wouldn't trip—and got up on stage. It's pretty terrifying. You suddenly face 6,000 people, and the cameras are on, and they have this huge television monitor that they wheel in front of you, which basically flashes "30, 29, 28, 27 . . ."—how long you're allowed to speak. I think I thanked everybody. It was funny. I had gotten a seat for Garth Stein, my friend and the film's coproducer, and he was seated up in the balcony. When I thanked Garth, I said something like, "I'd also like to thank Garth Stein." And I looked up and said, "Who's somewhere up there." I think a lot of people imagined Garth had passed away or something.

The moral of this story about the film is that it does take on a life of its own. I would say to any student out there: Don't be discouraged if you don't get into your first couple of festivals. It is important to try to give the film a chance.

Adam

appendix A

Genres

This book focuses primarily on the short narrative and documentary film and video. Some of the many other variations of the short work are discussed in this appendix. It begins, however, with a brief history of the short form.

A HISTORY OF THE SHORT FILM

The short film played an important part in the development of the modern cinema. From Thomas Edison to George Lucas, filmmakers have depended on the short format to exhibit new technology, advance artistic ideals, or simply catch the eye of the ever-important audience.

It was the audience that first motivated Thomas Alva Edison to commission his assistant, William K.L. Dickson, to begin research in 1889 on a device that would enhance his earlier invention, the phonograph. Photography had become increasingly popular since its inception in the 1860s, and with the invention of rolled celluloid film by George Eastman, the time was right. In 1891, Dickson projected the first motion picture images for his boss. Edison was granted a patent in 1893 for his Kinetoscope, an odd cabinet with a peephole viewer, and cinema was born.

Edison's first films were necessarily short. The Kinetoscope's compact design limited the length of the first films to 50 feet. The limitation was a commercial one. Edison knew that to make motion pictures financially viable, he needed to distribute not only films, but also miniature theaters.

These early Edison films were simple: one shot of a simple action. The photographic record of a sneeze, gloriously entitled *Fred Ott's Sneeze*, is thought to be the oldest remaining motion picture film. The Kinetograph, Edison's camera, was a clunky contraption that could not be moved beyond the walls of its dark studio, the Black Maria. This was not a problem for Edison. His films were novelties, short glimpses of a new technology for a price.

The creative constraints of Edison's distribution and production were soon resolved by two brothers on the other side of the Atlantic. Auguste M.L.N. and Louis Jean Lumière developed a motion picture camera that could also develop and project film. The Cinématographe was portable and depended on a hand crank, rather than electricity, for power. In 1895, the brothers produced their first film, *Workers Leaving the Lumière Factory*, a short static exterior shot of workers leaving their factory. The Lumière brothers opened their first public theater on December 28, 1895, in the basement of the Grand Café. At the showing of *L'Arrivée d'un Train en Gare*, the audience screamed and ran from the theater as a train barreled toward them on the screen.

Early filmmakers continued to use the convenient and economical short film format. Improvements in cinematography and a growing sophistication of content led to multishot narratives. An excellent example is George Melies's *A Trip to the Moon* (1902), which involved several static shots at different locations edited together. Edwin S. Porter's short film, *The Great Train Robbery* (1903), innovated continuity editing to build the narrative.

Motion pictures were by this time big business. Edison's company and others, including American Mutoscope and Biograph, began to compete for a piece of it. Nickelodeons, large store theaters, began spreading across the country after the first opened in Pittsburgh in 1905. The nickelodeons created an additional demand for films and kept the short film alive until great directors like D.W. Griffith insisted on creating feature-length films. By 1914, the feature film (four or more reels) had become the dominant form, and the studios began to relegate the shorts to the role of filler in a feature program. There were few exceptions.

The demand for product was a catalyst for the creation of serials. These short episodic films were centered around a few key characters, and they were exhibited in installments. In 1912, Edison's Kinetoscope Company began the first serial, *What Happened to Mary*. With a unique publicity campaign involving *The Ladies Home Journal*, which printed the new story each week, the format became highly successful. The clichés of the cliff-hanger soon appeared. Studios like Selig Polyscope Company and later Metro-Goldwyn-Mayer capitalized on the format to become major contenders in the business.

A young director named Mack Sennett, unable to produce comic films under Edison or Biograph, formed the independent film company Keystone Pictures. The Sennett shorts were characterized by their sight gags and slapstick humor. In 1913, British actor Charlie Chaplin joined Sennett. Chaplin later created several great shorts, including *One A.M.* (1916), *The Tramp* (1915), *Easy Street* (1917), and *A Dog's Life* (1918). The Chaplin comedy shorts were unique in that they presented social commentary under the guise of silliness. Later, the short film became a vehicle for other comic giants, including Buster Keaton (*The Goat,* 1922) and Laurel and Hardy (*Putting Pants on Philip,* 1927).

All was not comical in the early years of the twentieth century, however. Artistic movements triggered by World War I and the Russian Revolution influenced all media, including film. Directors became proponents of German Expressionism (Erich von Stroheim, Ernst Lubitsch, and Fritz Lang) or Soviet Montage (Sergei Eisenstein and Vsevlod I. Pudovkin). The short film became an experimental form for these new cinematic ideas.

Documentary, which had been reduced to travelogues and novelty films, gained momentum as a genre with Robert Flaherty's *Nanook of the North* (1921). Flaherty's work gave legitimacy to the documentary form and began an important artistic tradition.

Sound was the next major technical hurdle. There had been several attempts to synchronize sound and film during the early years of motion pictures. By 1919, a workable system had been devised. Lee de Forest, inventor of the vacuum tube used for amplification, began showing the first sound films, which he called *Phonofilms*. These were short demonstrations by famous personalities speaking or singing on screen. Vitaphone (the first commercial sound film company) and later William Fox's Movietone both began to distribute short sound films.

An example of one of these early sound shorts is Movietone's *Shaw Talks for Movietone* (1927). In 1927, Fox-Movietone premiered the first newsreels.

At the end of the twenties Disney introduced its first *Silly Symphony* entitled *Skeleton Dance*. These animated shorts coupled recent advances in film sound with Disney's unique artistic vision to create fantastic musical revues.

While Disney was busy with his favorite mouse in *Steamboat Willy* (1928), the avant-garde movement was awakening, led by such filmmakers as Jean Renoir, Man Ray, and Luis Bunuel. Classic short films like *Ballet Mecanique* (Fernard Leger, 1924), *Un Chien Andalou* (Luis Bunuel and Salvador Dali, 1928), and *Entr'Acte* (Rene Clair, 1924) revealed the strong intellectual influence on film from painting, psychology, and other areas.

Television changed films in general, but especially short films. With the inception of television, the 30-minute and 60-minute format became popular. In 1951, Columbia formed Screen Gems to produce product for television, marking a new area for studio dominance.

During the fifties, several independent animators experimented with techniques like pixelation and drawing on film. With his experimental shorts, *A Chairy Tale*, *Neighbors*, and *Pas de Deux*, Canadian director Norman MacLaren is the best known of this group. Animation techniques further influenced directors like Albert Lamorisse (*The Red Balloon,* 1956).

In the wake of World War II, a new wave of filmmakers emerged in France. A strong documentary tradition pushed these new filmmakers toward fresh artistic expression in documentary shorts. The stylistic devices of the documentary—location shooting, direct sound, and hand-held cameras work—further influenced their narrative work. Leaders in this movement included Alain Resnais (*Night and Fog*, 1955), Chris Marker (*La Jetée*, 1962), Jean-Luc Goddard (*All the Boys Are Called Patrick*, 1957), and Francois Truffaut (*Antoine and Colette*, 1962).

The sixties, a time of social and cultural change, saw the growth of the underground independent short filmmaker. Many classic short films were produced during this era, including Roman Polanski and Jean-Pierre Rensseau's *The Fat and the Lean* (1961) and Robert Enrico's *An Occurence at Owl Creek Bridge* (1962). The introduction of the 8mm and 16mm formats made film more accessible and affordable to more people. Andy Warhol, the famed pop artist, was one of those who crossed over into film as an alternative medium.

The accessibility of film to the public allowed younger and younger people to dabble in filmmaking. Film schools began to appear throughout the United States and the world. George Lucas's student film, *THX 1138*, inspired his later science-fiction feature with Robert Duval. Francis Ford Coppola, Steven Spielberg, Oliver Stone, and others began as student short filmmakers in the late sixties and early seventies.

Today, the short narrative and documentary film survives in film schools and festivals throughout the United States and in the booming European film community. Other forms, including music videos and television/film commercials, have given new filmmakers applications for their cinematic ideas. With the continued growth of film schools and the proliferation of video technology, the short format probably will continue into the future.

ANIMATION

Animation has been a part of our visual and popular culture since the turn of the century, mostly in the form of cartoons. Hanna Barbera, Disney, Fleischer, and Chuck Jones are names that represent a rich and dense creative body of work.

Most animation projects are short. The production principles are similar to those for live-action film and video, except that instead of actors, an animator employs characters drawn on paper or clear acetate *cels*. Creating an animated film involves creating an entire world from scratch. Anything that can be manipulated in space can be animated. Animation characters range from stick figures and paper cutouts to three-dimensional clay figures and elaborate Disney-style cel animation. The work of creating an animated film is time-consuming and requires great patience.

The styles of individual artists can be as varied as their imaginations. Norman MacLaren, John and Faith Hubley, and Frank and Caroline Mouris are animators who developed their unique non-Disney styles with great success. Clay animation, perfected by Will Vinton and others, has been incorporated into mainstream entertainment. Year after year animated features, a popular form of entertainment that is accessible to all ages, are traditionally the highest-grossing films. Some of the most original and visually dynamic films of all time were animated.

We are now experiencing technological revolutions in this field. Computer techniques and the enhancement of existing images are creating a branch of animation that will be available to everyone. The use of home computers for applications such as morphing and image manipulation will allow more of us to storyboard, animate, and tell stories in a visual manner unlike anything we know today.

EXPERIMENTAL OR ALTERNATIVE

The short film or video has been an ideal form for experimentation. Filmmakers have been experimenting with the possibilities of what film can do since George Melies's time. Many major European directors who became famous in the thirties and forties began their careers in the twenties with short films: Jean Renoir, Rene Clair, Luis Bunuel, and Julien Duvivier are among them. The artists Man Ray and Marcel Duchamp both explored the possibilities of film's pure visual form. Many early experimental pieces relied on seemingly random images, with no apparent story or narrative expectations to engage the audience. These filmmakers played visual tricks with the medium, dealing with surrealistic film fantasies. They later incorporated into their features many of the filmic ideas explored in these short experimental films.

The independent avant-garde, or underground, movement in the United States began as a protest of Hollywood's conventions and standard narrative expectations. Many of the early short films in the twenties focused on pure images and had little form or content. It was Maya Deren in the early forties who realized that noncommercial, personal short films could do more than just photograph a series of shapes and forms. She created a series of surreal films that played with the perception of space and time as well as the line between dream and reality. Her films greatly influenced the underground movement in the United States in the fifties and sixties. Aided by the increased availability of 16mm and 8mm film equipment, new filmmakers like Stan Brakhage, Robert Breer, Shirly Clarke, Bruce Conner, Kenneth Anger, Bruce Baille, George Kuchar, Jonas Mekas, Ed Emshwiller, and Andy Warhol emerged as explorers in "personal filmmaking."

The availability of portable video in the seventies and eighties allowed a new generation of artists to emerge, aided by the technological ease with which images could be created and the endless possibilities for electronic manipulation. No longer were images relegated to one screen. Installations became an intricate part of experimental presentations, embodied in what are referred to as *video walls*.

Multimedia, which mixes live performances with video and film, became an effective tool for musicians and dancers like Meredith Monk, Joan Jonas, and Bob Flanaean to use in expanding the reach of their art. Media organizations and artist support groups have sprouted up across the country to support new generations of visual artists who are expressing themselves in radical new ways. The lines between film and video are beginning to blur in the nineties with the impact of digitizing images.

CORPORATE

Businesses and other types of organizations (including nonprofit institutions and government agencies) use short films and video for a variety of purposes: to introduce new products or services, to explain new ideas or strategies, and to educate and train employees. Today, such works are generally known as *corporate*, rather than *industrial* (which is what they had been called for decades).

The objective of most corporate media is to communicate organizational information and messages to specific audiences in a consistent, clear, and memorable way. Most corporate work is produced in video, rather than film, and uses a variety of creative approaches, including computer graphics, animation, documentary, and dramatic narrative. The finest corporate work can transcend specific business objectives and achieve the status of art. One such film, *The Powers of Ten* (1978) by Charles and Ray Eames, was sponsored by IBM to help audiences understand the scale and power of large computers.

In the current constantly changing, culturally and geographically diverse organizations, video has become an important and ubiquitous means of communication. Many businesses maintain extensive production facilities; others contract with production companies that specialize in corporate media. Many writers, producers, directors, graphic designers, and others find corporate work both creatively and financially rewarding.

The size of the corporate film and video industry was $7.5 billion in 1993, according to a market research firm. Of that total, video production accounted for $6.5 billion, film for $1 billion. After years of growth, the video segment of the industry is now slowly shrinking, while multimedia and video conferencing are growing.

COMMERCIALS

A commercial is a short. It has a beginning, a middle, and an end. It sets up conflict at the beginning and tries to persuade us that the only way to resolve that conflict is to buy a particular product—and it does this in as few as 15 seconds. Commercials are small, succinct stories that carry a great deal of weight. For many young people, the television commercial is their only opportunity to experience an idea expressed in less than a half hour.

The one thing that can be said about any commercial, whether "good" or "bad," is that it has tremendous power. Commercials disrupt our regular viewing, creating a hostile relationship, but then are able to sway us emotionally and sell us something. The power of a television commercial is in its manipulation of the medium for one purpose. There are different kinds of commercials, including political commercials, which are designed to sell a candidate, and public service announcements (PSAs), which are designed to communicate an important issue. Whether they are designed to tell us whom to vote for, about the dangers of AIDS, or what detergent to use, commercials are about the power to persuade.

Since television commercials were first introduced in the early fifties (when they were broadcast live), they have managed to manipulate contemporary technology and current social and economic trends to successfully sell their wares. They exploit popular icons and ideology in an effort to access our personal psyches—all this to promote toothpaste or beer. Millions of dollars are spent on 30 seconds of screen time. During the sixties, there was a renaissance in commercial activity, and commercials were almost considered the best thing on television. This soon stopped. People were so entertained by the commercial that the product went almost unnoticed.

MUSIC VIDEOS

Music videos are short films, but their action is driven by the music, not a story. The music and the lyrics supply the narrative drive for which the images are mostly an embellishment. However, many film- and videomakers get their start making music videos. It has been a successful training ground for many directors.

appendix B

Screening List

The following is a partial list of recommended short films and videos. We have included distributors and rental catalogs when possible. Many of these are also available at public and school libraries.

SHORT FILMS AND VIDEOS

The Lunch Date. Directed by Adam Davidson, 12 minutes, B&W, Academy Award—Best Live Action Film, 1990, USA.. (The Lantz Office)

Truman. Directed by Howard McCain, 12 minutes, color, 1992, USA. (Direct Cinema)

Mirror Mirror. Directed by Jan Krawitz, 17 minutes, color, 1990, USA. (Women Make Movies)

All the Boys Are Called Patrick. Directed by Jean Luc Godard, 21 minutes, B&W, 1957, France. (Biograph Entertainment, Kit Parker Films)

Amblin. Directed by Steven Speilberg, color, 24 minutes, 1968, USA. (Kit Parker Films)

An American Time Capsule. Written and directed by Charles Braverman, 3 minutes, color, 1968, USA. (Pyramid Film/Video, Biograph Entertainment)

Bambi Meets Godzilla. Directed by Marv Newland, 2 minutes, animated, B&W, 1969, USA. (Picture Start, Biograph Entertainment)

The Battle of San Pietro. Directed by John Huston, 32 minutes, B&W, war documentary, 1945, USA. (Biograph Entertainment)

Betty for President. Directed by Max Fleischer, 7 minutes, color, 1932, Betty Boop cartoon, USA. (Biograph Entertainment)

Big Business. Directed by James Wesley Horne, 20 minutes, B&W, music track, 1929, USA. Cast Members: Stan Laurel, Oliver Hardy. (MOMA, Biograph Entertainment)

The Big Shave. Directed by Martin Scorsese, 6 minutes, color, 1968, USA. (Available on laser disc)

A Chairy Tale. Directed by Norman McLaren, 10 minutes, B&W, 1957, USA. (Biograph Entertainment)

Un Chien Andalou. Directed by Luis Bunuel, 20 minutes, B&W, silent, 18 fps, 1928, France. (Picture Start, Biograph Entertainment)

City of Gold. Directed by Wolf Koenig, Colin Low, 21 minutes, B&W, produced by the Canadian Film Board, 1956, Toronto, Canada.

The Critic. Written and directed by Ernest Pintoff, color, 1963, USA. (Biograph Entertainment)

The Cure. Directed by Charlie Chaplin, 19 minutes, B&W, music track, 1917, USA. (Biograph Entertainment)

A Day in the Country. Directed by Jean Renoir, B&W, 37 minutes, 1949, France. (MOMA)

The Dove (De Duva). Directed by George Coe and Tony Lover, 15 minutes, B&W, 1968, USA. (Picture Start, Biograph Entertainment)

Dr. Ded Bug. Directed by Ethan Cohen-Sitt, 10 minutes, B&W, 1989, USA. (Picture Start)

Dream of the Wild Horses. Directed by Denys Colomb de Daunant, 9 minutes, color, 1960, France. (Biograph Entertainment)

Entr'Acte. Directed by Rene Clair, 20 minutes, B&W, silent, 18 fps, 1924, France. (Biograph Entertainment)

The Fat and the Lean. Written and directed by Roman Polanski and Jean-Pierre Rousseau, 15 minutes, B&W, 1961, France. (Flower Films, Biograph Entertainment)

Fei Tien: Goddess In Flight. Directed by Christine Choy, 23 minutes, color, 1983, USA. (Third World News Reel)

Frank Film. Directed by Frank Mouris, 9 minutes, color, Academy Award—Best Animated Short, 1973, USA. (Direct Cinema, Biograph Entertainment)

A Game of Catch. Directed by Steven John Ross, adapted from short story by Richard Wilber, 15 minutes, color, 1990, USA. (Pyramid Film & Video)

A Girl's Own Story. Directed by Jane Campion, 27 minutes, B&W, Best Direction—Australian Film Awards, 1986, Australia. (Woman Make Movies)

The Great Train Robbery. Directed by Edwin S. Porter, 10 minutes, tinted, music track at silent speed, 1903, USA. (MOMA, Biograph Entertainment)

Hardware Wars. Directed by Ernie Fosselius and Michael Wiese, 13 minutes. color, 1978, USA. (Biograph Entertainment, Picture Start)

La Jetée. Written and directed by Chris Marker, 29 minutes, B&W, 1962, France. (Biograph Entertainment, Kit Parker Films)

Leon's Case. Directed by Daniel Attias, 25 minutes, color, 1982, USA. (Picture Start, Independent Film and Video)

The Life and Death of 9413, A Hollywood Extra. Directed by Salavko Vorkapich and Robert Florey, 12 minutes, B&W, experimental, 1928, USA. (Biograph Entertainment)

L'toile de Mer. Directed by Man Ray, 15 minutes, silent, 18 fps, B&W, 1928, France. (Biograph Entertainment)

The Man Who Planted Trees. Directed by Frederic Back, 30 minutes, color, animated, Academy Award—Best Animated Short, 1987, Canada. (Direct Cinema)

Meshes in the Afternoon. Directed by Maya Deren, 20 minutes, B&W, 1943, USA. (Picture Start, MOMA, Biograph Entertainment)

Minors. Directed by Alan Kingsberg, 36 minutes, color, USA. Winner Student Academy Award, 1st Prize FOCUS Awards, 1984. (ADR Films, 212-529-2440)

Les Mistons. Directed by Francois Truffaut, 18 minutes, B&W, in French with English subtitles, 1957, France. (Biograph Entertainment, Kit Parker Films)

Moods of the Sun. Directed by Slavko Vorkapich and John Hoffman, 10 minutes, B&W, 1942, USA. (Biograph Entertainment)

Moonbird. Directed by John and Faith Hubley, 10 minutes, color, Academy Award—Best Animated Short, 1960, USA. (Biograph Entertainment)

Night and Fog. Directed by Alain Renais, 30 minutes, color, subtitled documentary, 1955, France. (Biograph Entertainment)

No Lies. Directed by Mitchell Block, color, 16 minutes, 1972, USA. (Direct Cinema)

Number Our Days. Directed by Lynne Littmam, 29 minutes, color, Academy Award—Best Documentary Short, 1976, USA. (Direct Cinema)

NY, NY. Directed by Francis Thomson, 16 minutes, color, Academy Award—Best Short Film, 1957, USA. (Pyramid Film/Video, Biograph Entertainment)

An Occurrence at Owl Creek Bridge. Directed by Robert Enrico, 27 minutes, B&W, 1962, France. (Biograph Entertainment)

One Week. Directed by Buster Keaton and Eddie Cline, 20 minutes, B&W, 1920, USA. (Biograph Entertainment)

Pas de Deux. Directed by Norman McLaren, 14 minutes, B&W, experiment with dance, 1969, Canada. (Biograph Entertainment)

Passionless Moments. Directed by Jane Campion, 13 minutes, B&W, Best Short Film—Sidney Film Festival, 1988, Australia. (Woman Make Movies)

Peege. Directed by Randal Kleiser, 28 minutes, color, 1974, USA. (Biograph Entertainment)

Peel. Directed by Jane Campion, 9 minutes, color, winner of the Palme d'Or at Cannes Film Festival, 1990, Australia. (Woman Make Movies)

La Poulet (The Chicken). Written and directed by Claude Berri, 15 minutes, B&W, subtitled, Academy Award—Best Short Film, 1963, France. (Biograph Entertainment)

A Propos de Nice. Directed by Jean Vigo, 23 minutes, B&W, silent, 1929, France. (Biograph Entertainment, Kit Parker Films)

Rain. Directed by Joris Ivens and Mannus Franken, 12 minutes, B&W, documentary with music track, 1929, Holland. (Biograph Entertainment)

The Red Balloon. Written and directed by Albert La-morisse, 34 minutes, color, nonverbal, 1956, France. (Biograph Entertainment)

The Rink. Written and directed by Charles Chaplin, 19 minutes, B&W, music track, 1916, USA. (Biograph Entertainment)

Screen Test. Directed by Frank and Caroline Mouris, 20 minutes, color, 1975, USA. (Biograph Entertainment)

A Shocking Accident. Directed by James Scott, 25 minutes, color, Academy Award—Best Short Film, 1982. (Direct Cinema)

The Short and Curlies. Directed by Mike Leigh, color, 17 minutes, 1987, England.

Sticky My Fingers, Fleet My Feet. Directed by John Hancock, 23 minutes, color, 1973, USA. (Biograph Entertainment)

String Bean (Le Haricot). Directed by Edmond Sechan, 17 minutes, color, 1964, France. (Biograph Entertainment)

Sundae in New York. Directed by Jimmy Picker, 4 minutes, clay animation, Academy Award—Best Animated Short, 1983, USA. (Direct Cinema)

Sweet Sal. Directed by Tony Buba, 25 minutes, B&W, documentary, 1979, USA. (Picture Start)

THX 1138. Directed by George Lucas, color, 1969, USA. (Swank)

A Trip to the Moon. Directed by Georges Melies, 10 minutes, B&W, 1902, France. (Biograph Entertainment)

Two Men and a Wardrobe. Directed by Roman Polanski, 15 minutes, B&W, 1957, Poland. (Biograph Entertainment)

What Do People Do When They Think of the Bomb? Directed by Elizabeth Swados and John Canemaker, 26 minutes, color, 1984, USA. (Direct Cinema)

What's a Nice Girl Doing in a Place Like This? Directed by Martin Scorsese, 9 minutes, B&W, 1962, USA. (Kit Parker Films)

DISTRIBUTORS

At least one distributor per short where these films and videos can be found has been noted in their descriptions. Some of them are also carried by other catalogs in the following list, and some shorts are now available at your local video outlet.

Biograph Entertainment
2 Depot Plaza, Suite 202b
Bedford Hills, NY 10507
(914) 242-9838

Direct Cinema Ltd.
P.O. Box 10003
Santa Monica, CA 90410
(310) 396-4774

Films Inc.
Public Media Education
5547 N. Ravenswood Avenue
Chicago, IL 60640-1199
(800) 323-4222

Flower Films
(510) 525-0942

Kit Parker Films
1245 Tenth Street
Monterey, CA 93940
(408) 649-5573

Museum of Modern Art (MOMA)
11 W. 53rd Street
New York, NY 10019
(212) 708-9600
Contact: Bill Sloan

National Film Board of Canada
1251 Avenue of the Americas
New York, NY 10020-1173
(212) 586-5131

Picture Start
c/o Chicago Filmmakers
1543 West Division Street
Chicago, IL 60622
(312) 384-5533

Pyramid Film and Video
P.O. Box 1048
Dept. GR94
Santa Monica, CA 90406-1048
(800) 421-2304

Swank
350 Vanderbilt Motorpark
Suite 309
Hauppauge, Long Island, NY 11787
(516) 434-1560

Third World Newsreel
335 West 38th Street, 5th Floor
New York, NY 10018
(212) 947-9277

The Lantz Office
888 7th Avenue, Suite 2500
New York, NY 10106
(212) 586-0200

Women Make Movies
462 Broadway, 5th Floor
New York, NY 10013
(212) 925-0606

appendix C

Case Study Scripts

Included in this appendix are a synopsis and a screenplay or transcript for each of the three productions used as case studies in this book.

THE LUNCH DATE

Written and directed by Adam Davidson, 12 minutes, black-and-white film (1991).

Concept

A well-to-do woman's unusual encounter with a homeless man while waiting at a train station to return to the suburbs.

Synopsis

A well-attired and seemingly elegant older woman arrives at Grand Central Station after shopping in New York City. While she is waiting to return to her home in the suburbs, her purse is knocked out of her arms, spilling her possessions all over the floor. She quickly picks up her personal effects and runs to her track, only to just miss the train. She checks her purse and finds that her wallet is missing. She seems lost and close to tears.

With time before her next train, she buys a salad with her remaining small change at a nearby cafeteria. She places the salad and her packages at a booth and goes back to the counter for a fork. She returns to discover a homeless man eating her salad. Indignant, the woman plants herself in the booth and grabs for her salad, but the man refuses to let go. She spears a piece of lettuce with her fork. She keeps picking at it, but the man doesn't protest. In fact, he eventually gets up and brings the two of them coffee. This is their "lunch date."

The woman hears her train being called and gets up to leave. On her way to the platform, she realizes that she has forgotten her packages and rushes back, only to find the homeless man and her packages gone. Pacing back and forth, the woman finally sees that her untouched salad and packages were at the next booth the whole time. Realizing what's happened, she grabs the packages and heads for the train. This time she makes it.

The Lunch Date

Adam Davidson

FADE IN

INT. GRAND CENTRAL STATION - AFTERNOON

A middle-aged "Waspish" WOMAN walks across the station. Her appearance is refined but subdued—a dark winter coat with a mink stole, a lace-collared blouse.

She carries several shopping bags from Bloomingdales and others.

The woman stops to check the schedule board on the wall. She rustles through her pocketbook and removes her ticket.

CUT TO:

The woman hurries by a homeless man begging in the station.

In her rush she collides with a BLACK MAN. An explosion of pill bottles, lipstick, and knickknacks from her purse sprinkles to the floor.

WOMAN
Oh, oh my Lord!

She kneels down to collect her stuff.

The black man kneels beside her. His appearance is professional but rough enough for New York commuting—a silk tie and mirrored sunglasses.

BLACK MAN
I'm sorry. Let me get you that.

He begins picking up the loose items.

WOMAN
No. No.

BLACK MAN
Let me give you a hand.

She rushes to claim her belongings.

WOMAN
No, don't, you're making me miss my train.

The woman grabs her stuff and runs toward the platforms.

CUT TO:

INT. GRAND CENTRAL TRAIN PLATFORM - AFTERNOON

A train rolls down the tracks as the woman arrives. She is left alone on the platform.

Out of breath and slightly disheveled, the woman reaches for her bags.

Her wallet is gone. She collects her bags and walks back toward the station.

INT. GRAND CENTRAL STATION - AFTERNOON

The woman returns to the station floor where she looks up to the schedule board as the times change. Light tears appear in her eyes which she quickly dries with a white handkerchief. She stares ahead, lost in thought.

A black MUMBLING MAN walks by playing a harmonica. He stares into an imaginary audience. He is homeless. He rambles as he passes the woman.

> **MUMBLING MAN**
> Lord have mercy! Ha! Ha! Ha!
> He know it, he know it! How you doing!?
> You know who it is this morning! I know who are . . . Hot dog!
> You know who you are!
> Happy New Years. God bless ya!

The woman walks away.

INT. LUNCHEONETTE - AFTERNOON

The woman walks into a station luncheonette. It is a simple place—a grill, some booths, and rows of refrigerated cabinets filled with salads and sandwiches. She reaches into a glass case and removes a salad.

A COOK stands behind a white linoleum counter. He fiddles with his white paper hat and white apron.

> **WOMAN**
> How much is this salad?

> **COOK**
> Two dollars.

She puts the salad on the counter. She rustles through her pocketbook.

> **WOMAN**
> Well, I'm not sure that I have that much.

The woman empties a dollar and some change on the counter.

> **WOMAN**
> One dollar . . . here's some.

The cook fingers through the change.

> **COOK**
> A dollar-fifty . . . two dollars.
> Here ya go, lady.

She grabs the salad plate and her bundles.

> **WOMAN**
> Napkin.

The cook hands her a napkin. She walks towards the booths.

INT. LUNCHEONETTE BOOTH

The woman walks down the aisle looking for a suitable booth. She places her salad plate down and pushes her bags into a booth.

She sits but does not settle. She stands, carrying only her napkin.

INT. LUNCHEONETTE

The woman walks to the front of the luncheonette. She reaches into a steel bin and takes a fork. She examines the fork, wiping it with a napkin.

Fork in hand she searches for her booth and suddenly stops in her tracks.

ᵴ

CUT TO:

INT. LUNCHEONETTE BOOTH

A HOMELESS BLACK MAN sits opposite the woman eating a salad. He is dressed in a thick wool coat and a flannel shirt. On his head, a winter hat still has the tag attached. He looks up to her.

The woman sits across from him in the booth.

> **WOMAN**
> That's my salad.

> **HOMELESS BLACK MAN**
> Get out of here.

> **WOMAN**
> That's my salad.

She reaches for the plate. He pulls it back.

> **HOMELESS BLACK MAN**
> Hey!

The woman watches him chomping away at the bits of lettuce. He ignores her.

Moments pass.

She reaches over with her fork and swipes a piece of food off the plate. The woman quickly chews while keeping her composure. He goes on eating.

She takes another bite. Then another. And another.

The man does not respond. Suddenly he stands and walks down the aisle. She continues munching away at what remains.

He returns with two cups of coffee with saucers. He places the cups on the table and sits.

He offers her sugar.

> **WOMAN**
> No, thank you.

He offers her a packet of Sweet & Low from his coat. She accepts.

> **WOMAN**
> Thank you.

Checking her watch she stands with her purse and leaves. He watches her exit, somewhat disappointed.

INT. GRAND CENTRAL

The woman walks quickly through the station and then stops. She left her bags in the luncheonette! She runs back toward the luncheonette.

INT. LUNCHEONETTE BOOTH

She arrives at the booth and the bags are gone. Only two empty cups of coffee and a plate remain. She begins to pace the floor nervously.

She paces back and forth. In the next booth we see her shopping bags and her salad uneaten. The woman discovers her bags and the salad. She sits down and laughs to herself. Realizing the time, she grabs her bags and runs out of the luncheonette laughing.

INT. GRAND CENTRAL - NIGHT

The woman runs quickly through the crowds to her platform. She passes a BEGGAR on crutches.

BEGGAR

Spare some change. Please, please ma'am. I'm starving.

She ignores him and continues through the crowd.

INT. GRAND CENTRAL - NIGHT

The woman runs down the platform to the train.

INT. TRAIN - NIGHT

The train rolls down the tracks into darkness.

FADE OUT

THE END

Shooting Order

The following is a sample of the order in which the scenes could have been shot.

Monday

24. Scotty gets on train
16. Train leaves, S in frame
25. Train leaves, nobody in frame (?)
17. CU S after train missed
18. Med shot S straightening up

Lunch

9. Master of accident action
9A. Post train master
8. Super dolly of entire action
6. Dolly on face
7. Dolly on purse
10. Tight 2 shot collision
15. After all p/u, Bernard hands S last stuff, she rushes off
12. Med Bernard p/u
14. CU Bernard p/u
11. Med S p/u
13. CU S p/u

·(NOTE: If low on time after shot 8, shots 6 and 7 should be moved to end of day. It would be nice to get the entire action in these shots, but accident coverage is more important.)

Tuesday

1. Scotty enters, dolly
22. Scotty enters, again, dolly
23. Scotty enters, last time, dolly
2. Scotty takes out ticket
4. Panhandler approaches—wide
5. Panhandler talks—2 shot
19. Ladies room sign
20. Ladies room door
21. Scotty decides not to go in

Wednesday

6:15	Crew call—266 West 43rd Street
6:30	Load in to location
7:30	Talent call, rehearse
8:30	First shot
11:30	Crew break lunch
12:00	Talent break lunch, crew in
12:30	Talent in
5:00	Crew break dinner
5:15	Talent break dinner
5:30	Crew in
5:45	Talent in
9:30	Last shot, talent break Begin wrap
10:30	Wrap

TRUMAN

Written and directed by Howard McCain, 12 minutes, color (1991).

Concept

An eleven-year-old boy confronts his imaginary fears while attempting to climb a rope during gym class.

Synopsis

Truman, a timid eleven-year-old boy feigns a stomachache to get out of climbing the rope during gym class. The coach doesn't buy it and threatens to make the whole class run a mile if Truman doesn't climb. Suddenly feeling much better, Truman starts to climb but then imagines that the rope turns into a noose, the coach into an officer of the Civil War, and the students into his prisoners.

Truman keeps climbing and he imagines the rope starting to unravel and the students bringing out an old fireman's safety net. His imagines the rope snapping, the net being pulled away at the last moment, and Truman falls to the ground, missing the gym mat and bloodying his nose.

The coach then gives Truman a final ultimatum: He must hang onto the rope for one minute only, and if he does not, the whole class will have to run a mile. Truman is determined to give it his best, and the whole class pulls for him. He climbs, and as the seconds wind down, he imagines that the coach is the Sheriff of Nottingham, one student is Robin Hood, and the class is Robin's Merry Men. They shoot their longbows, and as the sheriff falls, so does Truman, one second away from victory.

As the class leaves to run the mile, the coach empathizes with Truman's dilemma. The coach asks Truman to clean up and leaves. Alone in the gym, Truman regards the rope with determination. He runs and attacks the rope with a vengeance. Meanwhile, the class and the coach return in time to see Truman reach the ceiling. A proud Truman looks around and smiles. An amazed coach yells at Truman who, looking down for the first time, gets queasy. Realizing how high up he is, Truman throws up all over the coach. The class goes wild, the coach is dazed, and we leave Truman hanging on for dear life.

Truman

Howard McCain

FADE IN:

THE SCREEN is BLACK. We HEAR a military drum MARCH. Then the CREDITS.

The last TITLE CARD comes up, the MARCH abruptly stops, as we CUT sharply to:

SCENE 1   CUT TO:

INT. JUNIOR HIGH SCHOOL GYMNASIUM - DAY

WIDE: A dull, suburban gym. A SWISHING SOUND . . . and a long rope swings into FRAME.

The SOUND of WHISTLE.

SCENE 2   CUT TO:

MONTAGE

CLOSE UP: A man, 43, with hairy eyebrows and red face blows hard on a WHISTLE. He is obviously a GYM TEACHER.

TAYLOR, about 12, dressed in a maroon reversible and gold gym shorts—standard issue—runs forward. A brief second and another child steps up to replace him. WE can see a line of kids stretching out behind him.

CLOSE UP: TAYLOR grabs the rope and starts to climb.

WE HEAR the SHOUTS of the GYM TEACHER, an occasional CRY of encouragement from a fellow gymster, and, as always, the WHISTLE.

CLOSE UP: TAYLOR touches the cross beam.

CLOSE UP: GYM TEACHER BLOWS his whistle.

CLOSE UP: TAYLOR'S feet touch the gym floor.

The next KID in line rushes forward.

CLOSE UP: KID jumps on rope.

CLOSE UP: GYM TEACHER BLOWS his whistle.

CLOSE UP: The next KID is up.

CLOSE UP: GYM TEACHER BLOWS his WHISTLE.

TAYLOR steps up into line again. Everyone has gone.

OFF SCREEN: The urgent CALL of the WHISTLE.

TAYLOR just stands there. WE HEAR the WHISTLE a second time. Still . . . no one moves. A final WHISTLE BLAST and the CAMERA PANS DOWN to reveal a scrawny boy, 11, at the front of the line. This is TRUMAN, and his eyes tell it all—he's terrified.

SCENE 3   CUT TO:

The climbing rope stretches up into the distance. The CAMERA begins to TILT DOWN, TRACKING BACKWARDS as it does so. The CAMERA continues down to the bottom of the rope to find it knotted in a hangman's noose.

WE linger on it only a second, and then the CAMERA RACK-FOCUSES through the noose to find TRUMAN standing on the other side, paralyzed. He clenches his eyes shut.

The SOUND of the WHISTLE OFF screen, as a figure moves into FRAME. TRUMAN remains still.

CUT TO:

CLOSE: The GYM TEACHER spits the whistle from his mouth and storms forward, calling.

GYM TEACHER
All right! What's going on, Truman?

The CLASS immediately straightens up. He pulls TRUMAN from the line.

GYM TEACHER
Well?

TRUMAN slowly opens his eyes and looks up at the intimidating figure before him.

This is MR. SPARROW, and he is the wrong man for the job. He has all the mannerisms of a football coach, although he's not. He carries a small playground ball in one hand.

TRUMAN
(weakly)
I feel sick.

The CLASS, obviously a little frightened by this man, does its best to remain stone-faced, but a few giggles slip out.

TRUMAN bows his head, and for an instant MR. SPARROW can't decide whether he is really dealing with a sick kid or not. But the CLASS's mockery makes it all seem to be a joke at his expense.

MR. SPARROW
All right, back of the line, Truman.

TRUMAN looks at him for a moment. He is not sure whether he is being punished or forgiven. MR. SPARROW eyes him coldly, and TRUMAN, now feeling the former, heads for the back of the line.

The CAMERA TRACKS with TRUMAN down the line. He does his best not to look anyone in the eye.

SCENE 4

MR. SPARROW
Next.

TAYLOR is next.

TAYLOR
But I already went, Mr. Sparrow.

TRUMAN slides into the back of the line, chagrined.

MR. SPARROW
That's right. Everyone's going again . . .
(pausing for effect)

The CLASS groans.

MR. SPARROW
. . . until Truman decides it's his turn.

Silence. He has just dropped the bomb. MR. SPARROW smiles coldly back, waiting and watching Truman's face, as if it might crumble at any moment.

The CAMERA TRACKS BACKWARDS from MR. SPARROW, revealing the rest of the line. Some KIDS groan, while others look back at TRUMAN. As the CAMERA reaches the end of the line, it PANS back to face TRUMAN, head-on.

No one moves. TRUMAN looks at the class and then back to MR. SPARROW, and he knows that if he ever wants to survive gym class, he has got to go.

TRUMAN summoning his courage, steps from line.

> **TRUMAN**
> (barely)
> I'm feeling better.

His CLASSMATES look suspiciously at him, not being sure if he is serious or if this is just another weak answer.

> **TRUMAN**
> (defensively)
> I am!

He is a little surprised by his own forwardness, but his confidence quickly fades with one look at MR. SPARROW, who seems utterly pleased by the whole situation.

> **MR. SPARROW**
> Well, then, let's get a move on.

SCENE 5

TRUMAN starts to walk forward. The CAMERA TRACKS with him as he walks down the line of kids, who are all now looking noticeably more compassionate toward their suffering comrade. The MARCH MUSIC from the opening CREDITS is heard.

TRUMAN fixes his gaze forward.

ANGLE FROM ABOVE: TRUMAN comes to a stop at the base of the rope and pivots about to face the class. The MARCH ceases.

The CLASS stares expectantly back.

LONG: TRUMAN, the CLASS, and MR. SPARROW—all waiting to see who's gonna make the first move.

CLOSE: TRUMAN looks ever so cautiously up.

HAND-HELD P.O.V.: The rope dangles above him, beckoning. The gym is silent.

> **MR. SPARROW (O.S.)**
> Are you ready?

CLOSE: TRUMAN closes his eyes and nods.

The instant he nods, the SOUND of DRUM ROLL commences.

> CUT TO:

SCENE 6

INT. SAME - FANTASY

CLOSE: TRUMAN gags. His eyes fly open like window shades. THE CAMERA TRACKS quickly back, as a noose is stretched over his neck.

The CAMERA is on MR. SPARROW, who is now a CIVIL WAR ARMY OFFICER, presiding over TRUMAN'S execution. He draws his sword from its sheath and raises it into the air.

The CLASS, shackled together at the wrists and ankles, is a beaten horde of Confederate prisoners. The CAMERA TRACKS quickly down the line of hollow faces.

CLOSE: MR. SPARROW nods and clicks his heels.

The CLASS tenses up.

MR. SPARROW drops his sword with a WHOOSH.

The CAMERA RUSHES in on TRUMAN'S face as the SOUND culminates in a loud SNAP. TRUMAN drops out of FRAME and the rope TWANGS tight.

CUT TO:

INT. SAME - REALITY - A SPLIT SECOND LATER

THE SAME SHOT: A beat. The rope creaks and twists, as if a small boy might indeed be hanging on the other end. Then, a hand suddenly swings into the FRAME and grabs a tight hold on the rope.

THE CAMERA begins to DOLLY back as TRUMAN climbs into FRAME. The noose is gone, and as we PULL further back, we find the CLASS still in line and MR. SPARROW circling close. All traces of TRUMAN'S fantasy are gone, and only brutal reality remains.

From the way TRUMAN struggles, it is obvious that this is not easy for him, further hindered by the fact that his eyes are still clenched shut.

SCENE 7

CLOSE: TRUMAN misses the rope with one hand.

> **MR. SPARROW**
> Hey Truman! Open your eyes. You can't go up like that.

TRUMAN continues blindly on.

> **MR. SPARROW**
> Hey Truman! Hey! I said open your eyes.

ANGLE FROM ABOVE: MR. SPARROW circles the rope. He has begun to wave his arms a bit out of frustration, trying to jump up and tug on TRUMAN'S leg.

TRUMAN, apparently unable to hear, continues upward.

> **MR. SPARROW**
> Open 'um . . .

TAYLOR, seeing a keen opportunity, starts jumping and waving his arms, in mock imitation of MR. SPARROW. He steps from the line and begins to circle TRUMAN.

The CLASS follows TAYLOR'S initiative, start to wave their arms and break formation.

> **MR. SPARROW**
> Now!

MR. SPARROW has managed to gain a hold of TRUMAN'S leg and he shakes it once.

MR. SPARROW catches sight of the class. Caught in mid-flap, they freeze, their expressions quickly melting.

SCENE 8

CLOSE: TRUMAN eyes fly open and look up.

HIS P.O.V.: The rope above unraveling.

TRUMAN looks down.

CUT TO:

INT. SAME - FANTASY

TRUMAN'S P.O.V.: His feet now dangle 30 feet from the ground. The SOUND of SNAPPING twine.

His CLASSMATES jostle into position with a large fire net, ready to catch stranded TRUMAN.

CUT TO:

SCENE 7

INT SAME - REALITY

Hustling the kids into line.

> **MR. SPARROW**
> Back in line! All of ya's. Move it.

The CLASS starts to slink back into formation.

CUT TO:

SCENE 8

INT SAME - FANTASY

CLOSE: TRUMAN.

Below, his would-be rescuers start to retreat with the fire net.

> **MR. SPARROW (O.S.)**
> I said move it!

The rope above his head is hanging by a thread, ready to snap at any moment.

CLOSE: TRUMAN sucks in his breath like a diver preparing for a great dive.

TWANG! The rope snaps.

CLOSE: TRUMAN lets go of the rope.

CUT TO:

SCENE 7A

INT. SAME - REALITY

MED SHOT: TRUMAN lets go of the rope and falls out of frame, landing with a DULL THUD. The CLASS and MR. SPARROW stare dumbfounded. A long pause.

> **MR. SPARROW**
> You missed the mat.

CUT TO:

SCENE 9

INT. SAME - REALITY - MOMENTS LATER.

CLOSE: TRUMAN stands rigidly upright. His nose stuffed with bloody Kleenex.

MR. SPARROW (O.S.)
Sixty seconds, Truman.

The CAMERA DOLLIES back to reveal MR. SPARROW moving into FRAME as he reaches over and pulls the Kleenex from TRUMAN'S nose.

MR. SPARROW
You couldn't cut it going up, so all you gotta do is hang on. Hang on for a minute, and you pass.

The CAMERA continues back. The CLASS circles around.

MR. SPARROW
But if you don't pass . . .
(pausing for effect)
everyone has to run a mile!

The CAMERA stops DOLLYING. The CLASS instantly erupts into cries of protest. "A whole mile!?"

MR. SPARROW
Five thousand, eight hundred and eighty-two feet . . . outside!

The CLASS gives MR. SPARROW the COLD snake eye. Their hatred of him and what he is putting TRUMAN through is obvious.

MR. SPARROW feels those stares drill right into him, but he is shaken for only a moment and quickly turns to TRUMAN and hoists him up, off the ground, by the shoulders.

MR. SPARROW
Are you ready?

MR. SPARROW and TRUMAN are now head to head. For the first time, TRUMAN stares MR. SPARROW directly in the eye. The room is silent. A beat. Then . . .

MR. SPARROW
Go!

He drops TRUMAN onto the rope.

TRUMAN gets an instant grip. He hangs there, three feet off the ground, twisting. MR. SPARROW starts to circle TRUMAN again, bouncing his playground ball.

MR. SPARROW
(reading from his watch)
Ten.

TRUMAN'S eyes are clenched shut. He's holding on with all his might.

The CLASS watches MR. SPARROW with utter contempt.

MR. SPARROW
Twenty.

CLOSE: TRUMAN'S grip is slipping.

TRUMAN'S feet are about a foot off the ground. Sensing the danger, he opens his eyes, looks down, and bends his legs back, giving himself another foot or so.

MR. SPARROW
Thirty.

HAND-HELD: TRUMAN looks out at the CLASS.

MR. SPARROW
Forty.

MR. SPARROW gets down on one knee. TRUMAN'S feet are barely above the pine.

MR. SPARROW
Ten . . .

Truman slips a bit more, clenching his eyes shut.

The CLASS winces.

MR. SPARROW
Nine . . .

The CAMERA begins to DOLLY in on TRUMAN'S grimacing face.

MR. SPARROW
Eight . . . seven . . . six . . . five . . .

The CAMERA moves in TIGHT, and suddenly we hear the SOUND of TRUMPETS calling. TRUMAN'S eyes fling open.

CUT TO:

SCENE 10

INT. SAME - FANTASY

CLOSE: TAYLOR rises into frame, dressed like a ROBIN HOOD ARCHER, with a long bow, arrows, and a look of death.

MED: He steps forward and lets fly an arrow.

THUNK! The arrow sinks into MR. SPARROW'S back. He spins around, gasping, his eyes popping from his head, to meet . . .

The WHOLE CLASS, rising in formation, with bows drawn and aimed. They fire . . .

LOW ANGLE: MR. SPARROW stumbles back, a DOZEN arrows now stuck in his chest. He falls out of FRAME in a bloody death.

THUD.

CUT TO:

SCENE 11

INT. SAME - REALITY

ANGLE FROM ABOVE: TRUMAN'S knees fall into frame and hit the gym floor. The CAMERA pans up to reveal TRUMAN'S face. He opens his eyes. The gym is silent. Slowly he looks down.

MR. SPARROW (O.S.)
(satisfied)
All right, everyone up. Pick up your gear and pack it in. Let's go! Let's go!

The CAMERA DOLLIES BACK to reveal the CLASS and MR. SPARROW. It is obvious that TRUMAN has failed.

The CLASS, now on the ground, rolls over and groans.

The CAMERA STOPS DOLLYING.

SCENE 12

MR. SPARROW starts to collect the rubber balls and put them into a movable bucket. TRUMAN pulls himself from the floor.

The CLASS begins to walk toward the gym door. TRUMAN hangs back, waiting for some final confirmation on his failure. Not getting any, he starts to exit with the rest of the CLASS. He gets about 20 feet.

MR. SPARROW
Hey Truman.

TRUMAN stops cold. Here it comes. MR. SPARROW pushes the rolling bucket up to TRUMAN. (The CLASS looks on.) MR. SPARROW looks directly down on TRUMAN.

MR. SPARROW
(incredulous)
You still feel sick?

TRUMAN
No.

MR. SPARROW
Good.

Without waiting to hear more, TRUMAN turns and starts to leave. He only gets two steps.

MR. SPARROW (O.S.)
Not so fast . . .

TRUMAN stops. MR. SPARROW wheels up the bucket of balls.

MR. SPARROW
(tone of familiarity)
. . . You know, Truman, today it was only the rope, but someday . . . when it's your big turn in life . . .

A beat. Suddenly, the SOUND of the SCHOOL BELL. The moment has been broken.

The CLASS automatically turns and starts for the door.

MR. SPARROW
HOLD IT! Where do you think you're going? You owe me a mile.

The CLASS really groans this time.

MR. SPARROW
What'd you think? I'd forget? Four times around the field. Let's go!

MR. SPARROW starts to wheel the bucket out the door along with the CLASS, leaving TRUMAN behind. The look on his face is a mixture of anger and hurt. The CLASS and MR. SPARROW exit.

MED: The expression on his face slowly melts. He takes one step forward, when the gym door opens again. It's MR. SPARROW. He leans halfway in.

MR. SPARROW
Don't bother running with the others.

A beat. MR. SPARROW retreats. The DOOR SLAMS shut.

SCENE 13

LONG: TRUMAN stands alone in the gym.

CLOSE: His face burns. There is nothing he can say and no one to say it to.

LONG: TRUMAN stands alone again.

CLOSE: He bites his lip and starts to take a small step forward and then, in midstep, stops. Another pause, shorter than the last, as if he is about to step in front of a speeding train. Then he wheels quickly around and is off like a shot, running for the rope.

The CAMERA DOLLIES with him as he speeds across the gym.

HIS P.O.V.: He rushes headlong at the rope.

THE CAMERA DOLLIES back with him as he leaps up and grabs hold of the rope. He swings back and forth once and then begins to climb upward.

CLOSE: TRUMAN struggles upward.

HIGH ANGLE: TRUMAN is nothing but an ant at the bottom.

CUT TO:

SCENE 14

INT. SAME - MOMENTS LATER.

The gymnasium door opens, and in steps TAYLOR. He picks up a sweat shirt, left lying near the door, and then looks up. A smile breaks over his face.

CUT TO:

INT. SAME - SECONDS LATER

HIGH ANGLE: TRUMAN struggles upwards.

CUT TO:

INT. SAME - MOMENTS LATER.

The CAMERA TRACKS down the faces of the entire gym class. They stand huddled near the door, staring silently upwards.

LONG: TRUMAN nearing the top.

CLOSE: He pulls himself up into FRAME, and suddenly the tremendous NOISE of CHEERING fills the air.

The CLASS is going wild. From down the hall comes sound of MR. SPARROW approaching, barking angrily.

The CLASS instantly quiets as he bursts through the door, totally unawares. Then he sees TRUMAN. His face goes blank with surprise.

TRUMAN, a foot or two away from success.

MR. SPARROW steps through the crowd and stops. His face still expressionless.

TRUMAN reaches out his hand and hits pay dirt: the cross beam. His journey over, TRUMAN is very still, breathing, smiling, his eyes still closed, as if the air, the wonderful air, was indeed different up here after all.

CLOSE: The CLASS is in silent awe.

CLOSE: TRUMAN just breathes in the air.

CLOSE: MR. SPARROW breaks into a wide grin and heads forward.

MED: MR. SPARROW positions himself at the bottom of the rope.

MR. SPARROW
Hey Truman!

TRUMAN, shocked to hear MR. SPARROW'S voice, opens his eyes.

> **MR. SPARROW (O.S.)**
> Truman!

Suddenly, the feet fall away beneath TRUMAN; for the first time he sees how high up he really is. Total vertigo.

> **MR. SPARROW**
> Hey . . .

CLOSE: TRUMAN. A shudder of fear. Then something begins to rumble deep inside him. A rushing he can't hold back.

> **MR. SPARROW**
> . . . I didn't think you had it in you.

TRUMAN vomits.

MR. SPARROW, exactly 20 feet below, his eyes popping from their sockets.

WE don't see it, but WE HEAR it—SPLAT! (The CLASS)

CLOSE: Vomit splatters over MR. SPARROW'S sneakers.

TRUMAN is horrified.

MR. SPARROW is stunned.

> **TAYLOR**
> Nasty!

MR. SPARROW lets drop from his hand the small playground ball.

TRUMAN, still in shock, wipes his mouth on his shoulder.

The playground ball rolls across the gym floor, towards the CLASS, where TAYLOR suddenly breaks rank and gives it a good swift kick. It sails across the room and . . .

School's out! With wild cries, the class surges forward, scattering in all directions. A gym class riot.

Half-blinded, MR. SPARROW spins about, lost in the onrushing mob.

CLOSE: The bucket of balls is overturned, sending them to be kicked, thrown, and bounced in all directions.

LONG: High above hangs TRUMAN, while below the melee erupts.

LONG: TRUMAN'S face slowly starts to register what is going on.

LONG: The crowd CHEERS and SCREAMS in wild abandon.

CLOSE: A funny look starts to break over TRUMAN'S face.

A flying playground ball beans MR. SPARROW on the back of the head.

> **MR. SPARROW**
> Who threw that ball! Who threw that ball!

But he is quickly drowned out in the rising cries of freedom.

CLOSE: OUR HERO. And the funny look on his face starts to grow into a wide smile. You could say it blossoms, like a time-lapse picture, only more perfect. TRUMAN just hangs there, twisting slowly, giving the world below the greatest smile of his career.

We linger on this for a moment, and then the PICTURE starts to fade and the CHEERING grows dim, as we slowly lose TRUMAN to the darkness.

THE END

THURSDAY MARCH 23, 1989

TIME	SHOT	CAMERA DESCRIPTION	TALENT	NOTES
8:00-9:00	4-3	TRUMAN POV ROPE OVERHEAD TO CIELING		HAND HELD: #1 POSITION FOR 2-1
	CHANGE ROPES			
	2-1	DOLLY: WS TRUMAN AND CLASS THRU NOOSE	TRUMAN/CLASS	RACK: MATCH #1-3 LINE UP CONTINUITY TAYLOR HOLDS KICKBALL
9:00-10:30	**PUSH IN CAMERA/LIGHTS FOR KID'S LINE UP**			
	1-3	WS KID'S LINE UP: MASTER SHOT	CLASS	NOTE LINE-UP ORDER FOR CONTINUITY!! TAYLOR HAS BALL AT END OF SHOT
10:30-12:00	**PUSH IN CAMERA/LIGHTS FOR TRUMAN/SPARROW 2 SHOT**			
	2-3	MS SPARROW GRABS TRUMAN/THEY TALK	ENTIRE CAST	LOTS O' COVERAGE: THIS IS MASTER SHOT
12:00-1:00	**CLASS LUNCH: 1/2 HOUR**			
	3-3	MS 2-SHOT TAYLOR/SPARROW: NO KCKBLL	TAYLOR/SPARROW	TAKES KICKBALL
	3-2	CU SPARROW: TAKES KICKBALL	SPARROW	CONTINUITY W/ 3-3
1:00-1:30	**CREW LUNCH**			
1:30-2:30	**MOVE LIGHTS/CAMERA FOR SHOT# 3-4: TAYLOR IN LINE-UP**			
	3-4	MCU TAYLOR WANTS KICKBALL	TAYLOR/CLASS	KICKBALL
	3-4A	MCU AMY DISAPPOINTED RE: KICKBALL	AMY/CLASS	ADDITION

TIME	SHOT	CAMERA DESCRIPTION	TALENT	NOTES
2:30-4:30	**MOVE CAMERA/LIGHTS FOR DOLLY SHOTS #3-1, 3-5**			
	3-1	DOLLY/ MS TRUMAN WALKS THE LINE	TRUMAN/CLASS	
	3-5	DOLLY/ CU SPARROW GLARING TO WS	ENTIRE CAST	SAME TRACK POSITION 3-1
4:30-5:30	3-6	WS CLASS GLARES AT TRUMAN	CLASS/SPARROW	NO TRUMAN
	RELEASE CLASS			
	2-4	OTS SPARROW: TRUMAN'S REVERSAL	TRUMAN/SPARR	FOLLOW 2-3 MASTER SHOT CONTINUITY
	TURN AROUND LIGHTS/CAMERA FOR SPARROW REVERSAL			
	2-2	OTS TRUMAN: SPARROW'S REVERSAL	TRUMAN/SPARR	FOLLOW 2-3 AND 2-4 CONTINUITY
6:00-6:30	**CREW DINNER**			

Figure C-1 Sample schedule for one day.

MIRROR MIRROR

Produced and directed by Jan Krawitz, 17 minutes, color (1991).

Concept

A documentary featuring women speaking about how they and others perceive their own bodies, intercut with historical footage of how the media emphasize women's bodies.

Synopsis

Thirteen women wearing white masks and leotards are interviewed on a stage in front of unclothed store mannequins and a poster of the "ideal proportion female." Because the women are faceless, the audience's attention is focused on their bodies. Each woman talks about how she feels about their body in relation to what she and society expect of it. Each woman eventually removes her mask and reveals her face. The interviews are intercut with shots of the mannequins and archival footage and voice-overs from

- A beauty contest from the forties, "the girl with the most beautiful gams"
- Shots from old magazines about the ideal form, "the gal who wins is the chick who is thin"
- Shots of women on antiquated exercise machines

The theme is women's dissatisfaction with their bodies, as influenced by the narrow range of beauty standards in society. Some of the specific issues addressed are

- The awkwardness of a developing body
- Sense of self as forged by one's perception of her body
- Comparison of one's body to others'
- Feelings about constant judgment of body appearance
- Positive and negative feelings about specific body parts and wishes that some could be different

Mirror Mirror

Jan Krawitz

DISSOLVE from BLACK to:

Nude female mannequin. Pan down over breasts, stomach, to waist.

CUT TO:

Shot of head of mannequin and bare breasts of another mannequin in profile.

WOMAN (off-screen, as shot dissolves several times to more shots of heads of mannequins): There are lots of ideal bodies that I think about. I guess the striking thing is that they're not mine.

CUT TO:

WOMAN 1(standing in front of "Ideal Proportion Female" poster): As a woman I'm always supposed to be aware of how I look. In any situation, in any environment, doing whatever, anything I'm doing, I'm supposed to be aware of how my body looks. How am I standing, you know, is my stomach in, are my—is my bust such and such, is my . . . And somehow I feel like if I had that kind of figure I would have to accept that, to go along with it, which is a funny thought.

CUT TO:

Newsreel "The Legs Have It"

NEWSREEL ANNOUNCER (off-screen, as women parade their legs and are examined): Beauty from the ground up parades for the title awarded, "The Girl with the Most Beautiful Gams." The girls are masked and air vents lift the skirts automatically, and oooh, let's look at the view. The contest at Palisades Park, New Jersey, unveils well-lined sights. And there are some modest girls who take no chances, you can bet. And now for the thrilling moment as 50 well-turned calves line up for the final judging. The judges are beauties of the nineties who once won contests of their own. They pounce on this pair as the shapeliest of them all.

CUT TO:

(Following are wide shots of each woman seated alone with nude mannequins in background.)

WOMAN 2: I think the first time I thought about how I look was in the seventh grade, in gym class. It was the first time I had to go somewhere in a big room and undress in front of other girls. And there was one girl who was in the class who had developed earlier than the other classmates. And she was actually quite pretty, and I envied her.

WOMAN 3: I came home one day from school. I was in junior high, and I was crying because kids were teasing me because I didn't have any breasts. And it seems that like the next year they just grew tremendously. So it was like one year I was crying because I didn't have any, and the next year I was complaining because I had too much.

WOMAN 4: There was something about being not noticed, being a sort of flat-chested, gawky girl—nobody really notices you, but once you start to sprout a chest, then people notice you. And there was a part of me, that despite the side of me that really was excited about getting a bra, this other side of me wanted to wear really baggy clothes all the time.

WOMAN 5: Well, my mother is very voluptuous. I always thought that that was real pretty, and then my sister came along, and she came out real voluptuous too, so I assumed that that was what I was going to look like, and when I didn't, this wasn't the best thing. I was pretty upset about it for a while. But that was about ten, eleven. Thirteen is when it really set in that I was never going to have breasts like my mother or my sister.

WOMAN 1: I think from very early adolescence, feelings of not quite knowing how to do it right, you know, not being this enough or that enough, and there were—and all the things you had to wear in order to be a woman, garter belts and stockings and brassieres and makeup and . . . I think most of my life I've had a feeling that I don't quite know how to do these things right, you know, the way other women do.

WOMAN 6: It seems like most of my awareness of myself as being different from other people was always called to my attention by a man pointing it out to me, like you know, look at, you know, Carol over there, she's really thin and real attractive—and not really saying, you're so overweight, you really ought to do something about that. At least maybe not at first. And I think that was, you know, those were the situations in which I became most aware that I was different than other people—that I was taller than they were, you know, not as thin as they were, or just general-ly I guess not as attractive.

Newsreel "Novel Method Used to Judge Beauty Winners"

NEWSREEL ANNOUNCER (off-screen, with shots of women waiting in line, being measured and judged): The form divine is well displayed by these modern Venuses at Steeplechase Park, Coney Island, New York. And they well know how to strut their stuff. It's a tough job with so much (unintelligible word) around to select a winner, but you can always pick a champion. They say a straight line, is oh well, with so much curvaceous beauty around, why both-er with straight lines? Hey, anybody got a ladder? No matter how pretty they come, there's always a winner. And the laurels go to Evelyn Peterson of Long Island, a mighty fetching modern Venus.

CUT TO:

(Following shots are all of women, each seated alone with nude mannequins in background; tighter shot than before, showing only head and shoulders of each.)

WOMAN 4: I don't look over at someone and say, "Oh what a nice body. Isn't it nice that this person has a nice body?" I can't just let them have a nice body not being relative to me. I have to look at their body and say, "What a nice body. Why isn't it mine? Why doesn't mine look like that?"

WOMAN 3: I think I'm pretty lucky in the sense that I have what people have termed a pretty face, so, and my height, and so it kind of, that initial impression is a good one, even though I am overweight, or my size is larger than I want to be.

WOMAN 1: In a funny way, I almost feel like I have more presence being big and that I don't look like a kid, and I don't look like a little girl.

WOMAN 7: People approach me as a sweet little Oriental woman. First of all, I'm not little. Physically, I'm pretty big for a Japanese, and often, I'm not sweet.

WOMAN 8: I'm not viewed with as much credibility as people who are an average height, and I think that, com-pounded with my blonde hair, is kind of a double negative.

WOMAN 9: People will look and see gray hair and think, old lady, and they don't go any further.

WOMAN 10: I think that because I am tall and that because that, combined with the fact that I am middle-aged and that I'm frankly middle-aged—I don't dye my hair, I haven't had a face lift or eye tucks or anything of these things—that this is fairly intimidating.

WOMAN 8: When I had blond hair, everyone thought I had an easy life, that it meant I was probably a cheerleader and had a real storybook life. When I died my hair brown, people were more accepting of my opinions. They thought I was more of an interesting person.

WOMAN 11: I am more aware of what other women will think of me and the way I appear than any consideration of appealing to men.

WOMAN 4: Like I feel badly that I look over at women who have a little bit fatter stomach, or, you know, their legs are a little bit heavy, and then I get some enjoyment out of seeing women whose bodies look less appealing than mine.

WOMAN 1: A friend and I had an experience. We went down to Port Oranges for the weekend, and we walked at about ten o'clock at night down to the beach, which was only a couple of blocks from where we were staying, and had the experience of having young men in pickup trucks yelling at us, yelling names at us: fat broads. It was a real shocker. I think partially because we neither of us expected to draw any attention whatsoever from that age group, particularly both of us forty-year-old ladies. But that whole thing, that we were committing some kind of crimes in their minds by being in the universe.

CUT TO:

Magazine cover of thin woman in bathing suit standing in front of heavy woman in bathing suit. Pan from legs to faces. (Song begins: "Now girls, a word of warning, I hereby do impart, now don't let an oversized physique, upset your apple cart . . .")

CUT TO:

Two semicircular B&W photos: woman in dress on left, woman in bathing suit on right. (Song continues without break: "Because ladies, we love you all . . .")

CUT TO:

Close-up of old B&W photo of woman in bra. (Song continues without break: "Big, fat, thin, and tall . . .")

CUT TO:

Magazine pages with photos of woman in bathing suit wearing sash. (Song continues: "But the gal that wins is the chick that's thin . . .")

CUT TO:

Old print ad with photos of women and headline: "You Can Improve." (Song continues: "Please listen to my call . . .")

CUT TO:

Old print ad with bathing beauty and headline: "It's Easy to Put on Lovely Curves Now." (Song continues: "Now she was neat and sweet and twenty-two, a solid sender . . .")

CUT TO:

Succession of B&W film clips of women exercising with machines. (Song continues: "Through and through, but her time is gone forever more, big and fat and forty-four, ain't no use in frettin', wastin' time and sighs, 'cause she keeps on gettin' heavier from diet and exercise . . .")

CUT TO:

Quick succession of print ads: "Reducing and how!" "What Type Overweight Person Are You?" "Girls with Naturally Skinny Figures," etc. (Song continues: "Now she's big and fat, and she can't get thin. She's gotta wrinkled neck and a double chin. She ain't like she was before. She's big and fat and forty four. . . . You know, my gal, boys she's a mess. Takes a circus tent to make her a dress. Feet so big she wears a ten. Her waistline is about to bust her skin. She goes to sleep and starts to spread . . .")

CUT TO:

Succession of film clips of women on exercise machines. (Song continues: "Darn near takes up all the bed. Still, at that, she means no harm. She might be fat, but she sure is warm.")

CUT TO:

Poster of "Ideal Proportion Female" (Music fades out)

DISSOLVE TO:

(Following shots are all of women, each standing alone in front of "Ideal Proportion" poster.)

WOMAN 12: You know, I'll see someone that's not necessarily real skinny, that I think is real attractive, or someone who is tall and kind of chunky and I think is real attractive, so I don't really have an ideal body that I think is attractive, but I don't feel like mine's it.

WOMAN 9: I look at pictures of myself when I was young, and I think, I was really quite slender and had a nice-looking figure, but I was never satisfied with it or happy with it.

WOMAN 10: I no longer am wistful about having perfect thighs or perfect breasts or a smaller waist or whatever it seems to be the ideal of the time.

WOMAN 13: I'm pretty content with the size of my body, that is, the proportion of my body.

WOMAN 4: I sometimes think it would be really neat to be petite, that I think of myself as too tall.

WOMAN 1: I think in some ways I'd like to be a big strong woman, but big more in the sense of muscular, large than fat.

WOMAN 7: I'd like to be much thinner.

WOMAN 3: As a matter of fact I'm trying to lose about 40 more pounds.

WOMAN 6: I like my hair. My hair is OK now because I have it colored, because there's a white streak that comes right here that I don't particularly care for.

WOMAN 4: Sometimes I think the gray makes me look sophisticated and trendy, and sometimes I'm really self-conscious about the fact that it's showing my age.

WOMAN 1: I like my hair, but it's too fine and thin.

WOMAN 8: I think my neck is OK. I feel pretty good about my neck.

WOMAN 2: My neck, I wish there was more to it, lengthwise.

WOMAN 9: I like my shoulders and my upper chest.

WOMAN 12: I like my shoulders, that, that's really the only part of my body that I think is totally acceptable.

WOMAN 8: My arms are probably what I like best about my body because they look toned.

WOMAN 6: Sometimes I think my arms are a little long. You know, you get the gorilla look.

WOMAN 4: I like the fact that my arms are the skinniest part of my body.

WOMAN 9: I don't like the way it's changed here.

WOMAN 5: I hate that when it gets flabby back here.

WOMAN 11: There is a bit of extra flesh down here.

WOMAN 3: My breasts are too large.

WOMAN 9: I'd just as soon they would be smaller.

WOMAN 5: I like my breasts right before my period because they're bigger and they're rounder.

WOMAN 6: It'd be nice if they were the classic up, just a little firmer.

WOMAN 4: I'm high waisted. I think my waist is too high.

WOMAN 9: I never have had a waist.

WOMAN 2: My waist, I wish there was much less of it.

WOMAN 3: My hips seem small because my stomach is large.

WOMAN 7: My hips always were a little bit too big.

WOMAN 12: My hips have always been too small.

WOMAN 8: I have a full bottom.

WOMAN 7: I always thought my bottom was real low.

WOMAN 3: My legs are pretty decent sized. I got those from my mother.

WOMAN 13: I would give myself nice long legs.

WOMAN 7: My legs are short.

WOMAN 11: My legs, I ignore them.

WOMAN 8: Probably what I don't like is this part right here.

WOMAN 4: I probably think my thighs are bigger than they should be.

WOMAN 6: Thighs are too large for my taste, too loose.

WOMAN 10: I always had good calves, good ankles.

WOMAN 4: A lot of exercise, so good calves.

WOMAN 9: I think I really have beautiful feet.

CUT TO:

Nude mannequin in front of mirror. Pan up to waist, breasts.

DISSOLVE TO:

Face of one mannequin partially obscured behind arm of another.

VOICE-OVER (unidentified woman; continues while women remove masks): I remember when I wanted to be smaller, more fragile, because then I thought that's what was attractive.

(Following shots are of each woman, seated alone in front of nude mannequins.)

WOMAN 8 removes mask.

WOMAN 9 removes mask.

WOMAN 7 removes mask.

WOMAN 3 removes mask.

DISSOLVE TO:

Breasts of nude mannequin and pans over other mannequin's

VOICE-OVER (unidentified woman begins to talk as WOMAN 3 is removing mask; continues after dissolve to mannequins): I think if it was up to me, it really wouldn't matter what size I was. But because society feels size is important, I think that has caused me to be very aware of my size.

DISSOLVE TO:

WOMAN 2 removes mask.

VOICE-OVER (unidentified woman): I don't think I'd like major changes. I'm OK the way I am.

WOMAN 10 removes mask.

WOMAN 13 removes mask.

WOMAN 12 removes mask.

WOMAN 5 removes mask.

WOMAN 11 removes mask.

WOMAN 6 removes mask.

WOMAN 1 removes mask.

VOICE-OVER (unidentified woman): I don't think anymore in my life I would even want to be a glamour girl.

WOMAN 4 removes mask.

VOICE-OVER (unidentified woman): It's just that I want to be different from who I am.

DISSOLVE TO:

Faces of mannequins

FADE TO BLACK

Credits

Interview Questions

Thirteen women were interviewed in *Mirror Mirror*. Filmmaker Jan Kravitz asked four questions of each woman, using a different camera setup for each question. Two sets were built in a single studio. In one set, each subject was seated in a row of theater chairs, surrounded by naked mannequins. Jan asked two questions in this location, one filmed in a medium close-up and the second filmed in a wider shot. The second set required the subject to stand in front of a mural that depicted the "Ideal Proportion, Female." Jan asked the following questions:

1. Seated mannequin set, wide shot: "At what point in your life did you first become aware of your 'body image'? Was this awareness catalyzed by a particular incident?"

2. Seated mannequin set, medium close-up: "How do you feel people respond to you or make assumptions about you based solely on your physicality?"

3. Standing mural set, wide shot: "Describe your body from head to toe, commenting on specific body parts—which parts please you and which displease you?"

4. Standing mural set, medium shot: "If you could redesign your body, what would it look like?"

Questions 1 and 2 resulted in distinct answers as predicted, so the responses to these questions were cut into two distinct sequences, using the jump cut aesthetic in which the composition and background remain constant while the subject changes in the foreground.

In the editing stage, Jan realized that there was often considerable overlap between the responses to questions 3 and 4. She ultimately constructed a single mural sequence in which the shots cut back and forth between the two compositions, dictated solely by the text of the interview.

appendix D

Forms

Included in this appendix are a talent release and a location contract. The appendix also contains samples of detailed budgets for a short film, an animated film, and a video.

RELEASE

Authorization to Reproduce Physical Likeness

For good and valuable consideration, the receipt of which from _____ is acknowledged, I hereby expressly grant to said _____ and to its employees, agents, and assigns, the right to photograph me and use my picture, silhouette, and other reproductions of my physical likeness (as the same may appear in any still camera photograph and/or motion picture film), in and in connection with the exhibition, theatrically, on television or otherwise, of any motion picture or motion pictures in which the same may be used or incorporated and also in the advertising, exploiting, and/or publicizing of any such motion picture, but not limited to television or theatrical motion pictures.

    I hereby certify that I have read the foregoing and fully understand the meaning and effect thereof, and intending to be legally bound, I have hereunto set my hand this _____ day of _____, 19__.

_____

WITNESS:

_____

LOCATION CONTRACT

Date: _____

Permission is hereby granted to _____

_____ (hereinafter

referred to as "Producer"), to use the property and adjacent area, located at _____

_____

for the purpose of photographing and recording scenes (interior and/or exterior) for motion pictures with the right to exhibit and license others to exhibit all or any part of said scenes in motion pictures throughout the world; said permission shall include the right to bring personnel and equipment (including props and temporary sets) onto said property, and to remove the same therefrom after completion of work.

The above permission is granted for a period of _____ from _____ at the agreed-upon rental price of _____.

Producer hereby agrees to hold the undersigned harmless of and from any and all liability and loss which the undersigned may suffer, or incur by reason of any accidents or other damages to the said premises, caused by any of their employees or equipment, on or about the above-mentioned premises, ordinary wear and tear of the premises in accordance with this agreement excepted.

The undersigned does hereby warrant and represent that the undersigned has full right and authority to enter into this agreement concerning the above-described premises, and that the consent or permission of no other person, firm, or corporation is necessary in order to enable Producer to enjoy full rights to the use of said premises, herein above mentioned, and the undersigned does hereby indemnify and agree to hold Producer free and harmless from and against any and all loss, costs, liability, damages, or claims of any nature, including but not limited to attorney's fees, arising from, growing out of, or concerning a breach of above warranty.

_____   _____
Signed   Company

_____   _____
Title   Signed

                                         _____
                                         Address

SHORT BUDGET – 2

		Detail	Budget	Actual Cost
001	SCRIPT & RIGHTS			
	Rights			
	Research			
	Script			
	Typing & Xerox			
	Travel			
	Other			
	TOTAL			
002	PRODUCER			
	Secretary/Assistant			
	Travel			
	Other			
	TOTAL			
003	DIRECTOR			
	Secretary/Assistant			
	Travel			
	Other			
	TOTAL			
004	CAST			
	Principals			
	Bit Players			
	Extras			
	Narrator			
	Welfare Worker / Teacher			
	Casting Expenses			
	Overtime			
	SAG Pension			
	Fringes			
	TOTAL			
005	PRODUCTION DEPARTMENT			
	Production Manager			
	Assistant Director			
	Location Manager			
	Production Coordinator			
	Script Supervisor			
	Production Assistant(s)			
	Fringes			
	TOTAL			

SHORT BUDGET – 3		**Detail**	**Budget**	**Actual Cost**
006	CREW			
	Director of Photography			
	Camera Operator			
	Assistant Camera			
	Second Assistant Camera			
	Sound Recordist			
	Sound Boom			
	Gaffer			
	Best Boy			
	Key Grip			
	Grip(s)			
	Driver			
	Overtime			
	Fringes			
	Other			
	TOTAL			
007	EQUIPMENT			
	Camera Package			
	Sound Equipment			
	Lighting Package			
	Grip Equipment			
	Dolly/Crane Rental			
	Generator Rental			
	Special Equipment			
	Expendables			
	Truck Rental			
	Gas, Oil			
	TOTAL			
008	ART			
	Air Director			
	Prop Person			
	Wardrobe Person			
	Hair/Makeup Person			
	Set Dresser			
	Prop Expenses			
	Wardrobe			
	Set Dressing			
	Hair/Makeup Expenses			
	Stage Rental			
	Set Construction			
	Construction Supplies			
	Petty Cash			
	TOTAL			

SHORT BUDGET – 4

		Detail	Budget	Actual Cost
009	LOCATION			
	Location Rentals			
	Permits			
	Police/Fire			
	Hotels			
	Meals			
	Craft Services			
	Car/Truck Rental			
	Gas			
	Petty Cash			
	Other			
	TOTAL			
010	FILM & LAB			
	Film/Tape Stock			
	Process			
	Print			
	Audio Tape Stock (1/4")			
	Transfer Dailies			
	Mag Stock			
	Stills, Stock, and Process			
	Video Transfer			
	Shipping			
	Other			
	TOTAL			
	PRODUCTION TOTAL			
011	EDITING			
	Editor			
	Assistant Editor			
	Edge Coding			
	Editing Equipment			
	Editing Supplies			
	Editing Room Rental			
	Stock Footage			
	Screenings			
	Fringes			
	Other			
	TOTAL			

SHORT BUDGET – 5		Detail	Budget	Actual Cost
012	SOUND			
	Sound Editor			
	Sound Effects			
	ADR			
	Foley			
	Composer			
	Studio Rental			
	Re-recording			
	Music Rights			
	Library Music			
	Mag Transfer			
	Mix			
	35 Full Coat Rental			
	16 mm Mix Mag			
	1/4" Protection			
	Shoot Optical			
	TOTAL			
013	LAB			
	Negative Cutter			
	Opticals			
	Titles			
	Answer Print			
	Second Answer Print			
	Optical Track			
	Interpositive			
	Internegative			
	Release Print			
	Video Transfer			
	Slop Prints			
	TOTAL			
	POSTPRODUCTION TOTAL			
014	OFFICE			
	Office Rental			
	Office Equipment			
	Supplies			
	Phone			
	Photocopying			
	Postage			
	Legal			
	TOTAL			
015	INSURANCE			
016	CONTINGENCY			
	TOTAL OVERHEAD			
	GRAND TOTAL			

ANIMATION BUDGET

	Detail	Budget	Actual Cost
PREPRODUCTION			
Director			
Storyboard			
Supplies			
Phone			
Other			
TOTAL			
PRODUCTION			
Director			
Design			
Layout			
Backgrounds			
Animator			
Animator #2			
Assistant Animator			
Assistant #2			
Assistant #3			
Track Reading			
Overtime			
Fringes			
Other			
TOTAL			
TECHNICAL SERVICES			
Inking			
Painting			
Checking			
Titles			
Supplies			
Other			
TOTAL			
CAMERA			
Camera			
Film Stock			
Process and Print			
Rotoscope			
Other			
TOTAL			
GRAND TOTAL			

VIDEO POSTPRODUCTION BUDGET

	Detail	Budget	Actual Cost
POSTPRODUCTION: OFF-LINE			
Equipment Rental			
Transfer			
Time Code			
Window Dub			
Tape Stock			
Operator			
TOTAL			
POSTPRODUCTION: ON-LINE			
Equipment Rental			
Operator			
Tape Stock			
Titles			
Animation			
Special Effects			
Paint Box			
Sound Track Building			
Sound Mix			
TOTAL			
GRAND TOTAL			

appendix E

Film and Video Festivals

UNITED STATES

Academy Awards/Documentary
Film Competition
    Academy of Motion Picture
      Arts and Sciences
    8949 Wilshire Boulevard
    Beverly Hills, CA 90211-1972
    Tel: (310) 247-3000
    Fax: (213) 859-9351
    Held: Early December

AFI Fest – Los Angeles
    2021 North Western Avenue
    P.O. Box 27999
    Los Angeles, CA 90027
    Tel: (213) 856-7707
    Fax: (213) 462-4049
    Held: Mid-June

AFI Video Festival
    2021 North Western Avenue
    Los Angeles, CA 90027
    Tel: (213) 856-7600
    Fax: (213) 462-4049
    Held: Early November

African American New Works
Film Festival
    Omega Media Network
    P.O. Box 4824
    Richmond, VA 23220
    Tel: (804) 353-4525
    Held: Late September

American Film and Video Festival
    8050 Milwaukee Avenue
    P.O. Box 48659
    Niles, IL 60648
    Tel: (708) 698-6440
    Fax: (708) 823-1561
    Held: Late May

American Indian Film and Video Competition
    State Arts Council of Oklahoma
    640 Jim Thorpe Building
    Oklahoma City, OK 73105
    Tel: (918) 747-8276
    Held: Mid-June

Ann Arbor Film Festival
    P.O. Box 8232
    Ann Arbor, MI 48107
    Tel: (313) 995-5356
    Held: Mid-March

Asian American International Film Festival
    Asian Cine Vision
    32 East Broadway, 4th Floor
    New York, NY 10002
    Tel: (212) 925-8685
    Fax: (212) 925-8157
    Held: Early June

Asian American International Video Festival
    Asian Cine Vision
    32 East Broadway, 4th Floor
    New York, NY 10002
    Tel: (212) 925-8685
    Fax: (212) 925-8157
    Held: Early April

ASIFA-East Animated Film Awards
    11 Admiral Lane
    Norwalk, CT 06851
    Tel: (203) 847-4740
    Held: Late January

Aspen ShortsFest
    P.O. Box 8910
    601 East Bleeker
    Aspen, CO 81612
    Tel: (303) 925-6882
    Fax: (303) 925-9534
    Held: Late February

Athens International Film and Video Festival
Athens Center for Film and Video
P.O. Box 388
75 West Union Street
Room 407
Athens, OH 45701
Tel: (614) 593-1330
Held: Late April

Atlanta Film and Video Festival
IMAGE Film/Video Center
75 Bennett Street, Suite J2
Atlanta, GA 30309
Tel: (404) 352-4254
Held: Early May

Big Muddy Film and Video Festival
Department of Cinema and Photography
Southern Illinois University
Carbondale, IL 62904
Tel: (618) 453-1475
Held: Late February

Black American Cinema Society Film
Festival/Independent Filmmakers Awards
Western States Black Research Center
3617 Montclair Street
Los Angeles, CA 90018
Tel: (213) 737-3585
Fax: (213) 737-2842
Held: Early April

Black Filmmakers Hall of Fame
Black Independent Film, Video
and Screenplay Competition
405 14th Street, Suite 515
Oakland, CA 94612
Tel: (510) 465-0804
Fax: (510) 839-9858
Held: Early April

Black Maria Film and Video Festival
Essex-Hudson Film Center of the East
Orange Public Library
South Arlington Avenue
East Orange, NJ 07018
Tel: (201) 200-2043
Held: Early January

Blacklight: A Festival of Black
International Cinema
Film Center of the School of the
Art Institute of Chicago
Columbia Drive at Jackson
Chicago, IL 60603
Tel: (312) 443-3733
Held: Early August

California Student Media Festival
1898 Bolsa Avenue
Seal Beach, CA 90740
Tel: (213) 430-1021
Held: Late April

Chicago International Festival
of Children's Films
1517 W. Fullerton Avenue
Chicago, IL 60614
Tel: (312) 261-9075
Fax: (312) 929-5437
Held: Mid-October

Chicago International Film and
Video Festival
415 North Dearborn Street
Chicago, IL 60610-9990
Tel: (312) 644-3400
Fax: (312) 644-0784
Held: Mid-October

Chicago Latino Film Festival
Columbia College
606 South Michigan Avenue
Chicago, IL 60605
Tel: (312) 431-1330
Fax: (312) 751-3422
Held: Late September

Chicago Lesbian and Gay Film Festival
Chicago Filmmakers
1229 West Belmont Avenue
Chicago, IL 60657
Tel: (312) 281-8788
Fax: (312) 281-0389
Held: Early November

CINE-Council on Non-Theatrical Events
1001 Connecticut Avenue, NW
Washington, DC 20036
Tel: (202) 785-1136
Fax: (202) 785-4114
Held: Early December/Early August

Cinequest
P.O. Box 720040
San Jose, CA 95172-0040
Tel: (408) 995-6305
Fax: (408) 277-3862
Held: Mid-October

Documentary Festival of New York
454 Broome Street
New York, NY 10013
Tel: (212) 966-9578
Held: Late June

Dore Schary Awards
TV Radio Film Department
Anti-Defamation League of B'nai B'rith
823 United Nations Plaza
New York, NY 10017
Tel: (212) 490-2525
Fax: (212) 867-0779
Held: Mid-January

Earth Peace Film Festival
P.O. Box 531
Burlington, VT 05402-0531
Tel: (802) 660-8201
Fax: (802) 658-3311
Held: Mid-April

Hometown USA Video Festival
The Buske Group
2015 J Street
Suite 28
Sacramento, CA 95814
Tel: (916) 441-6277
Fax: (916) 441-7670
Held: Mid-July

Houston International Film and Video
Festival/Worldfest–Houston
P.O. Box 56566
Houston, TX 77256
Tel: (713) 965-9955
Fax: (713) 965-9960
Held: Late April

Human Rights Watch Film Festival
485 Fifth Avenue, 3rd Floor
New York, NY 10017
Tel: (212) 972-8400
Fax: (212) 972-0905
Held: Early May

Humboldt International Film
and Video Festival
Theater Arts Department
Humboldt State University
Arcata, CA 95521
Tel: (707) 826-4113
Held: Early April

International Documentary Association (IDA)
Film and Video Festival
1551 South Robertson Boulevard
Los Angeles, CA 90035-9334
Tel: (213) 284-8422
Fax: (213) 785-9334
Held: Early November

Jewish Film Festival
26700 10th Street
Berkeley, CA 94710
Tel: (510) 548-0556
Fax: (510) 548-0536
Held: Late July

Los Angeles International Animation
Celebration
Expanded Entertainment
2222 South Barrington
Los Angeles, CA 90064
Tel: (310) 473-6701
Fax: (310) 444-9850
Held: Early January

Margaret Mead Film Festival
American Museum of Natural History
Department of Education
Central Park West at 79th Street
New York, NY 10024
Tel: (212) 769-5305
Fax: (212) 769-5329
Held: Late September

Marin County National Film and
Video Competition
Fairgrounds
San Rafael, CA 94903
Tel: (415) 499-6400
Held: Early July

National Latino Film and Video Festival
El Museo del Barrio
1230 5th Avenue
New York, NY 10029
Tel: (212) 369-3969
Held: Mid-November (biennial)

National Student Media Arts Exhibition
Visual Studies Workshop
31 Prince Street
Rochester, NY 14607
Tel: (716) 442-8676
Held: Late July

Native American Film and Video
Festival
Film and Video Center
Museum of the American Indian
Broadway at 155th Street
New York, NY 10032
Tel: (212) 283-2420
Fax: (212) 491-9302
Held: Mid-April

New Angle Intermedia Video Festival
  Angle Intermedia
  300 Mercer Street
  Suite 11N
  New York, NY 10003
  Tel: (212) 228-8307
  Held: Early May

New Directors/New Films
  Film Society of Lincoln Center
  70 Lincoln Center Plaza
  4th Floor
  New York, NY 10023-6595
  Tel: (212) 875-5628
  Fax: (212) 875-5636
  Held: Late March

New York Expo of Short Film and Video
  Flash Point Productions
  17 West 17th Street
  10th Floor
  New York, NY 10011
  Tel: (212) 226-7350
  Held: Early November

New York Film Festival
  Film Society of Lincoln Center
  70 Lincoln Center Plaza
  New York, NY 10023-6595
  Tel: (212) 875-5610
  Fax: (212) 875-5636
  Held: Late September

New York International Festival
  of Lesbian and Gay Films
  The New Festival
  80 Eighth Avenue
  New York, NY 10011
  Tel: (212) 807-1820
  Fax: (212) 807-9843
  Held: Early June

Poetry Film and Videopoem Festival
  Poetry Workshop
  Fort Mason Cultural Center
  San Francisco, CA 94123
  Tel: (415) 776-6602
  Held: Early December

Rochester International Amateur Festival
  Movies on a Shoestring Inc.
  P.O. Box 17746
  Rochester, NY 14617
  Tel: (716) 288-5607 (evenings)
  Held: Early May

San Francisco Art Institute Film Festival
  800 Chestnut Street
  San Francisco, CA 94133
  Tel: (415) 771-7020
  Fax: (415) 749-4590
  Held: Late April

San Francisco International Film Festival
  1560 Fillmore Street
  San Francisco, CA 94115
  Tel: (415) 567-4641
  Fax: (415) 921-5032
  Held: Late April

Santa Fe Film Exposition
  Center for Contemporary Art
  291 East Barcelona Road
  P.O. Box 148
  Santa Fe, NM 87504
  Tel: (505) 982-1338
  Held: Early March

Seattle International Festival of Films
  by Women Directors
  219 First Avenue North, #428
  Seattle, WA 98109-4893
  Tel: (206) 621-2231
  Fax: (206) 621-2232
  Held: Mid-October

Sinking Creek Film and Video Celebration
  1250 Old Shiloh Road
  Greenville, TN 37743
  Tel: (615) 638-6524
  Held: Early June

Student Academy Awards
  Academy of Motion Picture Arts and Sciences
  8949 Wilshire Boulevard
  Beverly Hills, CA 90211-1972
  Tel: (310) 247-3000
  Fax: (310) 859-9351
  Held: Early June

Sundance Film Festival
  3619 Motor Avenue
  Suite 240
  Los Angeles, CA 90034
  Tel: (310) 204-2091
  Fax: (310) 204-3901
  427 Main Street
  Park City, UT 84060
  Tel: (801) 645-7280
  Fax: (801) 575-5175
  Held: Late January

Telluride Film Festival
National Film Preserve
Box 1156
Hanover, NH 03755
Tel: (603) 643-1255
Fax: (603) 643-5938
Held: Early September

Three Rivers Film Festival
207 Sweetbriar Street
Pittsburgh, PA 15211
Tel: (412) 261-7040
Held: Late May

United States Environmental
Film Festival
1026 West Colorado Avenue
Colorado Springs, CO 80904
Tel: (719) 520-1952
Fax: (719) 520-9157
Held: Late April

United States Student Film
and Video Festival
Film Front
206 Performing Arts Building
University of Utah
Salt Lake City, UT 84112
Tel: (801) 328-3646
Fax: (801) 521-8513
Held: Late April

USA Film Festival
2917 Swiss Avenue
Dallas, TX 75204
Tel: (214) 821-6300
Fax: (214) 821-6364
Held: Late April

Videoshorts
P.O. Box 20369
Seattle, WA 98102
Tel: (206) 325-8449
Held: Early March

Women in Film Festival
6464 Sunset Boulevard, Suite 660
Los Angeles, CA 90028
Tel: (213) 463-0931
Held: Late October

Works by Women Film and Video Festival
Barnard College Library Media Services
3009 Broadway
New York, NY 10027-6598
Tel: (212) 854-2418
Held: Mid-October

INTERNATIONAL

Abitibi-Timiskaming Festival of
International Cinema
International Film Festival in
Abitibi-Teiscamingue
215 Avenue Mercier
Rouyn-Noranda, Quebec J9X-5W8
Canada
Tel: (819) 762-6212
Fax: (819) 762-6762
Held: Late October

Amascultura International Documentary
Film Festival
Encontros Internacionais de
Cinema Amascultura
Amascultura Departamento de Cinema
Centro Cultural Malaposta
Rua Angola-Olival Basto
2675 Odivelas
Portugal
Tel: 351 987 32 99
Held: Mid-November

Amsterdam International Documentary
Film Festival
Festival Office
Kleine-Gartmanplantsoen 10
1017RR Amsterdam
Netherlands
Tel: 31 20 627 3329
Fax: 31 20 638 5388
Held: Early December

Annecy International Animation Festival
Festival International du Cinéma
d'Animation
4 Passage des Clercs, BP 399
74013 Annecy Cedex, France
Tel: 33 50 57 41 72
Fax: 33 50 67 81 95
Held: Early June

Antwerp International Film Festival
Antwerpse Film Stichting v.z.w.
Theatre Centre, Theaterplein
B-2000 Antwerp
Belgium
Tel: 322 232 66 77
Held: Mid-March

Auckland International Film Festival
P.O. Box 1411
Auckland, New Zealand
Tel: 64 09 45 98 40
Held: Late July

Belgrade International Film Festival
Sava Centar
Milentija Popvica 9
11070 Belgrade, Yugoslavia
Tel: 3811 222-4961
Fax: 3811 222-1156
Held: Early February

Berlin International Festival
of Black Cinema
Fountainhead Tanz Theatre
Tempelhofer Damm 52
D-1000 Berlin 42
Germany
Tel: 49 30 782 1621
or c/o Stephan Gangstead
U.S. Embassy Office–Berlin
Unit 26738 (R.S.)
.A.P.O.A.E. 09 235k-550
Held: Late April

Berlin International Film Festival
Budapesterstrasse 50
1000 Berlin 30
Germany
Tel: 40 30 25 48 90/21 36 039
Fax: 49 30 25 48 92 49
Held: Mid-February

Bilbao International Festival of
Documentary and Short Films
Certamen Internacional de Cine
Documental y Cortometraje de Bilbao
Colon de Larreatequi, 37-4 Dcha
48009 Bilbao, Spain
Tel: 34 4 24 86 98
Fax: 34 4 42 45 624
Held: Late November

Bombay International Film Festival for
Documentary, Short and Animation Films
Film Bhavan
24, Dr. Gopalrao Deshmukh Marg
Bombay 400 026, India
Tel: 91 22 3864633
Fax: 91 22 3860308
Held: Early February

Cadiz International Video Festival
Muestra Internacional de Video de Cadiz
Fundacion Provincial de Cultura
Plaza de Espana, S/N.-Edificio Roma
11071 Cadiz, Spain
Tel: 34 56 24 01 03
Fax: 34 56 22 98 13
Held: Late November

Canadian Images Festival of Independent
Film and Video
Northern Visions
67A Portland Street, #9
Toronto, Ontario
Canada
Tel: (416) 348-9622
Held: Mid-June

Canadian International Annual
Film Festival
25 Eugenia Street
Barrie, Ontario L4M 1P6
Canada
Tel: (705) 737-2729
Fax: (705) 726-4655
Held: Early September

Canne International Film Festival
71, rue du Faubourg St. Honore
75008 Paris
France
Tel: 1 42 66 92 20
Fax: 1 42 66 68 85
Held: Mid-May

Cinema Jove International Festival
of Young Film Makers
Muestra International de Jovenes
Realizadores de Cine
Instituto Vanenciano de la Juventud
Avinguda de Campanar 32
46015 Valencia
Spain
Tel: 96 386 3212
Fax: 96 386 6507
Held: Late June

Cologne Film Festival
Film-Festival/NRW Köln
Am Malzbuchel 6-8
5000 Cologne 1
Germany
Tel: 49 221 25 32 41
Fax: 49 221 23 50 59
Held: Late September

Copenhagen Film and Video Festival
The Film Trade's Cooperation
and Idea Committee
Bulowsvej 50A
DK 1870 Frb. Copenhagen
Denmark
Tel: 45 3537 2507
Fax: 45 3135 5758
Held: Early June

Cork International Film Festival
  Hatfield House
  Tobin Street
  Cork
  Ireland
  Tel: 353 21 27 17 11
  Fax: 353 21 27 59 45
  Held: Early October

Cracow International Short Film
  Festival
  Festiwale Filow Krotkometrazowych
  Pl. Zwyciestwa 89
  P.O. Box 127
  00-950 Warsaw
  Poland
  Tel: 4822 260 849
  Fax: 4822 275 784
  Held: Late June

Edinburgh International Film Festival
  Filmhouse
  88 Lothian Road
  Edinburgh EH3 9BZ
  Scotland
  United Kingdom
  Tel: 4431 228 4051
  Fax: 4431 229 5501
  Held: Mid-August

FIPA International Audiovisual Program
  Festival
  Festival de Programmes Audiovisuels
  215, rue du Faubourg-Saint-Honore
  75008 Paris
  France
  Tel: 33 1 45 61 01 66
  Fax: 33 1 40 74 07 96
  Held: Mid-January

French–American Film Workshop
  Rencontres Cinematographiques
    Franco-Americaines
  23 rue fe la Republique
  84000 Avignon
  France
  Tel: 3316 90 85 50 98
  Fax: 3316 90 82 22 29
  Held: Early June

Funny Film Festival
  Via Monte della Farina, 54
  00186 Rome
  Italy
  Tel: 396 68 72 221
  Held: Late September

Golden Diana International Film Festival
  of Nonprofessional Films
  Hauptplatz 11
  9100 Völkermarkt
  Austria
  Tel: 42 36 2645
  Held: Early September

Golden Knight International Amateur
  Film and Video Festival
  Malta Amateur Cine Circle
  P.O. Box 450
  Valletta, Malta
  Tel: 356 442 803
  Fax: 356 225 047
  Held: Late November

Grenoble Festival of Nature and
  Environment Films
  Fédération Rhone-Alpes de Protection
    de la Nature (FRAPNA)
  5, Place Bir Hakeim
  38000 Grenoble, France
  Tel: 33 76 42 64 08
  Fax: 33 76 51 24 66
  Held: Late February (biennial)

Hamburg No Budget Short Film Festival
  Lag Film Hamburg e.V.
  No Budget-Buro
  Glashüttenstrasse 27
  D-2000 Hamburg 36
  Germany
  Tel: 49 40 43 44 99/49 40 439 27 10
  Fax: 49 40 430 27 03
  Held: Early June

Hiroshima International Amateur
  Film and Video Festival
  c/o Chugoku Broadcasting Co.
  Department of Business Promotion
  External Enterprise Division
  21-3, Motomachi, Naka-ku
  Hiroshima, 730, Japan
  Tel: 82 223 1111
  Fax: 82 222 1187
  Held: Early April (biennial)

Hong Kong International Film Festival
  Level 7, Administration Building
  Hong Kong Cultural Centre
  10 Salisbury Road, Tsimshatsui
  Kowloon, Hong Kong
  Tel: 852 3 734 2900
  Fax: 852 3 66 5206
  Held: Mid-April

Istanbul International Film Days
  Yildiz Kultur ve Sanat Merkezi Besiktas
  80700 Istanbul
  Turkey
  Tel: 901 160 45 33
  Fax: 901 161 88 23
  Held: Early April

Jerusalem Film Festival
  P.O. Box 8561
  Jerusalem 91083
  Israel
  Tel: 9722 724 131
  Fax: 9722 733 076
  Held: Mid-July

Leeds International Film Festival
  19 Wellington Street
  Leeds LS1-4DG
  United Kingdom
  Tel: 44 532 463 349
  Fax: 44 532 426 761
  Held: Mid-October

Leicester International Festival of Super 8
  Leicester Independent Film and
    Video Association
  11 Newarke Street
  Leicester, LE1 5SS
  England
  Tel: 44 53 35 597 11 x294
  Held: Late May

Leipzig International Festival for Documentary
  and Animation Films
  Leipziger Dok-Woche
  Box 904
  07010 Leipzig
  Germany
  Tel: 341 2 11 05 48
  Fax: 4 9 341 294660 (handwritten)
  Held: Late November

Leningrad International Non-Feature
  Film Festival
  12, Tolmacheva Street
  St. Petersburg 191011
  Russia
  Tel: 7812 235 5109
  Fax: 7812 235 5318
  Held: Early January

Les Enfants Lumiere International Film
  Festival on Childhood
  Les Enfants Lumiere Festival International du Film
  Sur L'Enfance
  7 rue Jules Chalande

31000 Toulouse
France
Tel: 33 61 23 33 37
Fax: 33 61 23 63 33
Held: Early April

London International Amateur Film
  and Video Competition
  c/o IAC
  Box 618
  Ealing, London W5 1SX
  England
  Tel: 37 22 76 358
  Held: Late March

London International Film Festival
  National Film Theatre
  South Bank
  London SE1 8XT
  England
  Tel: 071 815 1324
  Fax: 071 633 0786
  Held: Mid-November

Madrid International Festival
  of Films by Women
  Festival Internacional de Cine Realizado
  por Mujeres
  c/o Ateneo Feminista de Espana
  Barquillo, 44, 2 izq.
  28004 Madrid
  Spain
  Tel: 91 308 69 35
  Fax: 91 319 69 02
  Held: Early November

Madrid International Film
  Festival (IMAGFIC)
  Festival International de Cine
    Imaginario y de Ciencia Ficcion
  Gran Via 62
  Madrid 28013
  Spain
  Tel: 341 541 3721
  Fax: 341 542 5495
  Held: Mid-April

Maison's Laffitte International Short
  Film Festival
  Festival International de Court Métrage
  Culture Expo
  48 Avenue de Longueil
  78600 Maisons-Laffitte
  France
  Tel: 33 1 39 62 68 96
  Fax: 33 1 39 62 62 62
  Held: Mid-October

Mannheim International Film Festival
Internationales Film Festival Mannheim
Collini-Center-Galerie
D-6800 Mannheim 1
Germany
Tel: 0621 10 29 43
Fax: 0621 29 15 64
Held: Mid-November

MIFED International Film, Television
and Documentary Market
Mercato Internzionale Film e Documentario
Largo Domodossola, 1
20145 Milan
Italy
Tel: 39 2 499 7267
Fax: 39 2 499 77020
Held: Mid-October

Montreal International Festival of New
Cinema and Video
Festival International du Nouveau Cinema
et de la Video de Montreal
3726 Boulevard St. Laurent
Montreal, Quebec H2X 2V8
Canada
Tel: (514) 843-4725
Fax: (514) 843-4631
Held: Mid-October

Montreal International Festival of Young Cinema
Festival International du Jeune Cinema
Association pour le Jeune Cinema Quebecois
4545 Pierre-de-Coubertin Avenue
P.O. Box 1000, Station M
Montreal, Quebec H1V 3R2
Canada
Tel: (514) 252-3024
Fax: (514) 254-1617
Held: Late April

Montreal World Film Festival
1455 Maisonneuve Blvd.
W. Montreal, Quebec H3G 1M8
Canada
Tel: (514) 848-3883/933-9699
Fax: (514) 848-3886
Held: Late August

Moscow International Film Festival
Sovinterest
10 Hohklovsky Per.
Moscow 109028
Russia
Tel: 227 54 17 / 227 89 24 / 297 76 45
Held: Early July

Munich International Festival
of Film Academies
Türkenstrasse 93
D-8000 Munich
Germany
Tel: 49 89 38 10 40
Fax: 49 89 38 19 04 26
Held: Early November

Nature, Man and His Environment
Film Festival
Ente Mostra Cinematografica
Internazionale
"La Natura, L'Uomo e il suo
Ambiente"
Via di Villa Patrizi 10
00161 Rome
Italy
Tel: 06 8847 3218
Held: Early November

Norwegian Short Film Festival
Kortfilmfestivalen
Storengveien 8 b.
N-1342 Jar
Norway
Tel: 472 12 20 13
Fax: 4767 12 4865
Held: Mid-September

Nyon International Documentary
Film Festival
P.O. Box 98
CH-1260 Nyon
Switzerland
Tel: 4122 606 060
Held: Mid-October

Oberhausen International Festival
of Short Films
Internationale Kurzfilmtage Oberhausen
Christian-Stegerstrasse 10
D-4200 Oberhausen 1
Germany
Tel: 49 02 08 80 70 08
Fax: 49 82 52 81 59
Held: Late April

Rotterdam International Film Festival
Stichting Film Festival Rotterdam
P.O. Box 21696
3001 AR Rotterdam
Netherlands
Tel: 3110 411 8080
Fax: 3110 413 5132
Held: Late January

San Sebastian International Film Festival
P.O. Box 397
20080 San Sebastian
Spain
Tel: 34 43 481 212
Fax: 34 43 481 218
Held: Late September

São Paolo International Short
 Film Festival
  Festival Internacional de
   Curtas-Metragens de São Paolo
  Museu Da Imagem e Do Som
  Av. Europa 158
  01449 São Paolo
  Brazil
  Tel: 55 11 282 8074
  Fax: 55 11 853 7963
  Held: Late August

Sydney Film Festival
P.O. Box 25
Glebe, NSW
Australia 2037
Tel: 61 2 660 3844
Fax: 61 2 692 8793
Held: Mid-June

Tampere International Short
 Film Festival
  P.O. Box 305
  SF-33101 Tampere
  Finland
  Tel: 358 31 130034
  Fax: 358 31 230121
  Held: Early March

Tel Aviv International Student
 Film Festival
  Tel Aviv University
  Ramat-Aviv 69978
  Tel Aviv, Israel
  Tel: 972 0 341 1155
  Fax: 972 3 640 9935
  Held: Late May

Tokyo Film Festival of International
 Cinema Students
  Prem Sakuragaoka Bldg., 4F, 8-18
  Sakuragaoka-cho, Shibuya-ku
  Tokyo 150
  Japan
  Tel: 813 3770 1105
  Fax: 813 3770 6909
  Held: Early December

Toronto Festival of Festivals
 70 Carlton Street
 Toronto, Ontario M5 1L7
 Canada
 Tel: (416) 967-7371
 Fax: (416) 967-9477
 Held: Early September

Venice International Film Festival
 La Bieniale di Venezia
 Settore Cinema e Spettacolo Televiso
 Ca'Giustinian, San Marco
 30100 Venice
 Italy
 Tel: 3941 521 88 43
 Fax: 3941 522 75 39
 Held: Early September

Vienna International (Viennale)
 Internationale Viennale Filmfestwochen Wien
 Uraniastrasse 1
 A-1010 Vienna
 Austria
 Tel: 431 526 59 47
 Fax: 431 93 41 72
 Held: Mid-October

Wellington Film Festival
 Box 9544
 Te Aro
 Wellington, New Zealand
 Tel: 64 4 850 162
 Fax: 64 4 801 7304
 Held: Early July

appendix F

Contacts

AICE (Association of Independent Commercial
Editors)
  Robert S. Wollin
  666 North Robertson Boulevard
  Los Angeles, CA 90069
  (213) 659-0175
  Jim Smyth, Optimus
  161 East Grand
  Chicago, IL 60611
  (312) 321-0880
  Ed Friedman, DJM Films Inc.
  4 East 46th Street
  New York, NY 10017
  (212) 687-0111

AICP (Association of Independent Commercial
Producers)
  East Coast Chapter
  100 East 42nd Street, 16th Floor
  New York, NY 10017
  (212) 867-5720
  (They publish a commercial budget bidding form.)

ALPHA CINE LABORATORY INC.
  5724 West 3rd Street, #311
  Los Angeles, CA 90036
  (213) 934-7793
  1001 Lenora Street
  Seattle, WA 98121
  (206) 682-8230
  (800) 682-2510

AMERICAN ACADEMY OF DRAMATIC ARTS
  120 Madison Avenue
  New York, NY 10010
  (212) 686-9244

AMERICAN FEDERATION OF MUSICIANS
  Local 802
  1500 Broadway
  New York, NY 10036
  (212) 869-1330

AMERICAN FEDERATION OF TELEVISION
AND RADIO ARTISTS (AFTRA)
  350 Avenue of the Americas
  New York, NY 10019
  (212) 265-7700
  1717 N. Highland Avenue
  Hollywood, CA 90028
  (213) 461-8111

ARRIFLEX 500
  Route 303
  Blauvelt, NY 10913
  (914) 353-1400

ASCAP (The American Society of Composers,
Authors, and Publishers)
  1 Lincoln Plaza
  New York, NY 10023
  (212) 621 6000 or (213) 883-1000

ASTRO COLOR LABORATORIES INC.
  61 West Erie Street
  Chicago, IL 60610
  (312) 280-5500

AVID TECHNOLOGIES, INC.
  3 Burlington Woods Drive
  Burlington, MA 01803
  (617) 221-6789
  3900 West Alameda Avenue, Suite 1700
  Burbank, CA 91505
  (818) 972-1725

BMI (Broadcast Music Incorporated)
  320 West 57th Street
  New York, NY 10019
  (212) 586-2000 or (310) 659-9109

CIRCLE IN THE SQUARE THEATRE
  1633 Broadway
  New York, NY 10019
  (212) 307-2700

CFI (Consolidated Film Lab)
959 Seward Street
Hollywood, CA 90038
(213) 960-7444

CONTINENTAL FILM LABORATORY INC.
1998 N.E. 150 Street N.
Miami, FL 33181
(305) 949-4252

DIRECTORS GUILD OF AMERICA
110 West 57th Street
New York, NY 10019
(212) 581-0370

7950 Sunset Boulevard
Los Angeles, CA 90046
(213) 656-1220

DU ART LABORATORIES
245 West 55th Street
New York, NY 10019
(212) 757-4580

FOTO-KEM (LAB)
2800 West Olive Avenue
Burbank, CA 91505
(818) 846-3101

THE FOUNDATION CENTER
79 Fifth Avenue, Dept KM
New York, NY 10003
(212) 620-4230
(Will do a computer search listing for foundations.)

HERBERT BERGHOFF STUDIO
120 Bank Street
New York, NY 10014
(212) 675-2370

INTERNATIONAL PHOTOGRAPHERS OF
THE MOTION PICTURE INDUSTRIES
IATSE, Local 644
250 West 57th Street, Room 723
New York, NY 10017
(212) 247-3860

IATSE, Local 66
327 South LaSalle Street, Suite 1122
Chicago, IL 60604
(312) 341-0966

IATSE, Local 659
7715 Sunset Boulevard, Suite 150
Los Angeles, CA 90046
(213) 876-0160

IATSE, Local 667
6 Parklawn Road, Suite 200
Toronto, Ontario M8Y 3H8, Canada
(416) 252-6401

LAGUARDIA HIGH SCHOOL
108 Amsterdam Avenue
New York, NY 10023
(212) 496-0700

LEE STRASBERG THEATRICAL INSTITUTE
115 East 15th Street
New York, NY 10003
(212) 533-5500

MAKE-UP ARTISTS AND HAIR STYLISTS
IATSE, Local 798
790 Broadway, Suite 503
New York, NY 10019
(212) 757-9120

IATSE, Local 706
11519 Chandler Boulevard
North Hollywood, CA 91601
(213) 984-1700

MONACO FILM LABS & VIDEO SERVICES
234 9th Street
San Francisco, CA 94103
(415) 864-5350

MONTAGE GROUP, LTD.
4116 West Magnolia Boulevard
Burbank, CA 91505
(818) 955-8801

1 West 85th Street, Suite 4A
New York, NY 10024
(212) 580-7500

MOTION PICTURE EDITORS
IATSE, Local 771
630 9th Avenue
New York, NY 10036
(212) 581-0771

IATSE, Local 776
7715 Sunset Boulevard
Suite 100
Los Angeles, CA 90046
(213) 876-4770

MOTION PICTURE AND VIDEOTAPE
EDITOR'S GUILD
IATSE, Local 776
7715 Sunset Boulevard, Suite 220
Hollywood, CA 90046
(213) 876-4770

MOTION PICTURE AND EDITOR'S GUILD
IATSE, Local 771
353 West 48th Street
New York, NY 10036
(212) 581-0771

NEW YORK UNIVERSITY/TISCH SCHOOL
OF THE ARTS DRAMA DEPARTMENT
721 Broadway, 3rd Floor
New York, NY 10003
(212) 998-1700

PRODUCERS GUILD OF AMERICA, INC.
8201 Beverly Boulevard, Suite 500
Los Angeles, CA 90047
(213) 651-0084

PROFESSIONAL CHILDREN'S SCHOOL
132 West 60th Street
New York, NY 10023
(212) 582-3116

PUBLICISTS GUILD
IATSE, Local 818
1427 N. La Brea Avenue
Hollywood, CA 90028
(213) 851-1600

SAMPAC (Society of Advertising Music
Producers, Arrangers and Composers)
6 East 42nd Street, 8th Floor
New York, NY 10017
(212) 697-9805

SCREEN ACTORS GUILD (SAG)
1700 Broadway
New York, NY 10017
(212) 957-5370

7750 Sunset Boulevard
Los Angeles, CA 90046
(213) 876-3030

SCREEN EXTRAS GUILD, INC.
3629 Cahuenga Boulevard, West
Los Angeles, CA 90068
(213) 851-4301

SCRIPT SUPERVISORS, PRODUCTION OFFICE
COORDINATORS AND AUDITORS
IATSE, Local 161
251 East 50th Street
New York, NY 10022
(212) 688-8234

STUDIO MECHANICS
IATSE, Local 52
221 West 57th Street
New York, NY 10019
(212) 765-0741

STELLA ADLER CONSERVATORY
419 Lafayette Street
New York, NY 10003
(212) 260-0525

UNITED SCENIC ARTISTS
IATSE, Local 829
1540 Broadway
New York, NY 10036
(212) 575-5120

VIDEOTAPE PRODUCTION ASSOCIATION
63 West 83rd Street
New York, NY 10024
(212) 986-0289

VOLUNTEER LAWYERS FOR THE ARTS
1 East 53rd Street, 6th Floor
New York, NY 10022
(212) 319-2787

WRITERS GUILD OF AMERICA, EAST
555 West 57th Street, Room 230
New York, NY 10019
(212) 767-7800

WRITERS GUILD OF AMERICA, WEST
8955 Beverly Boulevard
Los Angeles, CA 90048
(213) 550-1000

appendix G

Film Schools

Everyone who received their acceptance letter and came to the first day of class thought that the guy next to them was the next Scorsese. After a few days you realize everyone is in about the same boat. That was a big relief to me.

Howard

The latter part of the twentieth century has seen the emergence and proliferation of film and television schools. Whereas in the middle part of the century it was the goal of many young artists to express themselves by writing "the great American novel," it is now their goal to make "the great American film."

And no wonder. Film and television are the two potent communication tools in the world today. There are now over 500 universities in the United States and Canada that have programs involving communications or media arts studies or film, television, or radio production. The magnetism, influence, and responsibility of the film and video communications artist is not to be taken lightly.

I'm a supporter of film schools because I think it's a quick and dirty way to get a lot of experience under your belt. If the school is run right, it teaches you to work under the kinds of constraints that will exist in the outside world, in terms of budget, deadlines and peer review.

Jan

Film and television programs offer the fledgling communications artist many educational opportunities not afforded in the past. At the core of the experience is a chance to experiment, to fail, to work out ideas, and to make contacts and liaisons that could last a lifetime.

The film and television industry is a tough nut to crack. We believe that a film school education can qualify a student not only for a career in film and/or television, but, also provide skills in communications, writing, and interpersonal conflict management that are useful for any of a number of fields·in the communication and media arts—politics, advertising, education, radio, social work, and so on.

Film schools can really choose, as I see it, between two things. One is to be a stepping stone into the industry. Now that the apprentice system isn't really in place any more in Hollywood there isn't any building up of one's craft. Film schools can say, "we're out here to be your stepping stone into the film industry. Come here, we'll make films that Hollywood will like. We'll teach you how to make them, and we'll show them off to Hollywood." Or it says the opposite, "we don't care what Hollywood is doing. We want you to come here to learn things and to try things and to fail. You're safe here."

I think that if a school chooses to do the latter, they will eventually get Hollywood's attention. Because Hollywood is always looking for material, and if there's a school, where suddenly things are coming out of it that are interesting and different, and some of it's bad, but some of it's really wonderful. Hollywood will take notice.

Adam

PROGRAMS

Film and television programs offer a variety of graduate and undergraduate degrees that concentrate on the study and/or writing and production of film, television, and radio. Also, there are many programs that offer degrees in such areas as mass communications, telecommunications, media arts, broadcast journalism, communications arts, and other specialties.

The undergraduate degrees offered are: Bachelor of Arts, Bachelor of Science, and Bachelor of Fine Arts. B.A. and B.S. degrees usually involve only two years of production or media study whereas B.F.A. programs involve four years of training or study in a major. There also are junior colleges that offer film, televison, and communications related programs.

Graduate programs offer Master of Arts, Master of Fine Arts, and Doctorates. The highest degree for programs concentrating on production is an M.F.A. Generally, a Ph.D. is offered for cinema studies and mass communications studies among others.

Among this list are "art schools" where the emphasis is on film, graphic arts, photography, and/or video. Certain programs focus on different disciplines within their curriculum such as documentary, experimental, narrative, or animation. Video production has taken the place of film in many programs; students wishing to make "films" should check out schools carefully.

Do your research by referring to the books in the references here. Pick a program that is in line with your overall goals. There are obvious advantages to schools located in major urban areas like New York, Los Angeles, Chicago, or Boston, but there are plenty of excellent programs in smaller communities around the country. Look at the size of the program as well. Big is not always better when it comes to the kind of individual nurturing and guidance needed for film and video courses.

> I did have a professor that I liked very much at Columbia, Vojtech Jasney. I had shown him the script. He was the one who encouraged me to go and make it.
>
> *Adam*

REFERENCES

Individuals interested in applying to a film and television program can begin by reviewing the first two reference guides. The *AFI Guide* has been out for several years, but the Pintoff guide is new to the market. Don't assume, however, that all the information in these guides is up to date. Check it out for yourself.

Laskin, Emily, Editor/Director. *The American Film Institute Guide to College Courses in Film and Television*, 8th ed. Englewood Cliffs, N.J.: Prentice-Hall, 1990.

Pintoff, Ernest. *Complete Guide to American Film Schools and Cinema and Television Courses.* New York: Penguin, 1994.

A list of some of the film programs in the United States and abroad follows.

UNITED STATES AND CANADA

American Film Institute
Center for Advanced Film and Television Study
2021 N. Western Avenue
Los Angeles, CA 90027
(213) 856-7600
Degrees offered: M.F.A.
Contact: Rod Merl

California Institute of the Arts
School of Film and Video
24700 McBean Parkway
Valencia, CA 91355
(805) 253-7825
Degrees offered: B.F.A., M.F.A.
Contact: Myron Emery

Canadian Centre for Advanced Film Studies
2849 Bayview Avenue
North York, Ontario M4W 3E2, Canada
(416) 445-1446
Contact: Carolyne Hew

Columbia College
Film/Video Department
Television Department
600 S. Michigan Avenue
Chicago, IL 60605
(312) 663-1600
Degrees offered: B.A., M.F.A.
Contact: Michael Rabiger

Columbia University
Film Division, School of the Arts
513 Dodge Hall
116th Street and Broadway
New York, NY 10027
(212) 854-2815
Degrees offered: M.F.A
Contact: Annette Insdorf

Emerson College
Mass Communication Division
100 Beacon Street
Boston, MA 02116
(617) 578-8800
Degrees offered: B.F.A, B.A., B.S., M.A. (video only)
Contact: Don Frey, Chair

Florida State University
Undergraduate Film Program
Tallahassee, FL 32306-2084
(904) 644-8747
Degrees offered: B.F.A.
Contact: Peter Stowell

Florida State University
Graduate Film Conservatory
Asolo Center for the Performing Arts
5555 North Tamiami Trail
Sarasota, FL 34243
(813) 359-5850
Degrees offered: M.F.A.
Contact: Dr. Raymond Fielding

Ithaca College, School of Communications
Ithaca, NY 14850
(607) 274-3242
Degrees offered: B.S., B.F.A.
Contact: R. William Rawly

Loyola Marymount University
Communications Arts Department
Loyola Boulevard and W. 80th Street
Los Angeles, CA 90045
(310) 642-3033
Degrees offered: B.A., M.A.
Contact: Donald Zirpola

New York University
Tisch School of the Arts
Department of Film and Television
Undergraduate Division
721 Broadway, 9th Floor
New York, NY 10003
(212) 998-1700
Degrees offered: B.F.A.
Contact: Ken Dancyger

New York University
Tisch School of the Arts
Department of Film and Television
Graduate Division
721 Broadway, 10th Floor
New York, NY 10003
(212) 998-1780
Degrees offered: M.F.A.
Contact: Christine Choy

Northwestern University
Radio/TV/Film
1905 Sheridan Road
Evanston, IL 60208
(708) 491-7315
Degrees offered: B.S., M.A., Ph.D., M.F.A.
Contact: Dr. Michelle Citron

Ohio University
School of Film
378 Lindley Hall
Athens, OH 45701
(614) 593-1323
Degrees offered: B.F.A., M.F.A., M.A.
Contact: David O. Thomas

San Francisco Art Institute
Filmmaking Department
800 Chestnut Street
San Francisco, CA 94133
(415) 771-7020
Degrees offered: B.A., M.A.
Contact: Janis Chrystal Lipzin

Stanford University
Communication
McClatchy Hall
Stanford, CA 94305
(415) 723-4700
Degrees offered: B.A., M.A., Ph.D.
Contact: Henry Breitrose

Sundance Institute
19 Exchange Place
Salt Lake City, UT 84111
(801) 521-9330

Temple University
Department of Radio/Television/Film
Broad and Montgomery Streets
Philadelphia, PA 19122
B.A. Program: (215) 787-8424
M.F.A. Program: (215) 787-1666
M.A./Ph.D. Program: (215) 787-6959
Degrees offered: B.A., M.F.A., Ph.D.
Contact: Dr. Howard Myrick

University of California
Department of Theater, Film,
 and Television
405 Hilgard Avenue
Los Angeles, CA 90024
(310) 825-7891
Degrees offered: B.A., M.F.A.
Contact: Gilbert Cates

University of North Texas
Division of Radio/Television/Film
P.O. Box 13108
Denton, TX 76203
(817) 565-2537
Degrees offered: B.A., M.A.
Contact: John Kuiper

University of Southern California
School of Cinema/Television
Office of Student Affairs
George Lucas Building, Room 208
University Park
Los Angeles, CA 90089
(213) 740-2892
Degrees offered: B.A., B.F.A., M.A., M.F.A.
Contact: Elizabeth Daley

University of Texas–Austin
Radio-Television-Film
Austin, TX 78712
(512) 471-4071
Degrees offered: B.S., M.F.A., M.A., Ph.D.
Contact: Johm Downing, Chair

York University
Department of Film and Video
4700 Keele Street
North York, Ontario M3J 1P3
Canada
(410) 736-5149
Degrees offered: B.F.A, B.A., M.F.A., M.A.
Contact: Dr. Evan William Cameron

INTERNATIONAL

Australian Film and Television School
Box 126, North Ryde
N.S.W. 2113
Australia

Deutsche Film- und Fernsehakademie Berlin GmbH
Pommernalle 1
1 Berlin 19
Germany

Dramatiska Intitutet (The Swedish Media School)
Filmhuset
Borgvagen
Box 27090, S-102
51 Stockholm
Sweden

Film and Television Institute of Tamil Nadu
Department of Information and Public Relations
Government of Tamil Nadu, Madras
Adya, Madras-600 020
India

Film and Television School of India
Law College Rd.
Poona 411 004
India

Hochschule für Fernsehen und Film
Ohmstrasse 11
8000 München 40
Germany

L'Institut des Hautes Études Cinémato-
graphiques (IDHEC)
4 Avenue de L'Europe
94360 Bry-sur-Marne
France

London International Film School
24 Shelton Street
London WC2H 9HP
England
Tel.: 01-240-0168

National Film and Television School
Beaconsfield Film Studios
Station Road
Beaconsfield, Bucks HP9 1LG
England
Tel.: 04946 71234

Panswowa Wyzsza Szkola Filmowa,
Telwizyjna i Teatraina
im Leona Schillera, U1
Targowa 61/63
90 323 Lodz
Poland

Vsesoyuzni Gosudarstvenni Institut
Kinematografi Ulitsa Vilgelma Pika 3
Moscow 129226
Russia

Everyone who received their acceptance letter and came to the first day of class thought that the guy next to them was the next Scorcese. After a few days you realize everyone is in about the same boat. That was a big relief to me.

appendix H

Grants and Financing Sources

ACADEMY OF MOTION PICTURES ARTS
AND SCIENCES / ACADEMY FOUNDATION
8949 Wilshire Boulevard
Beverly Hills, CA 90211
(213) 247-3000
Nicholl Fellowships in Screenwriting
 Purpose: To support screenwriters; recipients are
  expected to complete screenplay for a feature-length
  film during the year
 Eligibility: Previous recipients ineligible; professional
  screenwriters who have sold an original story, treat-
  ment, screenplay, or teleplay are ineligible
 Type of Support: $20,000 grant
 Number of Awards: 5–6
 Deadline: June 1
 Preferred Initial Contact: Send self-addressed, stamped
  envelope for application and guidelines

THE AMERICAN FILM INSTITUTE (AFI)
2021 North Western Avenue
P.O. Box 279999
Los Angeles, CA 90027
(213) 856-7600
Independent Film and Videomaker Program—
(213) 856-7787
 Purpose: To encourage the continued development of
  the moving image as art form through funding pro-
  ductions that emphasize creative use of the media
 Eligibility: U.S. citizen and permanent resident; profes-
  sional artists only; no students
 Type of Support: Grant of up to $20,000
 Number of Awards: 12–15
 Deadline: September 14
 Preferred Initial Contact: Call or write for application
  and guidelines
Directing Workshop for Women—(213) 856-7722
 Purpose: To offer mid-career professional women in
  the media arts their first opportunities to direct a dramatic project
 Eligibility: U.S. citizen and permanent resident; at least
  18 years old; women who have considerable experience in television, film, video, or the dramatic arts but
  have not directed dramatic films or television

 Type of Support: $5,000 grant to direct 30-minute
  narrative videotape; two weeks of seminars and
  hands-on training before start of individual production; access to production equipment and editing
  facilities
 Number of Awards: 12 grants during cycle of 18–24
  months
 Deadline: Spring
 Preferred Initial Contact: Write for application and
  guidelines
Academy Internship Program—(213) 856-7640
 Purpose: To provide opportunities for promising new
  directors to observe established film and television
  directors at work during the production of a feature
  film, mini-series, or movie for television
 Eligibility: U.S. citizen; at least 21 years old; must have
  directed at least one project on film or video; must
  demonstrate an understanding of the filmmaking
  process
 Type of Support: Internship with $250–$300 weekly
  stipend
 Number of Awards: 2–5 internships per year
 Deadline: June 30
 Preferred Initial Contact: Write for application and
  guidelines
Daniel Mandell Editing Internship—(213) 856-7640
 Purpose: To provide emerging filmmakers who are
  committed to pursing a career in editing with the
  opportunity to work with professional editors during
  the editing of a feature film, television series, or
  movie made for television
 Eligibility: U.S. citizen and permanent resident; at least
  21 years old; must have edited at least one project for
  film or videotape
 Type of Support: Internship with $200–$250 weekly
  stipend
 Number of Awards: 3 internships per year
 Deadline: July 31
 Preferred Initial Contact: Write for application and
  guidelines
Television Writers Summer Workshop—(213) 856-7623
 Purpose: To provide a learning environment for
  promising new talents to hone their scriptwriting

skills and to apply what they have learned by developing a script

Eligibility: U.S. citizen and permanent resident; at least 18 years old; preference to new writers with media or theater backgrounds who have no major commercial television writing credits

Type of Support: Workshop ($450 fee; scholarships with $1,000 living stipend available)

Number of Awards: 3 scholarships per year

Deadline: March or April

Preferred Initial Contact: Write for application and guidelines

ARTISTS FOUNDATION
8 Park Plaza
Boston, MA 02116
(617) 227-2787

Massachusetts Artists Fellowship Program

Purpose: To nurture the work of Massachusetts' best individual artists by recognizing the exceptional, completed work; disciplines rotate on a two-year cycle

Eligibility: Massachusetts resident for at least 6 months; at least 18 years old; no undergraduate students; no graduate students enrolled in programs related to the category of application; previous grantees ineligible for three years

Type of Support: $10,000 fellowship awards, $1,000 finalist awards

Number of Awards: 17 fellowship awards, 50 finalist awards in fiscal year 1991

Deadline: December

Preferred Initial Contact: Write for application and guidelines

Artists Emergency Assistance Program

Purpose: To provide loans or grants to artists confronted by medical emergencies, fire, or unexpected catastrophes, and to provide loans when emergency funds are needed to complete an arts project

Eligibility: Massachusetts resident for at least one year; professional artists only; no students enrolled in degree granting programs

Type of Support: Up to $500 grant or loan

Number of Awards: As many as possible from $5,000 revolving fund

Deadline: Funds distributed on first come, first serve basis; fiscal year begins in July

Preferred Initial Contact: Call to check on availability of funds

ARTS INTERNATIONAL (AI)
Institute of International Education
809 United Nations Plaza
New York, NY 10017
(212) 984-5370

Reader's Digest Artists at Giverny Program

Purpose: To give U.S. artists an opportunity to live and work in Giverny, France, home of Claude Monet

Eligibility: U.S. citizen; bachelor's degree or equivalent professional experience; recipients may not hold other fellowships or a regular job in France during residency

Type of Support: Six-month residency (April 1–September 30) residency, including round-trip transportation, housing, studio space, use of a car; $2,000 stipend before departure; $1,500 monthly stipend; $1,600 on return to United States

Number of Awards: 3 per year

Deadline: Early November

Preferred Initial Contact: Write for application and guidelines

ASSOCIATION OF INDEPENDENT VIDEO AND FILMMAKERS (AIVF) / FOUNDATION FOR INDEPENDENT VIDEO AND FILM (FIVF)
625 Broadway, 9th Floor
New York, NY 10012
(212) 473-3400

FIVF Donor-Advised Film and Video Fund

Purpose: To support independently produced social issue media projects that combine intellectual clarity and journalistic quality with creative film- or videomaking

Eligibility: Applicant must be affiliated with a nonprofit organization; institutional projects for internal or promotional use, public television station productions, and student productions are ineligible

Type of Support: Grant of $5,000–$10,000

Number of Awards: Total of $57,000 granted in 1989

Deadline: July

Preferred Initial Contact: Call or write to check on availability of funds; FIVF does not administer this fund every year

Programs of Special Interest: AIVF offers reasonably priced group health, life, and disability insurance. The Festival Bureau maintains information on over 400 film and video festivals in the United States and around the world. AIVF's resource files contain sample proposals, contracts, press kits, and information on funders, distributors, exhibitors, and television markets. The Association maintains a library and sells hard-to-find books and pamphlets on topics ranging from feature film production to copyright law. Seminars and workshops address business, technological, and aesthetic issues. AIVF's magazine, the *Independent*, is a national publication devoted exclusively to independent productions. Some AIVF services are for members only; individual memberships are $45.

BOSTON FILM/VIDEO FOUNDATION (BF/VF)
1126 Boylston Street
Boston, MA 02215
(617) 536-1540

New England Film/Video Fellowship Program

Purpose: To foster the production of independent film and video by New England media artists through funding works-in-progress

Eligibility: Residency for at least one year in Connecticut, Maine, Massachusetts, New Hampshire, Rhode Island or Vermont; at least 18 years old; artist must have complete creative control over project; commercial and instructional projects are ineligible; no students; previous recipients ineligible for two years

Type of Support: Up to $6,000 in cash, equipment usage, or combination of the two; grantees supply a copy of their completed work for the Boston Film/Video New England Film/Video Program Archives

Number of Awards: $45,000 in cash; $7,000 in non-cash equipment usage access in 1991

Deadline: April 1

Preferred Initial Contact: Call or write for application and guidelines

Equipment Access

Film: Production for 16mm, Super 8; postproduction for 16mm

Video: Production for Hi-8, Video 8, VHS, S-VHS, 3/4"; postproduction for VHS (off-line) and 3/4" (on-line and off-line)

CALIFORNIA ARTS COUNCIL (CAC)
2411 Alhambra Boulevard
Sacramento, CA 95817
(916) 739-3186
Artists Fellowship Program

Purpose: To recognize and honor the work of California artists who are primary creators of their art; disciplines rotate on four-year schedule among new genres, literature, visual arts, and performing arts

Eligibility: California resident for at least one year; must be professional artist with at least five years of experience; no students enrolled in degree granting programs; previous applicants ineligible for three years; previous grantees ineligible for seven years; originating artists only

Type of Support: $5,000 grant

Number of Awards: 63 in fiscal year 1989–90

Deadline: October

Preferred Initial Contact: Write for application and guidelines

Artist in Residence Program

Purpose: To offer long-term interaction of professional artists in many disciplines with the public in workshops sponsored by schools, nonprofit arts organizations, government units, and tribal councils

Eligibility: Professional artists with at least three years experience; artists must apply with sponsor; no full-time students in degree programs

Type of Support: 3- to 11-month residency; artist earns $1,300 per month for 80 hours of project time

Number of Awards: 185 residencies in fiscal year 1989–90

Deadline: February

Preferred Initial Contact: Call or write for application and guidelines

THE CENTER FOR NEW TELEVISION
912 South Wabash Avenue
Chicago, IL 60605
(312) 427-5446
NEA/AFI Great Lakes Regional Fellowship Program:
Film and Video Production Grants

Purpose: To assist independent film and video artists whose personal work shows promise or excellence

Eligibility: Residency of at least one year in Illinois, Indiana, Ohio, or Michigan; full-time students ineligible; commercial and instructional projects and projects associated with a degree program ineligible; applicant must have overall control and primary creative responsibility for project; previous grantees must have completed projects or production stages for which they received funding

Type of Support: New Project Grants of up to $15,000 for any stage of production of new projects with total budgets up to $60,000; Work-in-Progress Grant, up to $7,000 for projects where at least half the shooting is completed or the editing is underway; Encouragement Grants (targeted to emerging artists) of up to $3,000 for new projects with total cash budgets up to $10,000; recipients supply one copy of their finished work to the CNTV library for a one-time screening and/or broadcast

Number of Awards: $20,260 in New Project Grants, $30,000 in Work-in-Progress Grants, and $15,000 in Encouragement Grants in 1991

Deadline: May

Preferred Initial Contact: Call or write for application and guidelines

Retirement Research Foundation National
Media Awards

Purpose: To identify and promote the visibility of outstanding films, videotapes, and television programs for and about aging or aged people and to encourage excellence in media productions on issues related to aging

Eligibility: Work must have been produced in the United States and must deal primarily with concerns that are of specific interest to aging or aged people or those working in the field of aging; work that primarily promotes a particular organization, institution, or product is ineligible; completed work only

Type of Support: $500–$5000 awards; recipient is asked to donate a copy of his or her work to the Retirement Research Foundation National Media Awards Library for in-house use only and to attend an awards ceremony in Chicago or designate a representative to attend

Number of Awards: Up to $33,000 available in 1991
Deadline: February 1
Preferred Initial Contact: Call or write for application and guidelines

New Television Awards
Purpose: To provide access to facilities in order to encourage independent videomakers to produce and complete project
Eligibility: Project must be an independent production
Type of Support: Access to the center's equipment
Number of Awards: Up to $46,000 worth of equipment access available in 1991
Deadline: Fall
Preferred Initial Contact: Call or write for application and guidelines

CONTEMPORARY ARTS CENTER
900 Camp Street
P.O. Box 30498
New Orleans, LA 70190
(504) 523-1216

Regional Artists Projects (RAP)
Purpose: To provide funding for experimental or multicultural projects that would not be considered in other arts discipline categories because they are considered new or nontraditional forms
Eligibility: U.S. citizen residing in Louisiana, Mississippi, Alabama, or Arkansas
Type of Support: Project support of $1,500–$6,500
Number of Awards: $30,400 budget in 1991
Deadline: December
Preferred Initial Contact: Write for application and guidelines

CORPORATION FOR PUBLIC BROADCASTING (CPB)
901 E Street, NW
Washington, DC 20004-2006
(202) 879-9740

General Program Review
Purpose: To support television projects in the research and development, scripting, preproduction or postproduction stage, or any combination thereof
Eligibility: Organizations and independent producers are eligible; emphasis on multicultural and children's programs; programs must be appropriate for national PBS schedule; projects may be submitted only once
Type of Support: Up to $250,000
Number of Awards: Proposals reviewed quarterly; CPB anticipates no more than one grant per quarter
Deadline: Ongoing; quarterly review
Preferred Initial Contact: Call for application and guidelines

Multicultural Programming Solicitation
Purpose: To support programming by producers from the five ethnic minorities (African American, Asian American, native American, Latino, and Pacific Islander) and on subjects that could be of special interest to their indigenous communities
Eligibility: Organizations and independent producers are eligible; producer and director of independent production teams must be ethnic minorities; priority to projects that have significant representation of minority personnel
Type of Support: Grant for project support
Number of Awards: $2 million available each funding cycle
Deadline: April 15, August 15
Preferred Initial Contact: Call or write for application and guidelines

Content-Specific Solicitations
Purpose: To solicit from diverse sources high-quality programs of a specific nature that may be broadly or narrowly defined and range from one-hour documentaries on a particular theme to miniseries concepts
Eligibility: Organizations and independent producers are eligible; student, instructional, and industrial projects are ineligible; priority to children's programming, news/outreach/public affairs and arts, and cultural programming; programs must be able to command a national public broadcast audience and have the potential to be broadcast by a majority of PBS stations; other requirements may apply
Type of Support: Grant for project support
Number of Awards: Information not available
Deadline: Announced when requests for proposals are issued
Preferred Initial Contact: Call or write for application and guidelines

Program Challenge Fund
Purpose: To ensure that high-visibility, prime-time limited series are available each year for the national PBS schedule
Eligibility: Organizations and independent producers are eligible; priority to series with potential for above-average viewership and critical attention; series may be documentary or drama and should cover subjects of significance
Type of Support: Grant for project support
Number of Awards: $10 million available annually
Deadline: None
Preferred Initial Contact: Call any senior programming staffer at PBS or CPB for general information

DISTRICT OF COLUMBIA COMMISSION
ON THE ARTS AND HUMANITIES
410 8th Street, NW, 5th Floor
Washington, DC 20004
(202) 724-5613

Arts-in-Education Grants
Comprehensive Arts Development Grants
Grants-in-Aid Fellowships
Special Constituencies Grants

Purpose: Arts-in-Education grants fund professional artists' residencies in District public schools; Comprehensive Arts Development grants fund arts activities in traditionally underserved areas of the city; Grants-in-Aid provide fellowships and general operating support; Special Constituencies grants fund arts programming for populations such as senior citizens, the homeless, or the physically challenged

Eligibility: Resident of District of Columbia; at least 18 years old

Type of Support: For Arts-in-Education grants, up to $8,800; for Comprehensive Arts Development projects, $2,500; for Grants-in-Aid fellowships, $5,000; for Special Constituencies projects, up to $3,700 (all for fiscal year 1990)

Number of Awards: 13 Arts-in-Education grants; 8 Comprehensive Arts Development grants; 68 Grants-in-Aid fellowships; 4 Special Constituencies grants (all for fiscal year 1990)

Deadline: No specific dates

Preferred Initial Contact: Call or write for guidelines and application

FILM ARTS FOUNDATION
346 Ninth Avenue, 2nd Floor
San Francisco, CA 94103
(415) 552-8760

FAF Grants Program

Purpose: To aid experimental and independent media artists who have little recourse to traditional funding sources, or whose projects are at a stage where a small grant can have a significant impact

Eligibility: Resident of San Francisco, Marin, Sonoma, Napa, Solano, Alameda, Contra Costa, San Mateo, Santa Clara, or Santa Cruz counties, California; must have artist control of project; no commercial projects; previous grantees ineligible for two years

Type of Support: $3,000 Personal Works awards for new, short personal works that can be completely realized within this budget (funded projects must be available for Film Arts Festival); $1,000 Development awards for projects in the development and fundraising stages; $5,000 Completion/Distribution awards for films or tapes that can be completed or distributed with this amount

Number of Awards: 13 Personal Works awards, 5 Development awards, 2 Completion/Distribution awards in 1991

Deadline: May

Preferred Initial Contact: Call or write for guidelines and application

Equipment Access

Film: Production and postproduction for Super 8, 16mm

Comment: Members receive low-cost access to equip-

ment and editing facility for noncommercial projects ($35 membership fee).

FILM/VIDEO ARTS
817 Broadway at 12th Street, 2nd Floor
New York, NY 10003
(212) 673-9361

Equipment Access

Film: Production and postproduction for 16mm, 35mm

Video: Production for Hi-8, 3/4"; postproduction for VHS, 3/4", Hi-8, S-VHS

Comments: Low equipment access rates are available to artists working on noncommercial projects. New York State artists may apply for week-long residencies at F/VA's Image Processing Studio.

THE FUNDING EXCHANGE
666 Broadway, Room 500
New York, NY 10012
(212) 529-5300

The Paul Robeson Fund

Purpose: To support the production and distribution of independent films and videos that focus on social issues, reach a broad audience, respect the intelligence of the viewers, and combine intellectual clarity with creative use of the medium

Eligibility: Must be affiliated with a tax-exempt organization; priority to projects on issues where there are local or national organizing efforts and issues that have received minimal coverage, and to distribution initiatives that seek to increase the use of social issue films and videos by institutional users, public-interest and community-based groups, cable and satellite programmers; no purely personal projects or strictly sociological or anthropological explorations

Type of Support: $5,000–$10,000 (average) for preproduction and the creation of samples/trailers, production, and postproduction

Number of Awards: $300,000 granted in fiscal year 1991

Deadline: December 1

Preferred Initial Contact: Write for guidelines and application, available after September 1; no phone calls please

JOHN SIMON GUGGENHEIM MEMORIAL FOUNDATION
90 Park Avenue
New York, NY 10016
(212) 687-4470

Purpose: To further the development of scholars and artists by assisting them to engage in research in any field of knowledge and creation in any of the arts

Eligibility: Citizens of United States, Canada, or a Latin American or Caribbean country; permanent residents also eligible; artists must have already demonstrated exceptional creative ability

Type of Support: $26,000 average grant for 1990
Number of Awards: About 50 artists funded in 1990
Deadline: October 15 (U.S. and Canada); December 1 (Latin America and the Caribbean)
Preferred Initial Contact: Write for guidelines and application

INDEPENDENT FEATURE PROJECT (IFP)

New York Branch:
 Independent Feature Project
 132 West 21st Street, 6th Floor
 New York, NY 10011
 (212) 243-7777

Los Angeles Branch:
 Independent Feature Project/West
 5550 Wilshire Boulevard, #204
 Los Angeles, CA 90036
 (213) 937-4379

Minneapolis Branch:
 Independent Feature Project/North
 1401 Third Avenue South
 Minneapolis, MN 55404
 (612) 870-0156

San Francisco Branch:
 Independent Feature Project/
  Northern California
 P.O. Box 460278
 San Francisco, CA 94146
 (415) 826-0574

Chicago Branch:
 Independent Feature Project/Midwest
 P.O. Box 148026
 Chicago, IL 60614
 (312) 902-5339

 IFP is a nonprofit, membership organization that provides information, support, and education programs to independent filmmakers. Services include seminars, workshops, screenings, advice, and referrals.

JEROME FOUNDATION
W-1050 First National Bank Building
332 Minnesota Street
St. Paul, MN 55101
(612) 224-9431

New York City Film and Video Program
 Purpose: To support emerging film and video artists who make creative use of their media and who have not had the support needed to fully display their work
 Eligibility: U.S. citizen or permanent resident; residency in the New York City metropolitan area; must have completed formal education; preference to projects in their early stages and to personal, low-budget work in which the artist exercises complete creative control over production; strong preference to projects with

budgets under $50,000; previous applicants ineligible for one year
 Type of Support: Grants of $8,000–$20,000
 Number of Awards: 15 grants in 1988–89
 Deadline: Applications reviewed three times a year
 Preferred Initial Contact: Call or write for guidelines and application

Travel and Study Grants
 Purpose: To allow artists significant time for professional development through artist-to-artist communications on aesthetic issues, the experience of seeing artistic work outside of Minnesota, time for reflection and individualized study, a chance to develop future work and collaborations, and opportunities for the presentation or development of their work in other locations
 Eligibility: Resident of Twin Cities, seven-county metropolitan area of Minnesota for at least one year; professional artists and administrators only
 Type of Support: Grants of $1,000–$5,000 for travel
 Number of Awards: $90,000 available in fiscal year 1990–91
 Deadline: No specific dates
 Preferred Initial Contact: Call or write for guidelines and application

JOHN D. AND CATHERINE T. MACARTHUR FOUNDATION
140 South Dearborn Street
Chicago, IL 60603

 Purpose: To support projects related to the foundation's programmatic interests in the world environment and resources, peace and international cooperation, education, mental health, and world population
 Eligibility: Open to broad range of arts and humanities activities including video and film
 Type of Support: Cash for project support
 Number of Awards: Information not available
 Deadline: None; applications reviewed monthly
 Preferred Initial Contact: Write for guidelines

MEDIA ALLIANCE
356 West 58th Street
New York, NY 10019
(212) 560-2919

Equipment Access
 Comments: The ON-LINE program gives professional producers creating noncommercial artist projects and documentaries access to state-of-the-art production and postproduction services at commercial facilities in New York State at rates 50 to 80 percent lower than commercial rates. Participating companies include Broadway Video, CGI, Editel, GBS Video, LRP Video, Manhattan Transfer/Edit/Digital, Technisphere, and TV-R Mastercolor. $30 member-

ship fee and $35 per project administrative fee required.

Technical Assistance Programs and Services

Programs: Media Alliance maintains a mailing list of independent producers, publishes a bi-monthly newsletter, and conducts workshops on managing and marketing the media arts. Some services for members only; individual member fees are $20–$30; additional fees required for workshops.

NATIONAL ENDOWMENT FOR THE ARTS— INTERNATIONAL ACTIVITIES OFFICE
Nancy Hanks Center
1100 Pennsylvania Avenue, NW
Washington, DC 20506
(202) 682-5422

United States/Japan Artist Exchange Fellowship Program

Purpose: To enable American artists to enrich their art by living and working in Japan, to observe Japanese artistic developments in their fields of interest, and to meet with their professional counterparts and pursue opportunities for artistic growth

Eligibility: U.S. citizen or permanent resident; no students; artists who have previously spent more than a total of three months in Japan are generally ineligible; artists may not earn additional income in Japan for lectures or demonstrations of their work

Type of Support: Six-month residency in Japan including 400,000 yen monthly living stipend, 100,000 yen monthly housing supplement, up to 100,000 yen monthly for professional support services, roundtrip travel for artist, spouse, and children; stipend for Japanese language study in the United States is available if necessary

Number of Awards: 5 residencies per year

Deadline: November for media arts

Preferred Initial Contact: Contact appropriate discipline program for guidelines and application

NATIONAL ENDOWMENT FOR THE ARTS— MEDIA ARTS PROGRAM
Nancy Hanks Center
1100 Pennsylvania Avenue, NW
Room 720
Washington, DC 20506
(202) 682-5452

Film/Video Production Grants

Purpose: To support the creation or completion of film or video artworks of the highest quality

Eligibility: U.S. citizen or permanent resident; must have substantial professional experience; instructional, promotional, and student projects ineligible; documentation or simple recordings of performances or events for archival purposes are ineligible

Type of Support: $10,000–$35,000 grants for individual producers

Number of Awards: $835,000 granted to individuals and organizations in 1990

Deadline: November 1

Preferred Initial Contact: Call or write for guidelines and application

NATIONAL ENDOWMENT FOR THE ARTS— VISUAL ARTS PROGRAM
Nancy Hanks Center
1100 Pennsylvania Avenue, NW, Room 729
Washington, DC 20506
(202) 682-5448

Purpose: To encourage the creative development of professional artists, enabling them to pursue their work

Eligibility: U.S. citizen or permanent resident; professional artists only; no students pursuing graduate or undergraduate degrees; previous recipients who received $15,000 or more ineligible for two cycles; artists may apply in only one fellowship area per cycle; eligible media rotate on two-year cycle

Type of Support: $15,000 fellowships in 1991–92

Number of Awards: $2.13 million awarded to 177 artists in fiscal year 1990

Deadline: January–March (exact date depends on medium)

Preferred Initial Contact: Call or write for guidelines and application

NATIONAL ENDOWMENT FOR THE ARTS— MEDIA PROGRAM
1100 Pennsylvania Avenue, NW
Washington, DC 20506
(202) 786-0278

Humanities Projects in Media

Purpose: To support the planning, scripting, or production of film, television, and radio programs on humanities subjects

Eligibility: U.S. citizen or permanent resident; projects must involve humanities subjects and be suited for a national audience; projects must involve collaborations among humanities scholars and experienced producers, directors, and writers

Type of Support: Planning grants of up to $20,000; scripting grants of $20,000–$60,000; production grants of $150,000–$600,000

Number of Awards: $9 million awarded annually

Deadline: Mid-September, mid-March

Preferred Initial Contact: Call or write for information

NEW YORK STATE COUNCIL ON THE ARTS (NYSCA)
915 Broadway
New York, NY 10010
(212) 614-2900 (general)

Individual Artists Program—(212) 614-3988
  Purpose: To provide support that allows artists to create, develop, and present new work
  Eligibility: New York State resident; at least 18 years old; no students; artist must find a sponsoring nonprofit organization to submit an application on their behalf
  Type of Support: Up to $25,000 for project
  Number of Awards: 146 awards in fiscal year 1990 (68 in film and media production)
  Deadline: March 1 (for sponsor's application)
  Preferred Initial Contact: Call for guidelines

PUBLIC ART WORKS
P.O. Box 150435
San Rafael, CA 94915-0435
(415) 457-9744
On-Site Exhibition
  Purpose: To commission an annual series of temporary installations in public places, usually outdoors
  Eligibility: Disciplines vary according to location and project
  Type of Support: $4,000–$4,500 commission and $1,500 honorarium
  Number of Awards: 4 commissions per year
  Deadline: No specific date
  Preferred Initial Contact: Call or write for information; artists on mailing list receive prospectus

ROCKEFELLER FOUNDATION
1133 Avenue of the Americas
New York, NY 10036
(212) 869-8500
Bellagio Study and Conference Center Residencies
  Purpose: To provide a site for artists and scholars who have significant publications, compositions, or shows to their credit to work on projects, particularly projects that will result in publications, exhibitions, or performances
  Eligibility: Priority given to arts projects that increase artistic experimentation across cultures; previous recipients ineligible for 10 years
  Type of Support: Five-week residencies at the Bellagio Center in Milan, Italy, including room and board
  Number of Awards: 135 residencies per year
  Deadline: Quarterly, one year before residency
  Preferred Initial Contact: Call or write for brochure
International Film/Video Fellowship Program
  Purpose: To encourage film- and videomakers whose work can advance international and intercultural understanding in the United States.
  Eligibility: Must be nominated by a designated nominator
  Type of Support: $35,000
  Number of Awards: 14 grants annually
  Deadline: No specific date

Preferred Initial Contact: Unsolicited applications or nominations not accepted; must be nominated by designated nominator
SUNDANCE INSTITUTE
10202 West Washington Boulevard
Columbia Pictures
Culver City, CA 90232
(213) 204-2091
Feature Film Program
  Purpose: To support original, provocative, daring scripts that reflect the independent vision of the writer or writer/director
  Eligibility: Sundance is particularly interested in supporting new talent, artists in transition (e.g., choreographers, actors, playwrights), and filmmakers who have already made a feature and are looking for a creative arena for the development of their next project
  Type of Support: Five-day Screenwriters Lab (January or June); Filmmaking Lab (June); Producers Conference (July) for filmmakers supported in June; airline travel, accommodations, and food for one writer/director per project is provided by the Institute, and Sundance will consider paying for accommodations and food for additional partners; if project is produced, Sundance asks writers/directors to contribute 1/2 or 1 percent of production budget to the Institute
  Number of Awards: 10–15 projects per year
  Deadline: July 15 (January Screenwriters Lab); November/December (June Filmmakers Lab)
  Preferred Initial Contact: Call or write for guidelines and application

WOMEN IN FILM FOUNDATION (WIFF)
6464 Sunset Boulevard, Suite 900
Los Angeles, CA 90028
(213) 463-6040
Film Finishing Fund—General Awards
CFI Services Awards
Loreen Arbus Award
  Purpose: To support film- and videomakers who have demonstrated advanced and innovative skills, whose work relates to WIFF's goals of increasing employment and promoting equal opportunities for women, enhancing the media image of women, and influencing prevailing attitudes and practices regarding and on behalf of women
  Eligibility: Los Angeles residency (for CFI award only); independent producers and nonprofit corporations eligible; substantial number of the creative personnel involved in the project must be women; project must be in progress; project must treat issues of disability (Loreen Arbus Award only)
  Type of Support: For General Awards, up to $5,000; for CFI Services Awards, up to $25,000 worth of film

postproduction services at CFI Labs in Los Angeles; for Loreen Arbus Award, up to $5,000 in completion funding

Number of Awards: Information not available

Deadline: May 10

Preferred Initial Contact: Send self-addressed, stamped envelope for guidelines

Lifetime Television Production Completion Grants

Purpose: To fund the completion of projects whose subject matter relates to women and is of general humanitarian concern

Eligibility: Professional film and video artists only; no student projects or thesis films; dramatic projects inel-igible; 50 percent or more of production personnel must be female; project must be approximately 45 minutes in length or producer must agree to cut work to acceptable telecast length as determined by Lifetime; exceptional 30-minute works are also eligible

Type of Support: $25,000–$50,000 completion grant; producer must grant Lifetime Television exclusive exhibition rights for one year or four telecasts

Number of Awards: Information not available

Deadline: Ongoing

Preferred Initial Contact: Send self-addressed, stamped envelope for guidelines

appendix I

Film Versus Video

A recent trend has been a merging of film and video. Video has become popular because it is less expensive, and with its new technologies, its quality is quickly approaching that of film. More and more projects shot on film are being edited on video. It is unknown whether film will eventually die out as a viable visual medium.

Choosing between film and video is really a matter of selecting the right brush for the right painting.

A good producer can read a script and know artistically whether it should be shot on film or videotape.

For assistance with choosing the medium on which you will shoot your project, consult the following chart. Bear in mind that the basic textural difference between these media is that video is cool; film is warm.

VIDEO		FILM	
Pros	*Cons*	*Pros*	*Cons*
Fewer lighting problems	Harsh in rendition	Quality picture, more mystery	Slow to work with
You can see immediately what you recorded	Sharp in depth of focus	Soft picture when needed	No way to see immediately what you filmed
Depth of field is great with little light	Picture can be flat	Depth of field can be part of frame	Lighting is long and tedious
	Tape can only be viewed on a monitor	Frame-by-frame inspection when needed	
Easy to ship and duplicate	Can be erased or recorded over easily	Once shot, cannot be altered	Difficult and costly to ship
Can shoot high shooting ratio	Editing can be expensive	Editing relatively inexpensive	Need eight-plate flatbed to screen cut
Video and computers interface well	In studio, cameras must match	Technical illusions continue to improve	Technical illusions are expensive
	Engineer needs to be on standby	Cameras are solidly built	
	Sound quality is not great	Can record wild sound without running camera	
HDTV is good substitute for 35mm	Projection on monitor, big screen TV, or video projector	Big screen projection in theater still the ultimate experience	
Equipment continues to improve		Film stocks continue to improve	Film industry is shrinking
Small crews			Large crews
Inexpensive			Expensive

appendix J

Distributors

AIMS Media
    9710 DeSoto Avenue
    Chatsworth, CA 91311-4409
    Tel: (818) 773-4300 / (800) 367-2467
    Fax: (818) 341-6700
    Area of specialty: Non-theatrical educational
        productions
    Contact: Mike Wright

Barr Films
    P.O. Box 7878
    12801 Schabarum Avenue
    Irwindale, CA 91706-7878
    Tel: (818) 338-7878 / (800) 234-7878
    Fax: (818) 814-2672
    Area of specialty: Educational films
    Contact: George Holland

Black Filmmaker Foundation
    375 Greenwich Street
    New York, NY 10013
    Tel: (212) 941-3944
    Fax: (212) 941-3943
    Area of specialty: African American film
        and video
    Contact: Monica Breckinridge

Bullfrog Films
    Oley, PA 19547
    Tel: (215) 779-8226 / (800) 543-FROG
    Fax: (610) 370-1978
    Area of specialty: The environment, children's
        films as well as a new strand of performing
        arts programs

Canyon Cinema
    2325 Third Street
    Suite 338
    San Francisco, CA 94107
    Tel: (415) 626-2255
    Area of specialty: "No-profit" cooperative distri-
        bution center
    Contact: Dominic Angerame

Carousel Film and Video
    260 Fifth Avenue
    Room 705
    New York, NY 10001
    Tel: (212) 683-1600
    Area of specialty: Social documentaries
    Contact: Michael A. Dash

Churchill Films
    6901 Woodley Avenue
    Van Nuys, CA 91406
    Tel: (818) 778-1978
    Fax: (818) 778-1994
    Area of specialty: Education/health
    Contact: Marilyn Engle

Coe Films Associates
    65 East 96th Street
    New York, NY 10128
    Tel: (212) 831-5355
    Fax: (212) 996-6728
    Area of specialty: Short films and documentaries
        to television exclusively
    Contact: Beverly Freeman

Direct Cinema Ltd.
    P.O. Box 10003
    Santa Monica, CA 90410
    Tel: (310) 396-4774
    Fax: (310) 396-3233
    Area of specialty: Outstanding short films
        (live action and animated), documentaries,
        specialized features
    Contact: Mitchell Block

Drift Distribution
    83 Warren Street
    Suite 5
    New York, NY 10007-1057
    Tel: (212) 766-3713
    Area of specialty: Socially conscious, avante
        garde independent work
    Contact: Brian Golberg

Electronic Arts Intermix
536 Broadway
9th Floor
New York, NY 10012
Tel: (212) 966-4605
Fax: (212) 941-6118
Area of specialty: Video art
Contact: Stephen Vitiello

Filmmakers Library
124 East 40th Street
Suite 901
New York, NY 10016
Tel: (212) 808-4980
Fax: (212) 808-4983
Area of specialty: Social documentaries
Contact: Linda Gottesman/Sue Oscar

First Run/Icarus Films, Inc.
153 Waverly Place
6th Floor
New York, NY 10014
Tel: (212) 243-0600
Fax: (212) 989-7649
Area of specialty: Political and social issue
    documentaries
Contact: James Lee

New Dimension Media
85803 Lorane Highway
Eugene, OR 97405
Tel: (503) 484-7125
Fax: (503) 484-5267
Area of specialty: Non-theatrical distribution
Contact: Steve Raymen

Phoenix Films Inc.
2349 Chaffey
St. Louis, MO 63146
Tel: (314) 596-0211
Fax: (314) 596-2834
Area of specialty: Full-service distribution in
    all markets
Contact: Robert Dunlop

Picture Start
221 East Cullerton Street
6th Floor
Chicago, IL 60616
Tel: (312) 326-6233
Fax: (312) 326-0075
Area of specialty: Short works
Contact: Ron Epple

Pyramid Films and Video
2801 Colorado Avenue
Santa Monica, CA 90406
Tel: (310) 828-7577
Fax: (310) 453-9083
Area of specialty: Health, safety, social sciences
Contact: Pat Hamada

Tapestry International, Ltd.
920 Broadway
15th Floor
New York, NY 10010
Tel: (212) 505-2288
Fax: (212) 505-5059
Area of specialty: Televison productions and
    international distribution
Contact: Nancy Walzog

Third World Newsreel
335 West 38th Street
5th Floor
New York, NY 10018
Tel: (212) 947-9277
Fax: (212) 594-6917
Area of specialty: Works by makers of color
    and third world social issues
Contact: Ada Gay Griffin

Women Make Movies
462 Broadway
5th Floor
New York, NY 10013
Tel: (212) 925-0606
Fax: (212) 925-2052
Area of specialty: Woman's films and videos
Contact: Sasha Berman

appendix K

Insurance and Legal Matters

INSURANCE

Insurance plays an important role in motion picture and video production. Having insurance is as essential as having film stock or the right camera. In the course of normal life, calamities can happen and life goes on. In the course of a production, a car accident, sickness, a robbery, or a fire can bring the production to a screeching halt.

A budget, even with a contingency of 10 percent, is not flexible enough to cover keeping a crew standing for days, even weeks, while the lead actor recovers from an accident. This is why you need some type of protection for the unexpected occurrences that could happen in the course of the finely orchestrated movement of material, equipment, and people. Think of it as insurance for the possibility that Murphy's Law will prevail and everything will go wrong.

Some insurance companies specialize in entertainment insurance packages. They will evaluate the needs of the production and provide a price for appropriate coverage. You might not be able to afford everything they recommend, but it is highly recommended that you carry at least equipment and comprehensive liability coverage. You don't want to be personally responsible for property damage or injury on the set. Equipment houses will not rent to you without equipment insurance. Some offer their own insurance, but many don't.

What follows is a brief description of the many types of coverage available to film and video producers. The most common types of insurance are covered here. There are also special types of coverage that reflect unique demands.

Comprehensive Liability

Comprehensive liability coverage protects the production company against claims for bodily injury or property damage liability that arise from filming the picture. Coverage includes use of all nonowned vehicles (both on and off camera). This coverage is required before filming on any city or state roadways or at any location site.

Comprehensive liability policies do not cover accidents arising from the use of aircraft or watercraft. This coverage must be purchased separately.

Miscellaneous Equipment

This policy covers you against risk of direct physical loss, damage, or destruction to cameras, camera equipment, and sound, lighting, and grip equipment owned or rented by the production company. Coverage can be extended to cover mobile equipment vans, studio location units, and similar units upon payment of an additional premium.

Third-Party Property Damage Liability

This coverage pays for the damage or destruction of the property of others (including loss of use of property) while the property is in the care, custody, or control of the production company and is used or is to be used in an insured production.

This coverage does not apply to the following: liability for destruction of property caused by operation of any motor vehicle, aircraft, or watercraft, including damage to the foregoing; liability for damage to any property rented or leased that may be covered under props, sets, or wardrobe, or miscellaneous equipment insurance (although loss of use of any such equipment is covered).

This protection is not included under the comprehensive liability policy. Property damage coverage written as part of the comprehensive general liability policy excludes damage to any property in the production company's care, custody, or control.

Errors and Omissions

Distributors usually require this coverage before the release of any production. It covers legal liability and defense against lawsuits alleging copyright infringement; unauthorized use of titles format, ideas, characters, or plots; plagiarism; unfair competition; and invasion of privacy. It also protects against alleged libel, slander, defamation of character, and invasion of privacy suits.

Cast Insurance

Cast insurance reimburses the production company for any extra expense necessary to complete principal photography due to the death, injury, or sickness of any insured performer or director. Insured performers or directors must take a physical examination before they can be covered. Coverage usually begins three weeks before the beginning of principal photography.

Negative Film and Videotape

This is coverage against all risks of direct physical loss, damage, or destruction of raw film or tape stock, exposed film (developed or undeveloped), recorded videotape, sound tracks, and tapes, up to the amount of insured production cost.

This coverage does not include loss caused by fogging; faulty camera or sound equipment; faulty developing, editing, processing, or manipulation by the camera operator; exposure to light, dampness, or temperature changes; errors in judgment in exposure, lighting, or sound recording; or from the incorrect use of raw film stock or tape.

Faulty Stock, Camera, and Processing

This policy covers loss, damage, or destruction of raw film or tape stock, exposed film (developed or undeveloped), recorded videotape, sound tracks, and tapes caused by or resulting from fogging or the use of faulty equipment (including cameras and videotape recorders); faulty sound equipment; faulty developing, editing, and processing; and accidental erasure of videotape recording.

Props, Sets, and Wardrobe

This insurance provides coverage for props, sets, scenery, costumes, wardrobe, miscellaneous rented equipment, and office contents against all risk of direct physical loss, damage, or destruction during the production.

Extra Expense

Extra expense coverage reimburses the production company for any extra expense necessary to complete principal photography due to damage or destruction of property or facilities (props, sets, or equipment) used in connection with the production. It protects against loss that delays production.

Worker's Compensation

State laws mandate that this coverage be carried. It applies to all temporary or permanent cast or production crew members. Coverage provides medical, disability, or death benefits to any cast or crew members who become injured in the course of their employment. Coverage applies on a 24-hour basis whenever employees are on location away from their homes. Individuals who call themselves *independent contractors* are usually held to be employees as far as worker's compensation is concerned. The failure to carry this insurance can result in having to pay any benefits required under the law plus penalty awards.

Hired, Loaned, or Donated Auto Liability

This insurance covers all company-owned, hired, or leased vehicles used in connection with the production. Only vehicles that are being rented under the company's name and are issued certificates of insurance are covered under this policy.

Hired, Loaned, or Donated Auto Physical Damage

This coverage insures company-owned, hired, or leased vehicles against the risks of loss, theft, or damage (including collision) for all vehicles used in company-related activities. It covers vehicles rented from crew or staff members when the production company has assumed responsibility for the vehicles.

Guild/Union Travel Accident

This coverage provides Motion Picture/Television Guild or union contract requirements for aircraft accidental death insurance to all production company cast or crew members. Coverage is blanket, and the limit of liability meets all signatory requirements.

Office Contents

This is "all-risk" coverage (subject to policy exclusions) on office contents, subject to a low deductible.

Animal Mortality

When animals are used in the production, consideration should be given to this special coverage. This policy insures against the death or destruction of any animal covered. A veterinarian's certificate is usually required for this coverage. If the animal is a principal character, the cost to be paid to finish principal photography might be covered under cast insurance.

LEGAL

Music Rights

All music is subject to copyright protection unless it is in the public domain. It is very important that before deciding on using a particular piece of music or a song in your film or video, you secure its clearance. Failure to clear the music might result in an injunction, large legal fees, and the reediting of your piece.

Clearance means determining who owns the copyright to a piece of music and negotiating a license to use that material for exhibition and distribution in specific territories and media in exchange for the payment of a fee to the copyright owner. If the clearance process is begun ahead of time, the producer can determine if the budget can accommodate the price of a particular song or musical selection.

Generally, songwriters assign or sell the copyright to their work to a publisher who pays the writer a share of the royalties if the song is used in a film or video. Recordings are usually owned by the record company that paid for the recording session or that had the recording artist under contract.

You must also acquire the synchronization rights if the material is recorded as part of a sound track in synchronization with the visual images. These rights can be obtained by approaching either the author; the author's estate, lawyer, publisher, or agent; or the organization that represents the publisher and licenses those rights on its behalf. One example of the latter is the Harry Fox Agency.

If you use a song that has not been cleared, you carry the risk of being caught. You may face an injunction, have to pay an out-of-court settlement, or have to make extensive changes to your show to remove the musical selection. Festival rights might not require any payment at all; however, festival rights are negotiated in the same manner as if you were seeking commercial rights.

Public Domain

Music created after January 1, 1978, is protected by copyright for 50 years after the death of the last surviving writer. Works that were made for hire, such as an original film score, are protected for 75 years from publication or 100 years from creation, whichever is less.

You might have heard that you can use a few bars from a song for free. This is false. "Fair use" is another questionable area. This is an exception to the exclusive rights of copyright owners. Fair use permits limited use of a copyrighted material in a number of circumstances. In theory, the public interest is served when the material is used for purposes of criticism, comment, news reporting, scholarship, teaching, and so on. Parodies using the material for humor or social commentary are also allowed, but this is an area of law that is constantly changing and should be reviewed carefully.

For help in this area, get some legal assistance. If you cannot afford an entertainment attorney, you'll find free legal aid groups in major metropolitan areas that can answer many of your basic questions. One example is Volunteer Lawyers for the Arts.

glossary

A and B cutting   A method of assembling original material in two separate rolls, allowing optical effects to be made by double printing (A and B printing).

A- and B-wind   When a roll of 16mm film, perforated along one edge, is held so that the outside end of the film leaves the roll at the top and toward the right, A-wind has perforations on the edge of the film toward the observer, and B-wind has perforations on the edge away from the observer. In both cases, the base surface faces outward on the roll.

above-the-line   The part of a production budget earmarked for the creative aspects of production, including the salaries of the producer, director, writer, and talent.

abrasion mark   A scratch on film caused by grit, dust, improper handling, emulsion buildup, and certain types of film damage such as broken perforations.

academy leader   A film leader, placed at the head end of a projection reel, that contains identification and timing countdown information for the projectionist and is designed to meet the specifications of the American Academy of Motion Picture Arts and Sciences.

AD   See **assistant director.**

ADR   See **automatic dialogue replacement.**

aerial shot   A shot taken from the air.

AGC   See **automatic gain control.**

agent/talent agent   An individual or company licensed by the state to represent a particular talent in the entertainment field and to seek employment and negotiate contracts in his or her behalf. The standard fee is 10 percent of the client's salary. Agents can represent above-the-line talent (actors, writers, directors, producers) or below-the-line talent (art directors, directors of photography, editors).

ambient noise   (1) Background noise. (2) A sound occurring naturally in a location.

analog   A recording system that creates modulations analogous to the modulations of sound or video waves.

angle   With reference to the subject, the direction from which a picture is taken—that is, the camera-subject relationship.

animation   The act of making inanimate objects appear to move. This can be done by exposing one or two frames of film, moving the objects slightly, exposing one or two more frames, and so on.

answer print   The first film print in composite form, which the laboratory offers for approval. It is usually studied carefully by the director, producer, and DP to determine whether changes are required before the lab makes any additional prints.

aperture   (1) In a lens, the orifice, usually an adjustable iris, that limits the amount of light passing through a lens. The width of a lens aperture is expressed in f-stops. (2) In a motion picture camera, the mask opening that defines the area of each frame exposed. (3) In a motion picture projector, the mask opening that defines the area of each frame projected.

aperture plate   A metal plate, containing an aperture, that is inserted into a projector or camera.

ASA   The exposure index, or speed rating, that denotes the film's sensitivity to light, as defined by the American National Standards Institution. It is actually defined only for black-and-white films, but it is also used in the trade for color films.

aspect ratio   The ratio of picture width to height, such as 1.33:1 (16mm), 1.85:1 (35mm), or 2.35:1 (70mm).

assistant director (AD)   In video production, the person who relays the director's commands from the control booth to the studio floor and who keeps an accurate account of time. In film production, the person who helps the production manager break down the script during preproduction and keeps the director on schedule during production. The AD also hires, controls, and directs background action, including extras and camera vehicles.

atmospheric effect   An environmental special effect such as fog, mist, rain, or wind.

attack (sound)   The beginning segment of an audio cue.

audio sweetening   Enhancing the sound of a recording with equalization and various other signal-processing techniques during the postproduction process.

automatic dialogue replacement (ADR)   A process during postproduction in which an actor replaces any of her lines in the film or video that were not recorded properly during production.

automatic gain control (AGC) A device that maintains a constant audio or video signal level on a videotape or audiotape recorder.

baby legs A small, miniature tripod for low-angle shots.

back lighting Lighting from behind the subject.

back story The events stated or implied to have happened before the period covered in the film or video.

barn door A frame with adjustable flaps that is attached to a lighting instrument to control unwanted spill light or the spread of the beam of light.

barney A lightweight padded covering that reduces the sound emanating from within the camera, such as noisy gears or take-up reels. Heated barneys are sometimes used to facilitate shooting under extremely cold outdoor conditions.

bars Standard color bars that are generated in video systems, usually by the camera.

base makeup Makeup that hides blemishes and creates a consistent overall texture and color on the performer's face, arms, and hands.

battery belt A belt containing a rechargeable camera battery.

battery pack A battery power source for a camera or other location equipment.

beat (1) The point in a scene where a character's tempo, meaning, or intention shifts. (2) A musical tempo used for timing motion picture action.

below-the-line The part of a production budget allocated to the technical aspects of production, including the salaries of the crew and equipment and material costs.

binary code A series of ons and offs (or ones and zeros) that digitally represent a wide range of values in coded form.

blimp A soundproof enclosure that completely covers a camera to prevent camera-operating noise from being recorded on the sound track. A blimp is similar to a barney but is made from a solid material.

blocking How the director positions the actors and the camera on the stage or set.

blow up To enlarge a portion of the original image to full frame size in the copy by means of an optical printer. Running the entire film through an optical printer can enlarge 16mm film to 35mm size.

boom A support pole, held by a boom operator, used to hang the microphone close to the performers but just out of the shot.

bounce light Light that is reflected off white cards, ceilings, or walls to illuminate a subject indirectly.

breakdown sheet A list made from a script that includes all elements needed to produce a sequence.

broad light A soft, floodlight-type lamp that cannot be focused.

business Activity invented by actors to identify their characters' behavior. Business is a physical action that arises from dialogue, silences or pauses, or audio cues (such as a doorbell or ringing phone). It might involve movement from one part of the set to another (crosses) or the use of props and set dressing. Examples: lighting a cigarette at a key moment in a scene or jiggling a set of keys to break a tense silence.

cable television A means of distributing television signals to receivers via a coaxial cable.

call back To ask actors to audition for a second or third time.

camera axis A hypothetical line running through the optic center of the camera lens.

camera car A specially equipped truck that can tow a picture vehicle and offers several shooting positions from the truck. This enables the actors to act and not drive.

camera operator The person who operates the camera. This person might also be the director of photography.

canted angle See **Dutch angle**.

cardioid microphone A microphone whose responsiveness to sound forms can be described by a heart-shaped pickup pattern.

catharsis (1) A purifying or figurative cleansing of the emotions, especially pity and fear, described by Aristotle as an effect of tragic drama on its audience. (2) A release of emotional tension, such as after an overwhelming experience, that restores or refreshes the spirit.

CG See **character generator**.

changing bag A black lighttight cloth or plastic bag used to load and unload camera magazines with film stock.

character A person portrayed in an artistic piece, such as a drama or novel.

character generator (CG) An electronic device that creates letters on a television screen for titles and other purposes.

chroma key A method of electronically inserting an image from one video source into the picture from another video source by selectively replacing the "key color" with another image.

cinema verité A documentary film technique in which the camera is subservient to real events.

clapsticks Two boards hinged at one end that are slapped together to indicate the start of a filming session (take). Editors use clapsticks in conjunction with a slate, which provides the corresponding visual cue, to synchronize sound and image.

close-up (CU)   A tight shot of an object or an actor's face and shoulders.

C-mount   A screw mount for 16mm film and video lenses.

coding   Edge numbers that are placed on the film and mag stock so that a number of picture and sound rolls will have the same sequence. This gives the editor a visual reference to maintain accurate sync.

color bars   The standard video test signal, which involves a series of vertical bars of fully saturated color: white, yellow, cyan, green, magenta, red, blue, and black.

color correction   Altering the color balance by modifying the ratio of the printing light values.

color internegative   A negative-image color duplicate made from a positive color original. It is typically used for making release prints.

color negative   A negative (opposite) image. The colors in the negative are the opposite of the colors in the scene: Light areas are dark, and dark areas are light.

color reversal film   Like photographic slides, reversal film uses a different development process from negative and yields a positive image that can be directly projected without the need of a print.

color temperature   The color quality of the light source, expressed in degrees Kelvin (K). The higher the color temperature, the bluer the light; the lower the color temperature, the redder the light.

composite print   A film print that contains both picture and optical sound track.

composition   (1) The arrangement of artistic parts to form a unified whole. (2) The balance and general relationship of objects and light in the frame.

compound lens   See **lens**.

concept   A general idea derived or inferred from specific instances or occurrences in a film. This idea drives the story.

conflict   Opposition between characters or forces in a work of drama or fiction, especially opposition that motivates or shapes the action of the plot.

contingency fund   A sum of money, approximately 10 percent of the budget, which is added to the overall production budget in case of cost overruns and production problems.

continuity   The smooth flow of action or events from one shot or sequence to the next.

continuity script   A script made for postproduction by the script supervisor. A continuity script contains a shot-by-shot account of the contents of the film.

cookie   A thin panel with regular or irregular shapes cut out, permitting light directed through it to form a particular arrangement on a part of the set. Also known as a *kukaloris*.

costume designer   The person who designs and supervises the making of garments for the actors.

coverage   The different angles from which a particular scene is shot.

cover set   A predressed location available in case inclement weather forces the company to move indoors.

craft services   The person or persons responsible for feeding the crew.

crane   A boom that supports the camera and can be raised or lowered during the shot.

cross fade   A transition in which one sound source is faded out while another is faded in over it.

crystal sync   A synchronization system in which separate crystal oscillators in the film camera and in the synchronous sound recorder drive the camera and the sound recorder extremely accurately, enabling double-system synchronous sound to be obtained without a cable connection.

CS   Close shot. See also **close-up**.

C-stand (century stand)   A tripod-based stand for holding lighting instruments, flags, gobos, and sound blankets.

CU   See **close-up**.

cutaway   A shot of an object or a view that takes viewers away from the main action.

dailies   Picture and sound work prints of a day's shooting; usually, an untimed one-light print, made without regard to color balance.

DAT   See **digital audio tape**.

day out of days   A detailed schedule of the days the actors will work on a film or video production.

deal memo   A letter between two parties that defines the basic payment and responsibility clauses and the spirit of what will later become a contract.

decay   The gradual diminishing of a concluding sound.

decibel (dB)   A unit of sound measurement.

depth of field   The range of object-to-camera distance within which objects are in sufficiently sharp focus.

deus ex machina   An improbable event imported into a story to make it turn out right.

dialogue   The portion of the sound track that is spoken by the actors.

diffuse light   See **soft light**.

digital An electrical signal encoding audio, video, or both into a series of assigned numbers or binary code rather than analog voltage.

digital audio tape (DAT) A superior recording system achieved through the conversion of sound into a binary stream of ones and zeros that are computer-stored for later signal conversion and amplification without the risk of distortion. The computer is able to record up to 44,000 units of sound per second. See also **binary**.

digitize To transfer an audio or video signal onto a computers drive.

director The person who interprets the written book or script and oversees all aspects of a film or video production.

director of photography(DP) In production, the person who directs the cinematography (the lighting and camera setup and framing).

dirty dupe A splice-free work print of the work print, also called a slop print. Used in the mix to avoid breaking splices. Using the dupe frees the workprint to be sent to the negative cutter.

dissolve An optical or camera effect in which one scene gradually fades out as a second scene fades in. There is an apparent double exposure in the middle of a dissolve sequence where the two scenes overlap.

distributor A company that sells, leases, and rents films.

dolly (1) A truck built to carry a camera and camera operator to facilitate movement of the camera during the shooting of scenes. (2) To move the camera toward or away from the subject while shooting a scene.

double (multiple) exposure The photographic recording of two or more images on a single strip of film.

DP See **director of photography**.

dress rehearsal The final rehearsal or technical drill for a production before actual filming. A dress rehearsal involves costumes, props, and dressed sets.

dub To copy from one electronic medium to another. Both sound and video picture can be dubbed.

dubbing The process of melding several sound components into a single recording.

dupe/dupe negative A duplicate negative, which is made from a master positive by printing and development or from an original negative by printing followed by reversal development.

Dutch angle A shot made with the camera deliberately tilted. Also known as a *canted angle*.

edge numbers Numbers on the edges of film that identify the film. They are used to help match original film and sound to the edited work prints. Latent-image edge numbers are put on by the manufacturer and appear during development. Also known as *key numbers*.

edit controller An electronic device used to switch among various video inputs to record on a videotape recorder. It controls the edit by preroll cuing, edit auditioning, and performing the edit by punching in and punching out.

edit decision list (EDL) A list of edits performed during off-line editing in video. The EDL is stored in hard copy, floppy disk, or punch tape form and is used to direct the final on-line editing assembly or negative cut.

editing The process of selecting the shots and sequences that will be included in the final product, their length, and the order in which they will appear.

editor The person who decides which scenes and takes are to be used, how, where, in what sequence, and at what length they will appear.

EDL See **edit decision list**.

end crawl The names of the cast and crew who worked on a production that rolls up or "crawls" vertically at the end of a film or video.

equalization (EQ) Altering the frequency/amplitude response of a sound source or system to improve the sound quality. Treble and bass are adjusted, as is the relationship of various frequencies.

establishing shot A shot that establishes a scene's geographical and human contents.

exposure The amount of light that acts on a photographic material. Exposure is the product of illumination intensity (controlled by the lens opening) and duration (controlled by the shutter opening and the frame rate).

exposure latitude The range between the lowest and highest exposures that will ensure a readable image on the screen.

exposure meter, incident A meter calibrated to read and integrate all the light aimed at and falling on a subject within a large area. The scale might be calibrated in footcandles or in photographic exposure settings.

exposure meter, reflectance A meter calibrated to read the amount of light, within a restricted area, reflecting from the surface of a subject or an overall scene. The scale might be calibrated in footcandles or in photographic exposure settings.

eye-line The line from an actor's eye to the direction in which the actor is looking. If the actor looks at co-performers and behind them is an audience, the actor might become distracted. It is important to keep crew members out of an actor's eye-line during auditions and principal photography.

feed   The part of a recording device that supplies tape or film.

fiber optics   A small cable through which information, carried by light, travels through a telephone line. Also used for lighting.

fill light   Light used to fill in shadows, either on a set or on a face.

film chain   See **telecine system**.

film gate   The components that make up the pressure and aperture plates in a camera, printer, or projector.

film perforation   Holes punched at regular intervals in the entire length of film. The perforation is engaged by pins, pegs, and sprockets as the film is transported through the camera, projector, or other equipment.

film-to-video transfer   The process of copying a film on videotape through a telecine or flying spot scanner.

final cut   The last editing of a work print before conforming is done and before sound work prints are mixed.

fine grain   Emulsion in which the silver particles are very small.

fish pole   A hand-held microphone boom.

flag   An opaque sheet that is separate from a lighting instrument but is used to shape the light and prevent light from falling on certain areas.

flare   A streak of light that is recorded on the film or video stock when the light of the sun or an artificial instrument shines directly into the camera lens.

flashing   A technique for lowering contrast by giving a slight uniform exposure to the film before processing.

flats   Relatively lightweight, flat, rectangular boards that can be lashed together to create a temporary wall in a studio.

floodlight   A lighting instrument without a lens that uses reflectors and diffusers to spread and soften the light it emits.

floor plan   A scale drawing of a location that is used to plan lighting, camera, and actor blocking.

f-number   A symbol that expresses the relative aperture of the lens. For example, a lens with a relative aperture of 1.7 would be marked f/1.7. The smaller the f-number, the more light the lens transmits. Also known as f-stop.

focus   To adjust a lens so that it produces the sharpest visual image on a screen, on a camera film plane, and so on.

footcandle (fc)   A unit of light intensity that equals the power of one standard candle at a distance of one foot. Footcandles are measured with incident light meters.

foreground   The part of the scene in front of the camera that is occupied by the object nearest the camera.

format   The size or aspect ratio of a motion picture frame.

freeze frame   An optical printing effect in which a single frame image is repeated so as to appear stationary when projected.

full coat   The original 1/4 inch sound is transferred to magnetic film, also referred to as mag film, mag stock, and full coat.

gate   The aperture assembly through which the film is exposed in a camera, printer, or projector.

gel   Translucent material in a variety of colors that is placed in front of lighting instruments to alter the color of the light. Gels are held in place by barn doors.

genre   A category of film categorized by a particular style, form, or content, such as horror, sitcom, Western, and domestic drama.

gobo   A panel of opaque material on a footed stand with an adjustable arm. Gobos are used to confine the area that a light illuminates or to keep light from shining directly into the camera lens.

golden time   A rate of pay equal to triple the base hourly wage.

grain   Fine photo-sensitive crystals of silver halides suspended in the gelatin of a film emulsion that become exposed to light and developed into an image.

gray card   A commercially prepared card that reflects 18 percent of the light hitting it. Visually, it appears as a neutral, or middle, gray halfway between black and white.

green room   A comfortable holding area for the actors.

grid   A system of ceiling pipes for hanging lighting instruments over a stage. See also **spreaders**.

grip   A person who performs a variety of tasks during film production, including helping to set up cameras, lighting equipment, and sets.

guillotine splicer   A device used for butt-splicing film with splicing tape.

hard light   Illumination made up of directional rays of light that create strong, hard, well-defined shadows. Also known as *specular light*.

HDTV   See **high-definition television**.

headroom   Compositional space in a shot above the actor's head.

hertz (Hz)   The number of vibrations or successive waves of sound that pass a specific point each second.

high-definition television (HDTV)   High-resolution television signals, which can produce wide-screen images that are roughly comparable to film images in terms of overall sharpness and detail (lines of resolution).

high-hat   A tripod head mounted onto a flat board. This allows the cameraman to place the camera on the ground or on a table for a low-angle shot.

high-key   A lighting style that produces an overall and even brightness with few shadows. The low contrast is created by a low lighting ratio of key to fill light.

highlights   The brightest areas of a subject. In a negative image, highlights are the areas of greatest density; in a positive image, they are the areas of least density.

HMI light   The high-intensity, daylight-balanced light produced by energy-efficient, portable, lightweight HMI lamps.

hook   A dramatic device that grabs viewers' attention and secures their involvement in a story.

hue   The sensation of a color itself, measured by the color's dominant wavelength.

Hz   See **hertz.**

image lag   An afterimage left on a video monitor, usually resulting from bright objects.

insert   A close shot of detail.

intensity (light)   The total visible radiation produced by a light source. The term refers to the power (strength) of the light source.

interlock   A system that electronically links a projector with a sound recorder and is used during postproduction to review the edited film with the sound track to check timing, pacing, synchronization, and so on.

internegative (dupe negative)   A color negative made from a color negative. Internegatives are used for making release prints.

interpositive   A color master positive print.

iris   (1) An adjustable opening that controls the amount of light passing through a lens. (2) An optical effect that starts with a small dot of an image and "irises out" with an expanding circle to fill the entire frame with the next shot. This iris effect can also be used in the reverse.

jib arm   A miniature unmanned camera crane that is remotely or manually operated. A video tap is often used because of the difficulty in seeing through the eye piece while a jib arm is in use.

key light   The main illumination of the subject.

key numbers   See **edge numbers.**

key-to-fill ratio   See **lighting ratio.**

kicker   A separation light placed directly opposite the key light to create side and back light.

kinescoping   See **video-to-film transfer.**

kukaloris   See **cookie.**

laboratory   A facility that processes and prints film and sometimes offers additional services, such as coding, negative cutting, editing, and film storage.

lavaliere microphone   Small lightweight, usually omni-directional microphones that are pinned under an actor's clothing or taped to the body.

lens   (1) A ground or molded piece of glass, plastic, or other transparent material with opposite surfaces, either or both of which are curved, by means of which light rays are refracted so that they converge or diverge to form an image. (2) A combination of two or more such pieces, sometimes with other optical devices like prisms, used to form an image for viewing or photographing. Also called *compound lens.*

lighting director   In video production, the person who designs and supervises the lighting setup.

lighting ratio   The ratio of the intensity of key and fill lights to fill light alone.

light meter   An electrical exposure meter for measuring light intensity.

linear   A term used to describe editing systems that are locked into a straightforward, or "linear," approach to putting scenes together, as in traditional video editing systems.

lined script   A script marked by the script supervisor to show the editor which take number was used to record each part of all scenes.

line item   A budget entry.

lip sync   The simultaneous, precise recording of image and sound so that the sound appears to be superimposed accurately on the image, especially if a person is speaking toward the camera.

liquid gate   A printing system in which the original is immersed in a suitable liquid at the moment of exposure to reduce the effect of surface scratches and abrasions.

long shot (LS)   The photographing of a scene or action from a distance or with a wide angle of view so that a large area of the setting appears on the film and the scene or objects appear quite small.

looping   The process of lip-sync dubbing.

low-key   A lighting style that uses intermittent pools of light and darkness with few highlights and many shadows. The contrast is created by a high ratio of key light alone to key and fill lights.

LS   See **long shot.**

magazine   A removable container that holds fresh or exposed film.

magic hour   This is the time between sundown and darkness when the quality of light has an especially "magic" or warm quality—twilight.

magnetic sound   Sound derived from an electrical audio signal recorded on a magnetic oxide stripe or on full-coated magnetic tape.

master shot   Usually a long shot in which all action in a scene takes place. Action is repeated for the medium shot and close-up, which may be cut into the same scene.

master tape   The tape to which other material will be added during videotape editing.

match cut   A cut made between two different angles of the same action using the subject's movement as the transition.

matte   An opaque outline that limits the exposed area of a picture, either as a cutout object in front of the camera or as a silhouette on another strip of film.

meal penalties   A fine levied against the production to pay additional money to actors who were not allowed to eat at the prescribed break time.

medium shot   A scene that is photographed from a medium distance so that the full figure of the subject fills an entire frame.

mise-en-scène   The totality of lighting, blocking, camera use, and composition that produces the dramatic image on film.

mix   To combine the various sound tracks—dialogue, music, and sound effects—into a single track.

mix cue sheet   A list of all dialogue, effects, and music cues for a sound mix. Mix cue sheets are organized sequentially for each sound track.

mixer   (1) Circuitry capable of mixing two or more sound inputs to one output. (2) The audio console at which mixing is done. (3) The person who does the mixing.

MOS   Short for "Mit out sound," which is what German directors in Hollywood called for when they intended to shoot silent.

Murphy's Law   The observation that "anything that can go wrong will go wrong."

music cue sheet   A list of all music cues and timings for the picture to be used for royalties and publishing.

narration   The off-screen commentary for a film. Also known as *voice-over (VO)*.

needle-drop fees   One means by which royalty payments for music library selections are made. A fixed fee is charged each time a phonographic needle is dropped on a particular recording—that is, each time it is played.

negative cost   The amount of money required to complete the film or video.

neutral-density filter   A filter that is gray in color and affects all colors equally. It is used to reduce the amount of light passing through the lens without affecting color.

noise   Distortions in a signal, such as "snow" in video and "hiss" in audio, that are created by multiple-generation duplication.

nonlinear   A term used to describe editing systems that are capable of working out of sequence or in a random manner, as in film editing.

NTSC   The American television standard system of 525 scanning lines of resolution and 30 frames per second.

off-line edit   Manual, noncomputerized video editing. Compare **on-line edit**.

omnidirectional   Responsive to sound from all directions.

180°-axis-of-action rule   A means of camera placement that ensures continuity and consistency in the placement and movement of objects from shot to shot.

on-line edit   Computer-assisted video editing in which the computer locates and lines up specific time-coded frames in the process of assembling a final cut. Compare **off-line edit**.

on-screen sound   A sound emanating from a source that is visible within the frame.

optical   Any visual device, such as a fade, dissolve, wipe, iris wipe, ripple dissolve, matte, or superimposition prepared with an optical printer in a laboratory or on-line for video.

optical printer   A printer that is used when the image size of the print film is different from the image size of the preprint film or when effects like skip frames, blowups, zooms, and mattes are included.

optical sound   A system in which the photographic (optical) sound track on a film is scanned by a horizontal slit beam of light that modulates a photoelectric cell. The voltages generated by the cell produce audio signals that are amplified to operate screen speakers.

optical track   Sound track in which the sound recorded takes the form of density variations (variable-density track) or width variations (variable-area track) in a photographic image.

original negative   The negative that was exposed in the camera.

outtake   A take of a scene that is not used for printing or final assembly in editing.

over-the-shoulder shot   A shot in which a camera is placed behind and to the side of an actor, so that the actor's shoulder appears in the foreground and the face or body of another appears in the background. This type of shot tends to establish a specific subject's physical point of view on the action.

overtime   Additional salary that is paid if someone is asked to work longer than his or her contracted hours.

PA   See **production assistant.**

pace   A subjective impression of the speed of the sounds or visuals.

pan   A camera move in which the camera on a fluid head appears to move horizontally or vertically, usually to follow the action or to scan a scene. In animation, the effect is achieved by moving the artwork under the camera.

perspective   The technique of representing three-dimensional objects and depth relationships on a two-dimensional surface.

pistol grip   A hand-held camera mount.

pixel   The smallest unit of a reproduced image. Short for picture element.

playback   Previously recorded music or vocals to be used on the set for the actors to perform to or mime. Playback is used when filming songs (music videos), instrumental performances, or dance.

playback head   A magnetic device that is capable of transforming magnetic changes on a prerecorded tape into electrical signals.

plot   (1) The plan of events or the main story in a narrative or drama. (2) The arrangement of incidents and logic of causality in a story. The plot should act as a vehicle for the thematic intention of the piece.

point-of-view (POV) shot   A shot in which the camera is placed in the approximate position of a specific character. It is often preceded by a shot of a character looking in a particular direction and is followed by a shot of the character's reaction to what he or she has seen. The latter shot is sometimes called a *reaction shot.*

pot   A dial that can be rotated to increase or decrease the sound level. The term is short for potentiometer.

POV shot   See **point-of-view shot.**

practical light   A source lighting instrument on the set, such as a floor or table lamp, that appears in the frame.

prerig   To set up the lighting instruments based on a lighting plan devised by the director of photography a day or two before the shoot date. Prerigging can be done by a "swing crew" the night before the shoot.

presence   A recorded sound track from the location used to fill sound gaps in editing.

production assistant   An inexperienced crew member who floats from department to department, depending on which area needs help the most. Duties can range from running for coffee or holding parking spaces to setting up lights and slating.

production supervisor   An assistant to the producer. The production supervisor is in charge of routine administrative duties.

prosthetic makeup   Makeup and latex pieces designed to transform the appearance of a performer's face or body. Examples: a long nose for Cyrano or stitches and a big head for Frankenstein's creature.

proximity effect   A poor-quality audio transmission caused by having the microphone too close to the sound source.

pull-down claw   The metallic finger that advances the film one frame between exposure cycles.

punch tape   A paper punch record of videotape edit decisions for a computer or for printing commands in film printing.

rack focus   A focus that shifts between foreground and background during a shot to prompt or accommodate an attention shift (a figure enters a door at the back of the room, for instance).

raw stock   Unexposed and unprocessed motion picture film, including camera original, laboratory intermediate, duplicating, and release-print stocks.

reaction shot   A close-up of a character's reaction to events.

reference white   A white card or large white object in the frame that can be used for white balance or the proper color adjustment in video.

reflected light   Light that has been bounced or reflected from objects, as opposed to direct or incident light.

reflected reading   A light meter reading of the intensity of light reflected by the subject and/or background.

reflector   Any surface that reflects light.

registration   The steadiness of the film image in the gate or aperture.

release   A statement giving permission to use an actor's face or likeness. It also releases a producer from future legal action, such as for slander or libel, which is signed by people appearing in a video program or film who are not professional performers.

release print   In a motion picture processing laboratory, any of numerous duplicate prints of a subject made for distribution.

research   (1) To study something thoroughly so as to present it in a detailed, accurate manner. (2) The process of uncovering sources of information about a prospective video or film topic or audience.

residuals A payment made to a performer, writer, or director for each repeat showing of a recorded television show or commercial.

reticle A grid or pattern placed in the camera viewfinder used to establish scale or position. See **TV safe.**

reversal film Film that is processed to a positive image after exposure in a camera or in a printer to produce another positive film. See also **color reversal film.**

RGB The primary colors: red, green, and blue.

room tone The natural acoustical ambience of the area around which the scene is shot. Room tone can later be mixed with the dialogue to smooth cuts and create a more realistic presence of a space.

rough cut A preliminary stage in film editing in which shots, scenes, and sequences are laid out in the correct approximate order, without detailed attention to the individual cutting points.

royalty fees Money paid to composers, authors, performers, and so on, for the use of copyrighted materials.

rushes Unedited raw footage as it appears after shooting.

SAG The acronym for the Screen Actors Guild. The SAG contract also covers members of Equity (stage actors), AGVA (variety members), and AFTRA (television actors).

scale The base union wage.

score Music composed for a specific film or videotape.

scratch mix A preliminary or trial mixing of sounds against picture.

scrim A translucent material that reduces, like a screen, the intensity of the light without changing its character.

script supervisor The person who maintains the continuity in performer actions and prop placements from shot to shot and who ensures that every scene in the script has been recorded.

setup The combination of lens, camera placement, and composition to produce a particular shot.

SFX See **sound effects.**

shading Adjusting the brightness level, light sensitivity, and color of a video camera.

shock-mounted microphone A microphone that is designed to minimize all vibrations and noise except those inherent in sound waves.

shooting ratio The ratio of the material recorded during production to that which is actually used in the final edited version.

shooting script The approved final version of the script with scene numbers, camera setups, and other instructions by the director.

shot An unbroken filmed segment; the basic component of a scene.

shotgun microphone See **ultracardioid microphone.**

shutter An opaque device in a film camera that rapidly opens and closes to expose the film to light.

sides Part of a scene given to actors to read during an audition.

signal-to-noise ratio The ratio of desired to undesired sound, the latter of which usually comes from equipment or tape noise.

silhouette An outline that appears dark against a light background.

slating The process of placing, at the beginning or end of a shot, a common reference point for separate but synchronous film images and sounds as well as an identification of the recorded material. See also **tail slate.**

slop print See **dirty dupe.**

slow motion The process of photographing a subject at a faster frame rate than used in projection to expand the time element.

SMPTE The acronym for the Society of Motion Picture and Television Engineers.

SMPTE time code A reference code for individual videotape frames that was standardized by the Society of Motion Picture and Television Engineers.

snip book A notebook used to store trims without identifiable edge code numbers.

soft cut A very short dissolve.

soft light Light made up of soft, scattered rays resulting in soft, less clearly defined shadows. Also known as *diffuse light.*

sound effects (SFX) Any sound from any source other than the tracks bearing synchronized dialogue, narration, or music. The sound effects track is commonly introduced into a master track during rerecording, usually with the idea of enhancing the illusion of reality in the finished presentation.

sound gain An adjustment to control the sound recording level.

specular light See **hard light.**

split diopter A special filter placed on a camera lens that allows portions of the frame to remain in focus, even though they are beyond the lens's depth of field.

splits A shooting period that consists of half a day and half a night of principal photography.

spotlight A lighting unit, usually with a lens and a shiny metal reflector, that is capable of being focused and produces hard light.

spot reading A light-meter reading of the intensity of the light reflected by the subject in a very narrow area, as determined by the angle of acceptance of the spot meter.

spreaders   A bracket system for placing pipe or two-by-four lumber to act as a lighting instrument grid.

sprocket   A toothed wheel used to move the perforated motion picture film.

spun glass   A flexible light diffuser made out of fiberglass.

staging   The process of planning how the action of a scene will take place.

stand-in   Someone who takes the place of an actor during setup or for shots that involve special skills, such as horse riding or fight scenes.

Steadicam®   A registered trademark for a servostabilizer camera mount attached to the operator's body to minimize camera vibrations when the operator moves with the camera.

sting   A musical accent to heighten a dramatic moment.

storyboard   Semidetailed drawings of what each shot will look like; similar to a multipanel cartoon.

stripboard   A scheduling device. Each shot is represented by a strip of cardboard on which is encoded all the pertinent breakdown information. The strips are put in the desired order of shooting and are affixed to a multipanel stripboard. This board can then be carried to the set in the event that adjustments need to be made in the schedule.

subjective point of view   A story told from the perspective of a specific character or participant in the action.

subjective shot   A presentation of images supposedly dreamed, imagined, recollected, or perceived in an abnormal state of mind by a character or participant in a videotape or film.

subtext   The underlying personality of a dramatic character as implied or indicated by a script or text and as interpreted by an actor in performance.

sun gun   A high-intensity, portable, battery powered light. It is usually used for news or documentary work.

supercardioid microphone   A microphone with a highly directional pickup pattern.

superimposition   Two images occupying the entire frame at the same time. Normally, one image is dominant and the other subordinate during a superimposition to avoid visual confusion. The more detailed the images, the less clear and visually pleasing the superimposition is likely to be.

super objective   The overarching thematic purpose of the director's dramatic interpretation.

swing crew   A team of gaffers or grips that sets the stage, lights, or both for a big or complicated sequence before the main production unit arrives.

swish pan   A rapid turning of the camera on the tripod axis, causing blurring of the image. A swish pan can be used as a transition device between scenes.

switcher   A video editing device that controls which picture and sound sources are transmitted or recorded. It can be used during multiple-camera production or during postproduction.

tail slate   A sync mark used when a scene begins in action or from an extreme close-up, making it difficult to slate from the beginning. After the director has called "Cut," the slate is clapped, upside down, to give the editor a sync mark.

take   A photographic record of each repetition of a scene. A particular scene might be photographed more than once in an effort to get a perfect recording of some special action.

TBC   See **time-base corrector.**

telecine system   An optical/electronic system for transferring film to videotape. Also known as a *film chain*.

telephoto lens   A long-focal-length lens that foreshortens the apparent distance between foreground and background objects.

telescope story   A script or editing device used to make a leap in time.

tent   (1) A tent of heavy black velour drapery that can be rigged around a window to allow a sequence shot during the day to simulate night. (2) A box built outside a window that is draped but allows enough room to place a light outside the window, permitting a constant light source to appear through the window.

theme   (1) A central concept, idea, or symbolic meaning in a story. (2) A repeated melody in a symphony or long musical composition.

three- or four-point lighting   A basic lighting technique that helps create an illusion of three-dimensionality by separating the subject from the background, using key, fill, and separation lights.

three stripe   The magnetic 35mm film on which the sound is mixed together. This fullcoat mag has three tracks—one for dialogue, one for sound effects, and one for music. Should a track need to be replaced, to make a foreign dub for example, the remaining two tracks will be undisturbed.

tilt   The process of swiveling the camera in a vertical arc, such as tilting it up and down to show the height of a flagpole.

time code   A frame monitoring system that provides an exact numerical reference for each frame of film or videotape. Time code is divided into hours, minutes, seconds, and frames.

time-base corrector (TBC)   A device that stabilizes pictures from videotape recorders.

timing   A laboratory process that involves balancing the color of a film to achieve consistency from scene to scene.

title search   A legal process whereby it is determined whether a show title is available for use.

trims   The unused pieces of film cut out of a scene. They are labeled and stored throughout postproduction until the final prints are stuck.

trompe l'oeil   A style of painting in which objects are depicted with photographically realistic detail that is sometimes used in interior decorating.

turnaround   The time between ending one day's work and beginning the next day's.

turret   A pivoted plate that allows a choice of lenses to be swung rapidly into position.

TV safe   The innermost frame outline in the viewfinder is called *TV safe*, or the area that will be seen when screened on a television monitor. Elements outside this frame line may be missed. See **reticle**.

Tyler mount   A helicopter or airplane camera mount that reduces vibrations.

ultracardioid microphone   A microphone with the most directional (narrowest) pickup pattern available. Also known as a *shotgun microphone.*

variable-speed motor   An electric drive motor for a film camera whose speed can be varied and controlled.

VCR   Videocassette recorder.

vectorscope   A special oscilloscope used to monitor hue and color saturation in video signals.

video assist   A video camera attached to a film camera for instant dailies, allowing the shot to be immediately judged on playback. Also known as *video tap.*

video gain   An adjustment to control the picture recording level.

video tap   See **video assist.**

video-to-film transfer   Copying a videotape on film. Also known as *kinescoping.*

viewfinder   An eyepiece or screen through which a camera operator sees the image being recorded. See also **reticle.**

visualization   The creative process of transforming a script into a sequence of visual images and sounds.

VO   Voice-over. See **narration.**

VT   Videotape.

waveform monitor   A display device for video signal information.

wedge test   When making an optical, a test is done in which the elements of the optical (lap dissolves, superimposition, mattes) are photographed with one frame of each f-stop. When developed, the laboratory can identify the exact exposure reading that will produce the best effect.

whip pan   A very fast panning movement.

white balance   Electronic adjustments to render a white object as white on screen.

wide-angle lens   A lens with a wide angle of acceptance. Its effect is to increase the apparent distance between foreground and background objects.

wild   (1) Picture shot without a synchronous relationship to sound. (2) Sound shot without a synchronous relationship to picture.

windscreen   A porous cover that protects a microphone's diaphragm from air currents.

wireless/radio microphone   A cordless microphone that transmits its output to a recorder via a receiver.

work print   A print derived from the original negative to be used in the editing process to establish, through a series of trial cuttings, the finished version of the film. The negative is later conformed to the work print when a final cut is achieved.

wrangler   An animal trainer and supervisor.

wrap   The period at the end of a day of shooting during which the crew must store the equipment.

zoetrope   An optical toy with a series of pictures on the inner surface of a cylinder. When the pictures are rotated and viewed through a slit, the toy gives the impression that the pictures are moving. This device, a precursor to film projection, was a popular form of entertainment in the nineteenth century.

zoom lens   A lens whose focal length varies between wide and telephoto.

bibliography

ACTING

Hagan, Uta, with Haskel Frankel. *Respect for Acting.* New York: Macmillan, 1973.

Moore, Sonia. *The Stanislauski System.* New York: Viking Press, 1965.

Podovkin, V. *Film Technique and Film Acting.* New York: Grove Press, 1982.

Stanislauski, Constantin. *An Actor Prepares.* New York: Theater Arts, 1948.

Stanislauski, Constantin. *Building a Character.* New York: Theater Arts, 1981.

ANIMATION

Blair, Preston. *Animation and How to Animate Film Cartoons.* New York: Walter Foster, 1989.

Canemaker, John. *Felix: The Twisted Tale of the World's Most Famous Cat.* New York: Abbeville Press, 1987.

Canemaker, John. *Windsor McKay: His Life and Art.* New York: Abbeville Press, 1987.

Solomon, Charles. *The Complete Kodak Animation Book.* Rochester, N.Y.: Eastman Kodak Co., 1983.

White, Tony. *The Animator's Workbook.* New York: Phaidow Press, 1986.

CAMERA

Almendros, Nestor. *Man with a Camera.* New York: Simon & Schuster, 1985.

Carlson, Verne, and Sylvia Carlson. *Professional Lighting Handbook.* Boston: Focal Press, 1985.

Clarke, Charles G., ed. *American Cinematographer's Handbook.* Hollywood: American Society of Cinematographers, 1993.

Elkins, David. *The Camera Assistant Manual.* Boston: Focal Press, 1991.

Fielding, Ray. *The Technique of Special Effects Cinematography,* 4th ed. New York: Hastings House, 1985.

Malkiewicz, Kris J. *Cinematography: A Guide for Film Makers and Film Teachers,* 2d ed. New York: Prentice-Hall, 1989.

Millerson, Gerald. *The Technique of Lighting for Television and Motion Pictures,* 2d ed. Boston: Focal Press, 1982.

Samuelson, David. *Motion Picture Camera Data.* London: Focal Press, 1979.

Schaffer, D., and A. Ritsko. *Masters of Light.* Berkeley and Los Angeles: University of California Press, 1984.

Underdahl, Douglas. *The 16mm Motion Picture Camera Helpbook.* New York: New York University/ Reprographics, 1989.

CRAFTS

Baker, Patsy. *Wigs and Make-up for Theatre, TV and Film.* Boston: Focal Press, 1992.

Dunn, Linwood G. *The ASC Treasury of Visual Effects.* Hollywood: American Society of Cinematographers, 1983.

Kehoe, Vincent J-R. *Special Make-up Effects.* Boston: Focal Press, 1991.

LoBrutto, Vincent. *By Design.* Westport, Conn.: Praeger, 1992.

Maier, Robert. *Location Scouting and Management Handbook: Television, Film, and Still Photography.* Boston: Focal Press, 1994.

Miller, Pat P. *Script Supervision and Film Continuity,* 2d ed. Boston: Focal Press, 1990.

Olson, Robert. *Art Direction for Film and Television.* London: Focal Press, 1993.

DIRECTING

Bare, Richard L. *The Film Director.* New York: Collier, 1971.

Bunuel, Luis. *My Cast Breath.* London: Flamingo Press, 1986.

Clurman, Harold. *On Directing.* New York: Macmillan, 1974.

Katz, Steven D. *Film Directing: Shot by Shot*. Studio City, Calif.: Michael Wiese Productions, 1991.

Kurosawa, Akira. *Something Like an Autobiography*. New York: Vintage Books, 1983.

Mamet, David. *On Directing*. New York: Viking Press, 1991.

Nilsen, Vladimir. *The Cinema as Graphic Art*. New York: Hill and Wang, 1985. Foreword by S. M. Eisenstein.

Terence, St. John Marner, ed. *Directing Motion Pictures*. New York: A.S. Barnes, Tantivy Press, 1972.

Truffaut, François. *Hitchcock*. New York: Simon & Schuster, 1967.

DISTRIBUTION

Bowser, Kathryn. *The AIVF Guide to International Film and Video Festivals*, 3d ed. New York: Foundation for Independent Video and Film, 1992.

Council on International Nontheatrical Events. *The Worldwide Directory of Film and Video Festivals and Events*, 4th ed. New York: Author, 1993–1994.

Franco, Debra. *Alternative Visions: Distributing Independent Media in a Home Video World*. Los Angeles, Washington, D.C., and New York: American Institute Press, 1990.

Gagney, Alan E. *Gagney's Guide to 1800 International Contests*, Glendale, Calif.: Festival Publications, 1993.

Reichert, Julia. *Doing It Yourself: A Handbook on Independent Film Distribution*. New York: Association of Independent Video and Filmmakers, 1977.

Wiese, Michael. *Film and Video Marketing*. Studio City, Calif.: Author. 1989.

DOCUMENTARIES

Baddeley, W. Hugh. *The Technique of Documentary Film Production*, 4th ed. New York: Hastings House, 1975.

Ivens, Joris. *The Camera and I*. Cambridge, Mass.: MIT Press, 1969.

Rabiger, Michael. *Directing the Documentary*. Boston: Focal Press, 1987.

Rosenthal, Alan. *Writing, Directing, and Producing Documentary Films*. Carbondale and Edwardsville: Southern Illinois University Press, 1990.

EDITING

Dancyger, Ken. *The Technique of Film and Video Editing*. Boston: Focal Press, 1993.

Dmytryk, Edward. *On Film Editing*. Boston: Focal Press, 1984.

Hollyn, Norman. *The Film Edition Room Handbook*, 2d ed. Los Angeles: Lone Eagle, 1990.

Ohanian, Thomas A. *Digital Nonlinear Editing*. Boston: Focal Press, 1992.

Reisz, Karel, and Gavin Millar. *The Technique of Film Editing*. Boston: Focal Press, 1968.

Rosenblum, R., and Robert Karen. *When the Shooting Stops . . . the Cutting Begins*. New York: Da Capo Press, 1979.

Rubin, Michael. *Nonlinear: A Guide to Electronic Film and Video Editing*, 2d ed. Gainesville, Fla.: Triad, 1991.

FILM AND VIDEO BASICS

Adams, William B. *The Handbook of Motion Picture Production*. New York: John Wiley & Sons, 1977.

Pincus, Edward, and Steven Ascher. *The Filmmaker's Handbook*. New York: New American Library, Plume, 1984.

Wiese, Michael. *The Independent Film and Videomaker's Guide*, rev. ed. Boston: Focal Press, 1990.

Wilson, Anton. *Cinema Workshop: The Basics of Film and Video from the American Cinematographer*, rev. ed. Hollywood: A.S.C. Holding Corp., 1983.

GRANTS

Gibbs, Lissa, ed. *National Alliance for Media Arts and Culture Member Directory*. Beverly Hills: NAMAC, 1992.

Niemeyer, Suzanne. *Money for Film and Video Artists*. New York: American Council for the Arts/Allworth Press, 1991.

Renz, Loren, ed. *The Foundation Directory*, 11th ed. New York: Foundation Center, 1987.

Warshawski, Morrie. *Shaking the Money Tree: How to Get Grants and Donations for Film and Video*. Hollywood: Michael Wiese Productions, 1994.

THE INDUSTRY

Eaker, Sherry, ed. *The Back Stage Handbook for Performing Artists*. Rev. and enlarged ed. New York: Watson-Guptill, Back Stage Books, 1991.

Kindem, Gorham, ed. *The American Movie Industry: The Business of Motion Pictures*. Carbondale and Edwardsville: Southern Illinois University Press, 1982.

Litwak, Mark. *Reel Power*. New York: William Morrow, 1986.

Mayer, Michael F. *The Film Industries: Practical Business/Legal Problems in Production, Distribution and Exhibition*. New York: Hastings House, 1978.

Squires, Jason. *The Movie Business Book*. New York: Simon & Schuster, Touchstone, 1983.

Vogel, Harold L. *Entertainment Industry Economics*. New York: Cambridge University Press, 1986.

PRODUCTION

Baumgarten, Paul, Donald Farber, and Mark Fleisher. *Producing, Financing and Distributing Film*, rev. and updated ed. New York: Limelight, 1992.

Behlmer, Rudy, ed. *Memo from David O. Selznick*. New York: Viking Press, 1972.

Chamness, Danford. *The Hollywood Guide to Film Budgeting and Script Breakdown for Low Budget Features*, 5th ed. Hollywood: Stanley J. Brooks, 1988.

Curran, Trisha. *Financing Your Film: A Guide for Independent Film Producers*. Westport, Conn.: Praeger, 1985.

Davies, Sally. *The Independent Producer: Film and Television*. London: Hourcourt, Howlett, Davies, Moskovic, Faber & Faber, 1986.

Goodell, Gregory. *Independent Feature Film Production: A Complete Guide from Concept through Distribution*. New York: St. Martin's, 1982.

Gregory, Mollie. *Making Films Your Business*. New York: Schocken Books, 1979.

Singleton, Ralph S. *Film Scheduling: Or, How Long Will It Take to Shoot Your Movie?*, 2d ed. Los Angeles: Lone Eagle, 1991.

Singleton, Ralph S. *The Film Scheduling/Film Budgeting Workbook*. Los Angeles: Lone Eagle, 1984.

Wiese, Michael. *Film and Video Budgets*, rev. ed. Boston: Michael Wiese Productions/Focal Press, 1990.

Wiese, Michael. *Film and Video Financing*. Boston: Michael Wiese Productions/Focal Press, 1991.

REFERENCE

Brook's Standard Rate Book. Los Angeles: Stanley J. Brooks, 1994. [Union rates and rules.]

Capogrosso, Eric, ed. *The 1994/95 Industry Labor Guide*. Los Angeles: Industry Labor Guide Publishing Co., 1993.

Detmers, Fred, ed. *American Cinematographer Manual*. Hollywood: ASC Press, 1986.

Konigsberg, Ira. *The Complete Film Dictionary*. London: Meridian, 1989.

Maitland, Ian. *Film Editing Glossary*. Dubuque, Iowa: Kendal/Hunt, 1990.

The New York Production Manual. New York: Producer's Masterguide, 1994.

Production Boards and Strips: For Features and Television. Los Angeles: Stanley J. Brooks, 1991.

Ranucci, Karen. *Directory of Film and Video Production Resources in Latin America and the Caribbean*. New York, 1989.

Singleton, Ralph. *Filmmaker's Dictionary*. Los Angeles: Lone Eagle, 1986.

SOUND

Alten, Stanley R. *Audio in Media*, 3d ed. Belmont, Calif.: Wadsworth, 1981.

Anderson, Craig. *MIDI for Musicians*. New York: Amsco Publications, 1986.

Carlin, Dan, Sr. *Music in Film and Video Production*. Boston: Focal Press, 1991.

Karlin, Fred, and Rayburn Wright. *On the Track: A Guide to Contemporary Film Scoring*. New York: Schirmer Books, 1990.

Kerner, Marvin M. *The Art of the Sound Effects Editor*. Boston: Focal Press, 1989.

Mott, Robert L. *Sound Effects: Radio, TV and Film*. Boston: Focal Press, 1990.

Nisbett, Alec. *The Technique of the Sound Studio*, 4th ed. Boston: Focal Press, 1979.

Nisbett, Alec. *The Use of Microphones*, 3d ed. Boston: Focal Press, 1990.

Pendergast, Roy M. *Film Music: A Neglected Art*, 2d ed. New York: W.W. Norton, 1992.

Thomas, Tony. *Music for the Movies*. South Brunswick, N. J.: A. S. Barnes, 1973.

Weis, Elisabeth, and John Belton, eds. *Film Sound: Theory and Practice*. New York: Columbia University Press, 1985.

VIDEO

Huber, David Miles. *Audio Production Techniques for Video*. White Plains, N.Y.: Knowledge Industry Publishing, 1987.

Mathias, Harry, and Richard Patterson. *Electronic Cinematography: Achieving Photographic Control over the Video Image*. Belmont, Calif.: Wadsworth, 1985.

Millerson, Gerald. *Video Production Handbook*, 2d ed. Boston: Focal Press, 1992.

Verna, Tony. *Global Television: How to Create Effective Television for the 1990s*. Boston: Focal Press, 1993.

Watkinson, John. *The Art of Digital Video*, 2d ed. Boston: Focal Press, 1994.

Wiese, Michael. *Home Video: Producing for the Home Market*. Westport, Conn.: Michael Wiese Film/Video, 1986.

Winston, Brian, and Julia Keydel. *Working with Video: A Comprehensive Guide to the World of Video Production*. White Plains, N.Y.: Knowledge Industry Publishing, 1986.

WRITING

Armer, Alan. *Writing the Screenplay for Film and Television*. Belmont, Calif.: Wadsworth, 1985.

Biro, Yvette. *The Language of Film*. Bloomington: Indiana University Press, 1982.

Cooper, Patricia, and Ken Dancyger. *Writing the Short Film*. Boston: Focal Press, 1995.

Dancyger, Ken, and Jeff Rush. *Alternative Screenwriting: Writing beyond the Rules*. Boston: Focal Press, 1991.

Eisenstein, S.M. *The Short Fiction Scenario*. Methuen: Calcutta, Seagull Books, 1988.

Field, Syd. *The Foundations of Screenwriting*. New York: Dell, 1982.

Goldman, William. *Adventures in the Screen Trade*. New York: Warner Books, 1984.

Phillips, William H. *Writing Short Scripts*. Syracuse: Syracuse University Press, 1991.

Seger, Linda. *Making a Good Script Great*. Hollywood: Samuel French, 1987.

PERIODICALS/NEWSLETTERS

American Cinematographer. ASC Holdings Corp., 1782 N. Orange Drive, Hollywood, CA 90028: (800) 448-0145 or (213) 969-4333.

Backstage. 1515 Broadway, 14th Floor, New York, NY 10036: (212) 764-7300; or 5055 Wilshire Boulevard, Los Angeles, CA 90036.

Cinéfantastique. 7240 W. Roosevelt Road, Forest Park, IL 60130: (708) 366-5566.

Film Comment. Film Society of Lincoln Center, 70 Lincoln Center Plaza, New York, NY 10023-6595: (800) 783-4903.

The Independent. Foundation for Independent Video and Film (FIVF), 625 Broadway, New York, NY 10012: (212) 473-3400.

Millemeter. Penton Publishing, Subscription Lock Box, P.O. Box 96732, Chicago, IL 60693: (312) 477-4700 or (312) 960-4050.

Premiere. P.O. Box 55387, Boulder, CO 80323-5387.

Variety (daily or weekly). 5700 Wilshire Boulevard, Suite 120, Los Angeles, CA 90036: (213) 857-6600; or 249 W. 17th Street, 4th Floor, New York, NY 10011: (212) 645-0067.

index